Years of Upheaval

Years of Upheaval

Axial Changes in Islam Since 1989

Raphael Israeli

Routledge
Taylor & Francis Group
LONDON AND NEW YORK

First published 2016 by Transaction Publishers

2 Park Square, Milton Park, Abingdon, Oxfordshire OX14 4RN
52 Vanderbilt Avenue, New York, NY 10017

Routledge is an imprint of the Taylor & Francis Group, an informa business

First issued in paperback 2020

Library of Congress Catalog Number: 2015019604

Library of Congress Cataloging-in-Publication Data

Israeli, Raphael.
Years of upheaval : axial changes in Islam since 1989 / Raphael Israeli.
pages cm
Includes bibliographical references and index.
ISBN 978-1-4128-5712-3 (acid-free paper) 1. Islamic countries--Politics and government--20th century. 2. Islamic countries--Politics and government--21st century. 3. Islam and politics--History--20th century. 4. Islam and politics--History--21st century. 5. Islam and world politics. 6. Islamic fundamentalism--Political aspects. 7. World politics--1989- I. Title.
DS35.I827 2016
909'.09767083--dc23

2015019604

ISBN 13: 978-1-4128-5712-3 (hbk)
ISBN 13: 978-0-367-59706-1 (pbk)

Dedicated to the Memory of My Daughter

Shlomit Israeli-Lerekh (1960–2015)
A Great and Original Mind
A Multifarious Talent
An Indomitable Spirit
An Uncompromising Achiever

Contents

Acknowledgments

The idea of this volume was born more than two decades ago, when one of my esteemed students, Jonathan Schanzer, now an American scholar and analyst of Middle Eastern affairs in his own right, wrote, under my guidance at Hebrew University, a graduate seminar paper on the rise of militant Islam among the Palestinians, dubbed Hamas, the acronym for the Harakat Muqawama Islamiyya (Movement of Islamic Resistance). While discussing the themes of his excellent paper, he raised the insightful point that 1989, which was the second year of Hamas militant activities, was an eventful year both in the international arena and on the Islamic front, and we naturally posed the question whether that was a coincidence or whether separate world axial events somehow interconnected in our global reality. In any case, while putting this volume together, I had the privilege of rummaging through the draft papers Jonathan left in his wake and using some of his ideas. The two concluding chapters of this volume are based on the data collected and analyzed by Jonathan in his paper, and I am indebted to him for his work and for his generous permission to use it, and happy to give him credit in this book for his creativity on a topic that might have otherwise remained obscure and ignored. Hamas, whose notoriety peaked during its repeated campaigns of terror against Israel, also connotes a religious sort of enthusiasm, meaning that to the cold and straightforward old notions of political science by which we analyzed the movement, a refreshing, if disturbing, element of human sentiment and devotion was added to the equation.

Karl Jaspers, the progenitor of the idea of an "axial age" referred to the period from 800 to 200 BC in which revolutions in religious and philosophical thinking had occurred across civilizations with no obvious communications between them. Robert Bellah after him explored the utopian visions of that time to spell out its consequences. The Axial Age connoted a cluster of mega breakthroughs of universal significance, which mark the boundary between the world that was and the new world that is. Events of that scope include the discovery of America, the

French Revolution, the acts and deeds of the founders of great religions, such as Buddha and Muhammad, the Communist revolution, and the fall of Communism. All of those events demarcate the clear watershed between the world that was waning into history and the new world, which is yet crystallizing and undefined in its details, that began to take shape thereafter. While the former world was so stable and predictable that we thought of it as the "Era of Sanity"[1] that would last indefinitely owing to its desirability and familiarity, we tended to regard the latter as a destabilizing and unpredictable venture that it was best avoiding. This, of course, brings up the entire idea of political stability, which is hallowed in conservative political circles, versus the commotion, change, and new political experimentations that often levy the heavy toll of revolution, violence, and loss of human lives; invoke the unreliability of alliances and friendships; and raise the uncertainty about what tomorrow might bring. For this, we will need to examine the entire idea of stability and gauge its benefits and the prices it levies on its pursuers.

In this volume, the idea is to explore the events that have occurred in the Islamic world since the end of the 1980s and their aftermath; these events have signaled the dawning of a new age of Islamic violence and fundamentalism, have stimulated the dissipation of state borders and the rise of transnational and transterritorial movements that have been extraordinarily attractive to young people in the Islamic world, and have replaced the hopeful Arab Spring (2010–2013) by a threatening Islamic winter. Unlike the mammoth dimensions of the classic "Axial Age," which has revolved and has become past, the new "axial era" in Islam, all proportions guarded, has been in the making, and there is no telling either where it might lead or whether it will deserve the epithet of "axial era" that we have accorded to it, maybe too prematurely.

I am, as usual, obliged to my institution, the Harry Truman Institute for the Promotion of Peace, and to its staff, its facilities, and its funding, for the decades of support that I have enjoyed under its comfortable and caring wings. I am particularly grateful to Jonathan for the many fruitful talks we had in those years and for the friendly relations we have maintained since. However, the full responsibility for any misapprehensions of facts and data and for any misinterpretations of views and opinions rests squarely on my shoulders alone.

Note

1. See this author's: *Israel's New Strategic Dilemmas: Survival or Revival*? Strategic Books, Texas, 2012, especially chapter 2.

Introduction

The New Axial Era in Islamic and World Events

Like a whirlwind, events in the late 1980s and 1990s, both worldwide and within local Islamic communities, did not stop stunning the incredulous and increasingly suspicious world populations who watched, with a mixture of fear, doubt, uncertainty, awe, and hope, the parade of successive happenings in the world of Islam that were revolutionizing our universe, but of which we seemed helpless to change the course. While in the West the great concerns were focused on the dwindling of the Cold War, the Gulf wars and the primacy of the United States in the emerging unipolar world, on the other side of the ideological aisle, there were the two giant Communist civilizations: the Soviet and the Chinese, which were undergoing shattering processes of change, each in its own style and pace. In the Soviet Union, Mikhail Gorbachev, the general secretary of his powerful Communist Party, who had experienced several confrontations with President Reagan over the Star War and who had also signaled his opening to the West and to liberalized reforms, was elected president (May 25, 1989). He launched his *glasnost* (transparency) policy, which meant a relative freedom of the citizenry to speak their minds, allowing Western media to be present in Soviet cities and talk to frustrated and critical Soviet citizens. But the economy was lagging behind, since *perestroika* (restructuring) would begin only later and would take time. In the meantime, the *konsum* government stores presented empty shelves, but the dissatisfied citizens could now complain freely to the Western media in Gorky Park and other central venues that they were hungry and that there was high inflation and no consumer goods to have. That signaled that the Communist economic system, which rested on a thin layer of veneer, had started to crack. A bitter humor began to develop, claiming that what New York and Moscow had in common was that in both nothing could be bought for rubles. Neither did the humiliating withdrawal of the Soviets from Afghanistan in that year help to enhance the Soviet dwindling prestige.

The taste of freedom, accompanied by the feeling in Eastern Europe that the Soviet superpower could and would no longer interfere by force in its satellite countries as it had done in Hungary (1956) and Czechoslovakia (1968), began to cause those satellites to dare to peel away, like the layers of an onion, from the visibly weakening carcass of what was once the Soviet Empire: first the outer layer of members of the Warsaw Pact (Poland, East Germany, Romania, Hungary, Bulgaria, and Czechoslovakia) and Outer Mongolia, then the second layer of the fifteen "federated" members of the Soviet Union: the Baltics (Estonia, Lithuania, and Latvia), Moldova, the five Muslim republics of Central Asia (Kazakhstan, Kyrgyzstan, Uzbekistan, Turkmenistan, and Tajikistan), the Caucasus (Armenia, Georgia, and Azerbaijan), and finally Belarus and the Ukraine, the latter still experiencing in our days the lingering effects emanating from the shattering of that vast empire into pieces. Russia, the extant body of what was the Soviet Union, remains a weakened, though still threatening, grumpy neighbor trying to rebuild its lost stature and prestige. To top it all, on November 11, 1989, the Berlin Wall fell, and the process of unification of Germany on the one hand and of dismantling the Cold War structure on the other began.

In 1989 in the Baltics the people forced democratic elections, which opted for separation from Russia; in Poland Solidarity presided over the first free elections; and in Prague, the parliament abolished the dominant role of the Communist regime in November and ushered in the "Velvet Revolution," with the Western-style liberal mood introduced by Vaclav Havel, the writer and playwright. He personified the 1968 short-lived "spring," introduced by Alexander Dubcek, but this time without the menacing "Brezhnev Doctrine" that had called for Soviet intervention in the previous instance, for the Soviet Union had been emasculated and thrown into chaos in the meantime. But in adjoining Romania, things turned violent. On Xmas Day of 1989, a popular uprising overthrew the government of Bucharest and executed the tyrant Nicolae Ceausescu and his hated wife, just as in the days of the French Revolution. These events also exposed the underground palaces where rulers lived in luxury in the midst of starving people and the opulence in which the privileged Communist *nomenklatura* thrived under the open eye of the oppressive Securitate.

By contrast, China, with the diminutive but dominant Deng Xiaoping at the helm in the post-Mao era, learned from the Russian fiasco and preceded restructuring to transparency; namely, it eliminated economic socialism, allowed private property, and encouraged capitalist development, but maintained a heavy fist on political liberties by continuing to champion the "dictatorship of the proletariat," which held the monopoly on power in the hands of the Communist Party. Unlike the Soviets, who had layers to shed and were forced by their satellites to do so, the Chinese, who had not been defeated or humiliated in any foreign venture, continued to profess from time immemorial the concept of a unitarian state, in which power stemmed from one center. There are cultural "autonomies" in various parts of China, but no idea of federation has ever crossed their minds. The Tibetans and the Uighurs in Xinjiang understood that, much as they would have liked to secede and accede to some sort of semi-independence, the Chinese system would not allow it. Therefore, economic reform and development was the only legitimate channel of change to which all the people of China could aspire. That pattern has indeed made China a world powerhouse of economic growth, manufacturing, technology, innovation, trade, and financing and has arguably produced such a level of contentment and national pride among the populace that major civilian unrest has been averted so far. The September–October 2014 unrest in Hong Kong, due to Beijing's announced intent to interfere in the promised democratic system ("one state, two systems") when the former British colony reverted to Chinese control in 1997, may signal a change of that orientation.

When Chinese students took over Beijing's Tiananmen Square in a rally for democracy in May 1989, there was no evidence of massive peasant support: the latter being busy making money and none of them being hungry, despite the one to twelve proportion between population and land in favor of the Soviet Union. Indeed, the Soviet Union was three times larger than China, whereas China's population was four times larger, but there was want and hunger in the Soviet Union in transition, while in China there was none. That rally of protest escalated as nearly 1 million people in Beijing demonstrated for democracy, and there was a danger that chaos might spread across the nation if the clogged thoroughfares were not reopened for traffic and public order were not restored. On June 4, the Chinese leadership thought that things had gone too far and that their extreme leniency toward the demonstrators, the likes of which had never been tolerated under any Communist regime, had been interpreted, with foreign encouragement, as a weakness of the regime and exploited accordingly. The authorities moved in with force, causing thousands of casualties, but the square was again in government hands and life gradually went back to "normal."

In November of that year, Deng Xiaoping, the progenitor of the Second Chinese Revolution, which put China back on the capitalistic road of prosperity, resigned the leadership of his country and passed the helm to the younger generation of leaders. He is remembered as the man whose two figurative slogans had turned his country around. The first was that "it was not important whether the cat was black or white, as long as it caught mice." That put to rest the old debate that had been launched by Mao and celebrated during the Cultural Revolution (1966–76), giving precedence to the ideologues (the party commissars who served at all levels of society and the military) over the experts (the professionals, engineers, and managers who had the talent and the skill to obtain rational results from the available resources. The second slogan was "When you open windows some mosquitoes might get in," which showed an understanding toward the problems of unemployment (breaking the "iron rice bowl"), urbanization, inflation, massive migration to the urban centers in search of work, the unprecedented growing gap between the new tycoons (it was no longer shameful to get rich) and the poor rural population, and the visible differences in the pace and depth of development between the booming coastal areas and the backward interior.

In the Islamic world, the great events of those years centered on the towering figure of Ayatollah (the Sign of God) Ruhollah (the Spirit of God) Khomeini, the founding father of the Islamic Revolution in Iran and the great innovator of Shiite doctrine. In contrast with the four prevailing schools of law in the Sunna, which constitutes about 90 percent of the 1.5 billion Muslims in the world and whose laws are fixed and immutable since their savior had been the Prophet Muhammad, the Seal of the Prophets, and no one after him was expected to reveal himself to humanity, the Shiites live in permanent expectation of the revelation of the Hidden Imam. This means that if in the Sunna the ideal utopia has already happened in the past, from which we can only keep distancing ourselves as the years and centuries revolve, in the Shia hope is placed in the return of the Hidden Imam in some indefinite future, in order to produce prosperity, justice, and happiness for all humanity. The great luminaries of the Sunna usually counsel their followers to submit to the rule under which they live, even if it is not satisfactory to their religious taste, for a bad ruler is always superior to chaos; in disorder no Islam can function.

The Shiite scholars, on the contrary, have always been rebellious, especially when they were not in power. This restlessness, which has always been tinged with messianic and utopian elements, has lent to the Shia the characteristics that we today identify in the Arab Spring. Therefore, the Islamic Revolution that we witnessed in 1978–79 in Iran, which was intended for exportation—indicating its universal and messianic import—must be seen as the precursor of the Islamist Spring, because it professed the exact goal that the current spring proclaims today: to remove the present illegitimate tyrant and establish in his stead a just Islamic order (like the Islamic parties in Turkey, Egypt, Morocco, Tunisia, and others that all have this element of *revival* and *justice* in their very names), which will precipitate the coming of the Imam Mahdi (the Guided Imam, the corresponding term in the Sunna with the Hidden Imam in the Shia). The fact that this dream has not yet come to pass does not reflect negatively on the missed and unfulfilled utopia; quite the contrary: the longer the waiting, the more acute its sense of urgency and imminence. There were many attempts made by Sunnite doctors of the Holy Law to invite the Shia to join the Islamic consensus by turning it into a fifth school of law, with the intent of unifying all currents of Islam and putting an end to its internal debates. But the Shia always rejected the preconditions of the union, for had it joined the consensus, it would have had to renounce during the Friday prayer the denunciation of the first three caliphs for having usurped the caliphate from Ali, the sole heir of the Prophet who deserved it, according to Shiite belief. It is evident that the Shiites would not accept that position, since Ali and his descendants were the central figures in their narrative of Islamic history, and their acceptance of Ali as fourth in the apostolic succession of the Prophet would mean admission and recognition that Ali was not wronged, and therefore there was nothing to redress.

Conversely, the entire Shiite martyrology is founded on the suffering inflicted upon Ali and his children by the two people they loathe most—the first Umayyad caliph, Muawiyah, and his son-successor, Yazid—who have become in Iran the paradigm of oppression and injustice for having murdered Ali and his sons together with their retinues. The Sunna, on the contrary, will not accept the Shiites' hatred of the three first righteous caliphs as usurpers, disrespecting and cursing them accordingly. The Shiites would not renounce the special status of Ali in Islam as the cousin of the Prophet and his son-in-law, while in the eyes of the Sunnites all four first caliphs deserve the title of righteous (*rashidun*), are equal in status, and are all second only to the Prophet, who was the most perfect of all humans, designated by Allah as his last messenger. When Ayatollah Khomeini declared his Islamic Revolution in Tehran in 1979, he tried to gather the Sunnite–Shiite rift under the umbrella of the world Islamic revolution that he was professing, as he intended to spread it to the entire world and sweep in its path all Muslim peoples. He thought that his revolution, his early version of the Spring, would overshadow all the theological differences that looked insignificant in his eyes, compared to the great unifying themes in Islam. He indeed had some success—when he harnessed non-Shiite Syria, Shiite Hezbollah in Lebanon, and Sunnite Sudan to his purposes—and turned Tehran into an international center of terror that attracted other fanatics, including Sunnites, Hamas, and Islamic Jihad.

Ayatollah Khomeini also changed the doctrine of the Shia. He had begun to develop his revolutionary ideas under the shah and was audacious and creative when one considers his élan, his out-of-the-box thinking, and the far-reaching political consequences that ensued. The first thoughts that Khomeini started to develop cost him, inter alia, fifteen years (1963–78) of exile in Najaf, Iraq, one of the holy places of the Shia because it is the site where Ali, the first imam is buried. It was there Khomeini brought to completion and published his *Islamic Revolution,* in which he outlined his positions and plan of action, a sort of *Mein Kampf* that he was to implement step-by-step. He was then compelled to leave Iraq by Saddam, who had sealed an agreement with the shah on the border between the two countries in the middle of the mighty Shatt al-Arab, where the Tigris and the Euphrates converge before they pour into the Persian Gulf. The main thought that would have appealed to the Muslim crowds today would have been the need to eradicate the bad rulers and to install in their stead Islamic regimes under Sharia law. Khomeini's Iran was the first to do that, by an Islamic revolution in which the clergy played a part, followed by the Taliban in Afghanistan in the 1990s, and then by Iraq, which, under American tutelage, applied that same principle through a Western-style democracy, until the new menace of ISIS appeared on the country's horizon in the 2010s.

Khomeini's doctrine was revolutionary from yet other aspects, because it provided the ideological infrastructure and underpinnings for a new model of rule in which the clergy are actively involved. For him, because the ayatollahs are the supreme sources of knowledge, wisdom, and inspiration, it is only logical that they should also be the rulers—somewhat similar to the prince who is also a philosopher in Greek and Western philosophy. Khomeini developed two concepts that anchored his suggested revolutionary change: *marja' taqlid* (the reference for emulation), that is that the supreme head of the clergy (*ayatollah uzma*), being also the supreme spiritual power, ought to be the reference all aspire to emulate, a modern manifestation of the supreme model of the Prophet that is current in the Sunna; and second—*wilayat al-faqih* (the rule of the jurist). These two principles turned the passive state of expectation of the return of the Imam Mahdi, who would bring salvation, into an aggressive initiative to precipitate such a momentous event. To those familiar with modern Jewish history, this could be comparable to the revolutionary doctrine developed in the 1920s and 1930s by Chief Rabbi Kook in Palestine, whereby it was not enough for Jewry to sit and wait in the Diaspora for the coming of the Messiah to provide redemption, but it had become necessary to rise and practice Zionism by settlement on the land, nation-building, development, and social and political action as an avenue for getting there. Khomeini probably viewed these two concepts as personified in him as a result of his scholarship, his lifelong struggle against the tyranny of the shah, and his spiritual qualities, which made him a mujtahid who is thus qualified to continue his innovative *ijtihad* and express the will of the Hidden Imam pending his return. Unlike the Sunna, for whom the gates of *ijtihad* had closed since the passing of the great luminaries, the founders of the four schools of law, by the tenth century the Shiite mujtahid had undertaken the task of innovative legislation, through which his verdicts ought to be the law. Hence it was only natural that membership to parliament in Iran was to be assigned to mullahs, who understand the matter of religious legislation and the will of the Hidden Imam. Khomeini wrote that only the mullahs were able to get people out into the streets and motivate them not only to die for Islam, but also to beg that they should be allowed to sacrifice themselves for Islam.

Khomeini, like Muslim Brother Sayyid Qutb, was full of hatred toward the Jews and turned his bigotry into doctrine by dubbing them "enemies of Allah," hence the extremely large, libelous, and imaginary pool of lies, blind contempt, and outright primitive propensity to fabricate anti-Semitic hoaxes that were extraordinary for two great luminaries of modern Islam. These exemplary and hallowed figures would have been expected to hold a higher measure of humanity, civility, and good judgment than the ludicrous and false statements made in the classic books of these two respected Muslim thinkers.[1] No wonder, then, that President Mahmoud Ahmadinejad, who considered himself their disciple and the devoted executor of their anti-Semitic doctrine, should have felt as compelled as Hitler to repeat on every occasion his nonsense concerning the extermination of the Jews and their state. Khomeini also included in his political activism a novel interpretation of the murder of Hussein bin Ali and his entourage in Karbala, which is commemorated as the central rite in Shiite liturgy (the tazia on the day of Ashura). It was no longer only a memorial for the most despicable murder of one of the greatest martyrs of all generations, with whom every Shiite ought to identify by reliving his suffering; instead the day put pressure on all Shiites to emulate the supreme martyr in the path of Allah, on his way to paradise, who will also recommend his followers for admission into the high heavens. When Iraq invaded Iran in October 1980, Khomeini, who was adored as if he were the imam himself, called his people to the defense of the land and mobilized more recruits than needed for the defense of the country, thanks to his reverence of Hussein's model.

Khomeini, who became a model of modest living for his people compared to the luxurious and profligate extravagance of the hated shah, became so popular and his image so merged with that of the Hidden Imam that he could practically decree what he wished and his words became holy law. So when in February 1989, he issued his death fatwa against the author of *The Satanic Verses,* Salman Rushdie, a Muslim Indian writer who had sought his literary career in England, the world was outraged. That was the first time in the modern era that the West had to deal with such a blunt and unforgiving decree that required that a death sentence, issued by a clerical authority, be implemented anywhere in the world, by any pious Muslim who could find the victim and summarily execute him. The laws of humanity, the civil laws of the West, human rights in general—all had to bend before the verdict of the grand imam. That verdict could not be appealed because it was divinely inspired, so Rushdie went into hiding and then left England for a safer shelter. A strict fanatical Islamic view, which was horrendous enough when applied to other "heretical" Muslims, had now transcended the borders of Islam and become universal.

The far-reaching significance of that decree, which was violently debated in the Islamic world and contemptuously rejected by the West, though no one could appeal it, was that it soon became a yardstick for measuring the application and desirability of Muslim legal norms in the West. Soon, the Muslims in Europe began requiring that Sharia law be incorporated into European law: now "honor killings" were claimed to be part of the Muslim cultural heritage and therefore they could not be prosecuted; the adoption of the veil by Muslim women was claimed as a matter of course; and demonstrations throughout Europe dubbed restrictions on Muslims as "Islamophobia" and "racism." The numbers of terrorist acts against host countries in Europe began escalating,[2] until some of those countries, such as the Netherlands and France, undertook measures to control the situation. But the worst would come in 2006, when, in retaliation for a cartoon denigrating the Prophet Muhammad in a Danish paper, Muslim riots across the world generated the burning of Western embassies in Muslim countries, the deaths of many individuals, both Muslim and Western, and a disruption of diplomatic and trade relations between Denmark and the Muslim world. For Muslims, the prestige and adulation of a prophet long dead was more hallowed in their value system than the lives of present-day human beings or the decimation of their property. It also indicated that Muslims could not bear the idea that another creed could be permitted to criticize theirs, although they were free to demand that their beliefs be respected, or else the deniers of respect should risk the consequences.

Khomeini's revolution did not end with his death soon after he issued his abominable Rushdie fatwa in 1989. Quite the contrary, his death made his legacy holy and untouchable, for only he could have altered anything from what he said or did. Therefore, the verdict remained valid as has the awe for the imam, who continues to supervise closely from above what is happening in Iran and in the world, pending his or the Hidden Imam's momentous return. Khomeini's vision that the Islamic Revolution should apply worldwide has at least maintained his lifetime achievements: an ideological foothold in neighboring Iraq, a firm base in Syria and Lebanon via Hezbollah, namely the maintenance of the Shiite Crescent to compete for hegemony with the Sunnite adversary in the Arab world in general and the Gulf in particular. Moreover, anyone who watched his funeral and the frenzy of people struggling behind his procession to touch a tail of his cloak could not help thinking that they were witnessing the death of a hero: an imam sent by divinity to revolutionize Islam, who would leave a void behind until his or the Hidden Imam's return to salvage humanity.

The year 1989 was also when Omar al-Bashir took power in Khartoum and began his practical dyarchy with Hassan al-Turabi—the one providing the military rule that is necessary to secure the backing to any Islamic rule and the other providing the ideological underpinnings of their joint rule. In those years, the Sudan became an Iranian base for extending its influence in Africa, despite its Sunnite affiliation. For both partners, the theme of Islamic Revolution and the active involvement of Khartoum in practical terrorist activities was more important than the hairsplitting doctrinal differences that separated them. Hamas too, though not yet receiving direct assistance from Iran in those years, was just one year after the divulgation of its charter (1988) and building up its following among the Palestinian people, which made it self-confident enough to resist the Oslo Declaration of Principles (DOP) signed in 1993 between Israel and the Palestine Liberation Organization (PLO).

Expectedly, there were many other significant events that rocked the world in those years, but they are not part of our design here or have had such a minor impact on other world events as to render them irrelevant. President P. W. Botha resigned the presidency of the apartheid state of South Africa, leaving it to President F. W. De Klerk to valiantly revolutionize the system there, free Nelson Mandela from his twenty-six-year captivity, and prepare the grounds for the transfer of power to the "black majority," as if the political system were henceforth based, once again, on race and not on individual merit. In the Bay Area of California, a 7.1-magnitude earthquake shattered houses and bridges and caused many fatalities at the end of 1989, and some famous world figures died, including President Ferdinand Marcos of the Philippines, the artist Salvador Dali, actor Lawrence Olivier, the Russian human rights fighter Andrei Sakharov, and boxer Sugar Ray Robinson. The Dalai Lama, who since 1958 had been exiled from his native Tibet, won the Nobel Peace Prize in 1989, the most valuable "consolation prize" available in the modern world.

Like in other momentous moments in world history, historians ask themselves whether there was any link, causal or incidental, between events that unfolded separately but simultaneously in different parts of the globe. See, for example, Karl Jaspers's "Axial Age," the era of the great thinkers in various cultures of the ancient world around the fifth and sixth centuries BC, when Confucius, Buddha, the Jewish prophets, the Greek philosophers, and others all created their streams of thought while ignorant of each other. In this instance of the modern Islamic context, one asks oneself whether—in view of the globalization of information, the paradoxical immediacy of the media; the intensive interaction between nations, cultures, and peoples; and the rapidity of the communications and transport systems—the great events of the current Islamic axial era are interconnected or should be tackled separately for what they are.

In the coming pages, we will be inquiring whether the existence of "axial events" that effect tectonic shifts in the world leave room for an independent foreign policy that we impute to individual nations, especially the great powers among them, and whether the scarecrow of instability still has negative effects on the relations between nations. The idea of foreign policy conjures up the vision of cabals of international relations experts who are specifically convened by the chanceries of the world to concoct secret plans of how to advance their nations' interests and how to deal with other countries through scheming, self-strengthening, trading, aiding, arm-twisting, threatening, posturing, squeezing, blackmailing, cajoling, and sometimes forcing and even purchasing the positive or submissive attitudes of others. But Jews who have suffered throughout the twentieth century and beyond from the myth of the *Protocols of the Elders of Zion*—that infamous czarist fabrication published at the turn of the twentieth century that accused the Jews of a conspiracy to rule the world and even provided fake protocols of their secret meetings to achieve their goal—know better than that. They know better because, despite the international trials that took place in various locations in the world (Bern, Moscow, Cape Town), where those protocols were put before panels of judges and the judgments uniformly and consistently condemned them as libelous hoaxes, they persist among anti-Semites, particularly in the Arab and Islamic worlds. These trials have shown that no group or even power can decide for itself how to deal with the affairs of the world, because no one single group or nation is capable of doing it—not even great powers.

Take for example the greatest world power, the United States of America: its world involvements in the twentieth century—namely the two World Wars, Korea, Vietnam, Afghanistan, and Iraq—were not deliberate decisions based on foreign policy but responses to outside triggers that were neither planned nor expected. If this is true for America, how much more so for lesser powers who have no power of decision anywhere at any time. Therefore, the entire notion of foreign policy is actually nonexistent—at least in terms of policy making on a grand scale; instead, what is tackled by foreign ministries is foreign relations between nations, which do their best to form alliances, to gain assistance or extend it to others, to manage crises when they emerge, and to respond the best they can to preserve their country's interests.

The pretense of developing foreign policy has disappeared subsequent to the Vienna and Berlin Congresses (1815 and 1878, respectively) and the Versailles Conference, which followed World War One. In the twentieth century, due to the establishment of the United Nations, the advent of the Cold War and its demise, and the emergence of globalization, other international fora of various sorts have taken over the task of dealing with foreign policies: nongovernmental organizations (NGOs), UN bodies, humanitarian organizations, G7/G8, NATO, the Warsaw Pact, the European Union (EU), the Scandinavian countries, the CENTO, ASEAN, and SEATO regional organizations, and other associations of American, Asian, African, or Pacific gatherings binding together to advance economic, security, and other interests. Add to the list ethnic- and religious-based organizations, such as the Arab League, the Organization of Islamic Cooperation, the Organization of African Unity: all by definition scuttle any attempt by any individual nation to develop its own foreign policy.

A twin fear underlines American and European foreign policy (if there is any): the concern for stability and a gripping anxiety lest the current turmoil in the Arab world lead to Islamic rule, which is wrongly termed *Islamist,* that is, one of the many manifestations of the Muslim Brotherhood and its many derivatives and affiliates, all coming under the often misleading umbrella of "Islamism." President Ronald Reagan defied the stability of the seventy-year-old Soviet regime and its allies in the Soviet Bloc and dubbed it the "evil empire," successfully striving to bring about its demise. He acted thus because he realized that causing temporary instability was a necessary step leading to stable, predictable, peaceful, and desirable situations. The year 1989 was an axial year in which Communism was beaten and Islam gained currency, the two processes not being unconnected. The yawning vacuum that the fall of Communism left behind has indeed resulted in the search for new identities in many places: consider nationalism in Eastern Europe or Islam in the former Central Asian and Caucasian Islamic countries. In Israel, the demise of the Communist Party, which had for years dominated Israeli–Arab politics, gave way to the dramatic rise of the Islamic Party.

So it goes with the myth of stability, before a distinction could be made between desirable and undesirable stability. A sort of evil stability was provided by Saddam Hussein for thirty years (1975–2003), in contrast to the dynastic stability that the Assad Alawite family provided for forty-five years so far, the monarchical systems in the Gulf and in

Jordan and Morocco, and the military regimes established by Mubarak, Ben Ali, Saleh, and Qaddafi for decades, which were not questioned by the West as long as they were considered its allies. Only when they began teetering on the edge toward perdition, as a result of the rise of the Islamic Spring and domestic revolutions, did the West remember that they were not democratic and therefore did not provide a desirable stability, and in fact created a new threatening instability. But when the specter of Islam appeared in the horizon, it caused the West to shudder. What if instead of deposed and forlorn Mubarak, the authoritarian, "solid and credible ally" of yesteryear, a Muslim Brotherhood government were democratically elected, even though those elections might very well be the last? By definition, an Islamic government might shun the Americans, except for their military aid until it was substituted for by some other power (Russia, or perhaps the mounting capacities of China or Iran). That scenario has unfolded in Egypt, Tunisia, and perhaps to be followed by Syria, Yemen, and Libya.

Israel too is deeply frightened by such a prospect, especially when it hears many candidates for office in those Arab countries and most parties running for parliament reconfirming the need to either abrogate the thirty-year-old peace between Israel and some Arab states (Egypt and Jordan for now, with the Palestinians teetering on the edge), or at least to revise it. That peace, which was signed between Israel and Sadat more than three decades ago, and with King Hussein two decades ago, has been resented by much of the populace, something which should warn all of us that a peace that is concluded at the whim of a dictator can also be cancelled at the whim of his successors. In other words, national and international stability is also contingent on the sort of regime that agrees on it.

For Israel, the choices are more difficult and the consequences more dire than a matter of foreign policy, from which one can just learn a lesson. In the unlikely situation that relatively stable, democratic, and moderate regimes rise in the Arab world as a result of the present turmoil, Israel will undoubtedly be exposed to untold pressures by the West to compromise with the new regimes because they are supposedly moderate and deserve Western sympathies. But in the more likely instance that doctrinal Islamic regimes, such as the Muslim Brothers or their Hamas branch, which has been recognized internationally as a terrorist movement, win elections or otherwise take over government, then Israel, who must face them, may gain some Western sympathy. Under such circumstances, perhaps the Islamic menace that is also feared by the West is better for embattled Israel than the sweet trap of the Arab "moderates," against which she might fight courageously to survive but would be abandoned by her allies. Like Poland, Israel would become, in Churchill's eternal words after September 1, 1939, "magnificent and forlorn."

In the poet's words: "There is nothing stable in the world; uproar is your only music."[3] There is an atavistic human quest for stability. The fear to lose what one has, the suspicion emanating from uncertainty, and the need for repetition of the known and the rehearsed are stronger than the curiosity to explore new avenues and more overwhelming than the daring it takes to change the familiar. Therefore, change and turmoil have been the domain of the outstanding few, while conservatism and stability are the region of the many. Not surprisingly, conservatism and stability have been safeguarded by those who could lose from change, whereas change has been the motivating force behind the have-nots, revolutionaries, and progressives who can only gain from change. In politics, national and international, the catchword is *stability*; namely, regardless of the nature of a domestic regime and of the uneasy coexistence between various powers on the international arena, everyone craves stability. In other words, better to have a stable evil government somewhere than to have a more benevolent administration collapse every now and then unpredictably, throwing the country into instability and chaos. With a stable regime, one asserts, one could do business and rely on continuity, expectability, and accountability; with a chaotic system one is afraid and reluctant to deal, lest investments be wiped out, alliances collapse, regional security be compromised, and trade halted. But one has to pause for a moment to ask whether stability is always desirable, possible, or even necessary; and whether change, especially if it is for the better, is not preferable even when it generates chaos, disorder, and unpredictability, at least in the transition phase. Hence, instead of taking stability as a paradigmatic axiom and as a prerequisite for peace and prosperity that one has to pursue at any cost and under all circumstances, one ought to differentiate between desirable and undesirable stability; there is a stability one ought to encourage and another that one must undo—a good stability and a bad one.

For decades, the Cold War was an element of stability between two superpowers: each could destroy the other many times over; each dominated its system of alliances that was pitted against the other's (NATO versus the Warsaw Pact; SEATO and CENTO against a potential Communist threat; ASEAN and the Shanghai Group to check China's growing power; EU, the Arab League, the Organization of African Unity, and the Organization of Islamic Cooperation to crystallize regional, ethnic, economic, and religious groups to resist the pressures of perceived rivals, and so forth). Each block undermined the other in overt and covert activities; each operated under the assumption that it ought to win over new allies and subtract them from the other; each competed with the other on the international scene in economics, ethics, politics, sports, propaganda, the military, and the production of weapons of mass destruction. And yet that stability, which had translated since the 1960s into "peaceful coexistence" and later into the various SALT talks, contained an element of instability inasmuch as each side proclaimed its upcoming victory by peaceful means over its rival. By definition, if you compete with your rival and wish to undo him or her, or change him or her to your liking, you introduce instability into the equation.

This exercise in unstable stability climaxed under the Ronald Reagan administration during the 1980s, when, on the one hand, frequent summitry with Secretary Gorbachev was proclaimed to diminish world tensions and eradicate the dangers of Armageddon; but, on the other hand, Star Wars was initiated by the Americans to stretch the Soviet economy to its limit and push it to abandon the arms race. This process, in retrospect, triggered changes within the Soviet Bloc and brought about its demise and the dismantling of Communist regimes everywhere thereafter—save in doctrinaire North Korea so far. So, as long as the seeming interpower parity prevailed, there was a similitude of stability that was constantly undermined by American ambitions to bring to an end the empire of evil and by the Soviets' desperate attempt to hold their own after becoming aware that the hollow structure of Communism was well on its way to creating a new instability of world proportions.

The American endeavor to create the instability that would bring down Communism was eventually replaced by a new quest for stability, once the new post-Soviet Yeltsin regime of the 1990s proved more to the liking of the United States insofar as it signaled the triumph of capitalism, which had prompted Francis Fukuyama to announce the "end of history." This new shift in American policy was also predicated on the assumption that, being the only remaining superpower, the United States could henceforth singlehandedly run the new world of Pax Americana, in which it would play the predominant role, hence its interest in perpetuating it through stability and economic prosperity. But there are indications that, when a forceful post-Yeltsin nationalist regime took over and the long and authoritarian reign of Putin, under various titles, came to the helm, Russia would not toe the Western line, and it would reassert, in competition with the United States, its superpower role in the world. The first signs of that were seen in the provision of Russian nuclear technology to Iran, in the Russian support for the Saddam regime in Iraq and the Assad rule in Syria, and since 2014 in the artificial crisis in the Ukraine, which has already regenerated the imperial instinct of the Russians in the brutal annexation of the Crimea to Russia, in defiance of the entire world. That means the re-creation, once again, of a new status quo of stability in the Russian sphere of influence under Putin, reminiscent of a mini-Brezhnev Doctrine that may generate a new balance of power and therefore a potential regional and world instability. But this time there is no Reagan in sight to challenge it.

The varying American responses go a long way to show that stability as a general proposition has little meaning unless it is qualified as positive or negative, and for whom. The dilemma of striving to attain a positive stability while seeking to undermine a negative one has had many antecedents in world history and in world affairs today, not only as part and parcel of "foreign policy" made by the powers, but also in the day-to-day decisions that every country undertakes. The seeming contradictions in foreign policy stem from the necessity to relate to other countries—not as the product of a preconceived strategy, concocted in armchairs behind the closed doors of some chanceries, but as a response to rising challenges from the outside. In this sense, it is erroneous to speak of foreign policy, but we should speak rather of foreign relations, within which every country attempts its best to respond to rising problems not of its own doing. When a power is shaken by what lay at its doorstep and is forced to react, it calls the situation "unstable," but when it responds as a matter of routine to the expected and predictable, it dubs the occasion as "stable."

During World War II, the United States, the Soviet Union, and China were allies against Germany, Italy, and Japan; immediately after the war, the United States and Japan became the closest allies in East Asia against the Soviets and the Communist Chinese; and the United States allied with Germany and Italy under NATO against the Soviet Bloc. The alliances forged during the war—in a period of turmoil and instability, which came in response to German, Italian, and Japanese aggression in Europe, Africa, and the Pacific—were reversed immediately after the war, with a view of establishing a new era of stability. But why were alliances shifted so radically? It was thought that while wartimes were inherently unstable, post-war developments could afford new alignments that would create stability. But that stability turned out to be temporary and undesirable until it was overturned, together with the Cold War, into a new chaos. The great ideas of a "new world order," proclaimed by President George Bush (senior) turned out to have produced a new world disorder. The Ukraine/Crimea crisis of 2014 might signal that the historical pendulum has swung the other way and put to rest the notions of stability and instability as it has been understood in the preceding decades.

Jerusalem, Winter 2014–2015.

Notes

1. Khomeini, Ayatollah, *The Islamic Republic*; and Sayyid Qutb, *Our War against the Jews.*
2. See R. Israeli, *The Spread of Islamikaze Terrorism in Europe,* Vallentine Mitchel, 2008; and R. Israeli, *The Islamic Challenge in Europe,* Transaction, NJ, 2008.
3. John Keats, *Letters,* January 13, 1818.

1

World Upheavals in the New Islamic Axial Era and Their Impact on Islam

There is little doubt that the most earth-shattering event that has impacted the thought, politics, society, and conduct of the Muslim world in recent times has been the collapse of the Soviet Bloc, and with it of Communism as a competing alternative to Western capitalism. The ramifications of those developments were multifactorial among the Islamic countries. Internally, old Communist parties simply shrunk into insignificance once it was shown that their promise had been a thin veneer of pretense, which waned under the burden of its own inefficacy and helplessness in the face of the contemporary world's requirements. In view of its traditional hatred toward the West, which had been forged by Muslim radical thinkers since Hassan al-Banna and Sayyid Qutb, the great luminaries of the Muslim Brothers who had accused the Western colonizers of oppression, exploitation, and penchant for laxity in social behavior that corrupted the Muslim youth, it was no surprise that the West was shunned by the Islamic world, at least in theory.

In those years, the Soviet Union, the loyal ally who had never failed its Muslim clients, seemed the alternative to counter the Western threat. Indeed, many promising young people in the Muslim world were invited or sent to Moscow to pursue their studies-cum-political-indoctrination. They enrolled in professions like medicine and engineering or underwent other training courses that prepared them for community or political work in their countries. They learned Russian, and the elite among them took advanced degrees, such as PhDs in Marxist theory, Marxist economics, and Marxist history as viewed and analyzed from the Communist point of view. The case in point was Mahmoud Abbas, otherwise known as Abu Mazen, then a senior PLO official and after Yasser Arafat's death the president of the Palestinian

Authority (PA). He chose a topic for his dissertation that suited both his dedication to fight Zionism and Israel and his host's propaganda line, which promoted anti-Semitism masquerading as "anti-Zionism." His thesis, later published as a book, claimed a collaboration between Zionism and Nazism and diminished the Holocaust by cutting down the number of victims from six to less than one million. In other words, the import of those studies was not to discover historical truth but to serve the propaganda campaign of both his organization and his host's.

The Muslim students who dwelt in Moscow in the thousands, as part of the large body of invited cadres from all nonaligned nations, were not necessarily committed Communists but had a vested interest in training for careers without incurring any cost. They not only learned what was needed for their training but were also indoctrinated with the idea that the Soviet Paradise, which promoted exemplary models of economic and social development, was also the international hub of world peace and fraternity between nations. After the devastating Muslim defeat in the War of 1967, it was the Soviet Union who helped rehabilitate the routed nations, replace their destroyed military equipment, and encourage native models of "socialism" that resembled the structure of the Soviet Union itself and of the Soviet Communist Party in their organization, centralism, and authoritarianism. It seemed then that the Islamic world, save for the very conservative monarchical regimes of the Gulf, was comfortably placed in the bosom of the Soviets and well disposed to enjoy that position indefinitely.

But 1967 also generated a countercurrent of religious revival throughout that Islamic world, especially following the October 1968 Cairo Islamic Conference, which convened chief clerics and scholars covering the entire span of the Muslim world, from Morocco to Indonesia. In the painful soul-searching deliberations, which attempted to ponder the reasons for that unprecedented "glorious Muslim defeat" in modern times, they came to the conclusion that, while Islam had reached its climax close to the time of the Prophet and thereafter, when it was upright and ruled by the standards set by the Messenger of Allah, it was the Western corrupting influence on Islam that had caused its demise. The lesson was inescapable: only a return to Islam and its ancient norms could rescue it from oblivion. In other words, while Western utopia for progress and improvement lay sometime in the future and may be attained gradually by determined social, political, and intellectual measures; Islamic utopia was projected into the time of the Prophet in the past, and all that was needed was to strive to approximate the achievements of the Prophet's generation by studying and applying them in the real world. Hence the spread of many Salafi movements, connoting a return to the era of the *aslaf*, that is the ancients.

The Islamic movements, which emerged under various appellations, were not at ease with the Soviet alliance that had been thrust upon them as a matter of convenience. Therefore, as soon as the Soviet Union collapsed and the Communist parties in the Arab world withered away for want of commitment to the idea of Communism, a giant vacuum was created that needed to be filled urgently. In Israel, for example, one of the few places in the Middle East where a Communist Party was legal, an Islamic movement emerged where local politics had been dominated by the Communists. But now, even those who remained within the Communist Party had to change their name, as other Communists in the rest of the world had done. The wedding of convenience between Islam and Communism came to an end. Russia, who inherited the Soviet Union, became a close ally to the least Islamic regime in the Islamic world, that is the Alawites of Syria, but also defended the cause of Iran in an attempt to regain what it had lost. But the defeat of the Soviets in Afghanistan in 1989, which put an end to their ten-year, "Vietnam-like" venture, only precipitated Soviet prestige to its lowest ebb.

For the world of Islam, the Soviet demise in Afghanistan meant more than that. It meant that Muslim mujahideen were able, by their primitive weaponry but with the aid of other Muslims, namely the Muslim volunteers who flocked in from the entire Islamic world, to beat one of the two superpowers and force her to retreat. The conclusion was swift and clear: the other superpower (the United States) could not be far behind, an assumption that was not off the mark in view of the upcoming retreat of the United States and the takeover by the Taliban in Afghanistan when foreign intervention ended in 2014 or 2015. Moreover, the very intervention of the Soviets on Christmas 1979 had been motivated by their fear, lest the Islamic upheaval that began with the Iranian Revolution one year earlier might seep into its five Islamic republics of Central Asia, which were adjacent to Iran (Tajikistan, Turkmenistan, Kyrgyzstan, Uzbekistan, and Kazakhstan), and the Islamic Republic of the Caucasus—Azerbaijan—which borders Iran. The Soviets had hoped to stem that danger by demonstrating that the Iranian Revolution had been a paper tiger, but they eventually failed, much to the delight of Muslim radicals worldwide, who seized the opportunity to organize their forces and launch their onslaught on the West and the Jews.

The end result was that those six Muslims republics were freed from the Soviet yoke and became independent once the Soviet Federation crumbled. It was tempting for Muslims across the world to conclude that it was *their* mujahideen who were to be credited for that achievement and that thanks to other Muslims, not foreign powers, their brethren were liberated, increasing the number of Muslim countries to 57, almost one third of the world count in those days, when membership of the United Nations amounted to 180. The Muslim mood in the world was upbeat, not only due to the numbers of believers approaching the billion mark, billing their creed as "one quarter of humanity," but also boasting Muslim identity and promoting its international success. Indeed, the Organization of Islamic Cooperation (OIC), which had made its debut in 1968 as a result of the arson of the al-Aqsa Mosque in Jerusalem, when Muslims across the world rushed to falsely indict Israel of its premeditation, was a manifestation of that newfound pride. The first Rabat Summit Conference of the organization in 1968, under the pretext that it was urgent to "come to the rescue of Jerusalem," was concluded with a unanimous decision to establish a Jerusalem Committee, headed by the host of the conference, King Hassan, who hastened to call the central square in Fez "the Jerusalem Plaza," to evince his loyalty to Islam, for he had been much maligned by many Muslim radicals for "selling off" to the United States, France, and Western values and for maintaining secret contact with the Israelis, all unforgivable sins in Islamic politics.

Since 1968, membership in the OIC continued to grow in leaps and bounds, and in 1976 the incredible happened: Turkey, which under her civil and jealously guarded secular governments had avoided any official involvement with religion, suddenly yielded to the public mood and agreed not only to join the OIC but also to host that year's conference in Istanbul. The symbolism could not be missed: what used to be the splendid capital of the Muslim Ottoman Empire and the seat of its glamorous sultan, who was also the caliph of all Muslims, unexpectedly admitted to her Islamic past and present Islamic identity and joined that great association of modern Muslim states. Not since the disappearance of the caliphate after World War One, when the Ottoman Empire was dismantled, had Muslims across the world experienced that feeling of great Muslim power converging together—as if the gathered heads of the Islamic world represented the corporate caliphate that was no more. Since the Istanbul encounter, the membership of OIC grew to include such countries as Uganda, who was not exactly Muslim but was ruled by a Muslim tyrant, Idi Amin Dada, and that was enough for him to draw his country into the fray. Naturally, since the rise to power of the Islamic Party of Tayyip Erdogan in Ankara in 2002, the feeling of exhilaration with growing Muslim power has heightened, as it did in the 1970s when Pakistan revealed its "Islamic bomb" and as the Muslim world is bound to boast again when Iran achieves its own.

Admittedly, the Iranian Revolution of 1978 has caused unease in some quarters of the Sunnite majority, which fears the aggression of the Shiite Crescent, constituted by Iran, Iraq, Syria, and Lebanon, to the point that some Sunnite clerics have dubbed the Shiites as "worse than the Jews," a compliment not easily disbursed to a rival in the Islamic world. But, beyond these divisions, which pit Iran and its satellites against Saudi Arabia and its cohorts, there is agreement between the two parties that the victory of Islam takes precedence over the theological differences between Shia and Sunna. For example, the Islamikaze acts of terror, which were invented originally by Shiites (and were wrongly dubbed "suicide bombings"), have become a favorite modus operandi of many Sunnite groups, such as Hamas; some PLO factions, such as the al-Aqsa Brigades; some terrorists in Iraq and in Afghanistan; and others. Hamas in Gaza has been relying on aid from Iran, and many Muslim terrorists convene for their annual meetings in Tehran, regardless of their Sunnite affiliation.

Those years that followed the Soviet debacle in Afghanistan also saw the rise of the Afghani phenomenon in the Islamic world. Tens of thousands of Muslim mujahideen had indeed been recruited by American encouragement and Saudi financing from all over the Islamic world to flock to Afghanistan and to fight against the hated Communist superpower until its capitulation. Those Moroccan, Saudi, Jordanian, Iraqi, Chechnyan, Bosnian, European, and other volunteers had gathered in camps financed by the CIA, and they kept the stream of reinforcements from drying up in that demanding ten-year fight against the Soviet Russians. But when dwindling Russia capitulated and the war was officially terminated, those Afghani outsiders returned home and began to pose a local problem for their governments. In 1989 and thereafter, those repatriated fighters, who had now become a roving international jihadist camp, ready to go where they were needed for the cause of Islam, soon became one major issue for their governments. They went to Iraq to fight the Americans, returned to Afghanistan to face their former American allies who had assisted them against the Soviets, and are now the major component of the Syrian rebels against the Assad regime and the ISIS movement in Iraq and Syria. One of them, probably the most renowned and the most influential, was Osama bin Laden.

Bin Laden contributed more than any Muslim at that time to debunk the myth that Muslim terrorism was due to poverty and disaffection. The South American favelas, those makeshift slums that surround all major cities in that continent, provide daily proof that material misery does not necessarily produce indiscriminate terrorism against innocent people. But bin Laden's personal wealth had attested to the contrary. He could have led an easy life, like his peers in Saudi Arabia, in the opulence of his palaces, but he elected to fight for his ideas in the mountains of Tora Bora in Afghanistan, pursued by American aircraft and Special Forces attempting to eliminate him for a decade or more before he was gunned down in his secret abode in the garrison city of Abbottabad in Pakistan in 2012. It also happens that the two most fundamentalist Muslim countries—Saudi Arabia and Iran—are also the richest, so that poverty could not have been the reason for their radicalism. While Iran continues to serve as the international hub of Muslim terrorism, it has been the massive participation of individual Saudi donors in the world jihadi effort that had first allowed thousands of Saudi volunteers to fight in Afghanistan against the Soviets, then for the 9/11 events to happen, and for the continued bloodletting in the Syrian civil war and in ISIS's onslaughts in Syria and Iraq.

In Afghanistan bin Laden met the militant Muslim scholar Abdullah Azzam, of Palestinian origin, who devoted his latter years to posing the ideological fundaments of the universal jihad that radical Islam had vowed against the United States and the Jews. He was, like others, thoroughly influenced by the knowledge, the political and theological acumen, and the total devotion to the cause of that scholar and was so swayed that he forewent his family life and his initially positive economic activity, which had made him wealthy. Upon returning to Saudi Arabia as an "Afghani," who had been hardened by his battlefield experience as a *mujahid,* bin Laden became restless and fanatically determined to overthrow the corrupt and elitist royal regime under which he had grown in Riyadh. But soon he was identified for the danger he posed to his peers in the kingdom, was stripped of his Saudi citizenship, which had caused much embarrassment to the relations between his country and the United States, and expelled from the country. He was on the road from then on, together with his nuclear family, on the lookout for a land of shelter that was Islamic enough to accept and protect him, poor enough to vie for the funds he could provide in return, and deserted and inaccessible enough for foreign powers to remain unable to locate him or to dislodge him from there. That land would serve as the physical base for his new organization, al-Qaida (literally, "the Base"), and as the metaphoric base of the world jihadi movement he was determined to found, lead, and fund by his own means.

The organization spoke about confronting "American arrogance" and world Jewry (not Israel or Zionism, as others who wish to dissimulate their anti-Semitism pretend), which were seen as close allies with Jews at the lead. They were accused of providing the ideological underpinnings for "controlling the world" under the well-known and widely diffused "world Jewish conspiracy" and other conspiracy theories that jihadi Islam, like Hamas and the Muslim Brothers, had liberally borrowed from the *Protocols of the Elders of Zion*. Powerful America, it was claimed, was the financial and military arm that was manipulated by world Jewry to achieve its goals. That was the reason that on September 11, al-Qaida attacked the Twin Towers and the Pentagon, the symbols of American economic and military power, and all over the Muslim world there was great jubilation. However, some Muslim quarters were so embarrassed by the scope of that horror that they tried to impute the CIA or Mossad, claiming that Jews were in any case involved in it.

After he was ejected from his homeland, bin Laden sought and found shelter in Sudan, which in 1989 came under the rule of General Omar al-Bashir, who later became involved in the Darfur massacre and was indicted by the International Criminal Court for crimes against humanity. That poor country was hungry for bin Laden's foreign currency and was itself too involved in horrific mass murdering to resent bin Laden's terrorist schemes. For that reason, bin Laden settled there until the 1998 al-Qaida's terrorist acts against the American embassies in Kenya and Tanzania, resulting in hundreds of fatalities, both American and African, raised the wrath of the United States. The Clinton administration retaliated with a few bombings of the Sudan and threatened the host country with more unless bin Laden and his group were expelled from the country. In his search for new asylum, bin Laden identified Afghanistan as such a target. Since 1996, the Taliban had taken over the rule in Kabul and established such a strict Islamic rule there under Mullah Omar as to make Saudi Arabia look like a bastion of liberalism. The mullah was an unknown cleric who had gained spiritual control of his Taliban during the Afghani civil war. Once bin Laden was introduced to him in Kandahar, they became close friends, and the determined Afghani mullah guaranteed asylum to his guest, whatever the price he would have to pay.

The unipolar world of the 1990s and the dramatic fall of the Soviet Union were accompanied by vast economic troubles and deep social problems. The rise of Islamic radicalism, which challenged Russia's hinterland and forced it to take harsh measures against its Muslims in Chechnya and the Caucasus, also helped shift world attention to a new vocabulary in the West that seemed to adapt to the idea that militant Islam was there to be reconciled, not to be fought, despite its many outrageous outbursts of violence against not only the West and Israel, but also against its own people. If we say, for example, that murdering Jews is the result of anti-Semitic hatred and contempt toward them and anti-Western violence is generated by a fanatic and intolerant Muslim creed, then how do we explain the mass killings of Muslims by Muslims, which account for the majority of fatalities in Islamic countries—Syrians against Syrians, Iraqis against Iraqis, Afghanis against Afghanis, black Muslims in Darfur by Muslim Janjaweed, and other mass killings in Algeria, Lebanon, Yemen, Pakistan, the Palestinian Hamas, and all the rest?

The inescapable conclusion is that some trigger-happy Muslims, who are propelled by jihad, display their disregard for human life—which renders execution of others, capital punishment, hijacking, kidnapping, robbery, hostage-taking, beheading, mass murder, mutilation of the living and the dead, and torture—as an acceptable norm of conduct. Implementing Sharia rules in domestic penal law, and even more so attempting to impose its standards on foreigners (like in the cases of Daniel Pearl in Pakistan, Salman Rushdie in England, the authors of the anti-Muhammad cartoons in Denmark, or the Christians of Nigeria by the Boko Haram), are the best indications of the low value of human lives in their eyes. When practiced against Jews, this view is rationalized in many ways—as "anti-Zionism," or vengeance for the "crimes against Palestinians," or "self-defense," or "reaction to Western arrogance and Islamophobia," to their "humiliation of Muslims," or "desecration of Muslim values," along with any other amount of trumped-up rationalizations. Underlying all those rationalizations is the burning desire by many Muslims to impose by force their ideals, values, and rules of conduct both on their own nationals, whom they view as apostates, thus deserving death, and certainly on their rivals, who are often considered as enemies of Islam and Allah and therefore are equally deserving of annihilation. No debates, negotiations, compromises, or arguments are possible with this "expression of the will of Allah," and therefore no perceived offense against or deviation from these rules is tolerable.

It is often claimed that this strict interpretation of Islam with its abuses, including a blatant anti-Semitism, is only the lot of "fanatic," "radical," "fundamentalist," or "Islamist" Muslims, usually quantified as some 15 percent of the 1.5 billion world Muslims, as if that were a different faith embracing different principles than those followed by the rank-and-file Muslims. In fact, even if that were true, we are talking about 200 million individuals, spread among all nations—from the Boko Haram in Nigeria to the Lashkar-e-Taiba in Pakistan—whose numbers are large enough to cause trouble for the entire world. In reality, all 1.5 billion Muslims belong to one creed, who uphold Sharia law to various degrees but champion the same tenets, though those who do not follow them to the letter are not adepts of another alternative faith known as "moderate Islam," which is sometimes dubbed by ignorant politicians as "a religion of peace" to distinguish from the violent and aggressive conduct of the "extremists." In reality, no such separate Islam exists, though there are certainly many truly moderate Muslims who have broken off from the bloody path of Sharia law, especially some of those dwelling in the West, who can from a safe distance criticize the recurring killings of "apostates," "traitors," the phenomenon of the Islamikaze bombers against Westerners and Israelis, the culture of death that is groomed in many Islamic lands, and indeed the unbridled anti-Semitic calumnies that are rife in their environments. But "moderate Muslims" have yet to produce an alternative doctrine and worldview that could rival official Islam or posit a creed and a set of rules to persuade Muslims to relinquish the Sharia and embrace another way, thus excluding themselves from the community of the believers in the eyes of established Islam.

Moderate Muslims often accuse the radicals, who are in fact Muslims who behave in accordance with the accepted rules of the Sharia, of having "hijacked Islam" or distorted its real meanings, or misinterpreted it, and they in turn are condemned by their rivals for having abandoned the path of Allah or for having themselves been corrupted by Western ideologies. But, for better or for worse, it is the standards of the radicals that prevail in the Islamic world. One can watch the mass demonstrations in the streets of Gaza, Quetta, Casablanca, Durban, and Jakarta, or in the Muslim neighborhoods of Paris, London, Sydney, Amsterdam, and Toronto to realize how alive, universal, and popular are the Muslim mantras that are uttered, along with the rampages that are performed daily by men, women, and children, including leaders and clerics. Are they all Islamists? No, they are simply Muslims, and the common denominator that links them in their hatred of the West and the Jews is Islam, standard Islam, under the justification of the Sharia, which is promoted by their imams. While some moderate and courageous Muslim individuals will be there to save the honor of their faith when they raise their lone voices against the abuses perpetrated in the name of their creed, mainstream Muslims, including Westernized and modern professionals, intellectuals, and students, will also always be there to glorify in the executions of Westerners and Jews by Muslim terrorists, to write or broadcast in favor of the Islamikaze, and to distribute sweets in the streets to celebrate the deaths of Americans and Jews.

The champions of the spurious distinction between the so-called Islamist minority and the peaceful Muslim majority—who became entrapped in their reluctance from a carpet condemnation of Islam lest they be accused of Islamophobia or racism (as if Islam were a race and not a multiracial and multicultural creed) if they are non-Muslims and of treason if they are—are also enslaved by another distinction of their own making, which has equally no leg to stand on. That is "Judeophobia," a parallel to Islamophobia, to separate from anti-Semitism, which is universally condemned in those circles and is no longer in vogue in the West, at least not in public. They explain to us that Islam has never been anti-Semitic, which proves their ignorance of Islamic sources, and that the current dislike of Jews is no more than Judeophobia, which has no historical roots and has been a modern, circumstantial, and fleeting phenomenon that does not warrant uncalled-for anxiety. If flagrant and constant anti-Semitism is reduced to temporary and passing Judeophobia, it would merely become a junior counterpart of Islamophobia, and a lesser evil, making it less objectionable and more acceptable, on par with Islamophobia, as a collateral phenomenon in modern society. Generally speaking, they would simplistically argue: how can Muslims, specifically the Arabs, themselves Semites, be anti-Semitic?

It is exactly this war of words that has been engineered to obfuscate substance and increase the currency of Muslim terminology while at the same time depriving the Jews and their supporters from their traditional arsenal of words in the battle against anti-Semitism, which then needs to be clarified and understood. Could anyone explain in what way the Quranic condemnation of Jews as "descendants of pigs and monkeys"—which is routinely preached to all Muslims (not only

"Islamists") by their clerics in the Islamic world and in the West—can be construed as merely Judeophobic and not anti-Semitic? Is this hallowed reference, which is as eternal as the Word of Allah, a circumstantial and fleeting pronouncement? To say so would be a blasphemy. It is used by Muslim clerics, as a matter of course, in such "moderate" and "pro-Western" countries as Saudi Arabia, Egypt, and Jordan, as a continuation of the traditional way to demonize and dehumanize Jews in order to facilitate their annihilation. What more would it take to call this a plain manifestation of violent anti-Semitism?

Words were created to transmit conventionally agreed-upon meanings. If each actor chose to lend to his words a different significance or to accuse others of distorting their meaning, then we would no longer be able to call a spade a spade or communicate with others on any issue. Anti-Semitism is the irrational hatred of the Jews, and it has been called so since the onset of modern research on this sinister issue in the nineteenth century. No amount of manipulations of words or creation of parallels to dilute that terminology will succeed, exactly as no coupling of the unique term *Holocaust* with Armenians, Darfurians, or Rwandans (incidentally, the first two massacres were perpetrated by Muslims) can blunt the poignancy of the Jewish Holocaust or rob it of its uniqueness. No wonder then that the most frequent manifestation of anti-Semitism these days, both among Muslims and among their European anti-Semitic allies, has been Holocaust denial, meaning that the devalued term has acquired a generic usage for all sorts of massacres: the hated Jews cannot even claim to have acceded to the "honor" of having been the unique victims of that calamity.

The increased waves of recriminations of the Muslim world against the West and Israel during that axial era are also evident in the rise of Muslim parties in Turkey, Egypt, Jordan, Morocco, Sudan, and the Palestinian Authority. It has also found expression in the unbridled desire of the Iranians to go nuclear and in the thug-like rhetoric of its previous president Ahmadinejad against Western values and Jews, to the point of denying the Shoah in blatant terms, all indications of the spreading anti-Western antagonism in Islam. The zeal in the Islamic world has been directed not only against Israel and the West but aims primarily to sweep out of power their own Western-allied regimes, which are regarded as American stooges. As the major Egyptian paper *al-Ahram* put it, "Religious identity has replaced nationalist ideology,"[1] and that applies not only to Muslim countries but also amid Muslim minorities throughout their diasporas. This means that Muslim terrorism will continue to rise in both Europe and the Muslim world, hence the relevance of the present volume as a precursor and follow-up to the saga of September 11 and its aftermath. One has to realize, nevertheless, the distortions of the basic characteristics of Islam by both scholars and politicians, who wish to depict a more benign and less menacing picture of the Islamic rise than it is. This is done through the two distinctions that we have mentioned above, which have become conventional wisdom among both critics and proponents of Islam. One is the artificial bifurcation between the so-called Islamists or radicals, who are the minority "bad guys" who spoil the lot by their violent deeds, lend a bad reputation to the majority of their coreligionists, and wage war against the West and Israel and the majority, which is arguably "peace-loving," shunning violence and having no quarrel with the West. The other artificial, and equally spurious, distinction wants us to believe that Judeophobia, which is an attenuated sort of anti-Semitism posing as anti-Zionism and anti-Israel, has nothing to do with anti-Semitism; and that while Islam as a whole carries no traces of anti-Semitism, its present anti-Jewish manifestations are no more than a less lethal and vastly less threatening Judeophobia. It is clear that these "scientific" distinctions may have some empirical merit to them, but seem to have much more to do with political correctness—with a degree of sheepish dhimmi-like submissiveness or fear of being accused of racism—than with historical reality.

It is an unconvincing argument that Muslims are merely anti-Israel and anti-Zionist and not anti-Semitic, when Jews in the Western Diasporas are habitually attacked by Muslims and have been historically mistreated, beaten, massacred, or forced to convert until compelled to leave the lands of Islam, apart from the fact that they were Jews. French Jews, British Jews, and Belgian Jews are all citizens of the countries in which they live and cannot influence the policies of the Israeli government even if they wished to do so. To attack them is totally gratuitous and is undeniably an expression of the innate anti-Semitism in Islamic thinking. The equivalent in Jewish attitudes would be for Jews to attack their fellow Muslim citizens in European countries every time a Muslim country defames, vilifies, demonizes (or indeed physically attacks) Jews in the media or school curricula, or subjects them to individual or collective economic boycotts, all of which actually happens on a sustained, daily basis in Muslim lands. If it were Jews who committed the attacks, that would be a case of Islamophobia, and the fact that it does not happen proves first that Islamophobia, at least on the part of

Jews, is a figment of Muslims' imagination (bandied about precisely to combat the very notion of their pervasive anti-Semitism); and second that Jews, at least in the Diaspora, can distinguish between right and wrong and have never lost their sense of justice and civilized behavior, despite the relentless provocations of Muslims, and not only radicals, against them. When people are given the opportunity to express themselves freely in the Islamic world, such as in Algeria, Jordan, Egypt, Tunisia, and lately Palestine, it is almost invariably political Islam that gains votes, and since it is popular vote, it cannot be said to represent "radicals," exactly as it cannot be claimed that the more than 60 percent of Palestinians who voted for Hamas in 2006 were all Islamists.

After September 11, a talk show was held by Al Jazeera network (representing what is known as moderate and peace-loving Islam), in which the question was posed to the panelists and their viewers about whether bin Laden was a terrorist or a hero. The only moderate panelist, a Tunisian, was mocked and humiliated by his co-panelists and by the moderator of the show for daring to dissent from the otherwise unanimous opinion that crowned bin Laden as a national hero. Viewers who called or emailed from around the entire Islamic world were almost unanimous in the consensus. That was not a poll among Islamists, but among the rank-and-file Muslims, most of whom were supposedly the educated owners of PC computers. Yet their reaction was Islamist in substance.

So where is the distinction between the supposed moderates and the alleged Islamists? Yes, there are Islamikaze activists who are ready to blow themselves up for the cause of Islam, in the process of killing Westerners and Jews. But they are only a handful who are recruited, trained, financed, indoctrinated, and dispatched by a vast infrastructure of Muslim states, organizations, and individuals and surrounded by the sympathy and admiration, often adulation, of the vast masses of the Muslim public and the mainstream press, and in countries that are clients of the United States or have signed peace with Israel. Who is then an Islamist among all those activists and supporters, and who is moderate and peace loving? In the United States and Europe, several Muslim intellectuals, leaders, and clerics, who gained favor with the authorities and access to the highest echelons of power for their supposed moderation and their openness to dialogue were later arrested for their illicit fund-raising for Muslim terrorist organizations, for incitement to terrorism, and for suppressing women's rights. Did those leaders suddenly turn from moderate to radical? No, they were the same Muslims who were perceived previously as moderate when they acted a certain way and who became Islamists when they were caught red-handed engaging in subversive acts. In both instances they acted as Muslims in the name of Islam. It was Western scholars and Westernized Muslims who attached those epithets of "moderate" and "Islamists," which the Muslims themselves never recognized.

Similarly, clerics and other mainstream Muslims who dub the Jews "descendants of pigs and monkeys" based on a Quranic passage or cite the Hadith, which claims that on the Day of Judgment Jews will hide behind rocks and trees, but the rocks and trees will acquire the magic power of denouncing them and will invite the Muslims to come and kill them, are not exactly setting themselves apart from Islamists. All Muslims who cite those passages, and they all do regularly, are making blunt anti-Semitic and genocidal statements against the Jews, and no amount of rhetorical maneuvering can mitigate that fact.

Throughout the Muslim world, the legitimacy of Israel has been challenged, and the Holocaust is denied systematically, as evidenced by the popularity of such Holocaust deniers as Robert Faurisson, Roger Garaudy, or David Irving. Those countries also prohibited *Schindler's List* from their screens and condoned the violent declarations of the Iranian president on both scores. This is a common denominator among most Muslims, and just like the anti-Jewish stereotypes, nothing differentiates between radicals and moderates. That is the reason why we find Muslims contradicting themselves on the Shoah, denying it on the one hand and wishing Hitler had brought his annihilation plan to completion on the other; they also urge a "scholarly, free, and objective" research of the Holocaust, but only in order to prove that it never was. Similarly, the belief in and the spread of the *Protocols of the Elders of Zion,* the blood libel, the poisoning of wells by Jews, and conspiracy theories concerning the Jews are recurring themes in Palestinian (not only Hamas) as well as mainstream Egyptian, Jordanian, Saudi, Pakistani, and others' writings, systems of beliefs, and propaganda. Genocidal threats against the Jews have abounded not only in bin Laden's statements and in Ahmadinejad's delusions, but also in columns of Egyptian, Saudi, Palestinian, and other mainstream newspapers. Is this Judeophobia of the moderates or plain anti-Semitism of the Islamists? Words have a significance, and it is imperative to streamline our vocabulary; otherwise we are under the permanent threat of losing our ability to express what we mean or to comprehend what we are told.

Matters are further complicated by the paranoia and conspiracy theories that are widespread in the Muslim world among Islamists and others, whether modern and Western-educated or traditionalist and obscurantist. Those theories that are rampant even among Muslims living in the West would insist that world leaders who support Israel are Jewish (like presidents Reagan and Bush), that the United Nations, of all places, is the mastermind of the Jews, who utilize it as the tool for their world dominion, and that the major violent acts that have shaken the world, such as the World Wars, world revolutions, and September 11, are all the fruit of Jewish imagination and execution. Their minds are so permeated with these nonsense theories that they have become impervious to logical, rational debate. Therefore, the difficulty of dealing with Muslim minds consists not only in removing the mountains of pure delusion that choke their thinking, but also in persuading them that the very attempt to counter those untruths is not necessarily part of the world conspiracy that is being woven against them. It is possible to explain their imaginary picture of the world by their need to project on their enemies the analytical shortcomings that bewitch them, but it is impossible to move them out of the illusory scenarios that they have constructed around themselves, and then they cling to them with a tenacity that defies and contradicts Western standards of logic. The result is that even when Muslims initiate and launch an act of violence, they accuse the West or Israel of an act of aggression against them, of which they are the victims and which requires their retaliation or vengeance.

This reversal of facts is what characterizes the behavior of Muslim terrorists who seek refuge in the West, for the most part while on the run from their home regimes that they tried unsuccessfully to topple. Since they are persuaded that they fight for the path of Allah, they certainly do not regard themselves as terrorists, and, when they are arrested for terrorist activities within their host countries, which had generously, naively, and self-defeatingly given them shelter and provided for their needs, they accuse their benefactors and condemn their "barbaric behavior." This mechanism of denial, which posits Western democracy as a milking cow that owes them sustenance while they owe it nothing, allows them to deny the good and the protection they get and to even mount subversive cells that are liable to act in the heart of their countries of refuge. Their denial allows them to wreak havoc, death, destruction, and terror upon the nations that took them in, in spite of their repeated promises to the authorities that they will refrain from political or subversive activity as a condition of being accorded the status of refugees.[2] A sort of political denial is also adopted in the Western chanceries as well, under the belief that if they meant well for the Muslim refugees they would encounter exemplary behavior on their part in return. Even the al-Qaida entrenchment in the United States and Europe and their illicit activities were not enough to stir suspicions and to instigate the slumbering Western governments to take measures of self-defense until the Muslim radicals struck, first in the United States then in Europe. The new Muslim terrorists put the blame on the West for rescuing them from their own corrupt regimes, and therefore the host countries that have tried to fight terrorism are accused of racism, Islamophobia, an anti-Islamic drive, inhumanity, and the like. The democratic countries of shelter that have absorbed these streams of refugees, who have arrived uninvited, now become the oppressors of the poor and peaceful Muslims, like their original oppressive countries of Saudi Arabia, Egypt, Morocco, Yemen, Libya, and all the rest.[3]

Muslim diasporas in the West, which have vastly expanded since the 1990s and have acquired political power through sheer numbers of their coreligionists, have attempted to dislodge the older and more established, though far less numerous, Jewish communities from their advantageous positions. By doing so, they wish to eliminate the Jewish influence on the local governments and thereby shift the traditional political sympathies of the West from Jews and Israel to the Arabs and the Palestinians. This is why Islamic protests in Western societies almost invariably go hand in hand with anti-Semitic eruptions of violence. Again, this would seem an acceptable and legitimate way of political lobbying in any liberal political system, except that Muslim populations most often do not fulfill the two conditions that accompany political protest in the democratic West: they do not act in the interest of their host countries but rather against it, and they do not refrain from violence and the breaking of the law. For Muslim immigrants do not seem to have internalized these restrictions at the same pace that they have mastered the benefits they can extract from their countries of shelter. Many naturalized Muslims—for example some of the perpetrators of 9/11 and then the London attacks of July 2005—did not hesitate to act against their hosts, who had showered them with benefits; and many other Muslims who have sought shelter in Europe, Canada, and Australia devote their time not to assimilating into new environments but to cultivating their separate identities and building enclaves of Islam in their host countries. For example, far from accepting their host countries' Middle Eastern policies or their antiterrorist struggles, they protest against them, often violently.

The second count of using violence, which is usually shunned in Western societies, raises even more concern, because it ultimately hurts public order and value systems in host cultures. Since the outbreak of the Palestinian al-Aqsa Intifada in late 2000, thousands of violent demonstrations by Muslim immigrant populations have unfolded from Montreal to Sydney, from Sao Paulo to Durban (South Africa), from Oslo to Rome—apart from the usual anti-Israel and anti-Jewish demonstrations that have exploded throughout the Arab and Muslim world. Anti-Israeli demonstrations are certainly legitimate, but when they involve bouts of rage, the burning down of foreign embassies and flags, the pelting of rocks against houses of prayer, and sometimes murdering of innocent civilians or when effigies of American and Israeli leaders, who are often personal friends and certainly political allies of the local leaders are burnt and abuses hurled at them, this is the limit that the rule of law can permit, of which Muslim immigrants often seem to be unaware. Indeed, few Westerners participate in these acts of violence, and conversely no Jews have responded by committing the same acts against Western or Muslim countries with which the host society maintains relations. What is more, although Jewish communities worldwide have rallied around Israel, they have done so with dignity and full respect for the law and have not allowed harm to be committed against their home countries or against the violent crowds of Muslims and their supporters.

The most distressing aspects of these outbursts of violence have been that Western countries have been turned by their Muslim communities into violent arenas where the Middle Eastern conflict has been exported. Not content with attacking American and Israeli symbols in Western capitals, these hooligans who terrorize the downtown areas of their countries of residence turned to brutal onslaughts of the local Jewish communities in France, Britain, Germany, Belgium, and others, thus signaling to the world that Jews and Israel were to be equated and that anti-Semitism meant also anti-Zionism, or even pure and simple anti-Israeli outbursts. The worst hit were the Jewish communities in those countries, where hundreds of Jewish synagogues, cemeteries, schools, and other institutions were torched or otherwise desecrated; Jewish adults were attacked on their way to and from prayer; and children on their way to and from school. All this has happened under the eyes of the local police, who have not dared to intervene forcefully for fear of the politically correct politicians. One can only imagine what would have happened if a mosque or a church were likewise burned, or non-Jewish worshippers or children attacked and harmed. Other places have also experienced the full extent of this pogrom, which in many Jewish circles was reminiscent of the infamous Kristallnacht of 1938. In most, though not all, cases, these horrific anti-Semitic attacks were orchestrated by the Muslim communities of Europe, at times in conjunction with local inveterate anti-Semites.

The outcome of all this is that the Muslim communities in the Western democracies have shown since the 1990s that they can act in unison to undermine public order, to pose a serious threat to national security, and to harm their fellow citizens, Jewish and otherwise. This means that they can organize and demonstrate in the same fashion in their host countries when they judge an issue important enough or when local authorities are too lenient or reluctant to confront them. Polls organized in the United States after 9/11 found that Americans overwhelmingly tied Islam and Muslims to those horrific events: 68 percent of them approved of randomly stopping people who might fit the profile of suspected terrorists, 83 percent of Americans favored stricter controls on Muslims entering the country, 58 percent wanted tighter controls on Muslims traveling on planes and trains, 35 percent of New Yorkers favored establishing internment camps for individuals who the authorities identified as sympathetic to terrorist causes, and 31 percent of all Americans favored detention camps for Arab Americans as a way of preventing terrorist attacks in the United States.[4] This means that the threatened population found itself ahead of their authorities, which were more cautious in limiting civil rights, and the general public was prepared to a great extent to replay the unfortunate experience of the internment of Japanese Americans in World War II. It was to be expected then that if and when more major acts of terror unfolded in the West, the West would find itself compelled to curtail civil liberties and take radical measures against the Muslim minority in its midst. Only in this light did the very moderate measures taken by Israel against its demonstratively hostile Muslim minority, which had come under scathing criticism from the pre-9/11 world, look incredibly generous and even border at times on neglect.

All these developments, which have swept through both Islamic countries and Muslim communities in the West, have created a mood that has evolved since 1989 creating awe, and often outright fear, in the West from militant Islam and from the chaos it can create if not addressed. The 2006 Cartoon Affair, in which Denmark and other European nations shamefully capitulated to the violent and murderous attacks against them, are a case in point. Instead of defending the liberal ideas of the West, including the hallowed freedom of expression, as they were being dramatically and violently challenged, the Danes, the European foreign minister, and the United Nations elected to placate the hooligans and their supportive Arab governments, particularly Saudi Arabia, who threatened economic boycott of Danish dairy products. That show of muscular force, which ended up intimidating Europe, could not help but boost self-confidence in the Islamic world that their economic power could easily bring Europe to its knees, not only on the cartoon issue but on any policy that displeased them. How much more concerning when it involved the Arab-Israeli conflict, where unless the European Union took a clear-cut anti-Israeli position, the Muslim world would act, by force if necessary, to impose its views. And what has happened to Western ideas of fairness and support for freedom and democracy? Who cares? No one of consequence talks about that any more, and no one acts to stop the Western drift toward submitting to tyranny. So much so that Europeans have come to accept the Muslim thesis that the honor of the Prophet of Islam was more important than the lives of innocent people who were killed during the Muslim rampage as a result of the Cartoon Affair, or the material losses that were sustained by the boycotted countries.

Notes

1. *Al-Ahram Weekly*, "Beyond the Vacuum," April 13–16, 2006.
2. *Executive Intelligence Review*, September 4, 1998.
3. *Al-Ahram Weekly*, October 1, 2001.
4. See Daniel Pipes, "Fighting Militant Islam, Without Bias," *City Journal*, Autumn 2001. http://www.city-journal.org/htm/41/fightingmilitant.html.

2

The New Tripolar World—The United States, Russia, and China

In the heyday of the Cold War, the two world blocs were pitted against each other: the West, with the United States, Western Europe, and several regional alliances, arrayed against the Soviet Bloc, with its on-again, off-again Communist allies, including China, Yugoslavia, Albania, Vietnam, North Korea. The members of the Warsaw Pact countered them on a standstill deterrence governed by MAD (mutually assured destruction) that was based on mutual nuclear threats of extermination many times over. But already in the 1950s Tito's Yugoslavia took its separate path toward a more humane Communism, and the Sino-Soviet rift was occasioned by a more doctrinaire Chinese separatism that did not accept the Americano-Soviet path of coexistence amid the Cold War. That meant that each of the three powers could not converse with the other two, and this in fact turned the world into a tripolar competition, though admittedly China was the less competitive of the three. The collapse of Communism, which had momentarily allowed the world system to be dominated by the United States, has caused since 1989 the emergence of a tripolar world once again, with Russia, under Vladimir Putin, reasserting its place as a world power and China, with the engine of its spectacular economic success, emerging as a third leg in this new tripod of the world order. All three converse with each other and even engage in diplomacy concerning several world problems, but the potential for rivalry and even for confrontation between them continues to increase.

The tripolar world is being constructed not only as a consequence of the 1989 watershed in the world of Islam but is also dramatically influenced by it. Except for the Crimea and Ukraine crisis, which erupted in 2014 and scarred the US–Russia collaborative efforts, most of the other topics of disagreement between those two powers have either emanated from the radicalized Islamic world of post-1989 or remained linked to it in the long run. China's rifts with the West in the United Nations and other diplomatic arenas, while generally supportive of the Russians because of their common pro-Arab/Islamic policies, have strictly toed the line of their particular interests, especially in the economic and energy domains. While each component of the power tripod has its own axe to grind, there is no doubt that they all look for areas of convergence with each other, for it is always easier, cheaper, and more expedient to achieve a goal by agreement rather than under duress and amid controversy. For example, Russia, who has consistently supported the Assad regime in Syria in order to defend its own naval bases in the Latakia area, has deployed tremendous efforts to prevail on their client to dismantle its chemical weapons arsenal under the threat of American military intervention, rather than see Assad and his regime crumble and be taken over by the rebels. The most powerful of those rebels are radical Muslims from various denominations who are not likely to embrace Russia as an ally should they gain the upper hand. The Russians prefer to keep Assad in power rather than line up with his enemies. On the other hand, other Muslim radicals who are fighting on Assad's side, such as the Iranians and their Hezbollah clients, certainly feel blessed by Russia's support of them, as a superpower umbrella ensures the continued flow of arms from Russia and its unflinching diplomatic backing in international fora.

Due to its energy constraints, China has also backed Iran on the Syrian front and resisted any attempt to condemn it or impose sanctions against it, in spite of the ongoing massacres that are being committed against the Syrians by their government and vice versa. Worse, in its desperate attempts to lay its hand on future sources of energy wherever it can find them, China has even allied with the fugitive war criminal President Omar al-Bashir of Sudan, who has been indicted by the International Court in the Hague for the massacres in Darfur, in return for the rights to search for petroleum there. Also, in the context of energy thirst and strategic pursuits, China has adopted a reverse policy of fighting radical Islam in its own territory in the rebellious northwestern province of Xinjiang, where the Uighur population has been in effervescence since the 1980s. That question will be dealt with below in some detail, but here it is provided as an example to what length China, like other powers, is prepared to go in dealing with post-1989 Islam for the sake of advancing its perceived national interests. The Uighur unrest has also provoked China to improve its relations with long-term rival India, which has also suffered from Islam both domestically and in the adjoining territory of Kashmir, in spite of its traditional alliance with Muslim Pakistan, which has also been under the sway of Taliban and Lashkar-e-Taiba, both radical Muslim movements.

Until the Ukraine crisis of 2014, the United States and Russia, under weak and hesitant Obama and militant and vindictive Putin, respectively, had gone into a pattern of dealing with their most urgent frictions in Europe and the Middle East by discussing them peacefully, if not resolving them. All this while the United States has been disengaging from its expensive wars in Iraq and Afghanistan, from the Arab-Israeli conflict, and from the Arab Spring that turned Islamic Winter, while also turning its attention to the Pacific Rim, specifically to China, Korea, and the local conflicts in the South and East China Sea. But as long as the Middle East kept burning and the Arab Spring raging, the Russians were welcome junior partners in various peace processes as long as they were weak, and they could be made members of the inanimate "Quartet," that club of impotents that has achieved nothing so far, and when achievement appeared on the horizon, it was the Americans alone who negotiated it and dealt with it. For the other participants it was merely geared to maintain an eye set on the "political and diplomatic horizon," realizing full well that "horizon" referred to an imaginary line that ran farther away every time one seemed to reach it. But Russia, which has been entrenched in Iran and its proxy Syria, has been trying to reopen the doors of other Arab countries by posing itself as an alternative to disappointing America, which seems to be resolved to abandon the Middle East. Indeed, after the United States relinquished its old ally, Hosni Mubarak, and supported the Muslim Brothers instead, those who unseated elected President Mursi and took over from him were chastised by having part of the American aid to Egypt suspended, so Egypt turned to Russia for compensation. The Saudis, who were furious at the United States both for abandoning Mubarak and embracing Mursi and for the United States' failure to rein in the frantic Iranian effort to nuclearize, also began to talk with the Russians to create some compensating counterbalance. But even in that forum of P5+1, in which the three polar powers are supposed to collaborate on the Iranian nuclear program, a clear dichotomy is noticeable: the four Western participants are trying, more or less genuinely, to arrest Iran's race to the bomb, while Russia and China are being more lenient and protective toward it.

While the United States' reorientation toward the Far East has not been publicly resented by Russia, and that country may even regard that change of emphasis as relieving her from the US rivalry in the Middle East, China's considerations are different. She has been regarding American presence in the West Pacific as a penetration into her sphere of influence and a direct threat to her, something like 1930s Japan's, who resented faraway America as an impediment to her building of the Asian Co-Prosperity Sphere, which she thought belonged to her by right and nature. Japan has in the meantime turned from rival to ally of the United States, and China from ally of the United States under Japanese occupation into a rival that now contends for hegemony, out of a natural desire to translate her vast economic power into a political and strategic advantage. The stakes are high: not only does she have a vital interest in defending the islands in the South and East China Sea, which are also claimed by Japan, Korea, Vietnam, Taiwan, and the Philippines, but she also can revive and sustain her old revendications now that she is also capable of substantiating.

First and foremost among those claims is Taiwan, the American-supported dissident province that since the rise of Communist China in 1949 has posited a direct challenge to Beijing under the title of the Republic of China, based in Taipei and claiming sovereignty over the entire Chinese subcontinent. During the Cold War, the Taiwan Strait had been one of the most dangerous places in the world, with the American Seventh Fleet poised to defend the nationalist regime, which had placed its military outposts right on the islands of Quemoy and Matsu in the bay facing the Chinese mainland. But since President Nixon's visit to China in 1972 and the establishment of diplomatic relations with Beijing in 1979, the United States has relaxed its tight embargo on the China coast, and the relationship between the two countries has gradually improved, always at the expense of Taiwan. Sino-American relations have grown considerably, with the Chinese economy booming at the breakneck pace of approximately 10 percent a year in average for the past thirty years, and the American economy shrinking to the crisis ebb of 2008. That reversed the economic balance of power in the world: no longer was poor and backward China dependent on the United States' wealth and generosity to feed its own people, but it was the United States in crisis who needed the Chinese economy to wean itself out of the crisis. This reversed dependency inevitably raised the prestige of China in the world as a vast economic system, and correspondingly weakened the United States' stature. There were four major consequences to the reversal: one, the Chinese gamut of choices was noticeably diversified; two, the United States' options were narrowed; three, China has begun to upgrade its military stature to bring it to par with her economic and diplomatic successes; and four, China embarked on a more vigorous campaign to reinforce its grip on Xinjiang in view of its strategic and energy-wealthy resources.

Since China's first attempts to reach out to Israel for military and farming technology in the 1980s, which were kept under wraps due to China's fears of damaging its vast relations with the Muslim world, things have evolved. Israel's expert technical abilities in those two domains, which permitted China to upgrade its weaponry and agricultural output without undertaking any unbearable expenses that she did not have, have opened new opportunities for both parties to meet each other's needs without compromising much. China has continued to support the PLO and established diplomatic and commercial relations with almost the entire gamut of Muslim countries, while at the same time cultivating secret contacts and an advanced technical collaboration with Israel; in other words, Israel was for China a desirable concubine with whom a relationship was maintained as long as it was discreet; Israel, which unlike other Western nations, did not attach any strings to her aid program, found it expedient to impact Chinese military, economic, and agricultural development, pending the establishment of diplomatic relations sometime in the future. That happened in 1992, and within a few years the two countries' scope of collaboration had surpassed the thirty-year-long Sino-Arab trade relationship. By 1992, China had begun to understand that relations with Israel did not necessarily preclude good relationships with the Arabs or other Muslims. Twenty years after those relations were erected and despite the extraordinary intimacy they have achieved over the years until the AWACS crisis erupted, none of the Arab and Muslim countries have rescinded their relations with China. Moreover, China's unquenchable thirst for more sources of energy has produced an unusually close relationship between Beijing and Tehran and caused further Chinese inroads in East Africa, where sizeable Muslim populations dwell, including Darfur (Sudan), South Sudan, Ethiopia, Tanzania, Kenya, and others.

While Chinese relations around the world continue to prosper, the United States' failure in some Muslim states, notably Iraq and Afghanistan; its abandonment of its trusted clients in Muslim countries such as Tunisia, Egypt, and Yemen; and especially its helplessness in the face of the Iranians' race to the bomb have generated a vast estrangement of the United States among its most important allies in the Muslim world—Saudi Arabia and the Gulf states—and have raised some doubts in other countries, such as Jordan and Morocco, of the United States' ability to stand beside her allies when the chips are down. Some extremist movements, such as the Muslim Brothers, al-Qaida, and Islamic Jihad, have derided Muslim governments who have relied on the United States, comparing its inconsistent conduct with the firm and steady commitment of Russia to its allies, such as Syria, come what may. Concerning the issue of China upgrading its military capacities in order to assert its dominion in the oceans that surround it, several contradictions have emerged, as in the best tradition of Maoist ideology. On the one hand, it was Israel that ran to the succor of China since February 1979's rout of its forces on the Vietnamese border by enabling China to upgrade its military equipment without incurring unbearable and unaffordable outlays in foreign currency and keeping the affair under wraps in order not to raise the wrath of the Muslim world. On the other hand, exactly when Sino-Israeli relations were reaching the climax of intimacy in the mid-1990s, the Falcon/AWACS crisis came about, which forced Israel to cancel the deal and pay damages to the frustrated Chinese for violating the contract with them, thus threatening relations between the two countries, which had been slowly, secretly, and painstakingly built over the previous decade. It became evident that when the United States and China were put on the scale, US-dependent Israel had no choice but to conform to the US line, after it was threatened by its closest friends in Congress that they could not countenance that deal, which was based on Boeing platforms stuffed with Israeli electronics and would have yielded the most advanced early-warning systems to the Chinese in the Pacific, thus posing a threat to American national security there.

On the Xinjiang issue, 1989 was also a turning point for all parties concerned. More than a decade after the abuses of the Cultural Revolution (1966–76), in which lawlessness had thrown China into chaos, the post-Mao leadership was still trying to heal the wounds occasioned by the violent mistreatment of minorities, notably the Muslims, as manifested in the Shadian Massacre of Muslims in the province of Yunnan in 1976. In the summer of 1989, an extraordinary procession of several thousand Muslims, including some Chinese, marched through the streets of Beijing, while some shouted, "Allahu Akbar!" with men wearing their white caps and women hiding their faces behind veils. Similar processions took place in large Muslim communities in faraway provinces in the West—Qinghai and Xinjiang. In that tightly controlled regime, which permitted no demonstrations, the protests were allowed because they were not made *against* the government but *to* the government, in response to a tactless and plainly provocative Chinese book that had appeared in Shanghai, equating Muslim architectural features to sexual organs, suggesting that Muslims were obsessed with sex, a claim that had no leg to stand on, but Chinese readers were nonetheless elated to read about it, while Muslim citizens were provoked to respond. The book was eventually confiscated by the authorities, but a new awareness had been kindled among Muslims in particular and the general populace in general, despite the simultaneous events in Tiananmen, which had dwarfed the "Chinese Rushdie Affair," as the affair was dubbed there, and it illustrated the rise of a new consciousness.[1]

Throughout the 1990s, while in other places throughout China the relatively small Hui Muslim minority had kept quiet, knowing that it could be wiped out if it rebelled or rioted, in the outlying Xinjiang region, the Muslim Uighurs seized the moment to claim their rights, launch local uprisings, and even raise demands of autonomy, secession, and separatism under the slogan of "Free Eastern Turkestan," which could only be countered with repression by the Chinese regime. As researcher Lillian Craig-Harris has put it, "The Muslim groups of Xinjiang regarded Turkey, not China as their spiritual Homeland."[2] What raised the tensions between the host Han culture, and what it viewed as its "guest," Uighur culture, was the failure of this social paradigm in the cultural equation of their relationship. The Uighurs rightly felt that East Turkestan was theirs from time immemorial and that, though the Chinese dynasties had occasionally extended their dominion over that territory, they had never ruled it effectively, let alone continuously, for any length of time. Quite the contrary, not until the Ili Crisis of 1882, in which the Qing Dynasty won a battle against czarist Russia over control of Central Asia, did China lay a practical claim to that territory and encapsulate it into its administrative system, thus necessitating its renaming to Xinjiang (meaning new border). For the native Uighurs, however, who had experienced all manner of wars, occupations, and religious conversions, their country had been repeatedly invaded by various imperialists, the latest of which were the Han Chinese, but the predominating demographic prevalence had always been Uighur.

The Chinese concept of a unitary state ruled from one center, reinforced by the modern notions of sovereignty and effective rule, rendered Xinjiang every bit an integral part of the Chinese homeland as every other province of China, including Tibet. Even the fact that the latest transmutation of the Turkic Uighurs had made them Muslims did not convince the Chinese to categorize them on that basis, since the only differentiation between peoples they knew was ethnic. So as there were Hui Muslims in China proper, there were Uighur, Kazakh, Dungan, Kyrgyz, and other minority groups who believed in Islam in East Turkestan. But unlike the cultural autonomy promised to its minorities by the People's Republic, the Chinese state not only oppressed any sign of religious, linguistic, or ethnic autonomy but—due to Xinjiang's strategic importance—it intensified the settlement of Han youth in the province to dilute Uighur aspirations and frustrate their newfound nationalistic enthusiasm. The Uighurs then realized that not only could they not follow the example of their nearby compatriots (Kazakh, Kyrgyz, Tajik), who had been released from the Soviet yoke and become independent, but they were now bound to see their limited autonomy shrinking further in an attempt to choke separatism. The Uighurs were now outnumbered by the Han, to the point that they felt strangers in their own country, and their youth were being encouraged to seek work in Chinese big cities. Thus, dilution worked both ways, but the Uighur presence throughout China would facilitate their subversive antigovernment acts, as the 2013–14 bombings in Beijing and Kunming attest.

In this light, the current Uighur problem should be regarded as an international issue between the Han majority and the Uighur minority and not simply as a Chinese domestic issue. For, in spite of the lack of any chance for the Uighurs to achieve any sort of separation, or even a meaningful autonomy, their enthusiasm for self-determination did not wane. Second, there is evidence that the rebels received some aid, and not only spiritual, by other Muslims who regarded their struggle as an extension of the universal Islamic aspiration to assert itself and of the impact of the success of Afghanistan and of the independent Central Asian states. Indeed, Uighur riots have been triggered not only by Chinese oppression but also by the atmosphere of Islamic victory, first against godless Soviet Communism in Afghanistan and then against oppressive Western imperialism in Iraq and Afghanistan, and now against the rising second Communist superpower that has been trying to overwhelm them. The rebels certainly understood that, like their Tibetan counterparts, they stood no chance at bringing China to its knees. Their incapacity to posit a real challenge to China would nonetheless continue to kindle their hopeless enthusiasm, encouraged by the Uighur diasporas in the West and by Islamic bodies like al-Qaida.

The Uighur crisis in China rapidly overflowed into a wide array of Chinese interests, both with the Islamic world and the wider world in general, as part of those axial years and beyond. The Uighur protest escalated from a minor incident in Guangdong in 2007 to a demonstration of 3,000 Uighurs, including many high school and college students, in Xinjiang that summer. The riots turned violent, and the events reverberated through the world media as "breaking news," in spite of the Chinese information firewall that attempted to contain it, then to minimize it, and finally to justify it by explaining their circumstances. And though more Han people were victims of these events than Uighurs, the latter were inevitably conceived as the oppressed underdogs and treated by world media accordingly. Exiled Uighurs around the world, not only within China itself, propagated the outcry of the oppressed, magnifying it in the larger context of demands for an advanced autonomy, and even independence, occasionally conjuring up the Tibetan plight, which had garnered sympathy and criticism of the Han majority a year earlier. This context was also convenient for the comparison between Rebiya Kadeer, the exiled leader of the Muslim Uighurs and president of the World Uighur Congress, and the Dalai Lama.

Praise for Kadeer was coupled from within Xinjiang with another remarkable Uighur woman, Tursun Gul, who had been campaigning for the release of her arrested husband and his four brothers. She was concerned over his heart condition and, at thirty, had become a symbol of Uighur defiance. She acknowledged nonetheless that "thousands of Uighur men rampaged through the regional capital of Xinjiang (Urumqi), while her husband kept at home." She also admitted that "Uighur men set fire to hundreds of cars across the street where they lived. It was an act of bravery and defiance on her part that was spread around the world from the riot zone. The lone woman hobbling on her crutch toward ranks of militias and police, with their armored cars retreating as she approached shaking her fist"[3] was vividly reminiscent of the lone person who twenty years earlier had defied the immense roaring tank in Tiananmen Square.

The other symbol of Uighur protest, Mrs. Kadeer has been successfully wielding the power of the pen since her exile to Washington DC, where she heads the world organization of her ethnic group. She is often interviewed in Western media and has become the acknowledged voice of the Uighurs in the West. After the Urumqi riots broke out, she lashed out at the Chinese authorities and sought to exploit the crisis and to gain the support of the West to advance far-reaching demands, which would not likely contribute to pacifying the situation. In an article she published in the *Wall Street Journal,*[4] she confronted the Chinese government's claim that it clamped down on the riots in order to "maintain stability," stressing the courage of the Uighurs "to risk everything in order to speak out against injustice." She also claimed that hundreds of Uighurs were killed in the process, which grossly deviated from the number of forty-six dead Uighurs released by the government, and stated that they died "for exercising their right to protest." But by condemning both parties for the use of violence, she acknowledged that the Uighurs were not simply exercising their right to protest and that those who used violence could clearly expect violence to be used to control them.

Kadeer, who started her business empire in the 1990s with a laundry service, at first represented the success of Beijing's policies to assimilate the Uighurs and was pampered by the Chinese government accordingly. But in 2000 she was put in jail and served more than five years behind bars after being convicted of "disclosing state secrets to foreigners," a serious crime in a closed, secretive regime like Beijing's. She was freed in 2005 before a visit of Secretary of State Condoleezza Rice to China and swiftly deported to the United States. Rebiya, now in her sixties and mother of eleven children,[5] rose so fast to stardom due to her public activity for Uighur rights, that her autobiography, *Dragon Fighter,* became a bestseller and won her a nomination for the Nobel Peace Prize. She fell out of favor with her authorities partly because her husband, who lives in the United States, has been a staunch supporter of Xinjiang independence. Some of her children were mistreated by the authorities, and she was dubbed the mastermind of the Xinjiang disturbances, as if she were the head of a mafia clan. According to her narrative, which is at sharp variance with the government's and other press reports, students organized a protest in the Dong Korok (Erdaqiao) area of Urumqi to express discontent with the Chinese government's inaction in the face of the mob killing and beating of Uighurs and to express sympathy with the families of those killed and injured. She condemned equally the violence of the Uighurs and the "excessive use of force of the Chinese to quell the demonstrations," which, coming from her, also attested to the fact that the Uighurs had overstepped the boundaries of legitimate protest, which permitted the counter-use of force to quell them. But since she could not shoulder the entire responsibility for the violence, she resorted to the recurrent theme of "police excess of force," which would sound more logical and credible in the propaganda war than China's claim that it was the unarmed and underdog Uighur civilians who launched the violence in the first place. She also blamed the Chinese authorities for "years of repression" and Chinese officials, headed by Wang Lequan, the party secretary of the Xinjiang Uighur Autonomous Region, for not observing the rule of law, which was the root cause of Uighur discontent. But her previous acknowledgment that the Uighurs had used violence did not exactly present Uighurs as law-abiding citizens either.

In the propaganda war, even the number of fatalities were vastly different. According to Kadeer's sources, which may tend to exaggerate the numbers of her people's casualties and to ignore the Han victims, four hundred Uighurs were killed in Urumqi alone as a result of police shootings, and many more injured; she also stressed that a curfew was imposed, telephone lines were down, searches were conducted in Uighur houses, and males were arrested. As a result, the Muslim minority had to stay indoors, fearing arrest in the streets of their capital. Kadeer claimed that the cities of Kashgar, Yarkand, Aksu, Khotan, and Karamay "may have also seen unrest," which is a strange way to report such a large-scale incident, unless exaggerating data was her main agenda. Precision was exercised only regarding Kashgar, where one hundred Uighurs were reported to have been killed, namely the double of the overall Uighur casualties reported by the authorities. Kadeer claimed that two Chinese soldiers were posted to each Uighur house, which again seems wildly exaggerated, for that would have necessitated one million troops instead of the twenty thousand dispatched there for reinforcement. She imputed the outbreak of the riots to the nationalist streak that the authorities encouraged among the Han to replace the "bankruptcy of communist ideology." She invoked the Tibetan example to reinforce her case, by advocating the principle of "peaceful self-determination" and respect for human rights and democracy, ignoring the fact that China had never played by those rules.

Interestingly, Kadeer, who called for a government investigation of the events that had triggered the riots, also urged the United States to establish a consulate in Urumqi to serve as "a beacon of freedom in an environment of fierce repression" in order to monitor the daily abuses of human rights there. In other words, she believed that a permanent American presence in the heart of the Uighur-inhabited heartland would by necessity restrain the oppressive measures of the Chinese government and ease the stresses of everyday lives for the Muslims in Xinjiang. Her request was backed by reports that thousands of Han people had gone to the streets of Urumqi to take revenge on the Uighurs. These varying reports of the events only contributed to the widening chasm between the parties and made the pacification of Xinjiang even more unlikely. So much so that Kadeer, who is already intensely disliked by the Chinese government, was held responsible for the outbreak of violence, and she was dubbed a criminal, although she categorically denied any involvement. Chinese ambassador to Tokyo Cui Tiankai made representations to the Japanese government to prevent her from visiting Tokyo, arguing, "How would the people of Japan feel if a violent crime occurred in Japan and its mastermind were invited by a third country?"[6] He also hinted that the visit might harm the relations between Japan and China, something neither of them could afford, not only because they were major trade partners, but because they had difficulties settling the controversy over wartime history books, precisely as the PCR had been preparing for the sixtieth anniversary of the republic in October 2009, whose pageantry was to eclipse even the Summer Olympics of 2008.[7]

The Uighurs' cry reflected their deep concern of the Chinese threat to the very survival of Uighur culture, especially in light of the recent announcement of the government that it would tear down the old city of Kashgar, the Uighur cultural hub, and replace it with a new city. The Uighurs were also concerned about the limits imposed on the use of the Uighur language in schools and on the encouragement of Muslim state officials to relinquish the Ramadan fast. These measures were construed in Muslim eyes as geared to erase Muslim culture from their midst. Many of them also considered the massive arrests of some 1,500 Uighurs following the riots as arbitrary. The government's measure to impose night curfew on Urumqi and to cut the Internet connection, which had been the lifeline of Uighurs with their kin in the world, were viewed as government oppression. However, they also saw an improvement in government behavior, in that foreign journalists were allowed into Xinjiang, though they must be accompanied by officials, in contrast with the Tibetan riots a year earlier in which international journalists were expelled.[8] Expectedly, the Chinese government outlets blamed Uighur separatists and US-based Kadeer as the mastermind of the violence, as if the protests were a large-scale criminal act rather than a politically motivated outburst. For the Muslims, that meant a government-instigated retaliation using force by the majority Han Chinese. Indeed, thousands of Han Chinese, armed with homemade weapons, swarmed the streets of Urumqi calling for revenge. Police stopped them with tear gas, but not before they destroyed Uighur shops. Other acts of violence ripped across the city. The firm Chinese handling of the situation, which necessitated President Hu Jintao's immediate return home from a G8 summit in Rome, certainly stemmed from fears that the Uighurs wished to secede, and that, if they were intent on such a course, it would be more difficult for the authorities to put them down, let alone justify harsher measures against them.

The economic, strategic, and ethnic sensitivity of Xinjiang, together with the fact that it shares sensitive borders with Kazakhstan, Kyrgyzstan, Pakistan, and Russia, the latter had also been accused of meddling in Xinjiang affairs in the past, obviously make that remote heartland a focus of world interest beyond the local powers of Central Asia. Hence the world has some difficulty regarding that province and its affairs as a domestic Chinese problem and tends to judge China for its behavior and to castigate it for its policies, as if other nations have an innate right to tell another country what, where, and how to do within its territory. This situation is much reminiscent of Jerusalem, which is also a focus of interest to the international community, and about which nearly everyone asserts the right to interfere and give advice as to how Israel should handle its capital city.

For example, powers or international media, which presume to "understand" China's positions, would also jump to the conclusion that "China's fears are no excuse for its punitive and often violent suppression of the Uighurs,"[9] as if they would do better if they were faced with the same situation. Take, for example, the criticism of Israel worldwide for its devastating bombings in Gaza in the July–August 2014 Gaza War, which were occasioned by the indiscriminate launching of thousands of missiles from Gaza to Israeli cities and could not be arrested unless Hamas in Gaza were defeated and its hideouts among civilians there were destroyed. But the critiques of Israel were only concerned with the Palestinian victims of the war, though no one had any better idea of how to stop the missiles over Israel without destroying the recalcitrant Hamas bases in Gaza. China was caught in a similar situation of being blamed for the Uighur losses, though nobody had figured another way to regain peace and order. Therefore, the reverberation across the world was characterized by self-righteousness and hypocrisy, much like the ongoing conflicts in the Middle East, while when the United States, Britain, Russia, Turkey, and the rest are confronted with similar situations, they behave no better than China and Israel.

Uighurs are not interested in their homeland's importance to China. For them, discriminatory policies by the government, which do not permit them to boast their separate identity, are the key issues. For example, the prohibition of their language in schools; the adamant Chinese refusal to allow its Uighur employees to grow beards, wear headscarves, or pray or fast during working hours; or what they see as discrimination in education, health, housing, and employment—which force the young to migrate to Han-dominated remote provinces while Han outsiders are encouraged by government incentives to "invade" Xinjiang—occupy a much higher place on their ethnic and personal agenda. All the more so since dissent from these practices is harshly repressed by the Chinese government. After 9/11 and the worldwide scare of Muslim terrorism, the repression of Uighurs intensified in Xinjiang; many of their leaders were jailed, accused of having links with foreign Muslim terrorists, and draconian sentences were meted out to any group or individual convicted of terrorism, religious radicalism, or separatism. Nevertheless, claims a Western writer, "No *muftis* in the Islamic world have yet found the time to issue any fatwa (religious verdict) against China."[10] Again, compared to Palestinian Arabs in Israel, whose linguistic, religious, cultural, and social liberties are assured in Israeli democracy, the Uighurs have every reason to feel oppressed; nevertheless, there is much more international criticism of Israel on that score than of China.

Another issue that has inflamed the tempers in Xinjiang that was directly connected to the July 2009 riots was the Chinese policy, already mentioned above, of recruiting young Uighurs for work in the rapidly prospering coastal cities of the south and the southeast of the country. On the one hand, impoverished Uighurs could not resist the temptation of high salaries and promising futures. But, on the other hand, the alienation that their actual exile from their homeland and culture caused them, with the attending loss, or at least blurring, of their sense of identity in a predominantly Han environment make them wary. Chinese officials claim that by moving Uighurs to the cities they elevate their economic status. But some Han Chinese have also come to resent these policies, which they regard as favoritism (in the West this would be dubbed "affirmative action"), while the Uighurs in question are reluctant to be forced into integration, and they resent being discriminated against in government jobs.[11] This means that no easy or satisfactory solutions can be found. For what looks fair, and even a discrimination in reverse toward the minority, would look to the minority as oppressive and even culturally "genocidal." Therefore, to comprehend such complicated situations would always involve considering the constraints of ruling majorities and not only the distress of ruled minorities.

Considerable difficulties have developed as a result of this crisis in China's relations with major countries in the Islamic world, particularly with Turkey, where a major Uighur minority resides, and where historical, linguistic, religious, and cultural links have conditioned the fortunes of what Yitzhak Shichor has called the "Ethno-diplomacy in Sino-Uighur relations."[12] While Turkey, Saudi Arabia, neighboring Kazakhstan, and other Muslim countries have been displaying sympathy for their coreligionists in Xinjiang, discontent had been expressed by Beijing, which feared that its preciously cultivated relations with the Islamic world be harmed. Tayyip Erdogan, the fiery prime minister of Turkey, who in early 2009 accused Israeli President Shimon Peres of a "genocide" against the Palestinians in Gaza, where some 1,300 of them were killed, most during battle, and then callously walked out of the world-media attended panel, once again struck, this time against the Chinese. He accused them of "genocide" for the killing of two hundred people (most of them were Han), during the riots, insisting that there was "no point of interpreting this otherwise."[13] For Erdogan, who carries the terrible moral burden of the genocide of 1.5 million Armenians by his nation during WWI, hurling the same accusation against others, though the numerical disproportion is staggering, may perhaps thereby alleviate his own guilt. Like some Germans and Holocaust deniers who accuse Israel of the nonsense of having become the Nazis of our time or of committing genocide against the Palestinians in order to lighten their own burden of guilt, Erdogan's rhetorics can perhaps be dismissed as a displaced aggression against others to compensate for his own guilt, as he continues to deny the Armenian genocide and civil rights and independence to the Kurds, and in the recent past has launched attacks against them in both Turkish and Iraqi territory.

Thus, official Turkey stood out this time as an exception, compared with other foreign governments, including the United States, who responded cautiously to the crisis and did not rush to condemn the Chinese as a matter of course. Under the heading, "Turkey, Another Axis of Evil?" a Chinese writer lashed out at Turkey for its harsh position on China. He cited Erdogan speaking to a group of foreign ministers from the Gulf area on a visit to Istanbul as saying: "We have always looked to our Uighur brothers, with whom we have historical and cultural ties," and promising that as a member of the Security Council of the United Nations for 2009–11, his country would raise the issue at the United Nations. His foreign minister, Ahmet Davutoglu, emphasized that his country had concerns about developments in the Uighur Autonomous Region and "cannot remain silent in the face of what is happening there," an exact replica of what Erdogan had said about the Palestinians in Gaza half a year earlier. His country's trade unions and business associations went even further by urging a countrywide boycott of Chinese products, an escalation that would lead from a diplomatic to a commercial struggle, similar to what other Islamic countries had done to Denmark during the cartoon crisis in 2006. This anti-China path created the atmosphere in which the Ankara government permitted anti-Chinese demonstrations by Uighur groups dwelling in Turkey, in spite of Chinese support for Ankara in 2003, when it had firmly condemned the acts of terror that had rocked Turkey. Turkey was also taken to task by China for supporting the "separatist and terrorist thugs of Xinjiang, thus raising Chinese indignation."[14]

This state of affairs began to reflect Turkish attitudes to China. Over a dozen Turkish Uighurs gathered one afternoon in Istanbul to welcome a distant cousin and his family who had fled China's Xinjiang province after the 2009 communal violence. Their spokesman, fearing retribution from the Chinese authorities, insisted on using only his first name. The dining room table around which they gathered was laden with Uighur specialties—steamed dumplings, sesame-encrusted flatbreads, pastries stuffed with cheese and dates. "This [China] isn't our homeland," Abdullah, the host, said leaning on a mahogany cane, "but Turkey is our home. We are comfortable here." He fumbled with the Turkish ID card he carried in his shirt pocket and pointed to his place of birth: Xinjiang. Abdullah had received Turkish citizenship almost instantly when he first arrived, via Afghanistan, in 1981. Turkey once had an open-door policy toward its Uighur brethren, themselves a Turkic ethnic minority, who had begun arriving in waves from China in the late 1930s. In 1952, for instance, when several thousand Uighurs fled China's Communist regime into Pakistan, the Turkish government had stepped in and brought 1,850 of those refugees overland to Turkey. The new arrivals were settled in purpose-built housing—called the New Quarter—in the city of Kayseri in central Anatolia and were given jobs and citizenship. Such a welcome, however, is unimaginable today. Even though public sympathy still runs strong for the long-suffering Uighur population of what many Turks refer to as East Turkestan, Ankara has become increasingly wary of antagonizing Beijing. Several years earlier, President Abdullah Gul had visited China and oversaw the signing of $1.5 billion in Turkey-China business contracts. After the 2009 violence in Urumqi, one Turkish minister called for a boycott of Chinese goods, but that was quickly retracted; Prime Minister Recep Tayyip Erdogan, who in his usual outburst of anger labeled events there "tantamount to genocide," has had to tone down his temper and was soon smoothed over by apologetic foreign ministry officials.[15]

China's plight in the face of the danger of increasing world Muslim protest in the future against her Xinjiang policy was dramatized by its apologetic response to the Maghribi Al-Qaida (AQIM) threat to take revenge on China for the death of 46 Muslim Uighurs in Urumqi. No mention was made in that threat, as in its threats against Israel or the United States, of the 136 Han Chinese who had perished in those riots or of the offenses the Muslims had themselves committed to generate the confrontations that brought about those fatalities. Threats were also made of retaliation against the large numbers of Chinese employed in Saudi Arabia and other parts of the Middle East and North Africa.[16] It urged "to chop off their heads in their work places or in their homes, to tell them that the time of enslaving Muslims had gone." This was the first time that any al-Qaida group had threatened China and its interests so directly and so boldly. In fact, in June 2009, the al-Qaida branch in North Africa (AQIM) was reported to have ambushed an Algerian security team that protected a Chinese construction project and killed as many as twenty-four guards. It has also been noted that increased chatter on the Internet among active jihadists indicated that information was sought about Chinese interests in the Muslim world for targeting purposes, claiming to avenge the perceived injustices in Xinjiang.[17]

In pre-Spring Yemen too, where al-Qaida was seeking to topple President Saleh, Chinese interests were also threatened, though no significant link has been detected between the Uighurs and bin Laden or his organization as yet. That is perhaps the reason why, in spite of the vows of revenge against Beijing, no full-scale jihad has been urged against China. AQIM, which supports the idea of a Muslim state in Algeria and resents the unitarian and absolute control of the Chinese Uighur population by a government of unbelievers, has sharpened its harsh reaction and threats directed at Beijing. AQIM was presumed at the time to be buoyed by the Muslim fighters returning from Iraq who were seeking new jihadi frontlines. But it should be noted that even in such a moderate country as Indonesia, the largest Muslim country in the world, some Muslim groups called for a jihad against China, clashing with police outside the Chinese embassy in Jakarta. The anti-Chinese sentiment in the Muslim world was spreading, hence the absolute necessity for the Hu government in China to eliminate the crisis by pacifying it as rapidly as possible.[18] Perhaps in order to placate al-Qaida and escape its wrath, China took the precaution of putting a Uighur Christian on trial[19] to show that the prosecuted Uighurs were not singled out because they were Muslims. In spite of Turkey's and al-Qaida's occasional outbursts of rage against China, one writer asked, under the title "Mute Muslims," "Where are the *fatwas*? The angry marches in front of Chinese embassies, the indignant speeches? Where are al-Qa'ida's videos? In short what does China have that Denmark did not? China has been discriminating against Muslims, and recently a number of them have been killed in violent street riots." Given that so many fatwas have been issued on many international issues, from justifying Islamikaze (the so-called suicide bombing acts of terror) to convicting Salman Rushdie to death, it was surprising that, with regard to the Uighurs, Muslim imams and muftis kept almost silent.[20]

The Arab League and the Organization of Islamic Cooperation have also remained reticent, unlike in the Danish and Gaza cases, in which both organizations were active on all international forums to force a redress of what they viewed as a wrong done by the Judeo-Christian world against Islam. Even Turkey was at first tepid in its reaction, until swept by its own public opinion to embrace a more vigorous response.[21] Maybe the answer lies in the old enmity sensed by the world of Islam toward the Judeo-Christian tradition that it challenges on doctrinal grounds, while toward the Chinese order it has never entertained any fundamental rivalry, save against the Communist regime, which was itself in decline. Al Jazeera network, which is usually supportive of al-Qaida, Hamas, the Taliban, and other Muslim militants, insisted that the Xinjiang unrest "is not ethnic." It suggested that Turkey, which maintained linguistic and cultural links with the Uighurs, criticized Beijing for its "kind of genocide" of the Uighurs, while Iran mildly expressed the concern of the Muslim world, while the rest of Islam remained muted. Wu Sike, China's special envoy to the Middle East, told the network during his visit to its home base in Qatar that his country had always maintained good relations with the region and that these would not be harmed by events in Xinjiang. In his interview he sang the old refrain about "the links between the parties which lasted two or three millennia," and therefore he hoped that "our friends in the region would understand what happened," when "a minority of criminals tried to instigate violence against innocent civilians, in a bid to split the province from China." That statement confirmed that China's primary concern was to calm tempers and to persuade the world that the separatist Muslims stood no chance of succeeding and called upon the Arab world to support China's unity as in the previous cases of Tibet and Taiwan.[22]

Wu Sike pleaded that it was the duty of the security forces of China to "defend the integrity of the country," something that justified eo ipso the use of force. He stressed that no particular ethnic or religious group was targeted: China would take legitimate action only against criminals, any criminals. As if the Chinese constitution signified anything substantive to Chinese Communist Party leaders, Wu assured his interviewers that it "secures the freedom of religion for every Chinese citizen," backed by the presence of "thousands of mosques in China." (It did not occur to the interviewers to grill Wu on the embarrassing question of the simultaneous persecution of the Falungong). He denied that the Chinese government had tried to change the ethnic composition of Xinjiang through immigration and dismissed the question by remarking that "people move around everywhere," like the many Chinese who now live in the Persian/Arab Gulf, while others "have moved to Xinjiang out of their own volition." He also duly supported "Palestinian rights," the "liberation of occupied Arab lands," and emphasized that China did not consider Hamas a "terrorist organization" but supported dialogue between it and Fatah in order to move toward the Palestinian state.[23]

The Islamic Party of Turkestan (IPT), an illegal organization in the heart of Xinjiang that operates clandestinely and in concert with outside Muslims, has released an audio statement in the Uighur language in response to the riots. The voice was that of Sayf Allah (the Sword of Allah), a military commander in the group.[24] He was last seen in a video released in early 2009 titled "Steadfastness and Preparation for Jihad for the Sake of Allah." The recording was played over a still photo, and the statement was posted on jihadist forums in July 2009, the communiqué itself being dated July 7. The communiqué was released by the Islamic Army of Turkestan, formerly known as the Islamic Army of East Turkestan, which is a small jihadist Uighur group, believed to be based, like the beleaguered al-Qaida, in the tribal regions of western Pakistan. The group essentially threatened China over the Xinjiang riots, stating that "Allah's cavalry will soon fall upon you . . . Oh brave *Mujahideen* . . . kill the Communist Chinese wherever you find them."[25]

The wording is strikingly similar, with local adaptations, to al-Qaida and Hamas statements that are regularly voiced against Israel and the West. How far and wide might the Uighur issue reverberate throughout the Islamic world and affect the latter's foreign relations, but also how selective Muslims in the world might be about their outburst of rage was demonstrated in connection with the stabbing of a veiled Muslim woman in a German courtroom in early July 2009. This incident sparked anger across the Muslim world and fueled demands for a formal apology from Germany. But while the Muslim world was raging about this story of the "scarf martyr," holding her up as a symbol of persecution, the more extensive and lethal plight of Chinese Muslims has generally provoked a more sedate reaction. There was obviously not much interest in the Arab and Muslim worlds in these events, and news media covered them only sporadically. Even those writers who were prolific in defending the "headscarf martyr" had little to say about Chinese Muslims. The Saudi *Arab Times* compared the Uighur struggle to that of the Palestinians and the Han Chinese to the Jews. Only when events escalated in Urumqi, the Egyptian state-run *Al-Ahram*'s editorial urged the international community (not the Muslim world) to pay attention to the crackdown. But calls on Muslim leaders to condemn that repression remained conspicuously absent.[26]

This differential treatment of Muslim oppression might seem surprising. But one must remember that, to some Arab and Muslim regimes, especially in the pre-2011 Spring era, the bloody clashes of police with demonstrators in Xinjiang were sadly reminiscent of what happens routinely in their own homes. An Egyptian Muslim opposition leader made the remark that "in both cases they make the same systematic separation of opponents, of Islamic groups, of opposition groups and they arrest many and they kill many . . . How could they criticize the Chinese? They are in the same boat." Conversely, he believes that Turkey's harsh criticism of China is made easier because they have a democratic system. The US-funded *al-Hurra* network reported that in Jordan too there were some signs of protest, as forty Jordanian members of parliament submitted a letter to their speaker calling on the government to condemn the events in Xinjiang. The Islamic Party there asked the government to take a stance toward the "practices against Muslims in Germany and China." But no formal statement by the government came as a result. The reasons for this remarkable abstinence are usually placed with the economic and commercial interests that result from China's strong presence in the Muslim world. For example, China has been the major trade partner of Iran and Sudan and an important source of import to most of the other Islamic countries. Iran, which was itself busy quelling dissenters after the controversial presidential elections at exactly the same time, also remained relatively muted. But individual clerics and Islamic movements have nevertheless voiced their protests.[27]

Particularly striking was the case of Iran, which was the most vocal of Islamic countries criticizing Germany in the wake of the scarf martyr, Marwa al-Sherbini's death. That pregnant thirty-one-year-old Egyptian was stabbed eighteen times in a Dresden court by a man she was scheduled to testify against for allegedly calling her a terrorist. When her husband tried to protect her, he was also stabbed by the attacker and then shot by the court's security. As a result, some 1,500 Iranian women gathered in front of the German embassy in Tehran, chanting, "Death to the enemies of Hijab!" Iranian judiciary chief, Ayatollah Mahmoud Shahroudi, called for German court officials who were present at the attack to be sued, and the Iranian ambassador to UNESCO complained to the organization's director over what he called the "desecration of Islamic values in European countries." President Ahmadinejad called the event an "absolute proof of the brutality of the German Government." Conversely, Iran's and other Muslim countries' relatively mild reaction to China was as a rule—except for Erdogan's angry "genocide" accusation he hurled against China—limited to a phone call by Iranian Foreign Minister Mottaki to his Chinese counterpart and his denouncing the "foreign meddling" aimed at "undermining China's stability," thus implicitly blaming the West for the Xinjiang unrest.[28] The interpretation lent by Iran to those events was certainly calculated to justify its own muted reaction, by shifting the blame from China to the West. But Iran's commercial ties with China did not provide the entire explanation: if one takes into account that Germany is Europe's largest trade partner with Iran, including in matters of technology and chemicals, which may be contributing directly to Iran's nuclear program. Part of the explanation is that Iran was itself busy using its baton-wielding *basij* to quell the demonstrators who questioned the results of the rigged presidential elections of 2009, leaving twenty of them dead. Iran could not react harshly against Chinese police repression while her own security forces were acting no better. One cleric, Ayatollah Saanei, not a government spokesman, who condemned the Chinese government's "aggressive and inhuman stance," was in fact understood as obliquely referring to the repression in his own country, when he charged that "it is pretty much how they claim to be willing to join the international community, by putting down the protests of their citizens and answering their cries for justice with electric batons . . . bringing out their militia and silencing any protest." Another cleric, Ayatollah Hamedani, said that the situation in China was an even greater crime than what happened in Dresden with the veiled woman's wanton murder and demanded that Iran's authorities not remain silent.

An exiled Iranian analyst, Michael Wahid Hanna, was more explicit: "That is pretty much pointing a finger at their own regime." In denouncing Germany so vocally, claimed those analysts, Iran sought to divert domestic and international attention following the rigged elections. Besides, while China remained silent on the legality of those Iranian elections, Germany was one of the sharpest critics of the oppression of protesters in Iran. This quid pro quo had to be expected, for not only did it constitute a retaliation for Germany's criticism but also portrayed the Western world as "enemies of Islam" and drummed up support for the regime in its time of crisis. Add to that China's cordial relations with Iran and the fact that it blocked resolutions at the Security Council to tighten sanctions against it, and you have a plausible interpretation for this differential treatment of China and Germany by Iran.[29] One major exception, a cheerful one for China, was Sudan (in 2008 the trade volume between the two countries had amounted to $6.5 billion); the Sudanese could do no worse in rewarding their Chinese friends in the midst of world condemnation. In fact, Sudan was the only Muslim country to "reaffirm its support of the Chinese government in the handling of the July 5 riots by members of the Xinjiang Uighur [not Muslim, of course] minority." The Sudanese communiqué also claimed that the "ethnic unrest was planned and coordinated in a bid to ignite violence across the regional capital, Urumqi, thus echoing exactly the PRC's official position, which also charged that the rioters had stockpiled weapons for the occasion, were orchestrated from the outside by Rebiya Kadeer, and had updated the figures of casualties to 192." Sudanese defense minister Abdul Rahim Mohammed Hussein, who visited China shortly after the unrest, declared that his government firmly supported the measures adopted by Beijing to quell the disturbances in the "defense of its sovereignty, to safeguard social stability, and protect people's lives and property." To exonerate his government from Muslim rage, Khartoum's ambassador to China, Mohammed Saleh, emphasized that the "incident had an obvious political motivation and had nothing to do with Islam," adding that "China and the Islamic countries had forged a profound and traditional friendship."[30]

Externally, at least, the Chinese government hoped to make some headway in the Xinjiang crisis by explaining apologetically to the Muslim world that it was compelled by terrorism to act the way it acted. But even in terror-stricken countries like Turkey, the ethno-religious considerations seemed by far to outweigh the terrorism argument. Yet China's traditional ally in Pakistan, which was itself challenged by the Taliban, naturally sided with other Muslims; not to speak of Afghanistan, where the shaky government of President Karzai could not afford to remain indifferent toward the fate of the Uighur coreligionists across the border. China's erstwhile next-door rivals—Russia and India—who are themselves plagued by their own Muslim terrorists (Chechens, Dagestanis, and Tatars for the one; Pakistanis and Kashmiri Lashkar-e-Taiba for the other)—were paradoxically more disposed to show understanding toward China's current difficulties than her longstanding friends. Western countries, especially those with the closest relations to China, might have felt the greatest sympathy for China's difficulties, except that the large Uighur communities there, especially in the United States and Germany, led by a competent exiled leadership, have succeeded to sway public opinion to their side as a persecuted minority. Western public opinion in general was oblivious to the course of events this time, in which the Uighurs clearly took the initiative and the lead, and they killed three times the number of Han than the numbers they lost (136 versus 46).

Beijing was so nervous about its vast interests and investments in Africa, Asia, and the Middle East that its foreign ministry rushed to reassure Muslim countries that China pursued no policy of oppressing the Uighurs, their accusations notwithstanding. Its spokesman very apologetically and sycophantly stated that "We hope that our Muslim brothers can realize the truth about the July 5 Incident in Urumqi. Once they know the truth, they will support our ethnic and religious policies and the measures the Chinese Government has taken to deal with the Incident." The spokesman was also quick to deny the charge of genocide against the Uighurs that had been leveled by Turkey, which, together with Iran, has arguably emerged as Beijing's sternest critic over those events.[31] The Chinese government's effort to thwart those accusations has emphasized that it was a local (only in Urumqi) incident, having nothing to do with any general policy of oppression or genocide. To illustrate that point, the foreign ministry said: "In 1949 the population of Uighurs in Xinjiang was 3.29 million, and at present nearly 10 million, i.e., 3 times more than 60 years ago. What kind of ethnic genocide is this?" In fact, the numbers are currently estimated to be approximately 50 percent higher, but the Chinese spokesman totally omitted the overall demographic revolution that had evolved in Xinjiang, in effect tripling its Uighur population, but in so doing the Han minority population had increased much more rapidly and came to parity with the native Uighurs.

When the disturbances broke out, the government poured some twenty thousand security personnel into Urumqi. Armored cars patrolled the streets and squads of paramilitary People's Armed Police marched through the narrow alleys where the rioting occurred. The next day, work crews cleared the debris from the streets to give a similitude of normalcy to the ravaged neighborhoods. At some point, a group of several dozen demonstrators approached a group of foreign journalists who were being shown around the city by officials. The policemen reacted by showing them away by force. Police said that they arrested some 1,434 suspects in connection with the riots according to Xinhua News Agency, which cited Li Yi, a spokesman for the Communist Party in Xinjiang. The violent riots occurred throughout the city's Uighur district, with shops and vehicles destroyed. The government was caught in the usual dilemma: either it is blamed by foreign governments for its heavy-handed treatment of the minorities or condemned by its Han citizenry for its too-lenient stance, which permitted the rioting in the first place. Thus, the top concern of the government was to quickly quell the disorder before it could spread to other areas of the country.[32] The conflicting reports of casualties persisted. Chinese officials blamed the violence on the World Uighur Congress and its leader, who denied having anything to do with the unrest, which was all imputed to the police. They insisted that the situation turned violent only after police beat the demonstrators, while police said that violence erupted early that morning, after hundreds of protestors gathered at the city's People's Square. Witnesses said rioters smashed store windows and attacked buses. One Han man said that he was in his shop for hours while crowds rampaged outside. He said he could smell smoke and hear gunshots and explosions. The question remains the same: what constitutes the beginning of violence: the destruction of public and private property or the police attempts to arrest rioters by force if necessary, known as "police brutality" or "exaggerated use of force." An official of the region's People's Hospital said 291 injured people were treated there: 233 of them Han, 39 Uighur, and the rest from other minority groups. If these numbers can be confirmed, they point to the disproportion between the two rival groups and perhaps also to the changing patterns of Beijing's treatment of such situations.[33]

This energetic propaganda campaign by the Chinese government, which seems to have made some dent in the Muslim world, has been accompanied by firm measures of pacification at home. On the twelfth of July in Urumqi, the city hardest hit by Uighur rampages, two Uighurs were shot and killed by police and a third wounded in a street fight in which the parties were exchanging mutual accusations. Everyone in the city must carry his or her identity card or risk being taken away for interrogation. One prominent Uighur intellectual, an outspoken economist, Professor Ilham Tohti disappeared from his Beijing home amid the unrest, though a group of 158 Chinese writers, students, and intellectuals have issued a public appeal for his release. Tohti had recently sharpened his critique of the problems of Xinjiang, and his Website had become a lively forum for discussing Uighur life. Nevertheless, the Han demand for his release, which indicated that the boundaries of rivalry were not clear-cut along the Han-Uighur faultline, had emphasized his intellectual background and his "devotion to cultivate friendship between ethnic groups and eradicate conflicts between them," hence his desired exoneration from being treated as a criminal. Prominence was added to that public petition because it was led by Wang Lixiong, author and democracy activist, who had written about Xinjiang and viewed Tohti's Website as an important tool of dialogue between the Han and the Uighur.[34]To acquire some legitimacy for the harsh measures it adopted, Beijing rushed reinforcements, accompanied by armored cars into the city streets, but explained that the two Uighur casualties were "lawbreakers, who were shot after they attacked the police and assaulted another man with knives and rods" next to the People's Hospital in the heart of the city, an area where the Uighurs make up the majority of residents. Xinhua claimed that "Police on patrol fired warning shots before shooting at the three suspects." The official statements and the measures taken returned a semblance of normalcy to the streets, which were again clogged with traffic, and businesses reopened to customers. The government recognition of having resorted to firearms to restore order was at first justified in their eyes by the lawlessness of the instigators and the danger they posed to innocent passersby (presumably Han), who were assaulted with no provocation on their part. The casualties were extensive—184 dead and some 1,600 injured, including 74 gravely. It was claimed that the Han who sustained head injuries had been bludgeoned with bricks or staves, the most seriously wounded were admitted to intensive care at the hospital and access to them was barred by police. In response, furious vigilante Han Chinese, carrying metal pipes, wooden staves, and knives, took to the streets baying for Uighur blood. The government poured in thousands of police reinforcements to keep the two groups from further encroachments.[35] That was the primary gist of the propaganda spread to foreigners to calm tempers and to demonstrate the tight frame within which the Chinese authorities had to operate.

As the riots escalated, the officially acknowledged numbers of casualties increased. Nur Bekri, the governor of Xinjiang, who admitted that the casualty mark had attained 197, explained that police were compelled to shoot after the crowds ignored their warning shots, killing twelve rioters, three of whom died at the scene and nine others in the hospital. As proof of the Uighurs' aggressiveness, he cited the reports of the initially peaceful Muslim demonstrations, which turned violent once the Uighurs "indiscriminately attacked Han Chinese across Urumqi, who accounted for most of the dead. Only then did revenge attacks take place, which pushed the number of injured to 1700."[36] The brutal repression of the Tibet riots a year earlier served as notice to other minorities to lower their expectations of leeway and to raise their fears of retaliation by the government. This time the government had not only cut Internet communications, which were vital for Uighur support worldwide, but also arrested close to 1,500 Uighur militants who were picked up by police, some say arbitrarily as a deterrence, as an encouragement by the authorities to elect peaceful means of protest over violence. In addition, mosques were closed for Friday prayer in an attempt to calm tempers.

At the front gate of the White Mosque, not far from where the riots erupted, around a hundred Muslims gathered in white skullcaps to prepare for the Friday prayers. They demanded to enter, and the gates were finally opened. The policeman at the gate told a correspondent for the *Times:* "We decided to let them in because they were too many. There could have been trouble. When word spread, hundreds more converged on the mosque, and the authorities had no choice but to allow an abbreviated service."[37] The Chinese response showed that the Chinese preferred to avoid confrontation, caving in rather than arousing more discontent. In any case, it was feared that continued oppression and obliteration of Uighur culture would only galvanize the Uighurs' determination to resist government policy. However, the government's decision to relax its control and yield to some of the minority's demands could have been interpreted as helplessness to address the situation and could have prodded the dissidents to demand further concessions. This was a no-win situation, no matter what the government chose to do.

Tim Collard, a retired British diplomat who spent most of his career in China and Germany and an active member of the Labor Party, claimed in his blog[38] that China "was putting a Uighur Christian (a rarity in itself) on trial to keep Al-Qaida happy." He said that he was "wondering how the Chinese Government might respond since Al-Qaida and similar groups might be targeting China as a result of the murderous ethnic riots in Xinjiang." Things became clearer after the trial began. The accused's name was Alimujiang Yimiti. He had been in custody for the preceding eighteen months. As usual, his wife and mother had been told by the authorities that they would not be allowed to attend his trial. Although the general assumption was that his crime consisted of bearing witness among the Uighurs, he was also charged with "revealing state secrets." Well, he said,

> We are invited to reflect, for that's pretty serious. It's hardly a sign of tyranny for you get prosecuted for that anywhere. The problem is that, under Chinese law, any information which has not been specifically released by the government's information office is a state secret. The great dissident Wei Jingsheng got 15 years of prison in 1979 for "Revealing that China was fighting a war with Vietnam," although many Chinese families had already found this out the hard way. Chinese law is useful like that: most of the really severe laws from the Mao era have never been specifically repealed, only selectively applied. Until recently it was illegal to have sex outside marriage, which has frequently come in useful when persecuting off-message Chinese or blackmailing their lovers.

But back to Mr. Yimiti. Collard's blog concluded:

> Heaven knows what he might have revealed—probably that it's hot in Xinjiang in summer—but the timing of his trial came in very useful. The Chinese leadership could make it clear that they're not against Muslims, something in the vein of: "[H]onest, Osama, we're not," but just against Uighur troublemakers, who, it is implied, are quite likely to be Christians—and Christians who try to convert Muslims to boot! "Come on, Osama, you can't blame us for that!" Maybe that might keep Al-Qaida off the Chinese backs in North Africa. Either way, it's nice to be able to sock it to those who oppose the national religion: "There is no god but Mao, and Hu Jintao is his prophet."[39]

In an unusual move, the Party-owned *People's Daily* asked its readers in advance to look out for an editorial on July 9 in which it would call for the strict application of the laws against those found guilty and for strict measures to restore social order. It was important for the government to pursue a policy of transparency (something like the famous glasnost, which had ushered Russia into the post-Communist era) in order to show the world the brutalities committed by the Uighurs on July 5–6. This policy, which was adopted by Premier Wen Jiabao in the absence of President Hu Jintao, who was abroad, was approved and followed on Hu's return.

This was refreshingly different from the Lhasa uprising in March of the previous year. In the previous case, the authorities ordered all foreign journalists and tourists to leave and stopped issuing permits for foreigners to visit Tibet for three months, until the unrest receded. In this instance, on the contrary, the Chinese foreign and information offices in Beijing took the initiative in contacting foreign journalists and requesting them to go to Urumqi to report on the situation. Hence the wealth of Western-originating information available to the West on the Urumqi events, in contrast with the paucity of information on Tibet a year earlier, which had been similar to previous incidents that had been kept under wraps and were only slowly and partly leaked to the world much later. The only similarity in the treatment of the two cases was the equal demonization of the rebel leaders by the Chinese regime: the Dalai Lama then, and Rebiya Kadeer now.

Remarkably, in spite of the general sympathies for minority members and of the threats of the Muslim world against China for its claimed persecution of the Uighurs, the alleged number of the massacred Han people in this incident amounted to three times higher (138 versus 46). If these figures are true, one could hardly speak of a massacre of the Uighurs in Urumqi. If anything, the reverse has happened. This either points to the unusual ferocity of the Uighurs, perhaps related to the support they hope to find in the West and in the Muslim world, or to the extraordinary restraint of the Han authorities in trying to restore peace to that mixed and troubled city. In any case, a year after similar events in Lhasa, Tibet, the hard line used to suppress dissent while Beijing was bracing for the Olympics has fostered more dissent in other minority areas instead of driving minorities to submission and docility. Faced with the dilemmas outlined above, China will have no choice but to contain dissent and pacify it until the bottled-up tensions explode again. The fact that those explosions have not generated the unraveling of Chinese rule can only reinforce it, by the slow process of long-term Sinicization of those border areas, which serves to enhance Chinese control, regardless of the frictions encountered along the way.[40]

On December 6, 1993, the *South China Morning Post,* a major Hong Kong newspaper, laid out in detail the circumstances of the violent Muslim riots in Qinghai following a local paper's article about a Muslim woman reading from the Holy Quran to the attentive ears of her dog, something offensive to any Muslim. Those events, which had preceded the Xinjiang riots by a decade and a half, were nonetheless part of the post-1989 Muslim awareness in China, which was resolute to rebel when necessary, even when there were no hidden or manifest calls for separatism. According to new proposals at the United Nations to criminalize "defamation of Islam,"[41] China would have been condemned by the world community had these rules been valid at the time. But as these rules are now being adopted by the Commission on Human Rights in Geneva, which is dominated by Muslims, they will give more incentive to Muslim minorities to lodge complaints against their non-Muslim authorities and justify any violence against noncompliant governments. Consequently, the Muslim minorities in China will remain in a state of mind under which the following will occur:

a. They will continue, as they have always done, to live in a state of vague expectation that underlies their daily activities. They will go about their day-to-day business and pay lip service to the authorities when necessary, but this will not diminish their yearning to see their identity merge into that of the greater Islamic powers that be;
b. Ethnic nationalism does not provide the explanation for local Muslim unrest in various parts of China. Rather, Islam has to be viewed as an organic body in which every function, or dysfunction, affects the whole. For example, the Chinese Rushdie Affair of 1989, whose very name was borrowed from the Iranian experience, started in Beijing and soon spread to Qinghai; in 2009 the wounding of two Uighurs in a remote town of southern China was sufficient not only to trigger uproar in Xinjiang but also to elicit fury in the clerical circles of al-Qaida and Iran, the wrath of Turkey, and some measured criticism in all the rest of the Islamic world;
c. While Muslim-minority riots are usually a result of local concerns, underlying all of them have been anger, a spirit of revenge, and a personal and collective readiness to force the authorities to produce solutions. This reflects the new awareness of Chinese Muslims, which allows them to enjoy the advantages of the new Chinese openness, no longer allowing the blunt suppression of yesteryear. The Islamic conferences, the hajj to Mecca, the Muslim instructors who converge on China, the financial and political assistance the Uighurs can get

from the outside world, and the inroads by armed terrorists—all have converged to put an end to the state of isolation the Uighurs had suffered for years; Xinjiang and Qinghai, being geographically connected to the Muslim world, make it much easier for the Uighur (than, say, the Hui of the heartland), to advance claims of secession, even when they know that the unitarian, centralistic system of Beijing is not likely to yield on this matter.

d. Under the uncompromisingly strict Communist rule in Beijing of pre-1989, the government had exercised control over information and prevented the rise of any consciousness of human rights or any links between its citizens and the outside world. Internet, Facebook and Twitter, fax, mobile phones, the abundant flow of information, and the relaxation of civil liberties domestically have given minorities, notably the Tibetans and the Uighurs, the motivation, the means, the constituency, and the world support they need to allow their protest to be heard across the world and have correspondingly constrained the ability of the Chinese central government to react brutally without heeding world public opinion. Thus, dissidents are demonstrating more spontaneously, knowing that violent repression will stoke further unrest and that the authorities fear the reactions of the world.

e. The instantaneous spread—nationwide and worldwide—of any local incident, such as the incident at the toy factory in Guangdong that triggered the Urumqi riots, renders the containment of local incidents to their place impossible and allows them to become a cause célèbre, or "breaking news," within moments. Today, China lives the Xinjiang trauma, in contrast with the great Muslim rebellions of the nineteenth century, which had been barely known to the ruling hierarchy domestically, and only much later to anyone else externally. [42]

Since the resurgence of ethnicity and ethnic nationalism in China in the 1970s, in the post–Cultural Revolution era,[43] the government of China has adopted the policy of "two less and one lenient," which means that in handling Chinese minority criminals, the police should capture less, kill less, and be more lenient than toward the Han majority. Under this policy, the Uighurs can commit crimes without being punished. Many Chinese have noticed, for example, Uighur thieves beating up Hans in big cities like Beijing and Shanghai, while policemen dare not intercede due to the policy of "two less and one lenient." As a result, Hans and Uighurs have a different understanding of laws. The Uighurs, it is claimed by many Han Chinese, know that they can beat Hans up without being punished, and that if they kill Hans they won't be sentenced to death. Therefore, like many other minorities in the world (Muslims in Europe, Arabs in Israel) who feel protected by world public opinion and by the threat of being dubbed racist if one acts against them, they feel immune from punishment if they commit crimes. The state is there not only to protect them from the tyranny of the majority but also to defend them from its punishment. And if they commit a crime for which they deserve punishment, they always consider punishment as persecution, racism, Islamophobia, or discrimination. This would perhaps help to explain the larger numbers of Han casualties in the 2009 Xinjiang eruption and the likely increase in Uighur criminality. For if one fears no punishment, what would deter one from exercising violence?

These theories were confirmed during the Xinjiang riots of summer 2009. A Han man said he fled after seeing a group of young Uighurs chasing Han people on the street, pelting them with stones and stabbing them with knives. "Uighur terrorists are killing Chinese people," said another Han man, who was born and grew up in Xinjiang. "The police did not react quickly enough," he said, "I am crying for justice." According to Xinhua, the official Chinese news agency, a senior police officer in the province said that rioters had burned 261 vehicles, including 190 buses and 2 police cars, and several of them were still ablaze on the morrow of the rampage. According to doctors at the People's Hospital, 233 out of the 274 patients undergoing treatment in the follow-up of the riots were Han Chinese, 26 were Uighur victims, and another 15 Hui Muslims. Almost all the victims appeared to have been beaten, but some were knifed and 7 had been shot. (Though at Dosluk No. 3 Hospital, the majority of the 100 victims treated were Uighur.[44]) The Internet reflected the anger of the citizenry at police lenience. In one forum of the *People's Daily* Web, a user fumed that "only the hardest crackdown can quiet the people's anger." Another blogger called for the end to various government affirmative action programs for minorities.[45] Uighur rioters were seen on state television overturning roadside barriers, seizing police cars, and smashing their windscreens and then overturning them and setting them on fire. Rioters were shown near a bus station kicking a woman as she cowered on the ground. One man slumped against a railing, one side of his face swollen from beatings. Another lay dead, his throat cut. Both appeared to be Han.[46]

This was not the first time tensions in Xinjiang and elsewhere had burst into the open and produced violence. But some aspects of the 2009 chain of events suggest new developments that are likely to impact the future. First, the rapid spread of information and rumor through informal channels has quickly polarized the Han and Uighur rivals. Paradoxically, this process has been the result of the tight control of government over the official media; because Chinese common people do not always trust the official media, they are more inclined to give credence to information passed through the electronic grapevine. Moreover, even though the government has the means to censor online communications, it has never been able to stop the surge of information during a crisis. As discontented people latch on to the issue of the moment (Xinjiang in this instance), the industry of rumors tends to push the populace toward more discontent and to produce an atmosphere of fear, expectation, uncertainty, and instability. In the ambience of nationalism, which has been rising in China since the anti-Japanese demonstrations of recent years, this sort of discontent can spin out of control and stir more anti-minority sentiment.[47]

Chinese policy toward minorities has always sought to strike the balance between ideology and pragmatism, influenced by the nature of men in top leadership. Hu Jintao had come to prominence among the minorities of China, hence his high sensitivity in those matters and his rather surprising departure from the G8 summit in Italy, a gathering of supreme economic importance for China as a result of the extreme significance Hu attached to solving the Uighur eruption. He was aware that neither he nor his comrades could afford to let Xinjiang or Tibet slide into detachment from China, hence the urgency of dealing with the unrest and settling the crisis. He probably elected to stick to the modern Chinese pattern of treating the non-Han to economic development and intense Sinification, under the power of arms that the Uighurs have no chance to defy or challenge. But perhaps other members in the politburo who have not voiced their choices yet and the new leadership that took over from Hu in 2013 would ultimately introduce new ways of pacifying the Uighurs. But those ways too will become exhausted at some point, and the malaise will again emerge. The firm handling of the Hong Kong democracy crisis of October 2014 under President Xi Jinping does not seem to hold any new promise.

Already, in the immediate aftermath of the riots, a mythology was being woven around them that assures their transmission in the future to the growing generations of Uighurs. It has been claimed, for example, by the exiled Uighur leader Rebiya Kadeer, who is not even there to verify her facts, that 10,000 of her people were killed or detained in the month of July 2009 in "ethnic unrest in the Chinese city of Urumqi." Rebiya Kadeer, the US-based head of the World Uighur Congress, appealed to the United Nations to investigate their disappearance and said she was "perplexed" by the muted US response to the violence.

(On a visit to Japan, she has indeed emphasized that almost 10,000 people "disappeared" in one night on July 5 when authorities cracked down on the unrest in the Muslim region of Xinjiang.) "Where did those people go?" she dramatized. "If they died, where did they go?" She said Chinese police opened machine gun fire at Uighur people after dark once the electricity was turned off and that the following morning large numbers of Uighur men had gone missing. She cried out in public:

> The Uighur people who were there must have been either killed or taken away next morning, for the streets were cleaned up and the bodies of ethnic Han (Chinese) were left in the streets. I want to urge the international community to dispatch an independent, third-party investigation mission to investigate what happened . . . If China can confidently say that the Uighur people are at fault, then open up the area, tell the third-party commission what really happened.[48]

But Beijing continued to insist on its version. It escalated its accusations against Kadeer of being a "criminal" and a "separatist" who instigated the unrest. China has said that police opened fire only to prevent further bloodshed, killing twelve "mobsters," according to state media reports, and that more than 1,400 people were detained for their involvement in the unrest. Kadeer said she was not involved in fomenting the riots, which came after Uighur protests over violent clashes at a factory in southern China. China summoned Japan's ambassador in Beijing to protest Kadeer's visit, but the protest was politely rejected, and Kadeer visited there as well as Australia, who reacted similarly to protests from Beijing.[49] The question will always be who will win this struggle over memory and history. The continued controversy over fact and myth will ensure that the wound remains open. Wang Lequan, the hardline party secretary of Xinjiang, who is also a member of the politburo, said that the erupting violence there had been a "profound lesson learned in blood" and vowed "the most resolute and strongest measures to deal with the enemies' latest attempt at sabotage."[50] If that statement heralds another era of crackdown, there are no easy days lying ahead for Xinjiang and its Uighurs, and certainly not for China. If the reports of October 2014 about "One battalion of bearded Uighurs joining the Islamic state in Syria and Iraq" are authenticated, it may mean that we are facing a new escalation of the Xinjiang conflict, inasmuch as not only Uighur youth are throwing their lot with the thousands of other Muslim youth streaming to ISIS, but they are also announcing that they are now rallying to a world Islamic movement to salvage their otherwise forlorn cause.

Notes

1. See Dru Gladney, *Ethnic Nationalism in the People's Republic,* Harvard, 1991, pp. 1–7.
2. Lillian Craig-Harris, *China Considers the Middle East,* Tauris, London, 1993, p. 275.
3. "Tursun Gul, Symbol of Uighur Defiance: I Just Want My Husband Back," http://www.timesonline.co.uk/tol/news/worlf/asia/article6666787.ece, July 8, 2009.
4. *Wall Street Journal,* July 8, 2009.
5. Jane Macartney, "Rebiya Kadeer Accused of Being behind Uighur Violence in East Turkestan," *The Times,* July 7, 2009.
6. *BBC News,* July 27, 2009.
7. Peter Foster, *Daily Telegraph,* July 7, 2007.
8. "Uprising in Urumqi," *Wall Street Journal,* July 8, 2009.
9. "Uprising in Urumqi," *Wall Street Journal,* July 8, 2009.
10. Moises Naim, "Mute Muslims: Why Doesn't the Islamic World Speak about the Uighurs?" *Foreign Policy,* July 13, 2009.
11. Ariana Enjung Cha, "China Unrest Tied to Labor Program: Uighur Sent to Work in Other Regions," *Washington Post,* July 15, 2009.
12. Y. Shichor, "Ethno-diplomacy: The Uyghur Hitch in Sino-Turkish Relations," in *Policy Studies* 53, East-West Center, 2009, pp. 1–53.
13. Ross, Terrill, "The Empire Strikes Back," *Weekly Standard,* July 27, 2009.
14. Mo Lingjiao, "Turkey, Another Axis of Evil?" *Global Times,* July 10, 2009.
15. Pelin Turgut, "Turkey No Longer a Safe Haven for Chinese Uighurs," July 27, 2009, http://www.time.com/time/printout/0,8816,1912653,00.html (Istanbul).
16. In Algeria alone there are some 50,000 Chinese workers.
17. See Malcolm Moore, *Daily Telegraph,* July 14, 2009. See also Jane Macartney, *Times Online,* July 14, 2009.
18. Ibid.
19. Tim Collard, *Daily Telegraph* blog, July 29, 2009.
20. Moises Naim, "Mute Muslims," *Foreign Policy,* July 13, 2009.
21. Ibid.
22. Ahmed Janabi, "Xinjiang Unrest 'Not Ethnic,'" *Al Jazeera,* July 26, 2009.
23. Ibid.
24. Compare to the Izz ad-Din al-Qassam Brigades, the military arm of Hamas. Those terrorist groups found that differentiation expedient for reasons of denial and self-defense, as they can always accuse their rivals of retaliating against civilians who have nothing to do with terrorism.
25. Special dispatch 2450, *Jihad and Terrorism Threat Monitor,* MEMRI, July 17, 2009.
26. Abigail Hauslohner, "Uighurs: Middle East Ignores China's Oppressed Muslims," *Time,* July 16, 2009.
27. Ibid.
28. *Khaleej Times* (Dubai, the United Arab Emirates), July 15, 2009.
29. Ibid.
30. *Sudan Tribune,* July 26, 2009.
31. Malcolm Moore, op. cit.
32. Shai Oster and Gordon Fairclough, *Wall Street Journal,* July 7, 2009.

33. Ibid.
34. Jane Macartney, op. cit.
35. Jane Macartney, *Time Online,* July 13, 2009.
36. David Eimer, "China Admits That Police Shot Dead 12 Uyghurs during the Recent Riots in Urumqi," *Sunday Telegraph,* July 19, 2009.
37. Jane Macartney, "Han Chinese as the Main Victims as Urumqi Riots Death Toll Rises," *Times Online,* July 11, 2007.
38. http://blogs.telegraph.co.uk/news/timcollard/100004788/china-puts-a-uighur-christian-on-trial-will-that-keep-al-qaeda-happy/, July 27, 2009.
39. Ibid.
40. Hugo Restall, "The Urumqi Effect," *Wall Street Journal,* July 10, 2009.
41. UN Watch Briefing, News and Analysis from UN Watch in Geneva, Vol. 187, March 11, 2009.
42. Ibid.
43. See Nimrod Baranovitch, *China's New Voices,* UC Press, Berkeley, 2003, especially ch 2, pp. 54 ff.
44. Peter Foster in Urumqi and Malcolm Moore in Shanghai, "China Arrests 1,400 in Aftermath of Xinjiang Riots: Chinese Police Have Arrested 1,134 Suspects after the Worst Ethnic Violence in Decades Left 156 Dead in the Far Western Province of Xinjiang," *The Daily Telegraph,* July 7, 2009.
45. Shai Oster and Gordon Fairclough, *Wall Street Journal,* July 7, 2009.
46. Jane Macartney, "Blood on the Streets of Urumqi after 156 People Are Killed in Riot," *The Times,* July 7, 2009.
47. Hugo Restall, "China Enters a Period of Eruptions," *Wall Street Journal,* July 17, 2009.
48. http://www.telegraph.co.uk/news/worldnews/asia/china/5933478/Uighur-leader-says-10000-killed-or-detained-in-China-unrest.html.
49. Richard Lloyd Parry, "Exiled Uighur Leader Rebiya Kadeer in a Hurry to Bring Freedom to Her People," *The Times,* July 30, 2009.
50. Peter Foster in Urumqi and Malcolm Moore in Shanghai, "China Arrests 1,400 in Aftermath of Xinjiang Riots: Chinese Police Have Arrested 1,134 Suspects after the Worst Ethnic Violence in Decades Left 156 Dead in the Far Western Province of Xinjiang," *The Daily Telegraph,* July 7, 2009.

3

The Politization of Islam, the Rise of Islamic Radicalism

When one studies the timeline of the year of 1989 and the years surrounding it, one cannot help noticing that the dominating figure of Ayatollah Khomeini, both in Islamic events in particular and much of the world international discourse in general. For 1989 had symbolized both the height of Khomeini's one-decade rule as supreme leader in Tehran and also his death. However, contrary to what is known in authoritarian regimes, his passing did not weaken his legacy, but helped to crystallize what has become known as "Khomeinism," a notion fanatically followed by his successor, Ali Khamenei, and his cabal of ultra-conservatives who maintained their grip on power in Iran after his death. Similar to post-Marx Marxism, post-Lenin Leninism, or post-Mao Maoism, post-Khomeinism fossilized the way it was understood and imposed on the country, and the keepers of his heritage have grown even more fanatical than their predecessor in purporting to preserve it and rejecting any idea of reform. Particularly remarkable in this context is the infamous fatwa that was pronounced by Khomeini in 1989, condemning Salman Rushdie to death for his *Satanic Verses* bestseller, a theme that became central in Islamic discourse during that year and the years that followed in both Islamic domestic contexts and the international terror it sowed, in the clash of values it revealed between Islam and the West, and sadly in the sometimes capitulating dhimmi-like attitudes of Western individuals, institutions, and countries.

A detailed account of the domestic and international repercussions of that fatwa would be impossible to compile. But the main happenings connected to that unconscionable religious verdict would reveal a chain of incidents, many of them violent and costly in terms of human fatalities, all indicative of the unquestionable superiority of the honor of Islam over everything else, including human life. The Rushdie Affair and 1989 have served as a watershed: before controversies and differences had been ironed out peacefully, in an open and civilized manner, and intellectually superior ideas seemed likely to win. Thus, some naïve minds in the West had come to believe that negotiations with Muslim radicals could alter their fanatic attitudes and lead to coexistence between Muslims and their rivals. The problem was that dialogue was treated in the West as policy, whereas it was in fact a non-policy, designed only to fill an awkward vacuum and to make legislators feel virtuous for "doing something." But while Europeans had regularly entered such dialogues with Muslims in good faith, fully intending to find common ground with their often unruly Muslim interlocutors, for Muslims "dialogue" meant something else entirely. For them it meant the submission of lesser cultures and religions to their own superior one, hoping to inspire conversion to an Islamic worldview. Anything short of that was considered an abject "failure of dialogue."

Muslim negotiators between Islam and the West were practiced in both cultures, whereas the Westerners have literally become pushovers at this stage in their history. Except for the contemporaries of the pre-Obama United States, Westerners hardly believed that anything was worth fighting for. Nor did they have the stomach for a fight of unlimited duration. They would rather capitulate than investigate in-depth the meaning of tolerance, understanding, dialogue, and peace to radical Muslims of the post-1989 era. The problem lies in the juxtaposition of a resurgent militant Islam on one hand and a self-deprecating West on the other, unsure of itself or its values. Its people have made a virtue of instant self-gratification, and therefore they invest next to nothing in the future—hence they have stopped rearing children. Their preferred way of life amounts to a "credit card culture." They want everything, and they want it instantly. Never mind that their governments no longer raise sufficient funds to cover exorbitant welfare entitlements, which partly goes to pacify the Muslims that have settled in their midst, or that a bleak financial future awaits tomorrow's pensioners. In short, the West has become a disgrace to its own heritage, in sharp reversal of its fortunes when at the turn of the twentieth century the Muslim Ottoman Empire was considered the "sick man of Europe" and was therefore no match for a confident West. US defense secretary Donald Rumsfeld was onto something when he distinguished between the "old" and "new" Europe—except that in their eagerness to grab some (necessarily short-term) economic benefits after emerging from Soviet control, the headlong rush of "new Europe" to join the European Union will inevitably contaminate them with the prevailing Western disease.

There is another drawback to this constant resort to dialogue. It lulls the Western populations into believing that their governments are doing something constructive to avert violence or threats of violence in the future. In reality, nothing could be further from the truth, for this nonpolicy serves to embolden and empower those Muslims whom Western governments have chosen to act as intermediaries with the wider Muslim communities. Invariably, Western governments have elected these Muslims because they are prominent activists in the community, while the governments comfort themselves with the injudicious belief that these figures represent moderate Islam. However, these Muslims are familiar enough with the West to have learned to tailor their vocabulary precisely to whom they are facing across the table. They speak the language of peace, reconciliation, and goodwill to Westerners and reserve their true beliefs for fellow Muslims, in what we have often characterized as "double talk"—one for their domestic constituencies and another for their foreign interlocutors, one for their politics at home and another for their interviews with the foreign press. In other words, they have learned to work the system, and admirably so. In effect, these "moderate" Muslim leaders gradually extract one concession after another from Western policy makers, rendering dialogue a one-way street. They enter each session with the full intention of testing the limits of the concessions they can extract, and it is a rare Western negotiator who would risk disappointing them—or else the headlines in the papers the following day would be sure to inflame the Muslim public. Herein lies the value of the worldwide Muslim penchant for overreacting to every perceived slight by demonstrating their outrage loudly and violently. Temperament comes into play here too, for unlike other peoples who experience anger or humiliation, many Muslims are either unable or unwilling to contain those sentiments. One has only to recall the orchestrated "Days of Rage" in Gaza, Tehran, or Islamabad, in which Western flags and effigies are burned, foreign embassies and consulates are destroyed, and foreign diplomats and journalists are assaulted to understand that, in sharp contrast to Westerners, Muslims make a fetish of celebrating their anger. Such an uncontrolled behavior is unthinkable in the West, but not because of lack of provocation. Funerals are also manipulated to vent wrath and fury, emotion, general mayhem, and impromptu rifle shooting. The total and shameless lack of dignity, even at what should be a somber occasion, is jarring to Western eyes. Bodies are held aloft and bounced along the route in a manner that would be regarded as disrespectful to the deceased in other cultures. Bodies have been known to fall off the stretcher amid the melee, and other processions turn chaotic, as was recorded for posterity in the case of Khomeini's funeral in 1989.

This mood, which reigned supreme in those days of 1989 when the Rushdie Affair exploded into the open, signaled the abrupt transition from the civilized interaction between the West and Islam—with the exception of Iran who had mounted a violent attack against the American embassy in Tehran a decade earlier—to outright confrontation. Indeed, Khomeini's fatwa against Rushdie, delivered and made public just a few months before his death, not only declared an open war on Western values of freedom of speech but also universalized the scope of the conflict to bring in the entire Islamic world. Iran had quite isolated itself from the rest of Muslims by declaring its revolution as intended for export and confronting the United States all alone. The Rushdie Affair brought the conflict to its lowest Muslim common denominator, by positing any slight of the Holy Book, the Quran, the Word of Allah, as insulting to the entire Muslim community. Moreover, it was no longer acceptable to absorb in a dignified way the Western injuries to Islam: it became necessary to react in the most significant, harmful, and unforgiving way to that offense. So what Khomeini could not achieve by persuasion, to have other Muslim countries follow his revolutionary path, he succeeded in one stroke by launching his religious verdict that no Muslim could ignore. In February of that year, three attacks by Muslims were launched on American targets: an American Express travel office was bombed in Islamabad; the Associated Press Islamabad bureau was attacked and two reporters were killed; and an *Atlanta Journal Constitution* reporter was also killed. Moreover, 2,000 Pakistani rioters attempted to storm the American embassy in Islamabad in response to the Salman Rushdie Affair.

That was not enough, because insulting the Holy Book was so overwhelming for the Muslims who were on the lookout for a slight, that more sacrifices were required across the Islamic world as evidence that the offense was unforgiveable. To set the example, Iran declared February 15 as a national day of mourning in response to Rushdie's book, and a bounty was placed on the author's head. On the same day, England's House of Commons passed a motion condemning Khomeini for his verdict and passed another motion ensuring the safety of Rushdie. Iran's neighbor, Pakistan, its Sunnite doctrine notwithstanding (unlike Shiite Iran), banned all Viking/Penguin books, the publishers of the book. The triumphant mood in the world of Islam was bolstered as the Soviets began their withdrawal from Afghanistan in mid-February, and the link between the two events became inescapable in Muslim minds, as the mujahideen had not only beaten the Communist superpower but were now set to terrorize the West until it yielded to their demands to eliminate that apostate, Salman Rushdie, who had sold out to the West. On the same day Viking/Penguin's New York offices received their first bomb threat. Some Western firms immediately caved in, as bookstores B. Dalton, Waldenbooks, and Barnes and Noble decided not to stock Rushdie's book, and Viking/Penguin Books closed its offices in New York pending the installation of a new security system after repeated bomb threats.

Around the same time, Muslim radicals in Algeria announced the creation of the Islamic Salvation Front (FIS), which drug their country into a murderous war that caused hundreds of thousands of fatalities. The trend of Islamic triumphalism was climbing, and it seemed that no one could stop it. Some Western countries, like France and West Germany, were bold enough to announce the recall of their charge d'affaires from Tehran, and film directors from the Berlin Film Festival made a statement of solidarity with Rushdie. An international Rushdie Defense Committee was founded by writers, publishers, and journalists, declaring the violent fatwa an "armed censorship." The European community and Canada also moved to recall from Tehran their heads of mission, and President Francois Mitterrand published a special denunciation of the fatwa. To show their loyalty to Islam and their protest against the démarches that their host countries took publicly, thousands of Muslims demonstrated against Rushdie and for the fatwa in Paris and New York on February 26, 1989, as the Rushdie Affair picked up steam and became a worldwide cause célèbre. On the same day, William Nygaard, the publisher of the *Satanic Verses* in Norway, received a death threat, while Iran severed its relations with Denmark for not banning the book. This was a sign that the Muslims wished to impose their terrorizing standards on international diplomacy too, under the threat of cutting off relations with any renegades. Not only Westerners, but a growing number of Muslims started to pay with their lives for Khomeini's outrage, after a Pakistani guard at the British Council Library in Karachi was killed in a bomb attack, and several Muslim demonstrators against Rushdie were hurt in Srinagar, India.

Iran's closest ally, Syria, soon joined the ban of the book on February 28, while several American bookstores and the *New York Times* offices were bombed for supporting Rushdie's novel. The next day, a large demonstration was held in Dhaka, Bangladesh, to protest the book while the US Senate passed Resolution 72, condemning the threats against Rushdie by Islamic countries, organizations, and bodies. Muslim-populated countries, such as Kenya, Lebanon, Indonesia, Tanzania, and the tiny kingdom of Brunei banned the *Satanic Verses*, while violence erupted in Islamic Kashmir, where one person was killed and eighty-four injured. Even non-Islamic countries, such as Thailand, who feared the reaction of their Muslim minority, felt obliged to ban the book. In the heart of New York, bustling Fifth Avenue was blocked off due to a bomb threat to a large bookstore that carried the *Satanic Verses*.

The amok climaxed on March 16, when the forty-five-member Organization of the Islamic Conference, including the most moderate and pro-Western among them, convening in Riyadh, banned the book and lent to Khomeini's démarche a spectacular success that he never dreamt to gain across the Islamic world. The universal ban across Islamdom proved that the fatwa was not only the act of a fanatic regime in Iran, but was shared by the entire Islamic public. Even Muslim minorities in the West were swept into that wave of extremism, as two Muslims were killed in Belgium on March 29 after speaking out against the fatwa on television. A measure of the popularity of the Islamic uprising worldwide was revealed in the results of the election in pre-Spring Tunisia in April 1989, where 15 percent of the electorate, some say even up to 30 percent, lent their votes to Muslim parties, though the Ben Ali regime quickly annulled those scores.

In the West the upheaval did not rest either. Two London bookstores that carried the book were bombed on April 9, and three days later two Norwegian bookstores were similarly firebombed. On May 21 a bookstore was firebombed in Sydney for carrying the book, and a week later 30,000 Muslims demonstrated in Hyde Park, the inner sanctum of the freedom of speech, against the right that Rushdie had expressed by publishing his book. The death of Ayatollah Khomeini on June 3, the millions of mourning crowds in Tehran, and the chaotic funeral on June 11 only heightened the moods of violence in the Islamic world. A bomb exploded on June 10 at the Coca-Cola bottling plant in Kabul, and Iran's ally in South America, Venezuela, announced that it had also banned the book. Ali Khamenei's accession to power as the new supreme leader came on June 29, but there was no chance for the newly inaugurated and hardly known new leader to abrogate or suspend his great predecessor's fatwa, which became part of his heritage and an obligatory duty of his successors to uphold without appeal. On July 19 a new bomb threat was registered against the American embassy in Islamabad, and on July 30 the Organization of the Oppressed on Earth, a Lebanese group that had kidnapped US Marine Colonel William Higgins, threatened to kill him, and the next day his hanged body was shown on video that was delivered to a West Beirut newspaper. On August 3 a radical Muslim who was preparing an attack on Rushdie accidentally blew himself up in a London hotel room, and on September 3 a bomb exploded outside a London department store carrying the *Satanic Verses*, injuring an Irish tourist. On September 14 four Viking/Penguin bookstores were firebombed throughout England. All these frequent bombings were probably initiated by British Muslims, compatriots and coreligionists of Salman Rushdie. One is struck more by the ineptitude of the famous Scotland Yard to detect, arrest, and punish the culprits than by the daring and success of the Muslim enthusiasts to carry out their schemes in Britain, which had generously given them asylum in the hope of bequeathing to them its heritage of liberty. Instead, they imposed their anti-democratic standards on their host country and paved the way for the new wave of Muslim terrorism, which would sweep Britain in summer 2005 with even more grievous consequences.

Before we delve into the consequences of the 1989 escalation of Islamic rhetoric and violence, we should realize that the roots of Islamic radicalism go further back and wider across the Muslim world. In effect, jihadi Islam, that wide, amorphous, and unpredictable coalition of radical Islamic movements, showed that it could strike in the Middle East directly, via their Hamas, Hezbollah, and Islamic Jihad branches on Israel's borders, or in neighboring chaotic Syria, Lebanon, and the Sinai Peninsula, where al-Qaida, Jabhat al-Nusra, Islamic State (IS), and various others are struggling to replace the murderous Assad regime and to topple the Egyptian military government, without promising that they would replace them with more benevolent rulers. The sense of siege that these radical Islamic movements have imposed on Israel and in the West has been greatening as more and more relatively moderate Islamic countries, such as pre-Erdogan Turkey, pre-Mursi Egypt, and pre-Khomeini Iran, have shifted toward radicalism and turned their old alliances with Israel into virulent anti-Semitic and anti-Israeli stances. Worse, as the numbers of anti-Western Muslim countries and movements increase, the chances of accommodation between these clashing civilizations grows ever slimmer. While great powers and advanced countries can weave appropriate alliances to defend themselves and overcome threats, small and vulnerable countries like Israel—whose means are limited and whose very existence hangs on a patron state like the United States or another major power—perceive the emergence of radical Islam and the menace it poses to their existence as concrete, immediate, and overwhelming. In this state of affairs, terror groups like al-Qaida, who have shown in the past their mettle in destruction and death and in hatred and cruelty loom larger than life, and their followers are viewed as threatening the lives of non-Muslims.

Harrowing experiences that the Israelis have witnessed around them in these past decades make them all the more sensitive to these fears. They watched the evolution of the Shia in Iran under the Khomeini Revolution with horror, from passivity and expectation to activity and aggression. The new activism, brought about by the Islamic Revolution in Iran, took up the tragic death of Hussein, the son of Ali, the first imam, which used to be viewed as a murderous and cowardly act inflicted upon that "greatest of martyrs," and rendered it into an aggressive declaration of war against injustice in general, which has to be pursued in earnest by Hussein's followers. In this context, Hussein becomes not only someone to be mourned, but also a heroic leader in battle and a model worthy of emulation on the way of every Shiite martyr to paradise. The paradigm of martyrdom, Hussein will intercede on behalf of his worshippers to ensure the admission of the new generation of martyrs to heaven.

When Iraq invaded Iran in October 1980, millions of adults and adolescents flocked to the mosques of Tehran and heard the call for volunteers to the battlefront by the government. The lines of volunteers for martyrdom exceeded the needs of the military. Even children were urged to go to the front without their parents' permission and were used to clear minefields in a deadly trance that the naïve and unsuspecting youth were easily swept under. They rushed to the battlefront with their friends and classmates, under the promise that in paradise they would be able to reunite and pursue their worldly worry-free life.

The eagerness for death through martyrdom in that culture often prompts Iranian demonstrators to join processions, while covered by death shrouds to signify not only that they defy death but that they were also ready for it. When President Mursi was inaugurated in June 2012 in Cairo, his Muslim Brother supporters also showed up with iron bars and shrouds in their hands to proclaim their readiness to fight for Mursi if his legitimacy were rejected and to die for him if necessary in defense of his rights. Within the space of a few years, Shiite martyrdom practices had clearly seeped through the Sunnite–Shiite divide. For indeed the charismatic mullahs in Iran, like the venerated imams of the Sunna, injected in their followers the idea that life was illusory and merely a corridor to the real life in paradise, and therefore it was not worth living. The reenactment of the martyrdom of Hussein, which in Iran has involved a real change in the tazia ceremonies on the day of Ashura, has also transcended Iran's boundaries and been rendered a model to other Shiites, such as in Lebanon where Hezbollah, in its quest to internationalize the Islamic Revolution, has been adopting a militant and aggressive stance. Hezbollah not only routinely uses violence on the Israel–Lebanese border but is known to aid terrorism across the world against Israelis and Jews, such as murdering Israeli tourists in Europe, hunting down Israeli diplomats abroad, or blowing up the Jewish community center in Buenos Aires. Its close cooperation with Palestinians, notably with Hamas in Gaza, is expressed through collaboration in launching joint terrorist acts on Israel or in directly supplying arms or training in violence and in terrorist warfare. Since the outbreak of the civil war in Syria in 2011, Hezbollah has launched itself into the fray, fighting for Iran and its Assad client and against the radical Muslims who threaten to take over the country.

Above all, one ought to scrutinize the doctrine of Islamikaze that is erroneously called "suicide bombing" in the West and by other Muslims *istishhad* (martyrdom), which means active death in martyrdom, that had been sanctified by the Muslim Brothers in the 1930s and 1940s against the British in Egypt and Palestine and against the Jews in Palestine and Israel and was taken up by Hezbollah in Lebanon, against the US and Israeli presence there in the 1980s. As the Israeli presence in southern Lebanon continued, Hezbollah's operations were intensified until they became the routine trademark of violent encounters between Hezbollah and Israel, usually at the initiative of the former. It took another decade or so before that mode of operation was emulated by other Muslim, non-Shiite, groups, most notoriously the Sunnite Hamas, and to a lesser extent by Islamic Jihad. All it took for that transition to take place was for prominent, fundamentalist Sunnite scholars, such as Sheikh Yusuf Qaradawi in Qatar or Sheikh Tantawi in Egypt, to provide the missing link between the natural vying for suffering and martyrdom that radical Shiism has inherited from the tradition of tazia and pushed Shiite martyrs to emulate the martyrdom of Hussein and the generally hallowed Islamic idea of martyrdom and its rewards. This was not intended to self-inflict pain and suffering but was aimed at bringing death and destruction to the enemy, even at the cost of Muslim lives. The long succession of fatwas delivered to fill this gap has indeed provided the rationalization for the mostly Sunnite Islamikaze groups to launch their deadly and massive attacks. Hence the growing fears of Israelis, who watch almost helplessly as these unpredictable Muslim zombies surge and cause rampages and death around them.

It is quite amazing to watch the Sunnite radical groups adopt the Shiite ways, not only by embracing the Iranian and Hezbollah modus operandi, something that has been evinced in the collaboration of Iran and Hezbollah with Hamas and Islamic Jihad, and the latter with al-Qaida network, but also by creating their own version of the supreme sacrifice and suffering inherent in their tazia, only in reverse. In the battlefield of terrorism in the path of Allah, we have seen nineteen adepts of al-Qaida committing collective acts of Islamikaze within one hour of each other on American soil on 9/11. Al-Qaida fighters in Afghanistan and Iraq and now ISIS in Iraq and Syria have defied death in the face of American and international air power, like Hamas and Islamic Jihad operatives in Gaza or the Muslim terrorists of Lashkar-e-Tayiba in Kashmir or in India proper, who slay their own compatriots with the same senseless and blind zeal as they attack foreigners. This universalization of Muslim terrorism also carries with it a daring in the operations, yet it is becoming banal in its frequency, diffusion, and beastly cruelty. Not only have the massive attacks of 9/11 left their mark, but the almost daily attacks on Israel and its civilians during the 1990s and 2000s by Hamas, Islamic Jihad, and even PLO-related Palestinians, who have rendered these harrowing acts routine, to the point that they became "part of life," as if they were God-ordained and impervious to human prevention.

Even more worrisome, however, is that the non-Shiite radical groups do not content themselves with matching the Shiites in terms of audacity, sophistication, and the spread of Islamikaze worldwide. They are able to capitalize on being Sunni in order to draw other groups into the circle of self-sacrificing terrorists, like the Tanzim and the al-Aqsa Brigades among the Palestinians, who are not avowedly Muslim radicals. It was quite extraordinary to watch members of the Marxist-oriented Popular Front talking of jihad and martyrdom within their operations. Because they realized the high status of Islamikaze martyrs in Palestinian society, they had no compunction about gaining popularity through the use of the same radical Islamic vocabulary and discourse as their Islamic competitors. Thus, not only have the Sunni terrorist groups edged closer ideologically to their Iranian model, but they have done so even in some patterns of behavior. For example, the headgear around the foreheads of Hamas people parading in the streets of the Palestinian territories under the permissive eyes of their security forces and often in collaboration with them; the video cassettes the martyrs leave behind them and their parting speeches to their loved ones, which are often used as an educational tool to recruit others; and the slogans, citations from the Holy Scriptures, and words of praise about martyrdom and the martyrs—all are ominous imitations of the Shiite model.

Most intriguing, however, is the counter-example of the Sunnite tazia in reverse, widely and repeatedly practiced by Hamas, and perhaps by others, too. We have seen Shiite martyrdom associated with bitterness and suffering, first out of passive identification with the supreme martyr—the Imam Hussein—and then, even after the Islamic Revolution pushed the protest into the domain of action and the tazia grew more aggressive and became a rallying point for the martyrs, it remained essentially a self-pitying, introspective, self-sustained, self-consoling, and "within the family" sort of event. Within Hamas and Islamic Jihad, a new pattern has developed—namely to replay in slow motion to sadistically delight in the suffering they inflict on their victims. Indeed, when the Palestinian authority allowed these acts prior to the breakaway of the Gaza Strip in 2007 and following major acts of terrorism that left dozens of Israeli victims dead or maimed, local chapters of Hamas set up processions in the cities of the West Bank to celebrate their act of terror as a feat of heroism. With their hallowed *shahids* on, slogans of martyrdom shouted, Israeli and US flags burned, and puppets representing Israeli and American leaders stabbed by a frantic crowd, members of Hamas arrived at the end of the scary procession, during which, invariably, they shot wildly in the air with illegal weapons they should not possess in the first place. After Hamas broke off in its Gaza domain, they continued reenactment of such scenes as the kidnapping of Israeli soldier Gilad Shalit, which they viewed as a great victory while the family of the abducted soldier and all Israel were suffering and waiting to hear any news of the missing soldier. Similarly, in their missile attack on Israeli cities in July 2014, they initiated a campaign of curses, threats, and boasts against their Israeli targets, assuring them of their "coming end."

Even though Israel has become accustomed to the horrendous sights of Muslims celebrating over the spilled blood of their victims, it was shocked anew each time ecstatic crowds broke out in jubilation after news broke of successful attacks against Jews, Israel, or the United States. With no one in sight to rein them in, what followed in those orgies in the cities of the West Bank—that Israeli leaders had insensitively dubbed "the victims of peace"—was quite abhorrent. On those occasions, members of Hamas distributed sweets, danced in the streets amid cries of "Allahu Akbar!" as if to attribute to Allah their great feats of murder against their sworn enemies, and then went again into the repetitive ritual of burning the flags of their enemies or trampling them under their feet. Since the demonstrators were not usually participants in the real events themselves, who perished as *shahids*, they reenacted the horror symbolically to share it with the public, praising Allah for his intercession on their behalf. Outsiders paid little attention to the makeshift stages and structures erected at the terminal of those processions. Often, the largest target of the operation, for example, an Israeli bus loaded with civilian passengers or a restaurant where entire families sat to enjoy their lunch, was meticulously reconstructed in paper, cardboard, and cloth, collated and painted so as to imitate the original, and then set ablaze, to the sadistic delight of the watching crowd. All the while, any perpetrators of the original act, if any had survived it, or more likely their successors, who wished to cultivate the heritage of the deceased Islamikaze, ran around the stage in frenzy, shouting blood-chilling war cries, repeatedly invoking the power of Allah, smashing the burned carcass of the bus or the restaurant, and stabbing with their bayonets the remnants of their slain victims, whom they or their fellow Islamikaze had maimed or murdered.

But even those horrendous scenes, which seem foreign to civilized people, can be improved upon by Hamas. In Nablus, during the Palestinian intifada that broke out in October 2000, a most disturbing exhibition was presented to the general Palestinian public in the city public square: the replicas of detached limbs and body pieces of Israelis who had perished in a restaurant bombed by a Hamas terrorist, shown in graphic detail. It was only the reports of deeply disgusted foreign correspondents and the protests of Israelis who did not want to relive that horror by seeing it replicated on the screens that convinced the Palestinian Authority to move the exhibition indoors, yet still they chose not to close it down or arrest its promoters. By widening the scope of the viewers to the public, to the point of rendering it a sort of street theatre, even if most viewers were not part of the radical Hamas, the organizers expected to elicit respect and esteem for the self-immolating heroes and to encourage new recruits. In other words, unlike the stories of suffering enacted by the Shiites for the sake of commemoration, identification with the martyrs, and self-hardening in order to stand the excruciating trials to come, Hamas hardens its crowds and cultivates its audiences by boasting about the gruesome suffering inflicted upon the enemies. This change of focus, or a tazia in reverse, illuminates the difference between the Shiite universe of martyrdom—as the ultimate way to identify spiritually with Hussein, the ultimate martyr—and Hamas, whose most urgent aim is to bring down its Jewish enemies. In Palestinian thinking, the most atrocious act of injustice was dealt to them by the very birth of Israel, and its continued existence is untenable. For Israel's presence in their midst exposes their own hopelessness, helplessness, and haplessness. The Palestinians and Israel had begun from the same departure point half a century ago, but, while their sworn enemy has progressed, settled, prospered, and advanced to the forefront of modernity and technology, they are still rotting in refugee camps for the third or fourth generation; the gap between them and Israel continues to widen, and their refugees have remained dependent upon UN flour supplies and foreign aid (ironically mainly from the United States, who they love to hate). There is nothing more humiliating to the Palestinians than that. Therefore, they hate Israel and the Jews, who show them what they have failed to achieve, and they spurn the United States, to whom they must turn as beggars to improve their lot. In tortuous reasoning, instead of striving to come to parity Israel to reduce their dependence on the United States, they would rather attack them both in order to bring them down. That is the reason why, when the Oslo Accords were at their hopeful beginning, it was Hamas who rejected it lock, stock, and barrel, for fear that it might reinforce the superior stature of Israel. The result was the ensuing demonization of Jews and Israel, and the ruthless attacks against them are part of this externalized tazia in reverse, which focuses on the suffering inflicted on the enemies, instead of like the Shiites, extolling their own sacrifice and self-pitying their suffering.

How persistent are these trends in the vast Islamic world? We have observed that when part-time processes of liberalization are adopted, like in Algeria, Jordan, Egypt, and lately Libya and Tunisia, namely when people are given the opportunity to express themselves freely, it is almost invariably political Islam that gains votes, and since this is popular vote, it cannot be said to represent radicals, exactly as it cannot be claimed that the more than 60 percent of Palestinians who voted for Hamas in 2006 or the 70 percent who voted for Islamic parties in 2012 in Egypt were all "Islamists." If, as some claim, there is a certain percentage of Muslims who are "radical," "fundamentalist," or simply

"Islamists," while the majority are the good brand of Muslims, which politicians like Bush and Blair simply (and wrongly) called "peace-loving," then how are we to take those vast crowds, which seem to represent the local majorities, in every place where Muslims burst out in violence—be it in Cairo, Gaza, Quetta, Tehran, or Kabul—as during the Rushdie Affair in 1989 or the Cartoon Affair in 2006? What happened to those supposedly peace-loving majorities who are not supposedly represented by the violent crowds? And when Western-educated Muslim columnists write in the mainstream journals of the Muslim world, including in "moderate" and "pro-Western" countries, such as Egypt, Saudi Arabia, or Jordan, of genocidal wishes against Jews and Israel, virulent recriminations against the West, and expressions of joy after 9/11 or every time a bus or a restaurant blows up in the West or in Israel with dozens of victims, are those celebrating the representatives of radicals or Islamists?[1] Then, where is the difference between peace-loving Muslims and so-called Islamists? So while there are theological nuances between Sunnites and Shiites and within the Sunnites between the four schools of law (*madhahib*), for instance between the puritanical Wahhābis of the Hanbali cult and the more lenient Hanifites on matters of Sharia law, there appears to be unanimity among them with regard to jihad wars, the denigration of the Jews, and contempt and hostility toward the West, because they all draw from the same medieval Abu Yusuf and Ibn Taymiyyah scholars of Sharia, along with the more modern Hassan al-Banna, Sayyid Qutb, or Abul Ala Maududi, who authoritatively expressed those ideas. Understandably, not every Muslim would observe to the letter the strictest prescriptions of those scholars, but at the same time no sweeping, authoritative, alternative doctrine has emerged to challenge them, let alone replace them.

Those referred to as Islamists regard themselves simply as Muslims, who are perhaps more zealous than others and wish to fulfill Muslim ideals. But are they so distinguishable from other Muslims that they deserve to be treated as if they have invented a different Islam? All religious Muslims venerate the great masters of radical Islam, such as Hassan al-Banna, Sayyid Qutb, Maududi, and Yusuf Qaradawi, even if they do not fit into the categorization of "radicals." Radicals relate to the masses of common Muslims the way activists or militants in a political party refer to the rank and file of sympathizers who only vote when the day comes but are not involved in any day-to-day politics. But as we do not distinguish between radical and common party members, so must we with religious affiliation. Yes, they differ in both cases as far as the degree of commitment, activity, and observation are concerned, but we cannot set them apart ideologically, and they continue to belong to the same core of beliefs and convictions. For if there were a liberal or moderate tendency in Islam, it would be evinced, first of all by theologians of Islam who would stand up courageously and battle against the ideas of the Islamists. However, while truly moderate and daring individuals of Muslim descent (and sometimes conviction) do exist, principally in the safety of the West, we cannot discern any significant trend of moderation and peace-loving inclination that masses of Muslims rally behind. So what is erroneously dubbed moderate or non-Islamist Islam is actually the view of the silent majority who is, unfortunately, more likely than not to follow the general outbursts of jubilation when Jews or the West are harmed, to watch anti-Semitic series on television that depict Israelis (and Americans, for that matter) as blood-drinkers, world-conspirers, and children-killers, and to avidly absorb genocidal statements by their leaders and clerics and reiterate their beliefs in the same nonsense slogans and conspiracy theories that are circulated in their media. One year after 9/11, Dan Rather of CBS News undertook a worldwide survey of Muslim (not Islamist) reactions to those horrific events. From a sample of eight Muslim countries between Morocco and Pakistan, where he polled the literate population in remote villages in each one of those countries, the overwhelming majority of the populace, which was not radical, spelled out their conviction that the horror was perpetrated by the Jews and Mossad.

Did the Palestinians suddenly become Islamists when the radical Hamas won elections among them in 2006? No, they remained as Muslim as they were before the elections. They burst into unabashed joy when 9/11 happened, much to Arafat's embarrassment, who sent his security forces to disband those "radical" masses to avoid further disgrace. Why did they celebrate? Because they were indoctrinated by their school textbooks, which assured them of the imminent victory of Islam against the "corrupt and tyrannical" West. They burst forth in jubilation when Israeli and Western families were shown torn into pieces, and they reenacted harrowing scenes of explosions against Israel, showing cardboard buses or restaurants burning and limbs of children flying around, with huge crowds of children, passersby, shopkeepers, students, and policemen clapping and rejoicing. Even their universities and schools have staged such reenactments. Could all those citizens be Islamists? No, in their eyes, Israelis and the West are the enemies of Islam (not of Islamists), therefore one should rejoice at their defeat. And because they are not defeated often enough for the Muslims' taste, no Muslim can let the opportunity to rejoice slip by, instead replaying that defeat and savoring it in slow motion. The United States and Israel are particularly targeted and their national flags usually accompany each other when a Muslim frenzy of burning and destroying bursts forth in any part of the globe because both of those countries stand out as the consummate representatives of strength, modernity, prosperity, and success—something that only highlights the impotence and backwardness of the Islamic world. That is the source of "humiliation" that Muslims reiterate so often and so intensely, for only the existence of that successful world permits Muslims to grasp what they missed. A second reason Israel and the United States are targeted is this: the Muslim dream to create a global Pax Islamica has been scuttled principally by Israel in its immediate vicinity and by the United States worldwide, for the United States is the only power able and willing to stand up to them and obstruct their goal of establishing a world caliphate. These frustrations have been shared by Muslims in general, regardless of whether one categorizes them as Islamists or otherwise.

It seems that the fictional distinction that is drawn between Islam and Islamists, which is usually made either by Western scholars and politicians or by Muslim moderates who live in the West, emanates more from an instinct of their own self-defense and survival than from a sober observation of reality. In Muslim countries, it is often hard to tell who is who, inasmuch as Palestinian, Saudi, Egyptian, and Pakistani clerics who belong to the "moderate" establishment often issue fatwas and deliver sermons that are every bit as extremist as the "radical" ones, and even imported or homegrown Muslim clerics in the West do not make any effort to distinguish themselves from Islamists, because they themselves cannot tell the difference. Western scholars and politicians, who want to cater to Islam for electoral or other worldly perks, but cannot deny the rage of their own peoples against violent Islam, find shelter in a distinction that allows them to claim that the Islam they support or defend is moderate, while the violence that their peoples condemn emanates solely from the extremist Islamists. At the same time politicians and scholars critical of Islam need that distinction to shelter them from accusations of racism—as if multicultural and multiracial Islam were a race—or from Muslim bias and hatred. Muslim scholars and public figures who live in the West resort to that distinction in order to avoid a blanket condemnation of the Islam of which they are part and to escape suspicions by their coreligionists that they sold out to the West or that they committed an act of treason against their culture and religion. Many of them find it more expedient to claim that they are "secular Muslims," a notion that is unacceptable to Islam in all its nuances, and some of them convert to Christianity in order to feel free to lash out at their previous religion, though they know that they are handily offset by the much larger numbers of Westerners who convert to Islam.

Matters are further complicated to Western minds by the paranoia and conspiracy theories that are widespread in the Muslim world among Islamists and others, whether Muslims are modern and Western-educated or traditionalist and obscurantist. Those theories that are rampant even among Muslims living in the West insist that world leaders who support Israel are Jewish (like presidents Reagan and Bush); that the United Nations of all places is the mastermind of the Jews, who utilize it as a tool for their world dominion; and that the major violent acts that shook the world, like the World Wars, the world revolutions, and 9/11, are all the fruit of Jewish imagination and execution. Their minds are so permeated with these nonsensical theories that they become impervious to logical, rational debate that is open to argument, discussion, and persuasion. Therefore, the difficulty of dealing with Muslim minds consists not only of removing the mountains of pure delusion that choke their free thinking but also of persuading them that the very attempt to counter-argue those futilities is not necessarily part of the world conspiracy that is being woven against them. It is possible to explain their imaginary view of the world by their need to project on their enemies the analytical shortcomings that bewitch them, but it is impossible to move them out of the illusory scenarios that they have constructed and then cling to with a tenacity that defies and contradicts Western standards of logic and conduct. The result is that even when Muslims initiate and launch an act of violence, they accuse the West of it and dub it, or what led to it, as an act of aggression leaving them as the victims deserving a chance at retaliation.

As long as the Muslim anti-Western and anti-Semitic discourse was internal, little attention was paid to it in the outside world. But since the end of the Afghanistan War (1979–89), which also signaled the end of the Cold War and the return of the mujahideen to their Muslim home countries, tremendous energies have been released by the Afghanis (i.e., the foreign, battle-hardened graduates of the war in Afghanistan) and channeled both domestically (Islamist activity in Algeria, Saudi Arabia,

Sudan, Lebanon, Egypt, Jordan, Pakistan, and Taliban Afghanistan) and internationally to wage a worldwide jihad, led by bin Laden's al-Qaida but carried out simultaneously on Arab, American, African, Asian, and European soil. The rising prices of oil afforded some oil-producing Muslim countries and their rulers the possibility to finance the spread of puritanical and violent Islam in the West and to absorb some of the unemployed Afghani mujahideen, while the others were turned loose and ended up in the battlefields of Iraq, Lebanon, Bosnia, Chechnya, Syria, and Palestine or became mercenaries of violence in the United States and Europe. The Danish Cartoon Affair of 2006 proved a golden opportunity for Muslim regimes to redirect the rage and fury of the masses against the West and Israel, regardless of whether we define them as radicals or moderates, for Western institutions were attacked in Libya, Egypt, Palestine, Syria, and Lebanon, and the boycott of Danish products was launched by Saudi Arabia and other Gulf states, which are usually considered "moderate" and "pro-Western."

When one examines the spread of Islam into Europe in recent decades, one must come to the conclusion that it is not enough to account for Muslim immigration into the old continent and its transformation at their hands, but also must account for the European counter-measures after major acts of terror occurred there, and the Muslim worldview, which regards those Western defensive measures as aggression, persecution, racism, Islamophobia, and discrimination against the ever-docile and always poor, helpless, innocent, and victimized Muslims who had just come to seek work. When Britain or Germany idolized multiculturalism as a way to enrich European culture and celebrate the fake difference between moderate Islam of the mainstream and the few violent radicals, Muslims regarded that as an attempt to dilute Islam in order to dominate and eliminate it. As far as they were concerned, only their unrestricted and violent activity in Europe, in favor of recognition of their own mores and norms, such as wearing the veil, forcing marriage on their women, or pursuing "honor killings," would be acceptable as fair behavior of the host countries toward them. In other words, not satisfied with full equality of opportunity and freedom of speech and of religious cult, Muslims of the post-1989 era began to demand special privileges for themselves, like the prerogative to train terrorists or incite violence against other citizens. When they burned down a Jewish synagogue in Berlin or Paris or blew up trains in London and Madrid, they expected their adopted countries to accept that as a matter of course, and they were often aided in that belief by the local extreme-left or extreme-right organizations that boosted Muslim demands due to their common anti-Semitism or in order to appear as progressive multiculturalists.

In Iran, the bitterness of the Shia, which considers itself the downtrodden and persecuted branch of Islam (in fact a branch of them in Lebanon call itself the Downtrodden on Earth as a sign of distinction, not complaint), is best expressed in the anger and rush for self-sacrifice and the posthumous glorification of the martyrs after their death. So young Iranians were encouraged to clear minefields during the First Gulf War between Iraq and Iran (1980–88) with keys to paradise hanging on their innocent necks, and their parents were congratulated, not consoled, by family and friends for the martyrdom of their children. All those horrendous sacrifices were immortalized in the memorial for the martyrs in Tehran, a water fountain colored in bloodred, which symbolizes and eternalizes the endless flow of suffering and blood. Naturally, those groomed in that culture cannot be expected to recoil from the ultimate act of suffering—that is death. Quite the contrary, the stream of the Islamikaze has never dried in Iran, and it is diverted to flow in other lands of Islam as trends of radicalization proceed. There was a time when the most popular figures in the Islamic world were President Ahmadinejad of Iran and his proxy in Lebanon, Sheikh Nasrallah, who were the most militant and the most prepared for sacrifice. The attractive rationale reads: "The skies are shrouded in black, rivers of tears are flowing, Hussein arrives in Karbalah to sacrifice himself for Allah. This is the 'Ashura story, tend your ears to listen to its sadness, let your tears flow for the King of the Martyrs, because he will bring you to Paradise."[2] These are lyrics to one of the songs that constitute one of those mourning, musical passions that are reenacted in Iran and elsewhere to commemorate the martyrdom of Hussein. These reenactments, and the generally militant demands by the Shiites for their rights and for justice, had gone into abeyance or adopted a low profile for centuries (a state of *intidhar,* namely waiting and expectation), due to the principle of *taqiyya* (dissimulation) that was adopted after the mysterious disappearance (not death) of the twelfth imam (hence Twelver Shia), as a defensive measure of self-preservation in a hostile environment. That state of expectation for the return of the absent imam provided the entire rationalization and driving power behind Twelver Shiism, inasmuch as it encouraged the believers to suffer and wait, for the more they waited and suffered, the closer was deemed his return (like the pangs of the Messiah in Judaism), but if anyone at any time claimed to be the imam, he was immediately repulsed and condemned as an imposter and treated accordingly, because the faith was grounded in the waiting and expectation, not in its fulfillment.

The last decades of the twentieth century, however, saw the ideological and political quantum jump effected by the Shia, under the revolutionary impulse of Ayatollah Khomeini and his likes. The nature of the change, which has taken the Shia from passivity and expectation to activity and aggression, namely making the human will predominate over fate or the natural course of events, is indeed nothing short of revolutionary. This is inherent in Shiite theology, which recognizes the head of the clerical hierarchy as the *marja al-taqlid*, the supreme reference who commands the emulation of the believers. In fact this major figure, who gains his superior status through his scholarship and religious authority, is the supreme mujtahid, the "striver" to interpret the will of the Hidden Imam, who is the actual ruler of the world. The mujtahid thus acquires in the Shia the power of legislator, and his rulings are the law. This is the reason why Khomeini spoke about *wilayat al-faqih* (the rule of the jurist), for only such heaven- and imam-inspired jurists, who are the upper echelon of the mullahs, could be clairvoyant enough to detect the truth and pass it on to others. Khomeini himself wrote that "only the mullahs are able to take people to the streets and motivate them to die for Islam, and bring them to beg that they be allowed to spill their blood for Islam."[3]

Often young Iranian demonstrators were swept under the magic rhetoric of their leader, whom some saw as the imam, that is an incarnation of the Hidden One, when he said that life was illusory and merely a corridor to the real life in paradise—therefore it was not worth living. The reimagining of the martyrdom of Hussein, which in Iran has involved a real change in the tazia ceremonies on the day of Ashura, has also transcended Iran's boundaries and been made a model for other Shiites, such as in Lebanon, where Hezbollah in particular and the Amal Shiites in general have adopted the same style. Moreover, Hezbollah, the active, long arm of Iran in its quest to internationalize the Iranian Islamic Revolution, has been adopting a militant and aggressive stance in its pursuance. It not only routinely uses violence on the Israeli–Lebanese borders but is known to aid terrorism across the world against Israeli and Jewish interests, such as blowing up the Jewish community center and the Israeli embassy in Buenos Aires or its close cooperation with the Palestinian intifada, both in coordinating joint operations against Israel and in direct involvement in arms supplies, instruction to violence, and terrorist warfare. Above all, however, the doctrine of the Islamikaze, that is active death in martyrdom, was revived by Hezbollah in Lebanon. The first acts were performed in the early 1980s against US and Israeli presence in Lebanon, but as the Israeli presence in the southern part of that country wore on, those operations were intensified until they became the routine trademark of violent encounters between Israelis and Hezbollah, usually at the initiative of the latter. It took another decade or so before Islamikaze was emulated by other Muslim terrorist groups, most notoriously the Sunnite Hamas and to a lesser extent Islamic Jihad. All it took for the transition to take place was for fundamentalist Sunnite scholars, such as Sheikh al-Qaradawi, to provide the missing link between the natural vying for suffering that fundamentalist Shiism has inherited from the tazia tradition and practice and which pushed martyrdom to the top of the individual's striving to emulate the slain Imam Hussein and the general Islamic idea of martyrdom and its rewards, not with the goal of self-inflicted pain but aiming at inflicting damage onto the enemy, even at the cost of one's life. The long succession of fatwas delivered to fill this gap has indeed provided rationalization to the mostly Sunnite Islamikaze groups, like those of al-Qaida, to launch their deadly attacks against the West and Western interests.

It is quite amazing to watch the Sunnite fundamentalist groups adopt the Shiite ways, not only by embracing the Iranian and Hezbollah mode of operation, something that has been evinced in the collaboration of Iran and Hezbollah with Hamas and Islamic Jihad, and of Islamic Jihad with the al-Qaida network, but also by creating their own version of the supreme sacrifice and suffering inherent in the tazia, only in reverse. In the field of battle and terrorism for the sake of Allah, we have seen nineteen members of al-Qaida committing collective Islamikaze acts within one hour of each other on American soil on 9/11. Al-Qaida fighters in Afghanistan defied death in the face of US airpower, as do Hamas and Islamic Jihad operatives in the Palestinian Authority, or the fanatic Al-Gama'a al-Islamiyya in Egypt, or Abu Sayyaf in the Philippines, or the Muslim terrorists in Kashmir and India proper, or the fundamentalists in Algeria, who slay their own compatriots with the same senselessness and blind zeal as they do when they attack foreigners. This universalization of Sunni Muslim terrorism also carries with it a growing daring in the operations, to the extent of its banalization in the face of its frequency and diffusion. Not only the massive Islamikaze attack on 9/11 but especially the almost daily attacks in Israel by

Hamas and Islamic Jihad have rendered these harrowing acts routine, to the point that they risk becoming accepted as part of life, as if they were God-ordained and impervious to human prevention.

The paradox is that while in Shiite Islam, notably after the end of the First Gulf War (1988), acts of Islamikaze were restrained after they had peaked in the 1980s, it was precisely then that they were picked up by Hamas and other Sunnite groups. In Lebanon, where it all started, Hezbollah leadership came to the conclusion that the exaggerated use of overzealous youth had often ended in the death of the perpetrator without inflicting enough casualties on the enemy to justify that sacrifice. The spiritual head of the movement, Sheikh Fadlallah, has even issued a fatwa allowing acts of Islamikaze only on special occasions.[4] Sheikh Naim Qassem, the deputy secretary of Hezbollah, translated the guideline of his spiritual leader into specific directives, which he issued to the organization and released to the public in a press interview:

> First, one must obtain the authorization of an accredited Mufti. Anyone seeking to sacrifice himself, especially by car-bomb or blowing himself up, must first consult with a Lawyer of the Holy Law, because the soul is dear and can be expended only for the sake of the Islamic *Umma*.
>
> Secondly, after the religious authority delivers its verdict, the political leadership of the movement must deliberate on the political and military merits thereof. For when the same goals can be obtained without self-sacrifice, we do not send any Islamikaze to his death. The Islamikaze act is efficient only when other means are not deemed [by the leadership] to attain the same results.[5]

True, when the Islamikaze martyrdom was adopted by the Palestinians in the 1990s, there were tremendous debates among Palestinian scholars of the holy law over whether they should be sanctioned. Dr. Hamza Mustafa, the head of the Sharia College at Al-Quds University and a member of the Jerusalem-based Supreme Muslim Council, was emphatic in a press interview:

> Allah has determined that whoever commits suicide will end up in Hell. It is clear that suicide is unreservedly prohibited, because his soul is not his private property but belongs to Allah. There are those who believe that when suicide is committed as part of an act of war against the enemy, it is not forbidden, but most believe that suicide is prohibited in any case.[6]

A perception crystallized in those days, claiming that while the tiny Islamic Jihad group did opt for Islamikaze bombings as part of its world of self-sacrifice,[7] the larger and more popular Hamas did not encourage its membership to engage in this kind of operation. Sheikh Jamil Tamimi, one of the leaders of the Muslim Movement in the West Bank, for example, was often quoted as totally opposing these acts, not only due to the loss of life involved but mainly because of the categorical prohibition against self-immolation in Islam. He recognized that some Muslim scholars did permit this sort of operation in the context of war and of struggle against the enemy, though he emphasized that he personally was opposed to this interpretation.[8] At the same time, however, Izz ad-Din al-Qassam,[9] a hallowed name and symbol for both Hamas and Islamic Jihad, was cited as urging his followers to martyrdom, because "martyrdom is only the beginning of the road . . . Jihad is either victory or martyrdom . . ."[10] "Victory or martyrdom" as a slogan and battle cry, naturally encouraged and led people to sacrifice themselves. Indeed, after the first Islamikaze act against Israelis in Beit Lid in 1994, perpetrated by Islamic Jihad, one of the Gaza mosque's loud speakers proclaimed: "Islamic Jihad has announced long ago that we have hundreds of volunteers for martyrdom, ready at any minute to hurt the Zionist enemy and burn the land under his feet."[11]

So while no one of authority in Islam permits suicide per se, those who allow, indeed urge, the martyr to sacrifice his life, use the commonly held view that the soul belongs to Allah to facilitate its return to him. Because we are not talking here of a suicide, nor is it an accidental or incidental death incurred during battle, which is commonly dubbed *istishhad* (martyrdom), even when the martyr did not willingly or by choice embrace it, but it was an *amalyya istishhadiyya* (an *act* of martyrdom), meaning that the individual has taken the conscious decision to sacrifice his life for the Islamic cause. In this case, the martyr has considered his act as imperative to achieve his goal, he has "purposely thrown himself to his death, confident that he is rushing to Paradise."[12] And since he neither wished nor prepared any way of retreat, he has no other choice but perish together with his targeted, or incidental, victims. Even the Islamic Jihad's eagerness to martyrdom is, however, limited by the prohibition to kill innocent people, and the essence of the matter becomes the definition of who is right and who is wrong, who is innocent and who is the culprit. At any rate, the struggle of the Islamikaze has become so sustained that differences between Hamas and Islamic Jihad on the one hand and the nuances distinguishing the innocent from the culprit on the other have been totally blurred. Moreover, other Palestinian organizations who had thus far nothing to do with the Islamikaze have been joining the effort of martyrdom.

The author of the *Readings in Islamic Martyrology*[13] indeed addressed himself to these basic dilemmas. He cited Sharia sources that negate suicide from the Quran through the authoritative collection of Hadith edited by Bukhari and finally decreed that it was unlawful for any Muslim to commit suicide by poison, jumping from a high place, self-stabbing, suffocation, or cutting of hand or neck main arteries under the threat of hell punishment. He determined that Islam prohibits suicide out of despair from life, to avoid suffering due to illness or injury, or to debt, poverty, fear, disaster, imprisonment, or torture. Killing others can only be undertaken "justly," based on a Quranic injunction, namely for adultery, murder, apostasy, and those who deserted the company of the believers.[14] By avoiding generalizations and overarching and abstract principles and keeping strictly faithful to the detailed cases of prohibition mentioned in the sources, the writer of *Qira'a* thus prepares his readers to conclude that everything that is not expressly forbidden is allowed.

The most fascinating aspect of these prohibitions is that they rest on the strict requirement grounded in the Quran[15] regarding the sanctity of human life and the superior role of humans in Allah's creation. It is fascinating because it stands in stark contradiction to the seemingly unbearable facility with which the Islamikaze kill themselves and others. The resolution of this contradiction is the new convoluted interpretations undertaken by fundamentalist Muslim scholars. Man was created, according to the *Qira'a,* with the belief in Allah imprinted in his heart, and all his strength and spirit are devoted to the straightening up of the created world. In order to guide man to follow the right path, Allah sent prophets, apostles, and his messenger Muhammad, together with the Quran and the Sunna. Hence the purpose of man on earth is to worship Allah (*ibadat Allah*), which is more important even than human life. However, these two themes of the sanctity of human life and the worship of Allah are not contradictory.

This world is the scene of the struggle between good and bad, between the worship of God and the worship of Satan, the choice between a life of belief and disbelief. The right choice by man of truth in this world will bring him to eternal life in paradise. Namely, if man devotes his life in this world to worship Allah, he will end up in eternal life in the hereafter. Thus, the laws of jihad not only do not contradict the prohibitions of self-immolation and of killing others unjustifiably, but are even complementary to them. And this is precisely what makes Islam a perfect religion in terms of its regard for human life: namely, the preservation of human life on the one hand, but also self-sacrifice for the sake of Allah. For contrary to other doctrines, which permit killing in the pursuit of material benefit, Islam comes up with the value of human life. And contrary to the theories that regard human life as a supreme value, Islam comes with the value of the worship of Allah. For in the final analysis, according to this logic, setting human life as the supreme value permits injustice to persist without opposition, thus violating human dignity. Conversely, the worship of Allah that applies the tenets of justice and upholding right (*iqamat al-'adl wa-ihqaq al-haqq*) in itself constitutes the delicate balance between these two values. This kind of balance, which exists only in Islam, puts it as the supreme human and cultural model in existence. Naturally, when the author of this dissertation posits the worship of Allah as supreme and the way of jihad as the superior apex of worship, he inescapably comes to the conclusion that any believer who follows divine guidance with regard to jihad and emulates the Prophet in this respect must evince his willingness to die for Allah.[16] To support his conclusion, the author relates to a famous Hadith, where the Prophet undertook to die for Allah to come back to life and then die once again.[17] This means that there was no bigger goal in the Prophet's own existence than to die for Allah, and repeatedly so. Therefore, this tenet constitutes, in the author's mind, a divine guideline that applies everywhere at all times. Hence, the necessity for believers to embrace the road of self-sacrifice (*tad'hia*) and spiritual devotion (*badhl a-nafs*) becomes the central motif in the author's concept of jihad. He recounts many episodes from the life of the Prophet in which he proved his devotion to these themes in his jihad battles against his enemies.[18] This had necessitated the Prophet's readiness, indeed eagerness, to die in the course of jihad, which should be the standard behavior for all Muslims who seek battle at the highest level of risk. For this purpose, the author recognizes three kinds of battles, which must be graduated in accordance with the level of risk involved:

1. Where the chances to die or to emerge alive are even. In this case, the surviving fighter would deserve honor (*karama*), and if he should perish, his death would be considered martyrdom (*shahada*). An illustrious Muslim fighter, Khalid ibn al-Walid, was quoted as wondering every day of battle whether he was escaping from the day of *karama* or that of *shahada*. That meant that dying in this fashion was a winning proposition in any case.[19]

2. Where the balance of power is in the Muslims' disfavor, the Muslim fighter needs to display more audacity to overcome the enemy against all odds. Once again, in many such battles, in which the companions of the Prophet (*sahaba*) participated, the Messenger of Allah provided a personal example by fighting valiantly and near the eye of the storm, in defiance of the dangers the enemy posed to him. Such harsh battles—where some of the *sahaba* made the ultimate sacrifice after they sustained so many wounds that their corpses became unrecognizable[20]—became the high standards of combat to be followed by other believers.
3. A third category of battle is when self-sacrifice is not only hallowed but when it becomes imperative as the only way to win. This is where the act of jihad, itself highly regarded and lavishly rewarded in heaven, transcends into the domain of an act of martyrdom (*istishhad*). The difference between standard self-sacrifice and spiritual devotion and this sort of conscious and deliberate act of martyrdom is that here a special strategy is adopted by a special group of Muslims in order to rescue the entire Muslim army or the whole of the Muslim *umma* from dangerous straights, to disrupt the enemy's war plans or sow disarray in its ranks, to hurt the enemy's morale and boost the Muslims', or to bring such a disaster upon the enemy as to increase his losses and decrease the Muslims'.

One does not have to guess much in order to realize that the last mode of combat is assuredly the highest and most adulated and conforms typologically to the Islamikaze modus operandi that we have repeatedly mentioned in this volume. We learn from the author of the treatise that he regards the Islamikaze not as a routine strategy to fight the enemy in the battlefield, but as a tactical device to be used when conventional battles are about to be lost. In this context we may digress to find grounds to interpret the Twin Towers disaster or the daily attacks by Hamas and Islamic Jihad against Israel once the Palestinian intifada had failed to bring Israel to its knees. It is also noteworthy that when Yasser Arafat came to the end of his rope, when he realized that his campaign against Israel was falling flat on its face, he personally joined the fray by stating before crowds that he was ready to be a *shahid* for the sake of "liberating" Jerusalem, and he repeatedly urged his followers to launch the jihad to realize the evasive dreams of the Palestinians.[21]

In this ultimate model of self-sacrifice, it is the Prophet himself or his *sahaba* who make daring, self-sacrificing moves to save the entire Muslim strategy from failure. It is from cases of this sort, drawn from the personal histories of the most worthy Muslims at the time of the Prophet, that the author infers the implicit permission of Muslim fighters to sacrifice themselves for the public interest.[22] This is the stuff that the present-day Islamikaze hang on to justify their acts of martyrdom. The author connects the two concretely: he says that while today the Islamikaze can carry explosives on their bodies in order to carry out his mission, in the times of the Prophet the audacious fighter had to throw himself on the swords of the enemy, but both modes of action are essentially the same. Similarly, exactly as in early Islam, valiant Muslim fighters had to dismount their horses, which were no match for the elephants of the enemy, and handle those immense and frightening animals with their bare swords in their hands, even as they were trampled upon and slaughtered. Today, an Islamikaze can defy planes and tanks with his body and perish under their weight, or blow himself up on a minefield to facilitate the passage of his fellow fighters into enemy territory or their retreat into safety. In all cases, the gates of paradise were wide open to receive the new martyr.[23]

Thus, the author of this treatise, which gives license to acts of Islamikaze, builds his argument tier after tier: first, he designates the value of the worship of Allah over the value of human life; then the jihad as the supreme form of worship; and since the jihad involves self-sacrifice, three levels thereof are identified, the highest and most commendable of which is the act of martyrdom. All those stages are widely and soundly grounded on the precedents set by the Prophet himself or his companions, whom the believers hold in high esteem. Moreover, from examples in early Islam cited by the author, where self-sacrifice was not absolutely necessary,[24] one can deduce that the very defiance of death in the face of the enemy, in a battle for Islam and for Allah, is seen as a worthy act that allows the deceased fighter into the galleries of paradise. Moreover, as the author quotes the Prophet, determining that jihad is the "top of Islam's honey," he asserts that the martyrdom act is the "top of Jihad's honey," thus concluding that the higher the risk to perish in such an act, the more precious is the martyr's status in the eyes of Allah.[25] To illustrate his point, the author relates a sprinkling of Hadith that demonstrates that, in the eyes of the Prophet, defying death for its own sake is a worthy act, even when it was not absolutely necessary to achieve victory for Islam. For example, he cites the case of a Muslim fighter in the fateful battle of Badr, who took his armor off before the battle and was killed as a result, but he won praise from the Prophet for his audacity.[26]

The author of the treatise does not avoid confronting the contradiction between his sanctification of death and the Quranic injunction to preserve life and escape peril. Once again, precedents from the time of the Prophet and his companions were cited, for example of the fighter who threw himself literally to his death when he single-handedly attacked an entire Byzantine column, whereupon a discussion ensued about whether that hero had unnecessarily thrown himself into certain death. For the author, again through a tortuous manipulation of Hadith accounts, the real peril is not death in battle, but in turning one's attention to material life and neglecting jihad.[27] The same goes for the explicit Quranic prohibition of committing suicide,[28] and the author has to perform an intellectual summersault of sorts to circumvent the issue and manipulate it to prove his point. He says that while both suicide and the act of martyrdom require the express act of will of the Islamikaze, what matters is not the act but the intention (*nia*) of the martyr, which is what determines, in the final analysis, the quality of the act. And once again, the literature of the first Muslims is invoked as example and precedent. A case in point was of a martyr for Islam who appeared on the Day of Judgment and claimed that he fought for Allah, but Allah reminded him that his courage was displayed only so that it could be said of him that he was courageous; whereupon he was dragged on his face and consumed by the fire of hell.[29]

This turn of the argument is extremely important, for it leaves the final judgment to heaven, inasmuch as even when a man performs acts of extreme audacity and is considered by his peers, eye witnesses, and contemporaries as a hero of Islam and a well-deserved martyr, it is up to Allah to scrutinize his intention and decide, possibly otherwise. Conversely, a man may be considered by other humans to have committed a despicable suicide, but when Allah examines his intentions, he might be rewarded with the highest status in paradise. And this is precisely what sets suicide, a flight from the vagaries of life, apart from an act of martyrdom, which is a human response to the call of Allah to sacrifice oneself to inflict loss on the enemies of Allah. The question of whether martyrdom is the domain of the elected few who can cultivate the requisite pious intention or whether the choice is given to every willing Muslim. An analogy is suggested by the author with regard to laws of conversion. Muslims are allowed to renege on their faith outwardly, says the essayist, under duress or threat against their lives, as long that in his heart he did not budge from his creed.[30] However, insists the author, as against that permission (*rukhsa*), there exists also personal resolve (*'azima*), which is admittedly more difficult to attain and consists of refusing to abandon the faith, even in the face of certain death. Those who choose this course in spite of the allowance made by the Sharia in cases of imminent peril attain the highest levels of martyrdom and reward.[31] And since in every operation against the enemy there is a danger of death, the whole issue is determining the degree of the threat. Any act of Islamikaze martyrdom carries with it almost certain death, though everything is ultimately in Allah's hand, and this is what places it at the apex of martyrdom. But suicide it certainly is not.

Reverting to the right terminology, calling a spade a spade, is not only our duty to scholarship, which recognizes no biases, no self-serving ideologies, and no catering to political correctness, but it also reestablishes straight lines of communication between authors and readers and between scholars and their peers. It is unthinkable, for example, that ideology-driven volunteers, who are ready to make the ultimate sacrifice for their convictions, should be denigrated as suicide bombers, or that anyone who lacks the courage to criticize any aspect of Islam should hide behind the spurious labeling of "Islamism," while Islam pure and simple remains untouchable and beyond reproach. One should also recognize that injecting massive doses of Islam into an already difficult dispute has turned the Arab-Israeli conflict (not the erroneously dubbed Palestinian-Israeli issue) into an onslaught of Islam against Jews at large (listen to bin Laden and Iran's Ahmadinejad and note the execution of Daniel Pearl in Karachi and threats and attacks against Jews in Europe and on Israel's borders by Hamas and Hezbollah). The dispute was pushed up a notch because the quantitative conflict, involving territories, compensations, and other measurable, negotiable assets has grown into a qualitative problem, dealt with in absolutes, in Allah-given terms, which are not given to negotiation. Anyone reading the Hamas Charter or viewing Hamas's conduct on Israel's borders with Gaza, notably in the summer of 2014 when indiscriminate rocket attacks were launched on Israeli cities from Gaza, cannot have missed this trend, since the Palestinians have adopted it to guide their destiny.

The 1990s were the preparatory years for 2006, the year of the Cartoon Affair when, like the Rushdie antecedent, the values of Islam clashed violently with the West once again. But now the Muslims were much more experienced and battle-hardened, after blowing up the London and Madrid railways, causing hundreds of Western casualties, and forcing the Spaniards, under threats to dismiss the Aznar government in favor of a socialist, to become more docile to Muslim causes. This time, the Muslim militants were even more daring and vociferous, more militant and aggressive, than in the Rushdie case, for they had acquired the knowledge that the West would cave in to it. The underlying triggers were the same: insults to Islam. In 1989 it was the *Satanic Verses*, which had inexcusably mocked the Word of Allah, and in 2006 it was the Prophet of Islam who was unforgivably ridiculed. In both cases the flimsy self-confidence of the Muslims was so deeply shaken that they had to resort to violence, threats, and mayhem to rescue their desecrated honor, as if a movie or article criticizing Moses or Jesus should have provoked such reactions in the West. Muslims revealed the uncertain grounds of their convictions by signaling that any rock pelted at their idols risked to totter them completely. This conduct is the sort that puts a total ban on foreign missionaries in Muslim lands and is intolerant of non-Muslims in their midst as the persecution of Christians (and Jews in history) in Egypt, Nigeria, Syria, North Africa, and other Muslim countries attests to today. The idea of an open market of ideas is foreign to them, for they are not sure enough of their convictions to let them compete on equal grounds. Saudis and Kuwaitis build mosques and Islamic centers all over the globe, but woe to any Christian who would attempt to act similarly in their lands. In a Muslim rally in Los Angeles on February 18, 2006, one of the slogans waved by furious demonstrators was "Islam shall dominate!" In other words, they were not seeking accommodation as the Cartoon Affair raged on but victory; not calming their tempers but seeking vindication of their fanatic positions. Many movies and slogans had been produced in the West that could be interpreted as injurious to other faiths, but in no case had such a violent uproar exploded in which other people were attacked as in this alleged "harm" done to the Prophet of Islam. Nothing that the West can do will ever match the volume of abuse Muslims heap on Christianity and Judaism or their violent attacks against the followers of other faiths. It is Muslims and non-Muslims from Muslim regimes who flee for their lives to Western societies, and it is to Western consulates that long lines of visa-seeking Muslims form up, not the other way around—an indication in itself of where persecuted individuals feel safer. The cartoon controversy, which transcended the boundaries of a religious row, initially looked like a repetition of the Rushdie Affair, with a prize promised to whomever killed the blasphemous cartoonists who were seen as insulting the Prophet of Islam. There were also many clamors of vengeance resounding from one end of the world to the other. Western journalists were dismissed for supporting freedom of the press, politicians resigned or were castigated by a frightened Europe, and large-scale violence was used by Muslims against European national symbols, including flags and embassies. Only a clear death sentence by a cleric (a fatwa) was missing to make the comparison complete. There was nevertheless a world of difference between the two: the Rushdie Affair was directed at a Muslim individual who had apostatized in Muslim eyes, whereas the cartoon explosion was directed at a country (Denmark) and expanded into an anti-Western campaign of abuse and violence. Also, in the age of naiveté and candor, when the West differentiated between the vast majority of peaceful Muslims and a few extremists, political correctness assumed that if one could understand the offense done to Islam and apologize for it, even if that entailed sacrificing one individual (Rushdie) to appease Islam, then peace and tranquility would prevail. The Cartoon Affair taught the West that the more apologies and understandings (which are unfailingly directed unilaterally from Christendom to Islamdom, never the other way round), the more violent the explosions of anti-Western fury, because Muslims have convinced themselves that the infidels aspire to undermine Islam, and their apologies are proof of that admission.

In the 1990s, the ascent of oil-rich Islam was at its peak, Muslim immigration to Europe and the United States was gathering steam, and it seemed that Islam had become unstoppable. At the same time, a bitter, humiliated Islam—that has been repeatedly classified by UN development reports (all written by Muslim authors) as languishing at the bottom of the world scale—had been rendered more sensitive to its eclipse and therefore more prone to violence. Something had happened in the seventeen years between the Rushdie Affair and the cartoon days of rage, and that was 9/11, which shocked Westerners out of their illusions of an amicable coexistence with Islam. The dogged American determination to pursue wars in Afghanistan and Iraq (both Muslim countries) and then to democratize those countries, thereby putting in jeopardy the entire system of dictatorship into which the Muslim world had comfortably settled, was reason enough for the most directly threatened rulers of Iran and pre-Spring Syria to incite their crowds against the West. Iran's president—who was hugely popular among the Muslim masses due to his bluntness and the challenge he presented to the West by both his anti-Semitic rhetoric and denial of the Shoah—backed by his determined program to go nuclear, encouraged the Muslim crowds to defy the West and its values and attack Westerners when they could do so with impunity. The West had become accustomed to the sight of American and Israeli flags and effigies being burned in the name of Muslim political protest, which was considered legitimate throughout the Islamic world and in the Western democracies where Muslim minorities had settled, which would soon slide into open violence and cost lives. The fact that this sort of conduct offended Americans and Israelis no less than what Muslims consider a blasphemy when their symbols were desecrated did not matter at all to anyone bent on safeguarding those sacrosanct expressions of democracy. But no one had imagined that Scandinavian flags would also undergo the same disparaging treatment in Muslim lands, apart from the underlying hatred for the symbol of the cross in all Scandinavian banners. In other words, more than blasphemy was at stake: the burning of foreign flags was only one manifestation of a deep resentment against the West that had been waiting to erupt at the first opportunity.

It is baffling to witness the endless energy and resources Muslims expend at burning flags and foreign embassies and on desecrating the religious symbols of other faiths and the excess of wasted time that would have been better spent on educating, working, building, and creating. It seems that they are always on the alert to find reason for offense in order to demonstrate their anti-Western animus, sinking into inconsolable misery if such occasions for violent and vindictive demonstrations do not present themselves often enough. But they have no lack of such opportunities, for they manufacture them constantly. At the height of the Cartoon Affair, Sunni Muslims blew up a mosque in the ancient capital of Islam, Samara, just north of Baghdad, which is one of the most hallowed shrines for Shiites. It is the burial place of the tenth and eleventh imams in the line of the twelve adulated imams in the Twelver Shia of both Iraq and Iran, just before their descendent, the twelfth imam, went into hiding and assumed the identity of the Mahdi Messiah, who is expected to return and bring with him peace and justice to the world. The sanctity of the place is evident, judging not only from its objective place in Shiite hagiography, but also from the fury and rage that shook the Shiite community and was expressed by the equally outrageous outburst of violence in which dozens of Sunni mosques went up in flames. The enmity between Sunnites and Shiites in not new. What is striking is that, unlike the Cartoon Affair, in which no one was killed or physically hurt by the act of drawing the cartoons, the mosque desecrations and the massacres before and since have brought Iraqi society to the brink of civil war. Yet no outrage was heard in the Islamic world and no massive demonstrations were mounted against those murderous acts involving the Samara mosque. The only conclusion is that it not the nature of the insult that counts

dismayed Danish cartoonist at work, while a Muslim cleric, saber in hand, drew a line around the cartoonist's neck.[35] Another showed a Muslim cutting off the right hand of a Western cartoonist and exclaiming: "Maybe now you will learn tolerance and respect for the views of others!"[36] Still another decried the totalitarian regimes that hold Muslim populations under their grip, reproducing a dialogue between Assad of Syria and Ahmadinejad of Iran, in which they agree to instigate violence over the "blasphemous cartoons" because "our most sacred texts demand it."[37] The Iranian nuclear threat that dominated the headlines alongside the Muslim rampage caused some cartoonists to combine the two themes. A cartoonist was shown at his desk while an enormous nuclear bomb exploded next to his home, and he exclaimed: "What did I do now?"[38] Another showed Ahmadinejad holding a nuclear-headed missile in his hands, facing a Danish cartoonist, under the caption: "The battle of the world's greatest evil-doers."[39]

A keen response to these grievances in the context of the Cartoon Affair was provided by the Arab American psychologist Wafa Sultan in her interview with Al Jazeera.[40] In her forthright reaction she castigated millions of her Arab viewers:

> The clash we are witnessing around the world is not a clash of religions, or a clash of civilizations. It is a clash between two opposites, between two eras. It is a clash between a mentality which belongs to the Middle Ages and another mentality that belongs to the 21st century. It is clash between civilization and backwardness, between the civilized and the primitive, between barbarity and rationality. It is a clash between freedom and oppression, between democracy and dictatorship. It is a clash between human rights on the one hand and the violation of these rights, on the other hand. It is a clash between those who treat women like beasts, and those who treat them as human beings. What we see today is not a clash of civilizations, for civilizations do not clash, they compete . . .
>
> The Muslims are the ones who started to use this expression [clash of civilizations]. The Muslims are the ones who began the clash of civilizations. The Prophet of Islam said: "I was ordered to fight the people until they believe in Allah and his Messenger." When the Muslims divided the people into Muslims and non-Muslims, and called to fight the others until they believe in what they themselves believe, they started this clash and began this war. In order to stop this war they have to re-examine their Islamic books and curricula, which are full of calls for *takfir* [labeling others infidels, heretics, or apostates in order to justify war against them], and fighting the "infidels."
>
> [Some Muslims say] that they never offend other people's beliefs. What civilization on the face of the earth allows them to call other

people by names that they did not choose for themselves? Once they call them *Ahl al-Dhimma* (Protected Jews and Christians under Islamic rule); another time The People of the Book; and yet another time they compare them to apes and pigs, or they call the Christians "those who incurred Allah's wrath" [in fact, the opening sura of the Quran refers to the Jews as incurring the wrath of Allah, while Christians are dubbed as "those who went astray"]. Who told you that they are the people of the Book? They are not people of the book, they are people of many books. All the useful scientific books that you have today are theirs, the fruit of their free and creative thinking. What gives you the right to call them "those who incurred Allah's wrath" or "those who have gone astray"?, and claim that our religion commands you to refrain from offending the believes of others? . . . You are free to worship whoever you want, but other peoples' beliefs are not your concern, whether they believe that the Messiah is God, or that Satan is God . . . Let people have their own beliefs . . .

The Jews have come from the tragedy [of the Holocaust] and forced the world to respect them, with their knowledge not with their terror; with their work, not with crying and yelling. Humanity owes most of the discoveries and science of the 19th Century and 20th Century to Jewish scientists. Fifteen million people, scattered throughout the world, have united and won their rights through work and knowledge. We have not a single Jew who blew up a German restaurant or who destroyed a church, or who protests by killing people. The Muslims turned two Buddha statues to rubble. We have not seen a Buddhist burn down a mosque, kill a Muslim or burn down an embassy. Only Muslims defend their beliefs by burning down churches, killing people and destroying embassies. This path will not yield any results. The Muslims must ask themselves what they can do for mankind before they ask that human kind respect them . . .

Why does a young Muslim man, in the prime of his life, with a full life ahead, go and blow himself up? How and why does he blow himself up in a bus full of innocent passengers? . . . In our countries religion is the source of education, and is the only spring from which that terrorist drank until his thirst was quenched. He was not born a terrorist and did not become a terrorist overnight. Islamic teachings played a role in weaving this ideological fabric, into a thread to play a role. [41]

Notes

1. See R. Israeli, *Islamikaze: Manifestations of Islamic Martyrology*, Frank Cass, London, 2003, chapter 1, pp. 11–32.
2. Amir Taheri (a former pre-revolutionary editor of the daily *Kaihan*), *The Spirit of Allah* (in Hebrew translation), Am Oved, Tel Aviv, 1986, p. 148. See also Mahmoud Ayoub, *Redemptive Suffering in Islam*, pp. 148–58; Emanuel Sivan, *Muslim Radicals* (in Hebrew), Am Oved, Tel Aviv, 1985, pp. 192–95.

3. Amir Tahiri, p. 55. See also Hamid Algar, *Islam and Revolution,* UC Press, Berkeley, 1981, pp. 329–43; and Martin Kramer (ed.), *Protest and Revolution in Shi'ite Islam* (Hebrew), Tel Aviv University, p. 29.
4. Report by Guy Bechor, Arab Affairs commentator of *Ha'aretz,* December 6, 1995, p. b2.
5. Ibid.
6. *Ha'aretz,* January 23, 1995, p. 6a.
7. Meir Hatina, *Palestinian Radicalism: The Islamic Jihad Movement* (Hebrew), Tel Aviv University, 1994, pp. 79–80.
8. *Ha'aretz,* January 23, 1995.
9. Izz ad-Din al Qassam was the founder and hero of the Islamic movement in Palestine in the 1930s, which engaged in battle both against the British Mandatory forces and the Jewish self-defense groups, until his death in combat in Samaria in 1935. His name was picked up by Hamas, upon its foundation in 1988, and given to the military arm of the organization.
10. Hatina, p. 82.
11. A citation from an Islamic Jihad–distributed leaflet, *Ha'aretz,* January 23, 1995, p. 6a. The leaflet was reportedly headed by a citation from the Repentance Sura in the Quran, which promises paradise to those who kill and are killed in the battles of Allah.
12. *Qira'a fi Fiqh al-Shihada* (Readings in Islamic Martyrology), the very subtitle of this work, was published in 1988 as a special addendum to *al-Islam wa Filastin* (Islam and Palestine) that appears in Nicosia, Cyprus, but has been the ideological supporter of the Islamikaze operations against Israel. See *Al-Islam wa-Filastin,* June 5, 1988, p. 9.
13. See previous ftn.
14. *Qira'a,* op. cit. p. 3.
15. The Cow Sura, verses 28–36.
16. *Qira'a,* p. 4.
17. Citing Malik ibn Anas, *Ahadith al-Jami' al'Saghir,* in *Qira'a,* p. 4.
18. Ibid., p. 7.
19. Ibid., p. 8.
20. Ibid., pp. 8–9.
21. Palestinian Authority Broadcasting, shown on Israeli Television, January 24, 2002, 20:00 News Bulletin.
22. Qira'a, p. 12.
23. Ibid.
24. Ibid., pp. 10–12.
25. Ibid., p. 10.
26. Ibid., pp. 10–12.
27. Ibid., p. 10.
28. Quran, Women Sura, verse 29.
29. *Qira'a,* p. 6.
30. The Bee Sura, verse 108.
31. *Qira'a,* pp. 10–11.
32. See R. Israeli, *Islamikaze: Manifestations of Islamic Martyrology,* London, Frank Cass, 2003, especially chapter 8.
33. In a public speech by Ali Khamenei, February 20, 2006.
34. *CNN World News,* February 22, 2006.

35. John Branch, *The San Antonio Express News,* February 10, 2006.
36. John Cole, *The Scranton Times,* February 8, 2006.
37. Eric Devericks, *The Seattle Times,* February 10, 2006.
38. John Darkow, *The Columbia Daily Tribune*, February 9, 2006.
39. Mike Graston, *The Windsor Star*, February 10, 2006.
40. *Al Jazeera,* Interview with Wafa Sultan, February 21, 2006. See MEMRI, Special Dispatch Series 1107, March 7, 2006.
41. Ibid.

4

Nuclear Islam: Pakistan and Iran and Its Satellites

One of the preponderant elements of self-confidence, which helped propel Islamic radicalism and fundamentalist Islamic rhetoric forward post-1990s was the "Islamic bomb," which was considered a show of strength to emerge from its subordinate status on the world scene to a position of parity with the great powers. That effort had begun in Pakistan in the 1970s, when Prime Minister Zulfiqar Ali Bhutto, who spoke of "Islamic nationalism," also prepared to apply his ambitions into the real world.

Zulfiqar Ali Bhutto was indeed the founder of Pakistan's nuclear plans, and due to his administrative and aggressive leadership to lead this nuclear deterrence programme, he is known as the "Father of Nuclear deterrence programme". Bhutto's interest in nuclear technology was said to have begun during his college years in the United States when he attended the course of political science, discussing the political impact of U.S.'s first nuclear test, on global politics. While at Berkeley, Bhutto witnessed the public panic when the Soviet Union first exploded the bomb in 1949, prompting the U.S. government to famously launch the research on Hydrogen bombs. In 1958, Bhutto played a key role in setting up the Pakistan Atomic Energy Commission (PAEC). Soon, Bhutto offered a technical post to Munir Ahmad Khan, the real father of the Islamic bomb, in PAEC in 1958.

In October 1965, as Foreign Minister, Zulfiqar Ali Bhutto visited Vienna where nuclear engineer Munir Ahmad Khan was working at a senior technical post at the IAEA, informed him of the status of Indian nuclear programme and the options Pakistan had to develop its own nuclear capability. Both agreed on the need for Pakistan to develop a nuclear deterrent to meet India's nuclear capacity. While Munir Ahmad Khan had failed to convince Ayub Khan, at the time the President of Pakistan, to adopt his ideas, Bhutto assured him: "Don't worry, our turn will come." Shortly thereafter in 1965, Bhutto in a press conference, famously declared that "even if we have to eat grass, we will make a nuclear bomb. We have no other choice", as he saw India was making its way to develop the bomb. On 20 January 1972, Zulfikar Ali Bhutto, as the President and then Prime Minister of Pakistan, rallied a conference of nuclear scientists and engineers at Multan. While at the Multan meeting, arranged by Bhutto's Science Advisor Abdus Salam, scientists were wondering why the President who had so much on his hands in those trying days was paying so much attention to the scientists and engineers in the nuclear field. At the meeting Bhutto slowly talked about the recent war with India (1971) and the country's future, pointing out that the very existence of the country was in great mortal danger. With the academicians listening to Bhutto carefully, he said: "Look, we're going to have the bomb". Bhutto asked them: "Can you give it to me? And how long will it take it to make it?" Many of the senior scientists had witnessed the war, and were emotionally and psychologically disturbed. Therefore, their response was positive. There was a lively debate on the time needed to make the bomb, and finally one scientist dared to say that maybe it could be done in five years. Bhutto smiled, lifted his hand, and dramatically thrust forward three fingers and said: "Three years, I want it in three years". The atmosphere suddenly became electric. A junior scientist, Dr. S. A. Butt (a theoretical physicist), who under Munir Ahmad Khan's guiding hand would come to play a major role in making the fission weapon possible—jumped to his feet and clamored for his leader's attention, replied: "It can be done in three years". When Bhutto heard Butt's reply, he was very much amused and said: "Well . . . Much as I appreciate your enthusiasm, this is a very serious political decision, which Pakistan must make, and perhaps all Third World countries must make one day, because it is coming. So can you boys do it?" Nearly all senior scientists replied in one tone: "Yes . . . We can do it, given the resources and given the facilities". Bhutto ended the meeting by simply saying: "I shall find you the resources and I shall find you the facilities."[1]

Before the 1970s, a nuclear programme had long been established under the government of Suhrawardy, but was completely peaceful and devoted to civil power. Bhutto, in his book *The Myth of Independence*[2] in 1969 wrote that:

> If Pakistan restricts or suspends her nuclear deterrence, it would not only enable India to blackmail Pakistan with her nuclear advantage,

> but would impose a crippling limitation on the development of Pakistan's science and technology . . . Our problem in its essence, is how to obtain such a weapon in time before the crisis begin . . .[3]

After India's nuclear test—codenamed *Smiling Buddha*—in May 1974, Bhutto sensed and saw this test as a fatal threat on Pakistan's survival. In a press conference, held shortly after India's nuclear test, Bhutto said, "India's nuclear program is designed to intimidate Pakistan and establish '*hegemony in the subcontinent*.'" Despite Pakistan's limited financial resources, Bhutto was so enthusiastic about Pakistan's nuclear energy project, that he is reported to have said "*Pakistanis will eat grass but make a nuclear bomb.*" Pakistan Atomic Energy Commission's militarisation was initiated in 20 January 1972 and, in its initial years, was implemented by Pakistan's Chief of Army Staff General Tikka Khan. The Karachi Nuclear Power Plant (KANUPP-I) was inaugurated by Bhutto during his role as President of Pakistan at the end of 1972. The nuclear weapons programme was set up loosely based on Manhattan Project of the 1940s, under the administrative control of Bhutto. And, senior academic scientists had a direct access to Bhutto, and kept him informed about every inch of the development. Bhutto's Science Advisor, Abdus Salam's office was also set up in Bhutto's Prime Minister Secretariat. On Bhutto's request, Salam had established and led the Theoretical Physics Group (TPG) that marked the beginning of the nuclear deterrent project. The TPG designed and developed the nuclear weapons as well as the entire programme. Later, Munir Ahmad Khan had him personally approve the budget for the development of the programme. In January 1972, Bhutto chose the U.S. trained nuclear engineer Munir Ahmad Khan as chairman of Pakistan Atomic Energy Commission (PAEC), as Bhutto realized that he would want an administrator who understood the scientific and economic needs of such technologically giant and ambitious project. Since 1965, Khan had developed extremely close and trusted relationship with Bhutto, and even after his death, his children, Benazir and Murtaza Bhutto had been instructed by their father to keep in touch with Munir Ahmed Khan. In spring of 1976, Kahuta Research Facility, then known as Engineering Research Laboratories (ERL), as part of codename *Project-706*, was also established by Bhutto, and brought under nuclear scientist Dr. Abdul Qadeer Khan and the Pakistan Army Corps of Engineers' Lieutenant-General Zahid Ali Akbar.

By the time Bhutto was ousted, his crash programme had fully matured in terms of technical development as well as scientific efforts. By 1977, PAEC and KRL had built their uranium enrichment and plutonium reprocessing plants, and selection for test sites, at Chagai Hills, was done by the PAEC. The feasibility reports were submitted by both organizations on their works. In 1977, the PAEC's Theoretical Physics Group had finished the designing of the first fission weapon, and KRL scientists succeeded in electromagnetic isotope separation of Uranium fissile isotopes. In spite of this, still little had been done in the development of weapons, and Pakistan's nuclear arsenal was actually made by General Zia-ul-Haq's military regime, under the watchful eyes of several Naval admirals, Army and Air Force's generals, including Ghulam Ishaq Khan. In 1983, Bhutto's decision later proved to be right, when PAEC had conducted a cold test, near Kirana Hills, evidently made from non-fissioned plutonium. It has been speculated that Dr. Khan's uranium enrichment designs were used by the Chinese in exchange for some highly enriched weapon grade uranium. Later on, this weapon grade uranium was offered back to the Chinese as the Pakistanis used their own materials.[4] In all, Bhutto knew that Pakistan had become a nuclear weapon state in 1978 when his friend Munir Ahmad Khan paid a visit to him in his jail cell. There, Munir Ahmad Khan told Bhutto that the process of weapon designing is finished and a milestone in the complex and difficult enrichment of weapon-grade fuel has been achieved by the PAEC and Dr. Abdul Qadeer Khan of ERL. Bhutto called for an immediate nuclear test to be conducted, but no response was issued by General Zia or any member of his government.

From his jail cell in 1978, Bhutto made a plea for Pakistan to complete its nuclear program, arguing that he knew that Israel, South Africa, and India had full nuclear capacity, therefore it was unacceptable that while a Christian, a Hindu, and a Jewish civilization had this capacity, Islamic civilization did not. He was right; in 1987 Pakistan too became fully nuclear, though a decade and a half later than what he had expected in 1972, but he did not live to see his project through before he was executed by the ruling junta of Zia-ul-Haq.

India's 1974 testing of a nuclear "device" had given Pakistan's nuclear program new momentum. Through the late 1970s, Pakistan's program acquired sensitive uranium enrichment technology and expertise. The 1975 arrival of Dr. Abdul Qadeer Khan considerably advanced these efforts. Dr. Khan was a German-trained metallurgist who brought with him knowledge of gas centrifuge technologies that he had acquired through his position at the classified URENCO uranium enrichment plant in the Netherlands. Dr. Khan also reportedly brought with him stolen uranium- enrichment technologies from Europe. He was put in charge of building, equipping, and operating Pakistan's Kahuta facility, which was established in 1976. Under Khan's direction, Pakistan employed an extensive clandestine network in order to obtain the necessary materials and technology for its developing uranium enrichment capabilities. In 1985, Pakistan crossed the threshold of weapons-grade uranium production, and by 1986 it is thought to have produced enough fissile material for a nuclear weapon. Pakistan continued advancing its uranium- enrichment program, and, according to Pakistani sources, the nation acquired the ability to carry out a nuclear explosion in 1987. On May 28, 1998, Pakistan announced that it had successfully conducted five nuclear tests. The Pakistani Atomic Energy Commission reported that the five nuclear tests conducted on May 28 generated a seismic signal of 5.0 on the Richter scale, with a total yield of up to 40 KT (equivalent TNT). Dr. A. Q. Khan claimed that one device was a boosted fission device and that the other four were sub-kiloton nuclear devices. On May 30, 1998, Pakistan tested one more nuclear warhead with a reported yield of 12 kilotons. The tests were conducted at Balochistan, bringing the total number of claimed tests to six. It has also been claimed by Pakistani sources that at least one additional device, initially planned for detonation on 30 May 1998, remained emplaced underground, ready for detonation.

Pakistan's nuclear program was initially based primarily on highly enriched uranium (HEU), which is produced at the A. Q. Khan research laboratory at Kahuta, a gas centrifuge uranium enrichment facility. The Kahuta facility has been in operation since the early 1980s. By the early 1990s, Kahuta had an estimated 3,000 centrifuges in operation, and Pakistan continued its pursuit of expanded uranium enrichment capabilities. But in the 1990s Pakistan began to pursue plutonium production capabilities. With Chinese assistance, Pakistan built the 40 MWt (megawatt thermal) Khusab research reactor at Joharabad, and in April 1998, Pakistan announced that the reactor was operational. According to public statements made by US officials, this unsafeguarded heavy water reactor generates an estimated 8–10 kilotons of weapons grade plutonium per year, which is enough for one to two nuclear weapons. Khusab's plutonium production capacity could allow Pakistan to develop lighter nuclear warheads that would be easier to deliver with a ballistic missile. Plutonium separation reportedly takes place at the New Labs reprocessing plant next to Pakistan's Institute of Nuclear Science and Technology (Pinstech) in Rawalpindi and at the larger Chasma nuclear power plant, neither of which are subject to IAEA inspection.

In the past, China played a major role in the development of Pakistan's nuclear infrastructure, especially when increasingly stringent export controls in Western countries made it difficult for Pakistan to acquire materials and technology elsewhere. According to a 2001 Department of Defense report, China has supplied Pakistan with nuclear materials and expertise and has provided critical assistance in the construction of Pakistan's nuclear facilities. In the 1990s, China designed and supplied the heavy water Khusab reactor, which plays a key role in Pakistan's production of plutonium. A subsidiary of the China National Nuclear Corporation also contributed to Pakistan's efforts to expand its uranium enrichment capabilities by providing 5,000 custom made ring magnets, which are a key component of the bearings that facilitate the high-speed rotation of centrifuges. China is also reported to have provided Pakistan with the design of one of its warheads, which is relatively sophisticated in design and lighter than US- and Soviet-designed first-generation warheads. China also provided technical and material support in the completion of the Chasma nuclear power reactor and plutonium reprocessing facility, which was built in the mid 1990s. The project had been initiated as a cooperative program with France, but Pakistan's failure to sign the NPT and unwillingness to accept IAEA safeguards on its entire nuclear program caused France to terminate assistance. According to an American Defense Department report, Pakistan has also acquired nuclear related and dual-use equipment and materials from the Former Soviet Union and Western Europe. On several occasions, under the authority of amendments to the Foreign Assistance Act, the US has imposed sanctions on Pakistan, cutting off economic and military aid as a result of its pursuit of nuclear weapons. However, the US suspended sanctions each time developments in Afghanistan made Pakistan a strategically important "frontline state," such as the 1981 Soviet occupation and in the war on terrorism.

Pakistan has not signed the Non-Proliferation Treaty (NPT) or the Comprehensive Test Ban Treaty (CTBT). According to the Defense Department report cited above, "Pakistan remains steadfast in its refusal to sign the NPT, stating that it would do so only after India joined the Treaty. Consequently, not all of Pakistan's nuclear facilities are under IAEA safeguards. Pakistani officials have stated that signature of the CTBT is in Pakistan's best interest, but that Pakistan will do so only after developing a domestic consensus on the issue, and have disavowed any connection with India's decision." Pakistan does not abide by a no-first-use doctrine, as evidenced by President Pervez Musharraf's statements in May, 2002. Musharraf said that Pakistan did not want a conflict with India but that if it came to war between the nuclear-armed rivals, he would "respond with full might." These statements were interpreted to mean that if pressed by an overwhelming conventional attack from India, which has superior conventional forces, Pakistan might use its nuclear weapons.

In contrast with Pakistan, whose Islamic bomb is directed toward its archrival in the Indian subcontinent, Iran's nuclear program has been primarily targeting its hegemony in the Persian Gulf, while using the anti-Zionist pretext to enlist Arab and Muslim support for its nuclearization project. Both have been dubbed "Islamic bombs"—the one to justify Ali Bhutto's vision of an Islamic civilization deserving of a nuclear project, the other to back up by military power the dedication of a regime to ostensibly wipe out the Zionist presence in the Middle East, but actually to maintain its prevalence over the Gulf area. Both are openly committed to preserving and promoting Islamic causes. The Twelver Shia, which rules Iran today, had always promoted a particularly fanatic attitude toward Jews, and dhimmis in general, due to the impurity of unbelievers not to be tolerated among its followers. It is well-known, for example, that in medieval and early modern Iran under the Shia, Christianity was almost totally extirpated from the land, while the large Jewish community suffered limitations such as prohibition of walking outdoors when it rained or snowed, for fear of infecting the environment with their impurity.[5] Justice and purity will precipitate the coming of the Imam Mahdi, therefore those who block the way to redemption, such as the impure Jews, are to be discarded. The fact that this dream has not yet been realized in Tehran, and that Iran also entertains some national interests in the Gulf who might not accord with pure ideology, does not judge negatively the missed and unfulfilled utopia; this is what Max Weber called the "routinization of the charisma," or what others usually name "the deed that distorts and corrupts the ideal," or what revolutionaries have elected to express in the dichotomies of "theory and practice," "doctrine and praxis," "ideology and organization," or the "wings of vision versus the feet of reality."

The Shia has always been embroiled in rifts and differences, not only with its enemies but also within itself. Classical Shia, which was usually persecuted by its Sunnite environment, learned to bear its suffering quietly and passively and carried out its rituals within its mosques or in public without provoking rulers or the general Muslim population, especially before there was a Shiite state after the dissolution of the Fatimid Dynasty in Egypt in the twelfth century. In Safavid Iran (sixteenth to eighteenth centuries), Twelver Shia was finally established as the official faith of the empire, and in new Iran, where the empire was revived under the shah, the Shiite clergy—in contrast with the Sunnite, which has no clerical hierarchy—was hierarchical and an institutional religion:[6] namely it did not depend on the state for existence and did not fill any official role in the government. The rationale was overwhelming in its simplicity: In view of the belief that it was the Hidden Imam who managed the affairs of the world from his hiding, the proper functioning of society would be impossible without some sort of spiritual contact with him in order to receive guidance from him. Not every mullah (cleric) is capable of maintaining such a supreme contact with the Hidden Imam, therefore only the most senior amongst them, never more than two dozen in each generation, who have earned the title of ayatollah (the sign of Allah) and were so designated thanks to their scholarship, knowledge, and spiritual state deserve this status. A handful of them, the most path-breaking and imposing by their leadership, like Khomeini himself, were titled *ayatollah uzma* (grand ayatollah). Other senior clerics, with the titles of *hujat al-Islam* (militant for Islam, like, for instance, the second president Rafsanjani), and lower mullahs aspire all their lives to advance up the ladder of the hierarchy, similar to the Catholic Church, and the higher the clerical rank the more imposing the spiritual impact on society. After the Islamic Revolution, President Ahmadinejad was more influential than his predecessor President Khatami, in spite of the latter being one of a few ayatollahs while the former had no rank in the clergy. Conversely, Supreme Leader Khamenei, who was not among the top clerics, became the man whose decisions counted the most. In both Iran and Iraq, where the status of the ayatollahs was not dominant until recently, the mullahs were influential spiritual leaders but without any effect on state affairs, because they were often executed by Saddam Hussein or incarcerated or exiled by the shah.

Ayatollah Khomeini changed this, at least on the doctrinal level. He had begun to develop his revolutionary ideas under the shah, which, had they not preceded the Spring (2011) by one generation or more, could have served as its precursor, if one considers their audacious élan, their out-of-the-box thinking, and their far-reaching political consequences. The first thoughts that Khomeini started to develop cost him, inter alia, fifteen years (1963–78) of exile in Najaf, Iraq, one of the holy places of the Shia, being the site where Ali, the first imam, is buried, where he brought to completion and published his *Islamic Revolution,* in which he outlined his positions and plan of action. He was then compelled to leave by Saddam, who had sealed with the shah an agreement on the border between the two countries in the middle of the mighty Shatt al-Arab, where the Tigris and the Euphrates converge before they pour into the Persian Gulf. The main thought that would have appealed to Muslim crowds today would have been the need to eradicate tyrant rulers and to install in their stead Islamic regimes under Sharia law. Khomeini's Iran was the first to do that, through an Islamic revolution in which the clergy played a part, followed by Iraq which, under American tutelage, applied that same principle through a Western-style democracy, at least for now.

Khomeini's doctrine was revolutionary from yet other aspects, because it provided the ideological infrastructure and underpinnings for a new model of rule in which the clergy are actively involved. For him, in view that the ayatollahs are the supreme sources of knowledge, wisdom, and inspiration, it is only logical that they should also be the rulers—something similar to the prince who is also a philosopher in Western tradition. He developed two concepts that anchored the suggested revolutionary change: the first is *marja' taqlid* (the reference for emulation), that is that the supreme head of the clergy (*ayatollah uzma*), being also the supreme spiritual power, ought to be the reference all should aspire to emulate, a modern manifestation of the supreme model of the Prophet revealed in the Sunna; and second—*wilayat al-faqih* (the rule of the jurist). These two principles turned the passive state of expectation of the return of the Imam Mahdi to bring salvation into an aggressive initiative to precipitate such a momentous event. To those familiar with modern Jewish history, this could be comparable to the revolutionary doctrine developed in the 1920s and 1930s by Rabbi Kook in Palestine, whereby it was not enough for Jewry to sit and wait in the Diaspora for the coming of the Messiah to provide salvation, but instead Jews should practice Zionism by settlement, development, and social and political action as an avenue for redemption. Khomeini probably viewed those two concepts as personified in him, as a result of his scholarship, his lifelong struggle against the tyranny of the shah, and his spiritual qualities, which made him into a mujtahid who is thus qualified to continue his innovative *ijtihad* and express the will of the Hidden Imam pending his return. Unlike the Sunna, where the gates of *ijtihad* had been closed since the passing of the great luminaries, the founders of the four schools of law, by the tenth century, the Shiite mujtahid undertakes the task of innovative legislation, and his verdicts ought to be the law. Hence it is only natural that membership in parliament was to be assigned to mullahs, who understand the matter of religious legislation and the will of the imam. Khomeini wrote that only the mullahs are able to motivate people to die for Islam, and even persuade them to beg for permission to sacrifice themselves for Islam.

Khomeini, like Muslim Brother Sayyid Qutb, was full of hatred toward the Jews and turned his bigotry into doctrine by dubbing them "enemies of Allah," hence the extremely profuse, libelous, and imaginary pool of lies, blind contempt, and outright primitive ability to fabricate anti-Semitic hoaxes that are extraordinary for two great luminaries of modern Islam, from whom one could expect a higher measure of humanity, civility, and good judgment than the ludicrous statements made in the classic books of those two well-respected and adulated Muslim thinkers.[7] No wonder, then, that President Ahmadinejad, who considered himself their disciple and the devoted executor of their anti-Semitic doctrine, should feel as compelled as Hitler to repeat on every occasion his nonsense about the extermination of the Jews and their state. Khomeini also included in his political activism a novel interpretation of the murder of Hussein bin Ali and his entourage in Karbala, which is celebrated as the central rite in Shiite liturgy (the tazia on the day of Ashura). It was no longer only a memorial day for the most despicable murder of the greatest martyr of all generations, with whom every Shiite ought to identify by reliving his suffering through self-inflicted pain and torture, but a war hero whom it became incumbent on all Shiites to emulate as the supreme martyr in the path of Allah on his way to paradise, who will also recommend his followers for admission into the high heavens. When Iraq invaded Iran in October 1980, Khomeini, who was adored as if he were the imam himself, called his people to the defense of the land and produced more recruits than needed, thanks to his reference to Hussein's model.

Whether the main focus of the Middle East unrest has remained between Israel and the Muslim world, as Hezbollah, Hamas, and some other fundamentalists wish it, or has shifted to the Sunni–Shiite dichotomy, it is evident that, since the accession to power of Ahmadinejad in the 2000s, Middle East unrest has become centered on the issue of nuclearization of Iran, a matter equally feared by Israel and the Gulf states. Israel, having learned to count on no one for its fundamental security, has been preparing at least to damage the Iranian effort, if not to destroy it, while the Gulf state regimes, precisely those who are opposing the Muslim Spring, lest it sweep them away in its wake, are helplessly watching and waiting. In the meantime, these Gulf states are arming themselves to the teeth, to the full extent of what their wealth affords them, hoping that either the United States will interfere to destroy their nuclear capability, it being the only nation able to do so militarily, or at least that Israel will attempt to damage that ability through a limited strike within its means. Iran, undeterred by the economic sanctions and the military threats against it, has been pursuing its course frantically, aiming at getting to the point of no return so as to make itself immune to any attack by threatening to retaliate with nuclear devices.

During the Cold War, MAD (mutually assured destruction) was the key to deterrence between the nuclear powers: they understood that since each had the capacity to destroy the others many times over, none of them would dare to initiate an attack. The assumption was that the actors in both parts of the equation were rational and, for fear of bringing disaster upon their people, would certainly refrain from precipitating a nuclear conflict. For that reason, the presence of the ultimate weapons assured their definite unuse. But in Iran, the situation may be totally different. We know from Ahmadinejad's past in the Basij militia that he was a fanatic in the belief of the imminent return of the imam to earth, something that he had prepared for as mayor of Tehran when he ordered the widening of the main avenues of the city to absorb the millions who would flock to the streets to watch the return of the Hidden One. He also said that when speaking to the UN General Assembly as president of Iran he could feel the aura of the imam hovering over him and inspiring his speech. Since in Shiite eschatology the imam would choose to return after a millennium of hiding at precisely the worst moment of misery, injustice, and oppression—what in other eschatologies is called the "pangs of the Messiah"—then it makes sense that precipitating his return by an extreme and desperate tour de force, such as using nuclear arms, could be thought by rulers who do not ply to the MAD theory the best and most feasible avenue. In other words, in the minds of irrational leaders whose considerations and reasoning are obscured by religious fanaticism, mutual deterrence would not work.

Why would the Iranians wish to attack, and whom? Usually, when leaders concoct a plan of attack, they keep mute on it for the effect of surprise, and they may even try to create the reverse impression that they anchor no aggressive intent toward their victim. Ahmadinejad, since his advent to power, has not stopped, on the contrary, proclaiming his ambition to destroy Israel, to put an end to Zionism, which is another wording for the same, to deny the Holocaust, to instigate and dispatch terrorists against Israel and Jewish targets, to convene international conferences about Holocaust denial, to address the United Nations about his mad plan, to finance and instigate Hamas and Hezbollah against Israel, and to gather annual meetings of "Islamic Terrorism International" in his capital.

Is anything else needed to prove his intentions and to see to it that the lunatic man who was at the helm of Iran until 2013 must not possess nuclear arms? His intent was clearly aggressive against another member state of the United Nations, which instead of initiating harsh reprisals by ejecting Iran from the United Nations until it repents on the contrary attended the conferences convened by it and his convoluted speeches of nonsense at the UN headquarters. An attack of this sort on Israel would be one of indiscriminate extermination and genocide, motivated by hate and fanaticism, while an Israeli preventive attack to preempt such a disaster would be directed only against the threatening nuclear installations of Iran, though collateral damage and fatalities might unfortunately remain inevitable.

IDF chief of staff, Lieutenant General Benny Gantz, declared in an interview broadcast on Israel's sixty-fourth Independence Day (May 2012) that "The IDF is ready to move against Iran the minute it receives the green light." "The Iranians are determined to build a nuclear weapon while they continue to dupe the international community," Minister of Defense Ehud Barak added the following day. These fateful declarations were not gratuitous, for Israel's leaders have been facing a series of existential questions: should Israel attack Iran or pursue the diplomatic track? When, if ever, is the right time to launch an attack? How should it be executed? How will Iran's leaders react to an onslaught on their nuclear facilities? The most likely day-after scenario, as the international media see it, is a devastating Iranian response based mainly, though not entirely, on its long-range missile arsenal. This attack would be coupled with terrorist strikes against Jewish and Israeli targets abroad and backed by Hezbollah, Iran's proxy in Lebanon, and perhaps Hamas, its agent in Gaza. On the international front, Iran could wreak havoc on the global economy through fluctuations in oil prices, even though this could also ultimately harm Iran itself, which could respond via a four-way campaign with long-ranged counterfire against Israel, terror activity on Israel's borders, attacks on Israelis and Jews overseas, and a limited conflict on the Lebanese border of Israel. Israel is fully aware of the implications of the day after, but senior political security figures have increasingly alleged that Iran's response capabilities are limited due to international constraints and its distance from Israel. From Israel's perspective, it could withstand an Iranian retaliation, just as it has withstood missile attacks in the past (by Iraq, Hezbollah, and lately Hamas).

An unlikely voice is sounding the alarm on a nuclear Iran—the liberal Israeli newspaper *Haaretz*,[8] which is well-known for its opposition to official Israeli government policy. Columnist Ari Shavit, taking as his source an article in *The Economist* that declares it would be impossible to stop Iran from going nuclear, warns, "We're out of time. We're really out of time." Shavit writes, "Via the *Economist*, the mainstream of the international community has then admitted that its campaign against Iran's nuclearization has ended in failure. And via this journal, the school that favors containing a nuclear Iran came out of the closet." He continues: "What the world promised would never happen is happening at this very moment. What the top ranks of Israel's defense establishment promised would never happen is in fact happening. Iran is becoming a nuclear power, while Israel stands alone."

This was the strategy of Ahmadinejad, who put the elimination of Israel at the top of his agenda, and he was clear, open, and honest about it as a result of his visceral hatred of Jews, Zionism, and Israel. Dividing into two camps those who advocate containment or reject the severity of Iran's nuclear ambitions (the optimists) and those who warn of Iran's impending nuclear breakout (the pessimists), Shavit landed on the side of the latter. "The international optimists and the Israeli optimists were wrong, big time. And: Benjamin Netanyahu was right in his repeated warnings which were often derided by the international media and *Haaretz* itself," he wrote.[9] "While the optimists were misled by their illusions, the pessimists read reality correctly. While the defense establishment and the media establishment were smitten with weakness and apathy, the pessimists kept sounding alarms," Shavit wrote, adding, "Wolf? Wolf? Wolf! A strategic wolf with nuclear teeth is now at the gate." Meanwhile, a former research fellow at the London School of Economics wrote in Israeli daily *Maariv*[10] that Western sanctions against the Islamic Republic were having little effect.

Moshe Efrat wrote that Iran's foreign exchange reserves of roughly $96 billion, as well as other newly implemented economic policies such as raising minimum wage, will keep the country afloat and the middle classes happy for the foreseeable future, while Iran's supreme leader, Ayatollah Ali Khamenei, said on June 26, 2013, that the dispute over his country's nuclear program could easily be resolved if the West were to stop being so stubborn. "Some countries have organized a united front against Iran and are misguiding the international community and with stubbornness do not want to see the nuclear issue resolved," Khamenei's official Website quoted him as saying. "But if they put aside their stubbornness, resolving the nuclear issue would be simple," he said, without clarifying his demands of the Western nations.[11] Thus, after the victory of Hassan Rouhani at the presidential elections in Iran in June 2013, even if Iran's vitriol against Jews and Zionism recedes due to a tactical distancing from Ahmadinejad's aggressive and unbridled outpour of anti-Semitic rhetoric, the very success of the nuclearization strategy due to the capitulation of Western policies of appeasement will do nothing to reduce the anti-Semitic hatred toward the Jews, though there will prevail less need to manufacture new lies.

If Israel initiates a military strike and Iran responds, Israel will face a security challenge of a magnitude that it has never experienced. It will be the first time in history that Israel will face a non-Arab state with an entirely different culture, mentality, and historical legacy. The same is true for the Iranians—for the first time they will be confronting Israel and the West. Furthermore, Israel has never carried out a military attack against a state on the brink of nuclear capability. An attack against Iran would be far different than the bombing of the nuclear reactor in Iraq or the air strike against the reactor in Syria (attributed to Israel). For Israel, the element of surprise is already gone, which in effect has already enabled the enemy to carry out a series of cautionary steps. These steps range from instilling a state of awareness into their nation, political strategic maneuvering, and preparations for both an offensive and defensive military response.

When we examine the rationale behind an Iranian response, we should assume that the regime in Tehran will make every effort to cause the "Zionist entity" such severe damage that it would restore the Islamic Republic to the lofty position of a regional superpower. Iran's choice of targets and its method of attack will be a regional and international display of Iranian strategy and military might. Iran cannot allow the campaign to end with it appearing ruined and humiliated. Another

Iranian goal will be to safeguard its nuclear project so that it can quickly resume operations if damaged. An Iranian strike would probably be directed against Israel's population centers, since the Iranians believe that Israel would be hard-pressed to cope with a protracted campaign of attrition that weakens her home front.

Upon examining these goals against the scenario established by the media, we can see that the scenario the media portray would not attain Iran's objectives. What then is the modus operandi that Iran will choose to meet its goals? To understand how the Iranian leadership operates, we must go back to the 1980–88 Iran–Iraq War. Despite the extreme differences between that war and a possible Israeli–Iranian confrontation, it would be worthwhile to look at the way the ayatollah regime, then still in its infancy, waged its first war. At the time, following a break in relations with the United States, the Iranian regime was isolated and bereft of superpower backing. Iraq received lavish military assistance from the Soviet Union, while Europe exerted pressure on Iran for disrupting the flow of oil caused by the war. During the long and bitter conflict, Iran's Republican Guards displayed a high degree of patience, endurance, and determination. The nation proved that it could weather massive attacks from unconventional weapons (poisonous gas) and retain its trust in its leadership. This is the heritage that Khomeini bequeathed to the Iranian people: fighting and winning against all odds. Those who believe Iran's geographical distance from Israel will limit the Iranian response (the Iranians will mainly engage in long-range counterfire) fail to take into account the Iran–Syria–Hezbollah axis that enables Iran to bridge great distances, despite the current Syrian turmoil that has curtailed that capacity. Republican Guard ground forces could be deployed along Israel's northern border and could even engage the Israel Defense Forces (IDF) in a protracted guerilla campaign on the frontlines.

Israel must also take into account Hezbollah's role in such a scenario, since Israel could be tested in an unprecedented event. For the first time, Hezbollah would be completely subordinate to Tehran's leadership and Iranian military command, even though Hezbollah is a Lebanese organization supported by the country's Shiite population. In an Israeli–Iranian war, Hezbollah would take orders from Iran in its first and perhaps only real opportunity to repay the enormous debt that it owes to Iran for building up its military strength. Another possibility is that Iran could launch a preemptive strike and place responsibility on Hezbollah, since Tehran has no interest in becoming entangled in hostilities prior to an Israeli attack. After an Israeli strike, the scope of Hezbollah's rocket fire into Israel's depth could parallel the developments in the fighting between Israel and Iran. Israel should not be surprised if this time the rocket and missile fire is entirely different from the past. Instead of gradual escalation at the outset, Hezbollah could unleash a massive missile barrage into the heart of Tel Aviv. Israel has to proceed with great caution in light of Iran's policy and culture. A long and bitter guerilla struggle may ensue, one that could last for a year or a number of years against Iranian combat units on Israel's northern border.[12] The missile exchange between Israel and Gaza in October 2012, and especially the more severe confrontation of July 2014, both of which were initiated by Hamas, may in fact have been a rehearsal planned by Iran to test the soft belly of Israel in terms of missile defense and the reaction of the Israeli public when exposed to massive missile attacks.

These scenarios are not the product of an imagination run wild, but logical directions (where no logic applies) that Iran could take as it aspires to realize its goal to become a regional superpower. These alternative plans have been mocked by many, who contrasted Iranian military bombast—aggrandizing themselves and diminishing the enemy in an attempt to boost their people's morale and intimidate their rivals in ridicule—to Mohammed Saeed al-Sahhaf, the Iraqi information minister under Saddam Hussein during the US-led invasion of 2003, who was dubbed "Baghdad Bob" by the Americans and "Comical Ali" by the British. He spouted wildly inaccurate propaganda during his daily press briefings, praising the Iraqi troops and telling fabulous tales of how they crushed the foreign invaders, even as those invaders could be seen on the screen moving in on him.

For example, Brigadier General Hossein Salami, lieutenant commander of the Islamic Revolutionary Guards Corps, said: "The IRGC is never intimidated by the hugeness of the aircraft carriers and the roaring of missiles of U.S. and trans-regional enemies, and their equipment is nothing more than rusty iron in its eyes." Brigadier General Ahmad Vahidi, the minister of defense, in a telephone conversation with his Syrian counterpart, announced, just as he took over from his assassinated predecessor: "Iran is confident that Syria's powerful defense system will make the United States, its regional allies, and Israel back down from their plan of achieving their goals in the region." He said that "the Zionist regime and terrorists cannot affect the Syrian army's strong will and cannot build a stronghold for Israel through."[13]

Nevertheless and despite Israel's warnings, the West was relishing in being duped, since after ten years of negotiations and promises that the nuclear plan was only "for peaceful ends," and the counterthreats of the West, accompanied by sanctions that have had little effect so far, the program, if anything, has been accelerated in an effort by Tehran to get the bomb and thus constrain its rivals to containing the bomb instead of preventing it. Some US think tanks strongly argued against meeting Iran's demand in the negotiations that its "right to enrich uranium" should be acknowledged. The text of the Nuclear Nonproliferation Treaty documents no such right, and, moreover, Iran has violated the conditions the treaty sets out in order to receive "the right to peaceful use of nuclear energy." Those against Iranian negotiations go on to argue that Iran was using the demand for acknowledgment of the supposed "right to enrich uranium" because it places its P5+1 (the five Security Council permanent members and Germany) interlocutors in a lose-lose situation, and they should challenge this false claim more directly.[14]

Others exposed alleged Iranian nuclear intentions based on what appeared to be the Iranian position papers from the talks in Istanbul in July 2012. The document—whose authenticity is not independently verified—indicates that rather than being prepared to curtail its uranium-enrichment activities, Iran was actually planning to expand them, calling for four additional research reactors and new programs to sell nuclear fuel to other countries. The document also indicated that Iran was unwilling to consider closing the heavily fortified Fordow nuclear plant, as the international community has been demanding, and insistent on an unlimited right to enrich uranium to 3.5 percent—though perhaps showing some room for flexibility on the 20 percent enrichment (technically very close to weapons grade) taking place at Fordow. Still others argued that hoping that increasingly tight sanctions would soon bring greater Iranian flexibility at the negotiating table was probably a bad bet. Current and historical evidence suggested that while the sanctions are affecting Tehran's oil exports and therefore very important regime revenue streams, this effect is more likely to decrease rather than increase over time; therefore the way forward is to find other means to target the regime's vulnerabilities, including stepping up pressure on Tehran's allies in Damascus, increasing the regime's isolation, and bolstering the credibility of military threats against it, bearing in mind that as the threat remains a mere threat, Iran is increasingly tempted to call the bluff.[15]

Meanwhile, the Judeophobic legacy of Ahmadinejad will linger long after his departure, because his eight-year rule has established patterns of hatred and lies that cannot be easily erased: from Shoah denial to blunt delegitimation of Zionism and Israel; from direct threats to eliminate Israel "off the map," exactly as Hitler had pledged for Czechoslovakia and Poland, which the world, including the UN, has elected to ignore rather than confront to building nuclear power so as to implement those designs; from vocal public rallies in support of Palestinians and in condemnation of Israel to providing arms and finances to proxies to fight Israel, including Hezbollah and Hamas; from direct support of terrorist acts against Israel all over the world to direct supply of weapons and missiles to enemies of Israel. Except for Professor Bollinger, the president of Columbia University, who dared to tell Ahmadinejad to his face that he was a "petty and cruel dictator," and that his denial of the Holocaust was "either brazenly provocative or astonishingly uneducated,"[16] no governments or countries have come out openly to contradict that heap of hatred and lies. Ahmadinejad himself had repeatedly declared his hatred and violence to be "holy,"[17] making his international conduct unique. For, can anyone imagine any leader stating on international arenas his hatred toward a Muslim country or people and his determination to wage a (Jewish or Christian) holy war against it? Outrage would have kindled the entire Muslim world, which would have clamored: "Islamophobia!" Demonstrations would have erupted the world over, taking the lives of innocent civilians, and embassies would have been set aflame in vengeance, as happened during the Cartoon Affair of 2005–06. But when only Jews and Israel are at stake, who cares?

In the Shia, as exemplified in Iran, holy hatred that is sustained by religion and encouraged by clerics can not only attain peaks unknown in other cultures and cultivate the attending lies to support it, but also drive the conflict that results from it into a hopeless deadlock. For while resentments and angers that stem from quantitative disputes over territories or assets can be negotiated, hatred that is inspired by religion is usually absolute, cannot be resolved, and no compromise can lead out of it, because it is God-ordained. For example, while the PA leadership negotiates with Israel with the aim of coming to a compromise, divinely driven Hamas refuses any deal, recognition, or compromise with Israel. Similarly, while Sunni Islam, represented by Saudi Arabia, has offered the Arab Plan to settle with Israel, even if there are many problems and question marks to be resolved, and extremists like the Muslim Brothers still negate any compromise or negotiation with Israel, Shiites brandish the banner of total and unabated negationism stemming from their deep and unmitigated hatred toward Jews, Zionism, and Israel, which is reflected in the oft-repeated mantra: "You love life, we love death." For while the West believes in a life of construction, creativity, progress, and change, Shiites believe in hastening the return of the Hidden Imam by installing an adequate regime in preparation for it, and they detect the "pangs of the Messiah" in the difficulties and threats that surround them: the more difficult the circumstances and lethal the menaces, the surer and speedier is the coming of the redeemer.

Apart from expectation of the redeemer and nuclearization, the Iranian regime under Ahmadinejad (2005–13) seemed to concentrate on promoting anti-Jewish sentiments by resorting to the old Islamic and out-of-fashion European anti-Semitic stereotypes, and particularly stressing Holocaust denial, it being erroneously considered by the regime as the legitimacy-granting event to Israel. The rationale was that Zionism, which had illicitly implanted itself in Palestine during the Ottoman and then the British Mandate, obtained from the powers the stamp of approval to establish the Jewish state only in view of their sense of guilt for having failed to protect the Jewish population during World War Two. If it could be shown that the alleged Holocaust was a hoax, or at the very least grossly exaggerated, then the West would lessen its support to Israel and shift instead toward the Palestinians, who had been disinherited from their lands by Zionism. In June 2013, Hassan Rouhani was elected as the new president. While on the nuclear issue, which is under the direct supervision of Supreme Leader Khamenei, there seems to be no noticeable change, it is hoped that at least on the Judeophobia front the new president will evince more moderation as part of the smiling face that he wishes to present to the West, inter alia, as a way to pursue his nuclear program with acceptance, until such a time that he chooses to announce to the world that he has crossed the nuclear threshold and imposes the fait accompli that no one can interfere with any longer.

Iranians are not only bent on preaching their anti-Jewish hatred to their own people and to other Muslims, who are already sold to that conviction, but mainly to the world at large so as to hasten Israel's delegitimation worldwide. Hence, their former president's insistence in repeating every year his lies to the UN Assembly and to spread his bigotry through interviews in the international press. Another device has been to harness non-Iranian and non-Muslim anti-Semitic bigots who specialize in Holocaust denial in order to advance their cause. Besides the "research projects," the cartoon competitions, and the "scholarly prizes" that Iran confers on adherents of those beliefs, it also convenes in Tehran "conferences" at which the most infamous Holocaust deniers participate and spread their "research findings," including ultra-orthodox and anti-Zionist Jewish sects who abhor Zionism for its attempt to force redemption of the Jews before the divinely inspired arrival of the Messiah to redeem them in due course. So, in fact, these assemblies were gatherings of all the anti-Jewish, anti-Zionist, and anti-Israelis bigots, all usually under the guise of anti-Zionism, with the aim of delegitimizing Israel and bringing it to its demise, if the movement of national liberation of Jews is shown to be unworthy of existing due to its racism, demonic character, and its anti-Islamic, anti-Arab, and specifically anti-Palestinian bias. Those bigots, orchestrated by Iran, are perennially obtuse to the fact that saying that all people of the world possess the right of self determination, except the Jews, is in itself a racist and anti-Semitic concept.

Joachim Martillo, an economic analyst, participates in those conferences and often airs his anti-Semitic views in Iran's English-language press, where he blames the Jews for the American and global economic crisis. He claimed that there was a conspiracy on Wall Street and that the financial apparatuses for securitizing mortgages, which ultimately led to the subprime crisis, were the handiwork of a "rising class of East-European Jewish bankers" that had supplanted the older "German-American Jewish bankers on Wall Street" and was looting Arab oil money. He said that there was "an intimate connection between the collapse of the financial system in the US and the worldwide and US international policy and its manipulation by a class of hyper-wealthy Jewish Zionists." Martillo had also written against the Jews on previous occasions and claimed that "much of the mass murder of Jews during WWII was unjustified, but a very understandable reaction to, or collective revenge on, Jews for the part that East European Jewry played in the commission of Soviet mass murder and atrocities."[18] Even though Martillo finds the Holocaust "understandable," he at least attests to its veracity, while Ahmadinejad and his gang have opted to deny it altogether or at least to diminish it in its scope and significance. What is striking about Iran regarding the Holocaust and other anti-Jewish utterances is that the state and its higher institutions have embraced the cause of hatred, lie manufacturing, and propagation, while in other Muslim countries the authorities let their press take care of the issue, so that they can justify the publications by the imperatives of their "free press" whenever they are accused by the West of bigotry, incitement, or hate speech.

Iran's Vice President Reza Rahimi has been one of the channels for airing the country's unbridled anti-Semitism and incitement against Jews and Zionism. Any context is convenient, as long as Jews can be blamed and condemned. In June 2012 the Anti-Drug Day was marked in Tehran and that too was a good occasion for propaganda, as the vice president attributed the production and distribution of drugs to the Talmud, without of course citing any particular passage. He said that the Zionists have learned from that book how to suck the blood of and destroy non-Jews. The full citation of his words of wisdom deserves to be mentioned:

> The Zionists teach their Talmud where the production and distribution of drugs are advocated as a means to suck the blood of non-Jews and exterminate them. The economic part of the Talmud promotes illegal and legal fund-raising, like levying interest, robbery and pillaging other nations' wealth. This was the launching point of Zionism against humanity . . .
>
> Zionists are responsible globally for all conflicts, for example the October Revolution in the Soviet Union, which was launched by Zionists. Though not one Jews was killed in it . . . The Talmud was calculated to guide a handful of Zionists to destroy the entire world, for one of the goals of Zionism is to trigger conflicts between nations and between Sunna and Shi'a . . . Imagine that the money that they have spent in Afghanistan and Iraq would have sufficed to bring prosperity upon the entire world . . .
>
> Zionists consider themselves a superior race, and according to books published in Europe and other foreign countries, they use all other races as slaves in fulfillment of their own designs. 70% of the world capital is located in America, and 80% of it is controlled by Jews, who constitute only 6% of the population [they are in fact, hardly 2 percent]. Since their ultimate goal is to destroy the world [and how would they themselves survive?], they use their money to attain this aim. Zionists never use drugs themselves [they only invented the use of them], and they use opium just to undermine other societies. Iran is ready to spend the requisite budgets for research in order to prove that Zionists are the culprits in producing and spreading drugs . . . A Zionist doctor in America has sterilized 80,000 Indian women in order to help exterminate them . . . Zionists are set against humanity . . .
>
> Any conflict that unfolds in the world has necessarily Zionists roots . . . for they control the world media, which facilitate the fulfillment of their goals . . . Although Iranian religious education

> forbids nuclear weapons, the Zionists have used their control of the media to incite the world public opinion against Iran, thus bringing about a 32 year world boycott against it. Iran only enriches uranium for scientific and research purposes, and these are objectives that run counter to Zionist policy which strives to prevent from Iran information, knowledge and human science. [19]

This was the Iranian vice president, who certainly surpassed even his president in ignorance if not in bigotry, hatred, and lies. In the extreme ambience of hatred created in post-Khomeini Iran, anything claimed by the leadership is likely to be accepted and digested by the ignorant crowds, while the intelligentsia, who are better informed and did not lose their sense of criticism, either do not dare to speak up or elect to follow the general flow rather than risk their lives countering it. During the confrontation between Israelis and Palestinians in Gaza in November 2012, the official Fars News Agency disseminated a cartoon of the Israeli prime minister sucking the blood of a Palestinian child.[20] The common people of Iran feed on those lies, which are daily reinforced by a cataract of vicious hate-filled propaganda voiced by their leaders. One day earlier, President Ahmadinejad cited the founder of the revolution, Khomeini, who had said that Israel was a "cancerous growth," urging the people of the Middle East to excise it so that the area could exist without Zionism. He charged Zionists with the "damage they have been causing the Middle East for the past 400 years" [Never mind that Zionism was founded at the end of the nineteenth century], taking advantage of the "centers of power" that they control. He said:

> Today it is clear to all that Zionism opposes human society and constitutes the main reason for its decline . . . They are a small minority, well organized, corrupt and inhuman which opposes divine values . . . They are only interested in power, wealth and control . . . A small number of them have been causing the worst damage ever inflicted on humanity, part of which is irreversible . . . They had initiated WW I and II in order to control others, and since they have taken over America, all world matters are under their control . . . for all the strong governments, the banks and media are under their rule, and they use that power to destroy cultures, values, nations and states. They stand behind all large moral failures, and behind wars, conflicts and massacres . . .
>
> The existence of Zionism is an insult to the entire world . . . According to their racist education, only they are considered as humans while all other cultures and people are animals . . . They allow the murder of people, thus any opposition to Zionism and to the distorted

> Zionist regime is tantamount to safeguarding human rights, and to paving the way to rescue all humanity from colonialism, imperialism, poverty and misery . . . That is the reason why safeguarding Zionism is a commitment of most colonialist and imperialist countries . . . In America, candidates for the presidency must prostrate themselves before Zionists to have any chance to be elected. [21]

These themes, in addition to allusions to the *Protocols of the Elders of Zion* and numerous references to the "world Jewish conspiracy," are so widely and frequently repeated to the Iranian public, and from there distributed to other Islamic and anti-Semitic channels, that they become a matter of course, and anything contradicting them seems out of line with conventional wisdom.[22] Writers of these dispatches and "news items" are more bigoted than knowledgeable, and they hang on to any rumor or libel picked up abroad to duplicate it for further distribution. For example, one of them listed the "100 most important people in Hollywood," and found that the first twelve among them were all Jewish, who lend leverage to the international Jewish power. He, of course, found that Steven Spielberg devotes a percentage of his revenues to commemorate the Shoah (something that never happened, to his mind), and he contributes to the propaganda machine of Zionism, which gives it preeminence despite the fact that "Jews constitute only 4% of the American population" (in fact, they are hardly 2 percent.) Hence, the immoral import of Hollywood's movies, which contradict human and family values, is proven. The film industry invests lots of money lately for that purpose, and when one watches those movies one realizes that the main goal of Western, especially American, cinema is to spread perverse ideas.[23]

Naturally, demonization of Israel and Jews, which leads to aggrandizing those entities far beyond their size and capacity, tends to impute to them many of the troubles of the world, so as to present Iran's nuclearization program as the panacea for these troubles. Examples abound: Under the title "Greece Is Raped by Jewish Bankers," which was published by Press TV in July 2012 and where the "Jewish banking cartel, that is part of the Jewish mafia" was accused of responsibility for the economic crisis in Europe, especially in Greece. According to this article, this economic collapse was concocted by Jews, who influenced the decisions of the IMF in order to take control of the country's public assets . . . This argument also claims that the Jewish banking cartel was the true architect of the European monetary union, which knew that the union would damage the economies of southeastern Europe, but they hid this information from the French and the Germans . . . The article predicted that the Jewish cartel would end up expropriating airports and seaports at the lowest prices, so that the Greeks would become subjugated by them, thus allowing the Jewish mafia to enter the criminal arena, and eliminate the Greek religion, culture, solidarity and heritage of the Greeks.[24]

As part of Israel's conspiracies in the world, the Jews were also accused of Muslim massacres in Myanmar. None other than Ayatollah Karahi, the director of the Imam Mahdi Seminar in Tehran, said without blinking:

> The Muslim massacre in Mianmar has been allegedly committed by Buddhists, but we are sure that the murder and genocide are perpetrated by world Jewry and Zionism . . . For Buddhism derives from Judaism, and Buddhists have been tools in the hands of Zionists . . . Jews are also controlling America. Did it ever happen that any American President has failed to put on the *kippa* (head cover of Orthodox Jews) when he wished to be elected? . . . But since they know that Jews carry a stigma in the world, they prefer to hide behind other epithets, like Buddhists . . . So all lecturers in the universities and the media, must explain in various languages and in a way acceptable to the young people, that behind Buddhism hides a Jew. [25]

When one understands that this nonsense is not merely the invention of one deviating cleric but the same blind mantra repeated by the top hierarchy of that dark regime, both political and clerical, one begins to wonder about the sanity of those people and of that country. In fact, another ayatollah, one of those super intellectuals who are supposed to be in touch with the Hidden Imam, Hadavi Tehrani repeated the same garbage accusing the Jews of involvement in the massacre of Arakan (Myanmar) Muslims. That top cleric, who is a member of the Supreme Council of the World Assembly of Ahl al-Bayt and the president of the "Rawak Hikmat" Institute (ironically connoting wisdom), published an epistle in which he said:

> In Mianmar, cruel massacres against Muslims are unfolding. 19 years ago, I was there, and watched the people who had been taken over by Marxists and Maoists during the past 80 years . . . But when the population extricated itself from the claws of its executioners, and the people were enthusiastic about the newly-found freedom, the Zionists came in, to purchase lands and take root in the cheap land of Mianmar . . . I watched the Muslims of Mianmar, who have preserved their tradition under difficult circumstances and were proud of their

> Iranian roots . . . Nobody could have imagined that the Zionists would once again launch the country on a course of massacres of Muslims by Buddhists . . .
>
> The Jews have linked their small population to the large population of Buddhists and Hindis in the world, and they took root among them by taking advantage of their own wealth and the poverty of their hosts. They even put several Jewish figures as spiritual heads among some Buddhist and Hindi sects and set up temples for them in India and other countries in the area. Today, it is a Jewish arm that wears a Buddhist sleeve, to take vengeance on the freedom-fighting Muslims, by harming the Muslims of Mianmar and punishing them for the anti-Zionist activities in Egypt, Tunisia, Morocco, Lebanon, Syria, Bahrein and Hijaz. [26]

This obsessive and repetitive anti-Jewish attitude of the Iranian state and clergy is not just a collection of whimsical expressions by individual leaders who have a grudge following some unfortunate encounter with Jews, as President Sadat of Egypt had claimed in his experience. Its frequency, its mantra-like style, its virulence, and the uninhibited form in which it is couched, which is characteristic of Shiite Islam, suggest some underlying, deep-rooted creed that encompasses that entire culture and obscures any reasoning, logic, or good sense that might refute it. Often, this obtuse attitude toward Jews is anchored in a novel interpretation of Quranic verses and Hadith stories, as if the traditional (Sunni) interpretations were not loathsome enough. Nominally, the Iranian regime differentiates between Judaism as a faith, which is supposedly legitimate and acceptable, though it is often debased and humiliated, and Zionism, which as the expression of Jewish nationalism is objectionable and doomed to elimination. Nonetheless, since Iran became officially Shiite in the sixteenth century, the Jews there were afflicted by harsh persecutions before anyone had heard of Zionism. Not only were Jews considered inferior and impure, but they were imputed mysterious and devilish powers, which evolved under Khomeini into the "personification of evil," which sought to "control the Muslims" and saw the elimination of Islam as a prerequisite to attaining their goals. The verses in the Quran, the stories in the Prophet's biography (the Sira), and the Hadith stories that hint of Muhammad's disaccord with the Jews of Medina are amplified and made central to early Islamic narrative, as they are in other Islamic fundamentalist writings by Jew haters such as Sayyid Qutb, Sheikh Qaradawi, Sheikh Ra'id, and their likes. This reinterpreted history connects those events to the Jews' innate evil character, which drives them inexorably to constantly undermine Islam. Muhammad's policy of eliminating the Jews in Arabia and expelling the remainder of them from it, which is still valid today, has been hailed as a model to follow today vis-à-vis the state of Israel.[27]

Interestingly enough, we are now able to explore the roots of the Cartoon Affair of 2005–06 and realize that the contemporary hatred toward Jews and other unbelievers stems to a great extent from the complex of inferiority that has been afflicting Islam since its inception. In no other faith would followers go on rampage and kill, maim, and burn just because someone had insulted their creed or their prophet. The issue here is their lack of self-confidence in the power of their conviction, unable to withstand competition in the free market of ideas, as other faiths do. That is the reason why any apostate is deserving of death, no Christianity or Judaism is permitted in Arabia, and members of other faiths in Muslim lands are exposed to persecution and death everywhere there is a Muslim revival. Any insult to their holy book or their prophet is also punishable by death, and they constantly seek and proclaim the "superiority of Islam," something they would have certainly avoided if they were more confident of the self-evident dominance of their faith. In the Muslim rally in Los Angeles on February 18, 2006, at the height of the Cartoon Affair,[28] one of the slogans waved by the furious demonstrators was "Islam Shall Dominate!" In other words, they were not seeking accommodation among the host culture but victory over it; not seeking to calm their tempers, which had reached a boiling point, but vindication of their fanatic position; not seeking a free competition for their ideas on fair and equal grounds (something they do not permit in their own lands), but a statement of domination over all others. There is a paradox here: on the one hand, Islamic countries at large have been in the bottom of the heap of the UN annual development reports, something that does not inspire much pride, while the developed West's Christian culture has produced progress and development, which is totally rejected by Muslims. They feel threatened by it.

In a shame culture in which honor and prestige hinge on appearances and make-believe and where sycophancy and falsehood take precedence over reality and hard facts, one is more expected to confront humiliation and reject it than to reconcile to painful realities, even if that should bring damage and more pain. Dr. Duani, a lecturer at Imam Hussein University, stressed during a lecture on Islamic history the affront that Jews had caused to early Islam and the consequences that result. He said that the first action taken by Jews to undermine Islam was to mock it, especially its lack of a holy scripture, at a time when the Quran was only a series of unrelated oral revelations, not yet canonized and open to various versions. He emphasized that the Jews appeared at the mosque and mocked Muslim customs, to the point that the Prophet ordered to oust them. The Jews boasted that they possessed a holy book, contrary to Muslims, who had none, and regarded that as their election by God over other faiths. They also bragged that they had a day of rest a week, while others had none, until Muslims instituted their own Friday in response. This, of course, unwittingly posits Islam not as an original revelation but as a copycat who imitates others in order not to lag behind: first to put together a Quran to counter the Bible and then to institute a Friday to best the Jewish Saturday.

In those early days, said the lecturer, the Jews of Arabia, notably the famous poet Ka'b bin al-Ashraf, a son of the Banu Nadir tribe, wrote poems that insulted Muslims and Islam, and, when they reached Muhammad, he furiously sought to combat that "evil," and he entrusted Ka'b's half brother with that task. With a team of supporters, the brother proceeded to Ka'b's place, lured him out under some false pretense, and killed him. That was how the Muslims got rid of their critics and how the precedent was established that a critique of Islam deserved death. After all, the Prophet, the most perfect of men, created that inviolable precedent, and no one can contradict it. After that, a long series of ramblings accusing the Jews of wrongdoings, without any documented source, justified the murder of more Jews until they were all massacred or expelled from Arabia.[29]

From all this manipulated Islamic history, for which there is only oral traditions that were written down with a Muslim bias a century or more after the death of the Prophet, perhaps the most prominent parable is the one related to the story of Khaybar, which turns the residents' desperate attempt to defend themselves and their property from an aggressive and murderous Muhammad into a "Jewish plot to destroy Islam." Of course, the Jews were accused of having organized and incited the Arab tribes against Muhammad and Islam, as if they were marionettes easily manipulated according to Jewish wishes. Even to this day, anyone who defies the Prophet or his faith deserves death, and with this reasoning the Jewish population of Khaybar, which had been rooted there for centuries before the coming of Islam and engaged in peaceful farming, was slaughtered. Already in the 1990s, Hamas posters distributed in the West Bank and Gaza hailed the Khaybar events as a model for things to come, as they warned that "the time of

Khaybar has dawned," meaning that it was time for the Jews of Israel to think about the choice between deportation or slaughter. Iran's use of the same parable came lately from the mouth of none other than the Supreme Leader Khamenei, as he claimed that his country was combating the economic sanctions imposed by heathen America and its Zionist allies under "the same circumstances as in the days of the Badr (AD 623) and Khaybar (AD 628) battles led by the Prophet." In his words: "The front we face is of America and the Zionists, who have tried any avenue to combat Iran . . . We live today like in the days of Badr and Khaybar, we see only the upcoming victories."[30] In an interview, a senior official also resorted to that parable, this time based on the "great philanthropist and humanist" Hassan Nasrallah of Hezbollah:

> The Israeli vision of "from the Nile to the Euphrates" is over . . . This is the first time the Zionists feel they have no incentive to defend their artificial state . . . They are so afraid that they built a wall of separation between themselves and the Palestinians, and they will do the same due to their fear from the impact of the Egyptian Revolution . . . This is exactly the application of the Qur'anic verse: "They shall not burst forth to fight against you, but will hide behind fortified walls" (59:14) . . . The Supreme leader believes we are under the circumstances of Badr and Khaybar because we won the 33-day war in Lebanon [the Second Lebanon War in July 2006] and the 22-day War in Gaza [Cast Lead in Gaza 2008–09] under the same circumstances. As in Khaybar, the Jews hid behind walls in these battles, which means that the Jews are at the edge and cannot get out of their homes any more. As a very small and narrow state, Israel is unable to defend itself strategically and geopolitically, and it is likely to disappear at any moment. Then they will all run away collectively. In case of war, one million of them will flee from the occupied territories. [31]

The "inexcusable behavior" of the Jews and the Zionists is found even in such international art ceremonies as the Oscars, due to "their control of Hollywood and America." The 2013 recipient of the award, the movie *Argo*, which recounted the story of the rescue of six American diplomats from Tehran after the outburst of the Islamic Revolution, was condemned by Iran as "lacking any artistic or cultural value, distorts facts of history, as part of the Iranophobia led by Americans and Zionists." Prior to the awards ceremony and to counter it, a conference was held in Tehran by the Ministry of Culture, in which a suit was announced against the producers, the director, and the actors in the film, and a new twenty-episode television series was launched on the theme of "the conquest of the American spy nest in Tehran."[32]

In the same vein, some of the press, the Iranian ambassador in the United Nations, and some cartoons in the press all condemned the political bias of the movie, though some reformist and fairer minds admitted its artistic worth. But when all devices of propaganda and avenues of hatred are exhausted, there remains the mystic and magical supernatural means that the demonized Zionists can use. This means that as the Iranian regime proclaims to the world that it can defend against plots, conspiracies, and military and diplomatic threats, there is little it can do about supernatural charms. A selection of these bizarre statements—which parallel some of the mystical Palestinian and Egyptian accusations of Israel of "poisoning the land of Egypt," or of "luring sharks into the Sinai coast to frighten off tourists," or of "poisoning young Palestinian girls to affect their reproductive organs"—will throw some light on Iranian bigoted thinking rather than on Jewish conspiracies:

1. Mehdi Ta'ib, the head of a Khamenei's think tank, said in April 2013 that the Jews possess the "strongest magic powers in the world, which they use against Iran, either by way of imposing sanctions, where America serves as their tool, or by their abortive intervention with the Iranian elections in 2009." He warned that the Jews have not yet used all their potential for magic.
2. In March, 2013 the site Rassa News, which is linked with the religious seminaries in Qum, published an article on numerology and magic in Jewish mysticism, claiming that their charm power is transmitted genetically, with a view of taking over control of the world, of nature, and even of God's decisions.[33]
3. In the Websites of the Iranian regime, there are cartoons comparing Jews to wild beasts known for their cruelty, for the fears they engender in humans, and for the dangers they pose to them, like wolves and snakes. Hence the only way to counter them is to stand up to them and to kill them in order to save human life from their grasp.
4. "Israel is a cancerous tumor that will soon be finished off," that is how President Ahmadinejad addressed demonstrators protesting annually against the existence of the Jewish state. "Even if one cell of them is left in one inch of Palestinian land, the story will repeat itself . . . The nations of the region will soon finish off the usurper Zionists in the Palestinian land."[34]

The election of Hassan Rouhani in June 2013 to succeed Ahmadinejad, has inspired some optimism in the West that he might lead his country in a more pragmatic and less ideological fashion that his predecessor. However, in view of precedent "pragmatic" and "moderate" presidents, such as Rafsanjani (1989–97), and Khatami (1997–2005), who pushed forward with the nuclear program with sweet talk, unlike the confrontational style of Ahmadinejad, the newly elected president may also tread the same path. The question will remain whether that is good in terms of Iran's relations with the world. While one can appreciate a softer and more civilized dialogue with the world and a less openly hostile attitude to Jews and Israel, one may fear that soft conduct by the leadership in Tehran may be a lure to the Western powers, who will do anything to prevent a conflict, to continue to negotiate endlessly while Iran is pursuing its nuclear program without conceding an inch. Paradoxically, then, it will be a cleric like Rouhani, the only religious figure among the candidates to the presidency, who will follow the moderate course of his two "moderate" predecessors who were also clerics, while the doctrinaires among them, most of all Ahmadinejad, will continue to represent the civilian branch of the rule. One should not forget that the reins of power and of supreme control of the regime, including the nuclearization program, remain indisputably in the hands of the supreme leader, who by definition will always be a cleric, and not moderate.

While the overt Israeli pretext to justify Iran's obsession with its nuclear project prevails in international rhetoric, the deep worries that it provokes in Saudi Arabia and the Gulf states, which are literally scared by the prospects of being blackmailed by their Shiite rival across the Gulf, are more latent and mostly oppressed. They are drowned in the expressions of frustration voiced toward the United States, which has let them down by doing nothing to restrain Iran from realizing its nuclear dream, which is their nightmare. Sometimes those sentiments are accompanied by hints of covert cooperation with Israel, their only remaining hope that action might be taken to put an end to the second Islamic bomb. The most pessimistic Arab could never imagine the day would come when a US official would say, "If he covered the faces of top officials he met during the recent trip to Riyadh, Abu Dhabi and Tel Aviv, and listened to their perceptions on the issues and future of the Middle East, he would not be able to differentiate between the Saudi, Emirati and Israeli. Their views are the same on these issues."[35] This picture is not only bleak because Israeli and Gulf interests are the same, but because separate efforts to pressure the US administration into adopting positions that support this united regional vision are being expressed by Arabs in Washington. This is done through repeated praise (so far privately) and heavy reliance on activism by the Israeli lobby. A US expert justifies this situation by saying, "Israel, along with Arab Gulf states, has been the oasis of stability in the Middle East since the start of the Arab Spring three years ago. Naturally, they share the same concerns and fears about the elements of instability surrounding them."[36]

Both Israel and the Gulf states want to block an Iranian nuclear breakthrough through sanctions by Congress, despite White House objections. More importantly, repeated rumors exist concerning Iran's influence in the Arab Mashreq (East) as Tehran plays a greater role in the Syrian conflict. There are also repeated statements that Iran's Islamic regime has expanded to reach the shores of the Mediterranean Sea and Israel's borders. The Gulf and Israeli adversaries are highlighting the wide gap between the White House and Congress on the issue. They are also convincing Congress members to continue pressuring US President Barack Obama until it becomes impossible to reach any agreement with Iran.

Israel and the Gulf countries also adopt the same position with Egypt—rejecting any pressure from the Egyptian government and demanding the return of the entire military package to Egypt. It is noteworthy that the managing director of the lobby group hired by the Egyptian government in the United States is Arik Ben-Zvi, a former officer in the Israeli army, an Israeli citizen who served in the Israeli army, and a campaign adviser in several elections in Israel. The firm also works with Apple and Coca-Cola, and the Abu Dhabi Investment Authority is its top foreign client. Thus, Arabs in Washington are immersed in playing a role that does not in any way confront Israel or its lobby group. Arabs decided to exchange what needs to be done in the world's most important capital with an easy agenda, namely confronting their domestic political opponents and historic neighbors.[37] It may be that the energetic Arab lobbying in Washington against the Iranian nuclear project has drawn momentum toward the other manufacturer of the Muslim bomb—Pakistan.

Indeed, the Pakistani and Iranian navies have engaged in a four-day joint naval exercise east of the Straits of Hormuz, in April, 2014 in an effort to improve security cooperation between the two neighbors. The participating Pakistani warships, which arrived in Bandar Abbas on March 5, include the Agosta-70 class submarine *Hashmat* and the indigenously constructed missile boat *Quwwat*. They were returning from participating in the Doha International Maritime Defense Exhibition, which was held in Qatar.[38] Senior officers of both navies also met in the port of Bandar Abbas during the visit. The Iranian vessels participating are not known, but their exercise with Pakistan follows a similar exercise held with the Omani Navy previously. Iran is also increasing its naval presence closer to Pakistan with the announcement in February that it would build a new base in the Gwatr Gulf, close to the border with Pakistan. A spokesman for the Pakistan Navy, Commodore Irfan Ul Haque, said the presence of the Pakistani ships near Iran was part of a "normal visit" at the end of which a passage exercise would be conducted. Analysts agree, but are unconvinced the Iranian-Pakistan naval relationship will be expanded much beyond the current level. "These are just routine exercises and good for trust building and not much else," says analyst Usman Shabbir of the Pakistan Military Consortium think tank. However, when placed in the context of wider Iranian and Pakistani efforts to improve security cooperation, the exercises become somewhat more important. "These exercises are of course necessary to build better relations, and now are even more important considering the cross-border attacks by rebels in Baluchistan," Shabbir added. Iran-Pakistan relations have been strained over recent months mainly, but not entirely, due to the poor security situation along their mutual border. Iran has accused Pakistan of not doing enough to secure it against smugglers and militants that have attacked Iranian security personnel.

The most recent incident saw five Iranian border guards abducted by the *Jaishul Adl* (The Just Army) militant group in February. One was executed in March 2014 and the four survivors were released recently, reportedly swapped for eight *Jaishul Adl* members being held in Zahedan jail in Iran. Tehran claims the guards had been held captive in Pakistan, something denied by Islamabad. Iranian legislators, however, approved a bill to improve security between Iran and Pakistan. Among other things, the bill deals with setting out areas of cooperation, delegating responsibilities to various ministries and financial issues. This follows the signing of a bilateral counterterrorism security pact in February 2013 that involved agreements to counter drug smuggling, human trafficking and terrorism. Though admitting she is unfamiliar with the "fine print," Salma Malik, assistant professor at the Department of Defence & Strategic Studies, in Quaid-i-Azam University, Islamabad, said the pact "is a very good development, which was badly needed." "Iran is an extremely important neighbor and one time very good friend. Now the terms of endearment have converted into confrontation, and with US and Saudi Arabia as major stakeholders," she added. Due to the influence of Saudi Arabia and the US in Pakistan, she is uncertain just how deep this bilateral Iran-Pakistan security cooperation can become. However, she highlights that Pakistan desperately needs domestic and regional stability, and Iran is a part of ensuring this. "Pakistan wants to have a stable, peaceful and strong domestic set up. We have to have a pragmatic, realistic and solid building of relations with our immediate neighbors, of which Iran is an extremely important cornerstone" she says.[39]

Notes

1. "Multan Conference January 1972: The Birth of Nuclear Weapons Programme." *Pakistan Military Consortium* (Islamabad: Pakdef.info) 1 (1–2): 12–18. November 2006.
2. Zulfiqar Ali Bhutto, *The Myth of Independence*, Oxford University Press, 1969.
3. See ibid, the chapter on *Science in Pakistan*. See also Farhatullah Babar, "Bhutto's Footprints on Nuclear Pakistan," *The News*, (Islamabad) April 4, 2006.
4. "On the trail of the black market bombs," *BBC News*, February 12, 2004.
5. See Bernard Lewis, *Jews in Islam,* especially chapter 3, Princeton, 1984.
6. This distinction between institutional and diffused religion, see C. K. Yang, *Religion in Chinese Society,* UC Berkeley, 1967, chap XII, pp. 294–340.
7. Khomeini, Ayatollah, *The Islamic Republic, op. cit.;* Sayyid Qutb, *Our War against the Jews, op. cit.*
8. Ha'aretz Columnist, "Benjamin Netanyahu Was Right," on Iran, June 27, 2013, http://www.algemeiner.com/2013/06/27/haaretz-columnist-benjamin-netanyahu-was-right-on-iran/.
9. Ibid.
10. *Ma'ariv,* June 27, 2013.
11. Ibid.
12. This passage is based on an article published in *Israel Defen*se, issue 8 of 2012.
13. IRNA (Islamic Republic News Agency), July 19, 2012.
14. Michael Makovsky and Blaise Misztal, *Wall Street Journal,* July 8, 2012.
15. David Horovitz, *Times of Israel,* July 9, 2012.
16. In September, 2007, during Ahmadinejad's show at the UN GA in New York.
17. Mathias Kuntzel, "The Iranian Holy War," an address at Columbia University on March 6, 2008, under the auspices of Scholars for Peace in the Middle East.
18. MEMRI Special Dispatch 4824, July 10, 2012.
19. JAM News (Iran), April 4, 2012.
20. Fars News Agency, November 18, 2012.
21. In a speech delivered on Jerusalem Day, August 17, 2012, and reported by the major media of Iran on the same day, and by the written press the next day.
22. See, e.g., *Risalat* (Iran), June 26, 2012.
23. Ibid.
24. Presstv.com, July 10, 2012.
25. Interview with the Rasa News Agency, August 8, 2012.

26. Mahr News Agency, July 24, 2012. The same nonsense was parroted by the Basij commander, Mohammad Reza Naqdi, and reported on August 6, 2012, on the site yjr.ir.
27. See A. Zigron and A. Savion, "The Jewish Image in the Eyes of the Iranian Regime: Theological Roots," http://www.Memri.org.il/cgi-webaxy/sal/sal.pl?lang=he&ID=107345_memri&act=show&dbid=articles&dataid=3306.
28. For the complete story, see R. Israeli, *The Spread of Islamikaze Terrorism in Europe*, Vallentine Mitchell, London, 2008, especially chap. 5.
29. IRNA News Agency, June 15, 2012.
30. http:// farsi.khamene'i.ir, January 9, 2012.
31. www.farsnews.com, June 6, 2012.
32. www.memri.org.il, March 27, 2013.
33. www.memri.org.il/cgi-webaxy/sal/sal.pl?lang=he&ID=107345 memri &act =show&dbid=articles&dataid=3373, April 29, 2013.
34. Arab News, August 18, 2012.
35. Mohamed Elmenshawy, Thursday, April 10, 2014, http://english.ahram.org.eg/NewsContentP/4/98578/Opinion/The-Arabs-smitten-by-the-Israeli-lobby.aspx.
36. Ibid.
37. Mohamed Elmenshawy, Thursday, April 10, 2014, http://english.ahram.org.eg/NewsContentP/4/98578/Opinion/The-Arabs-smitten-by-the-Israeli-lobby.aspx.
38. April 11, 2014—09:53am by Usman Ansari, http://www.defensenews.com/article/20140411/DEFREG03/304110017/Pakistani-Iranian-Navies-Conduct-Joint-Exercises.
39. Ibid.

5

The Arab Revolt and Its Islamic Antidote

Unlike the two precedent-setting Islamic outbursts of fury—Rushdie and the cartoons—which were directed outwardly to vent rage against the Western world and its values, the Arab Spring that burst out in Tunisia on Xmas Eve of 2010 and spread to Egypt, Libya, Yemen, Bahrain, and eventually Syria, where it refuses to die, was meant to shake domestic systems internally. That series of rebellions in the Arab world was neither Arab nor had any characteristic to qualify as a "spring." For these riots were not restricted to the Arab world: they were symptomatic of the wider Islamic world, extending from Afghanistan in the east to Mali and Nigeria in the west. Nor were there any permanent signs of a fresh wind sweeping away the stale dictatorships of the Islamic world and heralding fresh starts and liberalizing tendencies. True, those movements began when young people crave open regimes and caring governments to resolve their problems of employment, poverty, and strict controls, but in the course of time those spontaneous outbursts of liberty were taken over by Islamic groups, like the Muslim Brothers, who found themselves the best organized to channel the popular outpour of resentment into a return to Islam. Extraordinarily, as exemplified by Egypt, the largest and most important country where that Spring erupted, and to a lesser extent in Tunisia, within one year two referenda were run in which the populace lent its majority first to the Muslim Brothers and a year later to banning them from power.

French philosopher and writer Albert Camus once wrote that "misnomers increase misfortune in the world."[1] It would therefore be advisable to rename that large phenomenon that has swept the Islamic world as rather an Islamic Winter, a continuation of 1989 and 2006—this time not challenging Western hegemony and their world of values but defying the dictatorships from within. Indeed, in almost all the demonstrations that were broadcast live from the Tahrir Squares of

Islamic capitals were the slogans: "We want democracy!" and the call upon all rulers in place to quit: "*Irhal!*" (Move on, or get out!) While they were certain they wanted the illegitimate rulers to go, they were not quite sure what they yearned for instead. "Democracy" sounded right to attract foreign correspondents and world sympathy, but none of them had any idea what it looked like, since none of them had ever experienced it. And when competition occurred after new "constitutions" were adopted in free elections, the votes went invariably to Muslim parties, whose legitimacy was established and deep-rooted. Though those Islamic winters did not last long and were reversed within a year, both in Tunisia and Egypt, the fact remained that free elections brought Muslims on top. That is the meaning of liberalism, to respond to the needs and the wishes of people, and people wanted Islam, for they knew nothing else. That was part of the legacy of 1989 and 2006, which strengthened the Islamic passion in the hearts of common Muslims across the globe. It is true that 9/11 also added some fuel to Islamic enthusiasm in the hearts of many Muslims, but in view of the violent American reaction in Afghanistan and in Iraq and the ultimate humiliating elimination of bin Laden in his den in Abbottabad, many common Muslims, realizing the price they paid for their enthusiasm, were rather sobered.

Since the end of 2010, the world has been watching the unfolding of what international politics and media have dubbed the "Arab Spring," which connotes renewal, revival, a new flourishing of thought and deed and should have resolutely directed it on the path of liberal democracy, peace with its neighbors, and the end to confrontations and tensions internally and with the Western world. But these hopeful signs were unfortunately missing, remaining only the wishful thinking of diplomats and the media, who are still hopelessly shackled to their political correctness. And like the Oslo peace process, which by now has fallen victim to similar false hopes, the Spring in question, which was erroneously connected to some sort of imaginary "democratic process" that had, as it were, suddenly swept through the Islamic world, has gradually died out as it becomes clear that a democratic endeavor was not taking place there but rather a power struggle to disinherit the long-standing tyrants who ruled Islamic countries and to replace them with something hopefully better, more legitimate, popular, and representative of the masses that would bring salvation to the alienated youth and to the desperate crowds from the depths of their social, economic, and identity crises.

This struggle is far from its conclusion, and it would smack of intellectual arrogance to predict either its longevity or its final outcome. But judging from the places where the dust seems to have begun to settle, such as Tunisia, and from the balance of power that seems to be in the making in others, such as Egypt, Yemen, and perhaps also Syria and Libya in the longer run, when the domestic upheaval and killing come to an end, it appears that Islam and traditional authoritarianism have been emerging as the main political forces from this Spring turbulence, while alternatives, comprising the democratic, liberal, and secular forces, have been badly beaten and discarded. Except for Tunisia, all those putative options have evaporated and gone with the wind or have been fighting for their lives in the midst of the present whirlpool in the Islamic world. What is worse, it seems that the West has relinquished its hopes of seeing democracy and freedom prevail and has made peace with the idea that Islamic governments must be accepted where they prevail and must be viewed as the lesser of two evils. The interim result has been that the tyrants who had barred the rise of Islamic governments were removed, and Islamic regimes were set up as the only viable alternatives, but at least in the case of Tunisia and Egypt, those too have failed after a brief interim period.

It is noteworthy, however, that even when defining the Islamic Spring, there is controversy about its significance, both within the Islamic world and outside of it. Hence the lingering debates concerning its course, its nature, and its consequences, and even on the very impact it is having on the various Muslim societies that have experienced it. For not only would the application of Sharia law mean depriving women of their basic human rights, imposing death on "heretics" or on anyone who dares to insult the Prophet or his memory, and flogging alcohol users in public, but clouds of war would gather over the skies of the Middle East, when incitement and jihad rise to new heights, directed against the West, and more specifically Israel. In other words, instead of peace, progress, development, democracy, and stability that the Spring was supposed to have triggered, we are entering an era of uncertainty, tumult, instability, unrest, and deprivation, as dramatically and devastatingly illustrated in the ongoing Syrian civil war. In the world of the Islamic Spring, the choices that are presented to the public are dichotomic: preserve the current tyrannical, corrupt, and oppressive regimes, which in some places are still fighting for their lives, or vie for a new order of the Sharia, which seeks a restorative revolution of classical Islam in the form of a revived caliphate. For, unlike Western revolutionary movements, which have placed their utopia in the future, to be attained through certain prescribed social and economic policies, a viewpoint that has collapsed in the meantime in Eastern Europe, Islam has always turned its eyes to the example of the Prophet in the far past: the Islamic regime he had set up in Medina in the seventh century remains the ideal one, which can hardly be emulated by anyone, therefore any Muslim rule thereafter can only strive to approximate it. In the Islamic setting of today, any revolutionary movement based on a set of ideals will always retreat if confronted by a restorative Muslim ideal anchored in the personality of the Prophet or modeled on his times.

The temptation is then presented to the Muslim public to adopt an Islamic regime that emerged in Muhammad's times: there is nothing more promising than to revive a close emulation of it. One can hardly dig up any arguments to counter the modalities of that regime, its ideal parameters being carved in stone in the Islamic tradition. Indeed, the Muslim Brothers in Egypt, Syria, Jordan, Algeria, Libya, Sudan, even in Europe and the United States, east of there in Asia, or throughout the rest of the world among the supporters of Hizb ut-Tahrir (The Liberation Party), and various Salafi tendencies all profess the revival of the caliphate, the regime that was installed by Muhammad's righteous successors, the caliphs, and has become the iconic model to be emulated by all future generations of Muslims. And to the extent that more militant Islamic movements—such as the Salafiya (the Rule of the Predecessors), Islamic Jihad, al-Qaida, and their sisters in Asia, including the Taliban in Afghanistan and Pakistan and Hamas among the Palestinians—are viewed as more extreme or radical than the others; this is more a matter of temperament than of any real doctrinal gap that does not actually exist between them. To wit, they all advocate the revival of the caliphate as the ideal Islamic state to be attained under Sharia law, and all endorse jihad as the means to attain that goal. However, the artificial distinction between moderate Islam and extreme Islam—or standard Islam versus the fundamentalist brand, or pragmatic Islam in contrast to the militant/radical/confrontational/ political kind, as if these were two rival doctrines competing for the souls of their followers—is unknown in the Islamic world.

In the real world, apart from personal jealousies and peripheral doctrinal matters that distinguish (but do not separate) these various factions, there are truly no contentious arguments between them. There might be nuances as to whether to take power by force when peaceful ways are blocked before them, as the Wahhābis had done in Arabia in the nineteenth century and their likes (al-Qaida, Hamas, the Taliban) have also attempted when the opportunity was open to them, or by peaceful means, as the Muslim Brotherhood in Algeria, Egypt, Tunisia, Jordan, and their likes have been attempting constantly through the existing political system. At one time or another, they had tried, but since they were crushed by the existing rulers whom they wished to eliminate and fearing for their survival, they embraced the peaceful way of propaganda (*da'wah*), social welfare, education, and participation in the democratic game to gain legitimacy among their constituents until they were able to take over the rule and impose the Islamic way of politicking.

There are, however, no salient doctrinal differences between the two tendencies, for the fundamental principles (e.g., the Five Pillars of the Faith [*Arkan*], or the obligation of aggressive jihad, which has been revived by the Muslim Brothers) are equally sacrosanct in the eyes of all brands of Islam. Certainly, the existence of moderate Muslims, who are distinguished from the fanatic ones, cannot be denied. However, both advocate the same Islam, respect its same tenets, more or less practice its requirements, and devotedly walk in Allah's path. But those who have chosen the moderate way to practice Islam do it patiently and with the long term in mind, and in the meantime they may be lax on the practice of daily duties, while the others want everything and now, and have no time for delaying tactics or patience for democratic niceties. Those practicing fanatical Islam are usually the militant types, those who demonstrate, often violently, call for jihad, and often participate personally in it. The moderate Muslims belong to the silent majority, who hail Islamic successes when they occur but usually prefer to stay on the sidelines and deal with their personal business. Even those who entertain relatively liberal or semi-democratic ideas usually elect to keep quiet, knowing what it has cost their peers who have the temerity of airing their more moderate views in public.

Some misguided Westerners have even gone as far as quantifying that putative difference between the two kinds of Islam, presumably as a way to gain credibility by emitting precise and "scientific" data. There are claims that about 15 percent of Muslims are radical, that is militant and jihad supporters, which even if true would amount to more than 200 million out of the Muslim population of 1.5 billion. This in itself would constitute a worldwide threat, thus undoing the intentions of the proponents of this theory who seek to minimize the negative impact of the extremists, in contrast to the "peaceful and quietist bulk of Muslims." Or perhaps, in order to avoid confronting the charge of Islamophobia, these well-meaning theoreticians have elected to diminish their criticism of militant Islam to 15 percent of the whole, letting the politically correct do-gooders comfort themselves that 85 percent are ideal neighbors who only seek peace and tranquility and therefore can be accepted with open arms in the West when they come in hordes, financed by Saudi Arabia and Qatar, to open mosques and Islamic centers, educational networks, and even hostile and subversive organizations that militate against the very foundations of Western culture and of their host countries.

These naïve people do not take into account that following every major slaughter of Westerners or Jews, the Muslim world celebrates, as when the Twin Towers collapsed in September 2001,[2] and Muslims from all countries and all walks of life, old and young, educated and illiterate, were distributing sweets, dancing in the streets, and boasting about their "outstanding achievements." At the same time, many of their spokesmen shamelessly denied that any Muslims could have committed those heinous acts and attributed them to the CIA, Mossad, or such. Could anyone who watched those mind-boggling events, live or on TV and the worked-up demonstrators in the streets of Casablanca, Paris, Quetta, or Gaza differentiate between which 15% were radical and which was the 85% moderate majority? One has to remember that the al-Aqsa Brigades, who belong to the supposedly moderate PLO, have performed no fewer acts of Islamikaze[3] against Israelis than the fanatic radicals of Hamas.

Another issue that has been brought up for debate in the context of the Islamic Spring has been the question of stability. As conventional wisdom has it, one should not disturb stability, even at the price of abstaining from intervention in areas of conflict or human rights violations. NATO chose to intervene with air bombing against Qaddafi in Libya but has been reluctant to act similarly in Syria. In both places, stability had evaporated into distant memory before the beginning of the turmoil, as it has been in all countries where this drama has been unfolding, producing new surprises every day, and causing more casualties than had occurred during the international wars in the area prior to the Spring. It is then ludicrous when the great powers intervene in the Spring, one way or another, but find ideological justifications to interfere or to refrain from interfering, usually under the same banner of "stability."

For example, America and the West state their support for democracy and human rights and rush to apply those principles when one Palestinian complains about their violation by an Israeli act of self-defense, even when those complaints refer to events happening within Hamas territory, where violation of human rights is rife. But at the same time, the West keeps silent when those violations occur on a daily basis in Saudi Arabia, the darkest and most regressive regime in the Arab world. In Bahrain, where a Spring uprising against the monarch had broken out rather early in the process, the autocratic regime, which is backed militarily by Saudi Arabia, did not raise any protest or objection from the West, in support of the sacred stability that had to be preserved. But in Libya, NATO airplanes bombed until Qaddafi was removed. How about stability there? If the powers were at least consistent in their support of their friendly, moderate, or pro-democracy allies for the sake of stability, one could still understand.

Prior to the Spring, Qaddafi had become again the darling of the West, after he gave up his nuclear program, despite having perpetrated the greatest horror when he permitted a Pan Am plane to be blown up above Lockerbie. But the direct perpetrator of the horror was released by the British for humanitarian reasons. No one in the West questioned Qaddafi's legitimacy after forty-one years of tyranny, because he had provided stability. So what happened when the rebellion against him erupted, first in Benghazi and then in Tripoli? Did he suddenly lose the legitimacy that he never had? So why did those same powers that befriended him, sold him weapons, and allowed him to plant his extravagant tent in the heart of Rome and Paris, end up bombing him to his bitter end?

Similarly, Mubarak, who served the West loyally for three decades, never condoned terrorism and provided stability in Egypt, which was well-known to the Americans. They were aware that he had converted the peace with Israel into a cold peace and that he rigged the elections in his country at every turn to get "reelected," but it kept silent for fear that an Islamic alternative might be worse. And then, suddenly, when the Spring broke out, he became illegitimate, lost favor with the West, and was thrown out like a "squeezed lemon," to use an expression of another champion of democracy—Josef Stalin, who was in the custom of using his allies until he needed them no more. The fate of Ben Ali, the president of moderate, stable, and pro-Western Tunisia, where the entire process had been kindled (literally), was no different. And in order to precipitate the replacement of those tyrants by others, the

West did not hesitate to delegitimize its allies of yesteryear, to ally to the new rulers whom it had shunned all those years, thereby undoing the famous stability they had supposedly been trying to preserve. Ali Saleh, the Yemenite president, suffered the same lot, while Bashar Assad, the son of Hafez Assad, who were both courted to be brought into the Western loop despite the slaughters they had committed against their own people, was tempted by the most liberal American administration in a century (Obama administration), to pursue his tyranny with impunity. In fact, the Bush presidency had boycotted Syria and forced it to evacuate its troops from Lebanon, cut off diplomatic relations with it, and threatened even harsher measures, but under Obama's watch diplomatic relations were restored to facilitate "engagement," and Assad took advantage of the opportunity to move as he wished, and he did, as long as the iconic "stability" was preserved.

When the Spring erupted, the Western supporters of the Arab tyrants of yesteryear suddenly began demanding the departure of their old protégés, even before ensuring the identity of the successors and before understanding that stability should not be a blind mantra, worth pursuing at any price, anywhere, and at any time. For there is a positive stability that supports democracy, legitimacy, and peace; and there is an evil stability that should be opposed and shunned. The Soviet regime had provided stability in Eastern Europe for forty-five years; nevertheless President Reagan called it evil and acted successfully to bring it down. And so were the regimes of Mubarak, Assad, Qaddafi, Saddam Hussein, and the Iranian ayatollahs and their ilk, in spite of being stable and enduring. It is no coincidence that only regimes that lack democratic legitimacy, such as the Russian and the Chinese, continue to support recalcitrant tyrants like Assad without worrying about their legitimacy, which they never had in the first place. Who has given shelter to Ben Ali and who is defending Bahrain from the turmoil of the Spring? Saudi Arabia, whose government also lacks legitimacy, but due to its illusory stability, the West keeps silent about it, especially since both provide petrol and military bases to the West. In sum, the Western delusion that by supporting the Spring they are preserving stability and cultivating democratization does not have any legs to stand on. It appears that the main contending orientation in many of these countries will be in the direction of Islamization, which if it completely materializes does not promise stability either.

The reaction so far in the Islamic world is nourished by either the confused initiatives of the Western world and the deep-seated suspicions toward it, or conversely by the determined refusal of Russia and China to accept the seemingly zigzagging and hypocritical nature of Western policies. Namely, the West supports stability and instability at the same time, negotiates with civil governments and Islamic fundamentalists, and deals with autocrats and revolutionaries, all at once. Developments on the ground are affected by both the domino and the snowball effects. The domino effect came into play in Tunisia, when an unknown peddler set himself on fire because he sensed that his government did not care for the plight of its citizens, something which signaled to next-door Egyptians, Libyans, Syrians, and Yemenites that they might try the same against their respective tyrants so as to obligate them to flee the country. All those people had watched, live on television screens twenty years earlier, as the autocrats of the Soviet Bloc fell one after the other, but they needed a courageous example in their midst to remove the obstacle of fear and launch the process, and that happened first in Tunisia. The snowball effect worked the moment the flame was kindled in every one of those countries, and others followed suit while there was no one able to stop it. So far, except for Tunisia, where things seem to have begun to settle, and in Egypt, which has embarked on a new rocky and uncertain process, in most other countries, more than three years after the initial explosion, with the autocrats removed and the realization of change sinking in, domestic disagreements have been raging over which alternatives to choose from. Destruction is by nature much faster than construction, and it will take time before we know where this Spring is going to take us.

From its historical inception, the Islamic government had to learn from the great imperial experiments of its time: the Sassanids in Persia and the Byzantines in Anatolia, which combined empire and religion. The Prophet Muhammad, consciously or not, adopted this model in his ten years of rule in Medina (AD 622–32), for without his experience as a preacher in Mecca he would not have been invited to Medina, and without his ruling experience in Medina, it is doubtful whether his prophetic experience in Mecca would have served any practical purpose and accorded him his fame as the founder of Islam. The mold of government developed by Muhammad through his Medina experience, while he was setting the first example of rule in the first Muslim polis, consisted of five functions: prophecy, legislation, administration, judiciary, and military. Muhammad's prophecy was his value-added quality over all humans, and when he moved from Mecca, where he was a mere apocalyptic soothsayer who predicted the end of the world and had not much to offer except to sermonize the bourgeois merchant population of his clan in his city, to Medina, where he was an invited ruler, his career changed completely. Now he had to care for the city's affairs, to deal with personal, clan, tribal, commercial, political, and military issues that sought settlement before him. His prophecies continued, but this time tailor-made to respond to the arising problems he had to resolve. Those revelations, as he and other Muslims came to see them, being imprinted in the Holy Book, served later as the base for the Prophet's legislation. But when he died, and having no successor as a prophet, it was clear that no caliph could legislate after the Prophet, that the Prophet and his Sunna contained all necessary legislation for all humanity for all time, and that only ulema (doctors of the Holy Law) could henceforth tell what is the law. Hence the important role the doctors of Islam have in the state as interpreters of the law: *faqih* (jurist) as religious verdict renderers (*mufti*) or as *quda* (sing. *Qadi*, meaning judge). Theoretically, the caliphs could not legislate because they lacked the understanding of the scholars, but they could make other scholars who obeyed them pronounce the legal sanctions they wanted.

In Muhammad's time, legislation was narrowly related to prophecy because as the Prophet's revelations were laws and were later included in the verses of the Quran, they became laws by definition. But after his death, who else could legislate who did not possess the power of prophecy? In theory, the jurists retained that right for themselves of legislation via interpretation, but not any more through divine inspiration, since the gates of *ijtihad* had been closed, and most certainly not via innovation (Allah forbid, the *bid'a*!) Except for periods of truly righteous and pious rulers, who would resort to the scholars of their time to determine right or wrong, most rulers could not resist the temptation of ruling daily on current matters and then asking their scholars to find rationalizations for their decisions.

In our days, there is supposed to be a modern legal code that is partly based on the Islamic sources (Sharia) and partly on the civil code (*qanun*), a distinction established by the Ottomans. But the body of laws in both systems is there to be violated by the rulers, who continue to play by the Islamic rules in public, but in private they do much what they like. Therefore, though no Arab dictator prior to the Spring would admit that he was the legislator and would assert that he made sure that every item of legislation passed the parliament, everybody knew that even the king of Jordan and the president of Egypt, who were among the mildest dictators, could suspend the parliament at will; conversely, anything they wished the parliament to pass was done without much foot dragging. That meant, in fact, that the dictators were also the legislators.

As far as executive power was concerned, the Prophet was truly limitless, even though his Medina Treaty, which he signed (metaphorically, since he was illiterate) prior to his arrival, had stipulated certain conditions and obligations on him. In fact, after he Islamized the city and subjugated it to his will and as his lifestyle became the model for all Muslims to emulate, who could question his wisdom in his executive functions, especially that being under the constant blessing of his divine revelations, he could not be contradicted or disobeyed. And so the Prophet, using his charisma and his leadership skills, could unite the Arab tribes, deal with the Jewish tribes quite harshly—expelling some of them, executing others, and Islamizing still others—subjugate his rivals from within, launch military campaigns against other tribes, reform the inner structures of the city, launch the new religion and much more, all in the space of ten years.

Executive powers are the area in which the present tyrants excel too: they make their own "constitution" upon ascending to power, thus taking over something from the legislative branch when there is one; they monopolize the appointments of all ministers and their prime ministers; hold the reins of power at all levels; decide upon the budget, the rate of taxation to be levied, and the persons and institutions who enjoy public budgeting; determine what the people will eat and at what price; and hold in hand all the entrances and exits to and from public power. Is this a continuation of the old privileges that the Prophet had enjoyed, or simply the place where all dictators are bound to slide? It does not matter, as long as there will always be people who find justification to their deeds in Muhammad's exemplary life. The sociopolitical conditions of those days had indeed required that all those authorities be concentrated in the Prophet's hands, regardless of whether he realized that his style was no different from the authoritarian rule that he saw or heard about in his environment, external and domestic.

The only model he was familiar with internally was the tribal one, in which the sheikh concentrated all authority in his hands, thus he could not deviate much from what was known without producing controversy around him. Naturally, the sheikh was also committed to his tribe and its values and to the consensus among the notables to preserve his dominant rule, therefore he could not turn his rule into a heartless and unrestrained tyranny without incurring the risk of losing it. There was an unwritten social pact, worded in terms of the classical *muruwa,* which included ruling justly (the judiciary aspect), managing wisely and effectively (the executive part), and leading heroically in battle (the military aspect). His constituents, in return, undertook to obey him and his orders and to follow his lead in all his endeavors. In other words, when the Messenger of Allah was asked to proceed to Medina and take over the rule there, it is reasonable to assume that he knew what was expected of him.

The authoritarian rule in Islam naturally followed on the footsteps of the Prophet, who was, and still is, considered infallible and the most perfect of men; therefore he could commit no fault, in government or in anything else. It is also reasonable to assume that while establishing the fundaments of Muslim rule according to his needs, he also learned something from the imperial models he knew or learned about. Being possessors of an acute sense of obedience to his example, the Arabs have always felt that the great precedents set by Muhammad in his lifetime had necessarily grown to become valid for all times, especially after he died and the Arabs sprang out of Arabia to conquer the world and were in need of a Muslim style of government that would respond to their growing and pressing needs.

One has to assume that they were convinced of divine assistance with their vast and exciting enterprise of conquest, which was done under the authoritarian regime of the time; after the death of the Prophet they pursued the same route, which was common to them and to the enemies they fought against. Moreover, at a time when their Sassanid and Byzantine rivals were tyrannical rulers living in luxury and opulence, to the point that one spoke of the legendary "Byzantine Court" and "Sassanid ostentation," the Muslim court was managed much more simply and modestly, at least in the beginning of Islam, for the authority of the ruler was institutionalized in the *bai'ah* (oath of fealty), without a need to resort to all the excesses that inspired awe and authority in the rule and succession of those ancient imperial houses.

That meant that the ruler in place, who had been designated by the *shura,* as in the times of the rightful caliphs, or who later inherited his mantle through dynastic inheritance, was recognized and accepted in the public square, as if the oath of allegiance to him had been given personally by each Muslim. For any time of rebellion or dissatisfaction with the ruler, dubbed *fitna,* meant that the oath (*bai'ah*) lost its validity. Then worshippers no longer mentioned the name of the ruler at Friday prayers, as if the weekly validation of the oath no longer held.

Thus, the outside symbols of power were very much personal, direct, and needed no elaboration.

The charisma of the Prophet in his time was undoubtable. Nobody put into question his sublime qualities and natural propensity to rule, as if he were a prince who had inherited those qualities. But what about those who followed him as rulers? Did they inherit his charisma? How was the balance preserved between their nature as pious and righteous men and their ability to govern the people and make their rule as beyond reproach as possible? Allah's Messenger, apart from serving in all the functions cited above, also created a systematic ritual, repeated many times daily, which became one of the sources of his power, in addition to being the Messenger of Allah and his last Prophet. The first pillar of the faith, the *shahada* (bearing witness), which repeats at the head of each prayer the formula that "there is no God but Allah and Muhammad his Prophet," when becoming the first of the articles of the faith, made inextricable the connection between the Prophet and the very belief in the religion. When repeated many times over every day in prayer and preceding each important act one does, this accorded a central place to the Prophet in one's life. As long as the Prophet lived and his contemporaries felt privileged to be around him, they could see in front of them the perpetual expression of Allah's grace in sending to them the Seal of the Prophets and the most perfect of men to serve them and to guide them. There was never a possibility that anyone could question that charisma. Even in moments of friction with his closest companions, for instance with Umar in Hudaibiya, Muhammad's unique quality remained, because he always had the last word.

When the Prophet suddenly died in A.D. 632, there was an urgent need to appoint a successor, lest his entire heritage disintegrate. The Shura elected Abu Bakr, probably by order or seniority since he was the oldest, but also the Prophet's father-in-law. What to make of his attribute of *siddiq* (the righteous)? Probably not much, because it was accorded to him after his death. After him came the three others (Umar, Uthman, Ali), each time following huge controversies and forceful lobbying for each candidate, which ended in compromises, horse trading, bargaining, and pressures. The main issue was to elect a successor, lest the charisma of the Prophet be discontinued and the authority of the caliph be so diminished that there would not be much left to inherit. At the same time, it was clear that the prophecy was sealed forever by Muhammad, and so were the divine legislative powers that emanated from it. Therefore, all that could be passed on to the caliphs were the remaining four functions of the Muslim ruler: civil legislation, executive and judiciary powers, and military command. This combination of so many top functions made sure that the caliph would be no less omnipotent than the Prophet in the practical domain of rule, while the special and unique level of prophecy would remain sealed. Hence the attribute of *khalif* (caliph) imputed to him, meaning a human figure, as the Prophet had insisted upon characterizing himself, who served as a replacement, or vicar in Christian parlance for the replacement of Jesus on earth. But in Christianity the vicars became infallible popes and divine figures, while the caliphs remain human all the way; otherwise the doctrine of the unity of Allah (*tawhid*) would be seriously compromised.

After the four righteous, many Islamic dynasties followed, often simultaneously and struggling against each other and sometimes the sons of the same ruler were fighting for the succession of their father, like the bloody struggles between Aurangzeb and his brothers for the succession of Shah Jahan in Mughal India, in which the imprisoned ruler helplessly watched as his sons butchered each other. This war to the finish continued with every generation, for a new king could not feel safe on his throne as an absolute ruler unless all the rival contenders were eliminated. In the Arab monarchies today, there are families on the throne who try to ensure an orderly succession, yet there is no telling when someone down the line might rebel and reverse the order, as had happened with the Nasser and Qaddafi revolutions in North Africa. There are certainly various degrees of absolutism, like the one perceivable between Saudi Arabia, without any institutions to palliate the royal house and where even the Shura is appointed by the monarch, and Kuwait or Jordan, who have some kind of parliament. Some kingdoms, like Jordan and Morocco, boast of their "constitutional monarchy," but either they understand the difference between their kingdoms and those of Benelux, Scandinavia, and England, and they continue nonetheless their fraudulent pursuit, or they don't and they just play with words. But absolutism in these countries is not confined to monarchies, for in Saddam's Iraq, Assad's Syria, and Qaddafi's Libya, there was also an extreme sort of absolutism, which even surpassed monarchies in cruelty and egotism of the rulers. Some of them are so full of themselves that they designated heirs among their sons to succeed them (Saddam for Iraq, Mubarak for Egypt, Saleh for Yemen, Qaddafi for Libya, and Assad for Syria, where Bashar actually inherited his father in 2000).

More moderate and human and less cruel and absolutistic authoritarianism was offered by Ben Ali of Tunisia and Mubarak of Egypt, and it was paradoxically they who first fell at the beginning of the Spring, but their lives were preserved or they escaped to a protective exile. It seems that the more cruel among them, who have also been ruthless in defense of their rule, including Assad, Qaddafi, and Saleh of Yemen, have had to fight the longest and kill the most of their own citizens to remain in place. Islamic history has known both types—tyrants who ran away and those who were killed under their watch. But even the more benevolent type, such as Mubarak, when too long in power (thirty years) tended toward corruption and monarchic rule. In effect, Mubarak was "elected" and "reelected" every time anew by an obedient parliament with no rival candidate allowed to run, lest he "caused division among the people." Lately, when old and tired Mubarak announced that his son would run for office after him, his people rebelled, because when they agreed to a republic in 1952 they did not mean a monarchical or dynastic republic. In Lebanon too, despite the full-blown election campaign, Sa'd Hariri ran to replace his father, who had been murdered by Hezbollah on behalf of the Syrians, exactly as the legendary Pierre Jumayel, the founder and commander of the Phalangs, was followed by his two sons: al-Bashir first, and, when he was slain by the Syrians, his brother Amin followed. Kamal Junblatt, the Druze leader, was replaced by his son Walid, who is far from reaching his stature and has even shown subservience to Bashar Assad, wrongly betting on the leader of Syria, who began to disappear during the civil war that has been tearing his country apart.

All these examples show that when it comes to authoritarian executive power, all the Arab countries of the Middle East have some affinity to it, one way or another. Only lust for power in this fashion can motivate a father to wish to bequeath his rule to his sons. It is not known what the Prophet himself would have done had he had a son. But since only Fatima his daughter survived and she married his cousin Ali, who also became a contender for power, it is difficult to conclude from that anything about the pre-Spring present-day rule of succession in the Muslim world. One strong suspicion has to be mentioned: the tyrants in place were so much afraid of what might happen to them or to their legacy after their death that their only way to guarantee the posthumous survival of their reputation was to ensure the rule of their sons after them, because

a) only the son can assure the memory of his father by making sure that he is properly commemorated and his heritage is respected and even worshipped: just imagine what would have happened to Hafez Assad's memorial in Qardahah had his son not been around to defend and cultivate it; and

b) without prearranged succession, fathers, especially coming from a minority group like the Assads, could not ensure that their children would succeed, or even survive. Imagine that Assad the father had been killed as a president-dictator: then his son Bashar would at best have remained an optometrist or continued to seek shelter in London, and his father's memory may have been totally erased. Conversely, had the successions of Saddam, Qaddafi, Saleh, and Mubarak succeeded, the dictators could still be in power or put on a pedestal as elder statesmen, and in any case allowed to die naturally.

As far as the judiciary is concerned, judges, who were all religious (*qadi*) in old days, served under the various caliphs and dynasties, and since they depended on the royal court for their appointment, they were also usually obedient, though they were supposed to enforce Sharia law. But since the Ottoman rule, which established the distinction between Sharia and civil law (*Qanun*), all independent Muslim countries then gradually adopted such a system, and pressures began as to the degree and extent to which the law of each country ought to depend either entirely, or to a large degree, on religious law. In either case the two systems exist side by side, and both are appointed by the administration in place. But under dictators the system does not matter, and things are usually decided according to the whims of the ruler. We have mentioned that the first legal document that every ruler in the Muslim world devises is a constitution, which instead of being left to the public or to assemblies of representatives to put together, is made by the tyrant or his underlings. Rather than constituting a legal framework that sets limits to the dictator's power and promises protection to the citizens and their rights, this sort of constitution only draws the guidelines for the future action of the ruler, to be altered by a new document when the next dictator comes along.

And finally the military field had been fulfilled with distinction by the Prophet as he launched periodical wars of expansion in Arabia, seized the holy shrine of Mecca to which he had not been allowed to enter by his fellow tribesmen of the Qureish, or raided Arabia. In those ventures, which his Medinan followers never hesitated to assist, he ensured for himself the title of *Amir-al-Mu'minin* (Commander of the Faithful), a title he seemed to like in particular due to the frequency of its usage when he was addressed by other Muslims. This was also the title preferred by all the caliphs and sultans who followed throughout the generations. There were even cases of Muslim minority rebellions in which the local commanders, who wished to rally larger groups of Muslim troops around them, made a summon to their public using this title or one similar to it.[4]

In the modern Arab and Islamic worlds, most dictators also put themselves at the head of the high military command in their country, either because they have mounted a coup as military men or because they wish to appear as generals, marshals, or admirals in their military uniforms. (Sadat was killed in a general's suit while watching a military parade; Idi Amin dressed like a marshal; Qaddafi liked to parade with either his officer's suit or his clown outfit; and Arafat appeared perennially with his military suit.) In that fashion, they seem to send a clear message that no matter the rank of their generals, the grades and the medals they wear are superior. For all these dictatorships, the army has been their main sustenance in power, and it is worth recalling that in Egypt, when the army abandoned Mubarak, he collapsed. In Syria, Bashar's army supported him so he could fight for a long time without faltering, mainly thanks to outside support by armies from Iran, Russia, and Hezbollah.

Even though dust is far from settling yet on all those countries, it is clear that what was will never be again, and that new and uncertain paths are being chartered that we cannot yet ascertain their directions. It is also clear that the masses of Arabs and Muslims are loath to sustain the tyrannical rule that has ruled them hitherto. Yes, they all shout: Democracy! as if they knew what it was; but what they mean is that they are tired of dynastic and absolute rulers. On the other hand, it is not easy to imagine in the Islamic world powerless "vegetarian" monarchical regimes like those in Europe, because for them a ruler is a ruler, a king is a king and an executive without authority is nobody.

Thus, Saudi Arabia, Morocco, Jordan, or the Gulf States, who are proclaiming their wish to adopt reform by instituting "constitutional monarchies" into their respective systems will have to go, because neither can they relinquish their power totally, without which there is no constitutional monarchy, nor would the nations enslaved by them for many decades let them continue their rule unchecked, for then the monarch, instead of being the symbol of the state, remains a power broker, and that is a recipe for friction and future crises.

Remarkably, after years of intimate knowledge of these heads of state—of business dealings and official representations in each other's countries, during which they had the chance to examine the regimes, gauge their feudalistic and dictatorial dimensions, and evaluate the degree of oppression, suppression, corruption, and exploitation that sustained them—Western powers, including politicians, diplomats, and scholars, hardly ever voiced one word of alarm, of warning of things to come. They allowed things to fully deteriorate, and only when open rebellion broke out and blood started to spill in the streets have they had the decency to say: "Oh yeah, we knew all along but were ordered not to speak up," or "We knew it was coming," or else "We would never have believed this rule would be so easy to remove."

We could even expect someone to cry out: "Remember the shah's island of stability that Carter had turned into a swamp of Iranian hostility. Where are all those presidents and foreign ministers who invited those dictators to their capitals, sold them weapons, defended them in the United Nations, formed alliances with them, pardoned their violations of every law, forgave their crimes, and allowed them to plant their tents (literally) in the hearts of Rome, Paris, and London? Didn't they know they were corrupt tyrants? If they did not know, they should have dismissed their ambassadors there, who had submitted false and biased reports. Their late reaction would expose them to two sorts of accusations that they would find difficult to refute: that they now admit their faltering policies in the previous years in lending support to corrupt and dangerous dictators and enabling them to survive for decades, knowing that they were robbing and exploiting their peoples and second, if that was the situation, why expect the countries of the Spring to have confidence in the Western powers that have disappointed them in the past?"

Many secondary questions pop up in the public squares of all those Muslim countries that have chosen to change course, all leading back to the main question of trusting once again the powers that have betrayed them before. For example, the United States and the West now promise to support democracy. What democracy? How can we be sure we are talking about the same democracy? For years the West had let Mubarak (and others) rig elections, so how can they be trusted to ensure fair elections now? They had let Saudi Arabia and Libya go without elections at all, and they were never heard urging those rulers to conform. What has happened now? Did Westerners suddenly mend their ways? Why did they let Egypt suppress the Copts for decades, the Syrians impose a regime of terror and interfere in their neighbors' affairs, and Hezbollah take over rule in Lebanon in submission to the Syrian and

Iranian tyrannies? And when the West intervened in oil-rich Libya, dropping bombs from the air without taking any risks on the ground, everyone expected to see the same happening in Syria. But NATO members knew the difference, because the Syrian army is large, comprising more divisions than NATO (except for the Americans) could field, its air force and air defenses are formidable enough to challenge Western air power, save the American, while Libyan forces posed no threat. No major European power could stand the domestic disaster of bringing home plastic bags filled with corpses from the Syrian battlefield; therefore no country volunteered to fight there. The United States, who could have done it, had her hands full in Afghanistan, and an election campaign approaching, and it was clear that it would not take additional risks.

The faults that the awakening Arab champions of the Spring complain about in the West are not only on the military level but on the diplomatic front as well. When the United States stated one year into the Syrian crisis that Assad had "lost its legitimacy," it simply revealed in public what it refused to recognize before (i.e., that Assad never had any legitimacy for power, exactly like the other dictators). Assad's father, who took over the rule by a coup and then bequeathed it to his son, had never been elected by anyone either. Bashar Assad's role in power has been sustained by Iran and by Hezbollah, two outlaws who never received legitimate rule.

Obama's administration stated its policy of engagement, which failed dismally. Before him, the Bush administration had successfully isolated Syria, cut off relations with it, put it under political siege, and forced it to evacuate its forces from Lebanon—all this to punish it for the al-Qaida forces who were allowed to infiltrate Iraq and damage the American forces there. Obama, with his new policy, went to Riyadh to prostrate before the king of that primitive and obscurantist country, notoriously corrupt and a denier of human rights. He then proceeded to Cairo, where he made an incredibly hypocritical speech to the Muslim world, which produced no positive result, apart from the Spring of 2011, which Obama did not want in the first place. Then he enlisted Turkey to also sponsor Syria back into the fold by granting her back her place among nations, reestablishing diplomatic relations with her. Assad and others came to believe that the United States needed them more than they needed it, and felt free to act at will on their domestic front.

Within one year, Mubarak was urged to go: he no longer represented the Muslim world, nor the much solicited stability. Assad was again boycotted, his legitimacy had gone, and, as he engaged in more killings of his own citizens, suddenly the United States discovered that he had formidable allies in Moscow and Beijing, even more so in Tehran and in Beirut, and that his allies would not let him fall. Who could take seriously that lukewarm policy? Least of all, the countries of the Spring, which look at pathetic Obama, one week supporting Mubarak, the next negotiating with his sworn enemies of the Muslim Brothers; one week boycotting and besieging Assad, then giving him long leashes with Turkish enthusiastic support, then banning him again. Did they know whom they would support instead? Of course not, and they called that "foreign policy," as if it were measured, calculated, and considered. They published the State Department report about human rights violations, where the most liberal guardian of human rights, Israel, was censured, but Saudi Arabia, the most grievous violator of those rights, was discreetly kept hidden behind the scenes. One wondered what was going on in Washington. In Bahrain, an uprising of the Shiite majority was quelled militarily, with several casualties, but no word of delegitimation, censure, condemnation, or blame came out from the State Department, much less the White House .

We have noticed several elements of authoritarian rule in Islamic tradition that have all found expression in this Spring. For example, the tradition of the sheikh, which generated the caliphate and the dictatorships that are still extant in our days and, by contrast, the other tendencies that palliate that harsh aspect, such as the *Ijma'* (consensus in religious practice), the Shura (principle of the council with notables participating), the lack of hierarchy in the clerical system, and the mystical equality between all believers on the floor of the mosque, from the king to the last worshipper. We are suggesting here a contradiction between principles that look proto-democratic, down to earth, and popular, and harsh autocratic principles of government. There is a tradition in Islam that the Prophet and the first caliphs were simple, accessible, and wary of elevating themselves over the masses when compared to the later kings, emperors, and sultans, who hid in their palaces and could hardly be seen by the public. Their behavior stemmed partly from the size of the growing empire and its bureaucracy, where it had to grow impersonal for the state to fill its pressing needs. But partly their response was due to the changing interpretations of things. For example, coffee was considered in the beginning of Islam as a drug or equivalent to alcohol or narcotics, and there were people who were arrested for using it. But popular custom was stronger, and at last coffee was not only permitted but became an essential tool of socialization. But one has also to pay attention to the fact that while *Ijma'* did gather momentum as a social and religious consensus, it was no longer possible to implement it in practice when the *umma* grew beyond the city of Medina, to extend over large parts of the medieval world, and then over the entire universe. It was then necessary to confine its validity to the scholars of each community only, since it was impossible that a consensus among all world Muslims be attained, especially under the transport and communications conditions of the time. But that too was too vast for a practical consensus, and in time it became imperative to consult the main scholars of each generation.

Of course, there was neither democracy nor anything resembling it. But this was the closest one could come to some kind of representative body. Moreover, unlike the Shura and other councils of appointed notables, the consensus of scholars was, and still is, meritocratic in essence because it is self-selected, just like the ayatollahs in the Shiite system, and elitist due to the participation of a select few. There is another limitation here: supposing a consensus requires at least a majority if not the totality of the main scholars, then the minority does not even have the right to express its minority view, let alone implement it under the inundating sweep of the majority. In other words, to seek democracy in this society is equivalent to sending a blind person to a dark room to look for a black cat that is not there.

In the West, legitimacy is achieved by freely electing a parliament and a government at the end of each term specified by law and when power is smoothly transferred from the incumbent to the elect. In the Islamic world there is no democracy of the Western type, though in Saudi Arabia one could hear arguments in favor of the Shura as the "mother of all democracies." So in what way would those who seize power justify or rationalize it? Except for the Prophet himself, who ruled by the grace of Allah who dispatched him as his Messenger, all his successors had to prove their legitimacy one way or another. One way to gain legitimacy today is to follow the spirit of the time and hold "elections," whose results are preprogrammed and whose unfolding is choreographed in such a style as not to betray the rigging.

In the Communist world, there were also elections, but with candidates from a single party, namely the ruling party, and they were "elected" without opposition, a pattern that has been generously and uncritically copied by most Islamic countries if and when elections were held at all. In Iran, there is a Supreme Screening Commission that decides whom to permit to run for elections and whom to ban. In that system, there is a permanent Supreme Spiritual Leader who does not run or stand for election, instead he supervises from above and nothing can be done without his agreement. The entire bureaucracy, from the president down, is supposed to be guided by him, due to his aura of sanctity, launched by Khomeini but allowed to continue even though no one was found so far to fill that position weightily.

In monarchic systems, kings and princes are not elected, and when they don their crowns they act as authoritarian and sometimes as absolute as the other sorts of dictators. They preserve their clan's laws of succession, going first through the collateral members of the family, brother by brother, and only when they are all exhausted does that generation skip one or two generations forward to start a new count of kings, heirs, and princes, the others becoming ministers, governors, military commanders, court councilors, ambassadors, and senior officials. In that system, proximity and loyalty to the king, rather than skill or proficiency for the job are the main criteria for senior appointments.

In other systems, like those of Qaddafi, Saddam, and Assad, there was no pretense of election or legitimacy: they simply took over and ruled, with the help of a military clique that supported them in return for benefits that accrued to them after the success of the coup. After they take over power, they organize "elections" to signify to the world that the Arab Middle East is no different from the American Midwest, and very often misinformed and naïve correspondents report those "elections" with enthusiasm, as if the data were ironclad and authoritative. This grotesque farce continued for decades and the West kept its silence, pretending it did not know. The Islamic regimes also pretended that all was well, since rarely did any Western country protest against any transition from fake elections to rigged power. Quite the contrary, every president who was thus "elected" was inundated by a cascade of greetings upon his "election."

Even before the coming of the Spring, the autocrats in place started feeling the push from the bottom, through Internet and social networks, to open up and democratize—something that compelled them to devise new rationalizations to their illegitimate rule because they realized that their previous pseudo-democratic measures had resulted only in contempt and anger in the street. So they at first reverted to their old and rusty pretexts. The president of Egypt boasted the "strongest military force in the area," which would stand fast in defense of all Arabs; the Syrians were proud of their resolute Arab nationalism and their unconditional support of the Palestinians; the king of Morocco invoked his descent from the Prophet, and so did the king of Jordan, who also added to his arrows the title of "the Curator of Al-Aqsa," which he obtained from his peace deal with Israel; and Saudi Arabia, as the curator of the Two Mosques of Mecca and Medina, the holiest in Islam.

They thought that if they were seen as wonderful, idealistic, and caring for their countries and peoples, who would want to replace them? But in fact, they were all illegitimate, because no one chose them; they took power either by royal inheritance or through succession of revolutionary leaders (Nasser, Sadat, Mubarak), and, if not for the Spring, which discontinued that apostolic chain, successions would have gone on to the sons of the leaders in place. During World War II, scholar Ferrero wrote his book *On Democracy*, which has since become a classic, in which he coined the idea of a "fraudulent democracy" to describe the fascist regimes in Europe (Hitler, Mussolini, Franco, and some of their short-lived supporters in the Arab world, such as Rashid Ali in Iraq, the Brothers in Egypt, and Haj Amin in Palestine), part of whom had experienced something of the democratic system but had ended up borrowing its rules in order to distort its substance. For example, "elections" were held technically, but only to leave the arena open to the autocrat and to him alone. In the Arab and Islamic world, which had almost never experienced democracy (even in Turkey, the classic border-case, the elected governments were removed by the army on several occasions), one can suspect a true ignorance of the essence of democracy. Indeed, how could they know what it meant if they had never experienced it?

If the UN wants to extend assistance to a new country to organize elections, it should not dispatch as its messengers the delegates of Syria, Sudan, or Iran, but those of Sweden, Britain, and Luxemburg, who know and have experienced something of it. In any case, even prior to the Spring, "democracy" has become a mantra repeated by every leader as part of his platform. In fact, it was meaningless, not only because those autocrats did not mean it, but also because they did not comprehend it.

Mubarak's party was called "National Democratic," which like the popular democracies in Eastern Europe, namely Bulgaria, Romania, Poland, Czechoslovakia, and so on purposely added to their names the appellation "democratic," knowing full well that they were not. Britain, France, or Sweden never needed to underline that they were democracies, because everyone knew it. China, similarly, boasts its "popular" attribute, intending to distance its image from the autocracy that it is, in fact. The bottom line is that where there is a democracy, autocrats cannot rise, and vice versa: where there is an autocrat there can be no democracy.

When Ariel Sharon headed the Israeli government in the 2000s, President Mubarak was interviewed by the international press. He stressed that, unlike "Sharon the dictator," he himself was a "real democrat," voted in by 90 percent of the parliament. It was clear that Mubarak never understood how democracy worked, nor the very stringent rules and controls over Israeli elections so that there should be no doubt or question over their results. What he said indicated more his ignorance than any flaw with the free and democratic elections in Israel, which are supervised by an impeccable Supreme Court judge. Or take Bashar Assad. He inherited from his father in 2000, following a speedy process of amending the constitution (as if it mattered) to make the young age of the successor (thirty-four) eligible for the presidency. But the members of parliament and the public at large who were interviewed after the amendment all pointed to the "democratic process" that regulated the succession. No one dared to raise the issue of an inexperienced son inheriting the mantle of his murderous father, proving once again a case of simple-minded fraud rather than a sophisticated and effective system of succession of the rule.

We have already mentioned the fleeting constitutions, introduced by every new tyrant as a way to lay his future plans before his constituency, which he did not consult when he seized power. He and everyone else knew that he will not be restrained by those rules and that he will pursue his autocracy with or without constitution. But lacking any other legitimacy for power, he feels that his proclaimed goal serves as some kind of justifier, and he will throughout his term hold on to it and show it as his achievement, even if there is no real substance to it. That constitution was aimed at replacing the previous one, which had been written and promised by the previous ruler, full of rosy wordings and sublime pledges, and when the day comes and the autocrat is removed, another paper of that sort will replace it. A plurality of constitutions, one succeeding the other, means that there is no one, binding constitution.

Only now, in view of the changing realities under the Spring, in which public commissions were established to assemble, discuss, and formulate a new constitution, is there any chance that it would be more open and liberal and not reflective of the ruler's whims. Two more obstacles stand in the way of removing tyrants: to return the armies to their barracks as has been done by Erdogan in Turkey and Mursi in Egypt and searching for some working compromises between the fundamentalist Muslim governments, who are getting the majority but are almost totally lacking in any governing experience, and those parts of the civil population that fear them, lest the entire infrastructure erected by the tyrants in the past decades comes tumbling down.

There is almost no Muslim fundamentalist movement in the Islamic world that, in spite of the uncertainties of the Spring, does not put forward its dream of establishing their Sharia state as part of the ultimate caliphate. What is the magic of this utopian state that is so much talked about? We have already explained above the contribution of the caliphate to the authoritarian state in Islam, and we have now to become aware that a caliphate would mean two contradictory trends: on the one hand, this is the ideal Islamic state that all Islamic society should strive for, but on the other hand this regime is only a replacement (*khilafah*) to the truly ideal one that occurred at the time of the Prophet. The time of the Prophet was unique in human history and will not repeat itself. But at the same time, the peak of human ambition cannot possibly surpass the original human endeavor as expressed in and by the caliphate. Thus, it is agreed that the caliphate is the most adequate regime to govern the *umma,* provide for its needs, and defend it. In the prenationalist world, when the caliphate succeeded Muhammad's rule, it was designed to become a universal Muslim administration, like the contemporaneous Sassanid and Byzantine empires, which were regarded as governing all Zoroastrians and all Christians, respectively.

The great questions remain: since no one could possibly emulate the Prophet, in spite of his unmistakably human nature, does one focus on the example of the caliphs only, particularly those worthy of admiration and imitation? Also, will the agreed-upon model remain applicable to all future generations of Muslims, in view that the Sharia is itself eternal and immutable? And lastly, are there other ways than the *bai'ah* to legitimize the rule, which creates a lasting social pact between the ruler and the ruled? At the beginning of Islam, the four righteous caliphs who succeeded the Prophet (Abu Bakr, Umar, Uthman, and Ali) were elected by the Shura based on their personal merit, though admittedly nepotism, lobbying, tensions, competition, and quarrels were part and parcel of the process.

But as the Prophet was the most perfect of created men, and he could not sin or act indecently, so were the righteous, known as second in sanctity to the Prophet, who came closest to perfection, though differences existed among them in Islam during their lifetime and certainly after their deaths. Three of the four were killed in the middle of their terms, creating a precedent of responding to disagreement by taking the lives of those who were thought to deviate from the crystallizing norm of government in post–Prophetic Islam. The last of them, Ali, absorbed most of the criticism, because, unlike others who accepted the choice of the Shura and served under the elected caliphs, he and his followers bitterly protested his discrimination, since on three occasions he was skipped over and disregarded, until he was elected as the fourth successor.

Even when Ali was elected, his election remained challenged, so much so that his brief caliphate of five years (656–61) was in itself controversial and ended with his death in battle, thus bringing to its close the Rashidun era of thirty years (632–61). Ali was supported throughout his repeated candidacy by a faction (Shia) of well-wishers and disciples, who brought out his personal and family qualities (*Ahl al-bayt*), rather than his governmental skills to function as caliph, for he was the Prophet's cousin and also son-in-law, since he married Muhammad's sole-surviving daughter—Fatima. The Shia also propagated an unconfirmed claim that on his deathbed the Prophet had designated Ali, his son-in-law, as his successor. It would have immediately had a tremendous impact on the inheritance of government in Islam, had the Prophet had a son who would have perhaps succeeded to him, which would have meant more of a reliance on blood succession than on merit.

This complication was further aggravated when Muawiyah, the nephew of the slain third caliph, Uthman, accused Ali's people of the murder, seized power in Damascus, ostensibly to avenge his uncle but in fact vying for himself and for the establishment of the Umayyads, the first dynastic house in Islam. Thus, it was not only Ali's life that ended in battle, but with him also the era of the righteous caliphs, who remain nevertheless deeply respected in Islam, second only to the Prophet himself.

As explained above, the Ali faction was created to sustain their patron's claim to the caliphate (i.e., it was a political expectation and demand to start with). It is possible that had Ali received what he wanted and the enormous opposition to him had been neutralized there would have been no major schism in Islam. However, as it happened, right after Uthman's murder in 656 and Ali's appointment to succeed, the mounting opposition to him led him on a collision course with the mainstream. For a great innovation was there, when Ali and his people claimed that family qualifications overrode personal merit. But

Muawiyah, who led the battle against Ali, did exactly what his sworn enemy wanted: to lend family priority to the rules of succession when he instituted his royal house of the Umayyads, where for decades rule passed from father to son, thus opening the road to blood succession in Islam, as in other royal dynasties in other cultures, lasting until the decline of the Ottomans in the twentieth century.

Nonetheless, Ali was accepted and venerated in Sunni Islam as the fourth caliph, while the Shiites continued to curse the first three as usurpers. The Sunnites, who made many efforts for the Shia to join Islam as a fifth school, naturally predicated the union on the Shiites' acceptance of the first three Rashidun, but the followers of Ali categorically refused. Through the years, the two factions of Islam have grown so far apart, both politically and theologically, that it is impossible to see how they can get closer or how their principles can be bridged over. The Islamic Spring has further deepened the gap between them, to the point of turning them into bitter rivals on either side of the divide.

The main sect of the Shia, the Twelvers who rule Iran, is founded on the principle of the twelve imams, the first of whom is Ali himself and then his two sons, Hassan and Hussein, and another series of nine imams, the last of whom disappeared as a child in the tenth century, and, as the Hidden Imam who rules the world from behind the scenes, he will reappear as the savior at the end of time, rescue humanity from misery, and inaugurate an era of justice and plenty. As long as this doctrine existed as an eschatological vision, it was not disputed so openly and bitterly, and the Shiite minority could live side by side with the Sunni majority in low profile, though no love was lost between them. But the Islamic Revolution of Khomeini of 1979, having shuffled the cards, in fact unwittingly served as the precursor of the Islamic Spring.

Khomeini in his time, and even more so Ahmadinejad, the president of Iran in the 2000s, have pressed for the acceleration of the messianic process. Like Rabbi Kook in religious Judaism, but unlike ultraorthodox Jews, who prefer the quietist approach of waiting and expecting the Messiah, the Iranian leaders have elected to precipitate the process through acts of piety, like the declaration of the revolution, the aid they extend to Syria, Hamas, and Hezbollah to fight for the cause of Islam, the convening in Tehran of the Terrorism International organization to battle against the West and Israel, all in order to hasten salvation. Khomeini professed that his Islamic Revolution was intended for export. He also revived and operationalized the doctrine advocated by the senior ayatollahs (*ayatollah uzma*), who are in constant contact with the Hidden Imam and get their guidance from him; therefore they are the best positioned to know how to manage the affairs of the state until his reappearance and how to hasten his return.

President Ahmadinejad, who despite his high position is not a cleric, is nevertheless one of the most zealous believers in hastening the coming of the imam. When he was the mayor of Tehran, he undertook the widening of the main avenues of the city to accommodate the large crowds that would flood the streets when the imam reappears. When he spoke at the United Nations, he said he sensed the aura of the imam, which enveloped him—all to mean that the return of the Hidden Imam was no longer an apocalyptic event to occur at the end of days but a concrete and imminent affair to be expected any day. Thus, when these visions and delusions are spelled out, coupled with the nuclear power that Iran has been frantically deploying a supreme effort to accomplish, they cause extreme concern in Israel and the world. Moreover, due to the historical division in the world of Islam between Sunna and Shia, Iran's current doctrinal precipitation of what was traditionally an eschatological thought, coupled with its stepped-up military preparations, nuclear and missile armaments, and unbridled bellicose statements, have raised deep security concerns among Iran's Sunnite neighbors and heightened the arms race in the region.

The following added to these worries: Unlike policy considerations of gains and losses, which are usually made within rational boundaries, the apocalyptic motive of Iran's leaders may distort their capacity to weigh pros and cons: the worse the situation, the closer the Day of Judgment and the return of the imam, which are foretold and signaled by the "pangs of the Messiah." In such a situation, they will not be deterred by threats they incur in pursuing their policy but may even wish to precipitate them, knowing that they would thus hasten the return of the imam. In other words, all the international reasoning based on accepted norms of restraint, diplomatic custom, rational debate, and logical argument are turned on their head.

The Iranians, who launched their Spring thirty years before all others, have in the meantime acquired some valuable allies in Iraq, Syria, Hezbollah in Lebanon, and Hamas in Gaza, thus forming the Shiite Crescent (despite the fact that Syria and Hamas are consummately Sunnite), a real threat to its neighbors with its well-armed 100 million inhabitants who can sustain their own long-term bellicosity without risk of depletion or exhaustion. They are perceived as so dangerous to the Sunnite countries (except for Syria, their ally, but that too can change with the eventual fall of Assad) that for many clerics in the Sunnite world they are "worse than the Jews," no mean compliment for both.

This is no longer a matter of bridging over the doctrinal gaps between Shiite and Sunnite, but a widening gulf that can produce a confrontation between the parties and push the Sunnites to developing nuclear weapons too. Turkey enjoys a special status in this regard, because as a senior Sunnite state that wishes to lead the rest, it also abhors the idea of a nuclear Iran. One has to recall that the removal of the Erbakan government from Ankara in 1998 was due to its rapprochement to Iran, and that Syria, which Turkey wished to co-opt into the alliance with Iran to form a new Middle Eastern front, has slipped into chaos and caused increased tension with Iran. For now, as the balance in the new Middle East seems to turn toward the Muslim Brothers and their ilk, it is difficult to predict what policy they might adopt after the dust settles.

This deviation from the main narrative to explain what has happened in modern Iran impels us to return to pursue the story of the caliphate. Shia continued after its schism from the Sunna to inhabit the eastern mountainous regions of Islamdom in Persia/Iran and Central Asia, with one exceptional foray into North Africa—the Fatimid Empire at the time of the Crusades, while most other Muslim territory was Sunni. Namely, when we talk about Muslim empires, we mean Sunnite. For the Shiites, that means that if three out of the four first caliphs are rejected as usurpers, then the entire model of the caliphate as the ideal form of rule collapses.

After those four, Muawiyah's family literally took over by force the kingship of the Arab/Muslim world, establishing the first dynasty of the House of Umayya, not only enforcing dynastic hereditary succession of the rule instead of the previously meritocratic system, but also determining that, since no dynasty can survive forever, there were going to be wars of succession in the years to come. After the Umayyads came the Abbasids, some of whose legendary rulers were immortalized in the *Thousand Nights and One Night* tales, and they were themselves demoted by the Mongols in 1259 when Baghdad was occupied and destroyed. But before it crumbled under the weight of its years, the dynasty had grown more Islamic than Arab, and its capital moved eastward to the Iranian area. However, the vast uncontrollable territories of the dynasty and the huge distances between them could not prevent new centrifugal forces from rising in the periphery: the Iberian Umayyads, the North African successive dynasties, the Fatimids and the then the Mamluks in Egypt, and then slowly the penetration of the Turkish Seljuks and Ottomans, who once Islamized contributed to the revitalization of the Islamic Empire.

The historical experience with so many caliphates, from the righteous to the Ottomans, even if we include the mighty Moghuls who paralleled the Ottomans chronologically, shows us that only seldom was the ideal of one Sharia law state inclusive of the entire *umma* close to being realized. The record also shows that the more *dar-al-Islam* expanded, the less was the caliphate able to exercise power over it. For example, when Islam reached East and Southeast Asia and black Africa and took root in places like Indonesia, Malaysia, Mali, Kenya, and Nigeria, it became clear that aspiring to one all-encompassing Muslim caliphate had become impractical. Then why the persistence of the single-mindedness of this kind of regime as the ideal one, when in the real world it could almost never enforce itself in view of the geographical, ethnic, linguistic, cultural, and political diversity?

Perhaps the modern dreamers of the renewed caliphate hope that improvements in communications and transport could make possible what was not in the previous centuries. In any case, this mythical ambition persists. Take for example the platform of Hamas, worded in 1988, which was supposed to respond to the Palestinian aspiration to rid themselves of what they saw as Israeli occupation but ended up peddling the idea of the caliphate, which larger and more secure states like Turkey and Pakistan are not dreaming of. The reason is that Hamas, being a branch of the Muslim Brothers, who have made the caliphate one of their main tenets, is bound to raise it as one of its principal goals. Now that Egypt, the homeland of the Brothers, has come under their aegis, it may be that this item will no longer be confined to a platform and grow to become a political blueprint.

The following references in the Hamas Charter are worth mentioning, bearing in mind the great strides the Brothers and their affiliates have been making in the world:

1. Article 11 of the charter refers to the land of Palestine as an eternal waqf (holy endowment): therefore it is not negotiable, even not by Arab kings, presidents, and other leaders, because the ban to negotiating is part of the Sharia. This formula leans on the caliphate of Umar (634–44), when the caliph was asked about the fate of Syria and Iraq, which had just been conquered, and he answered, after consultation with the rest of the Prophet's companions, that the land had to stay in the hands of those (not yet Islamized inhabitants living on it at the

time) as a *usufructus,* but its ownership and domination must stay as an eternal Muslim waqf for all generations to come until the Day of Judgment. It is clear that by recruiting such a prestigious source among the Rashidun to back their uncompromising demand for the entire land of Palestine, Hamas was addressing the entire Muslim audience and expecting their help. Knowing how much Umar was an exemplary caliph among caliphs and the image he created of a righteous and just ruler, it is clear why they chose his reputation and the institution of the caliphate to back their claim.

2. In Article 22, the Jews are presented as the enemies of the caliphate, because they triggered World War I to "wipe the caliphate out," a hint to the "Anglo-French conspiracy against the Ottoman Empire." This kind of accusation had been propagated by none other than Sayyid Qutb, the great guide of the Brothers until his execution in 1966 by Nasser. He had spent time in the United States and returned obsessed by hatred to the West and its values, which he viciously attacked in his writings. Prominent among them was his book *Our War with the Jews,* in which he dubbed them as the enemies of Allah and of Islam and, like other anti-Semites, imputed to them all the evils of the world, including the dismantling of the caliphate.

It would seem unrealistic today, that after the split of the Islamic world into fifty-seven separate countries, languages, and ethnic groups and in view of the prevailing personal, regional, and national jealousies among them that they could possibly unite under one rule. But it is a fact that the ideal persists, in any case among the fundamentalists who aspire to Sharia law in their countries. But among these groups that champion the caliphate, there are different orders and paces of execution. The Brothers, including Hamas, advocate the takeover of government in their countries and the enforcement of Sharia there, as they did in Gaza, before all countries who would have achieved the same could unite into a caliphate. But the Salafis and the Taliban profess the creation of a caliphate first, which would by definition be comprehensive enough to impose Sharia on all Muslims. The Brothers in Egypt have embraced a cautious and gradual method of introducing the Holy Law to all citizenry, lest sudden and all-encompassing Islamization deter and frighten hesitant and uncertain souls who have been corrupted by modernization, secularization, and Westernization. But there are also some aggressive currents, such as the Taliban in Afghanistan in the 1990s, the Gama'at in Egypt before they were wiped out by Mubarak, or the Armed Groups in Algeria, who fought and killed their countrymen mercilessly in order to impose their will.

Only now, as the Spring is beginning to show its fruits, for example in Tunisia and Egypt, will we be able to detect the method chosen by the new leaderships of those countries to implement their Islamization blueprint. Where there is no decision yet, like in Syria, Libya, and Yemen, it is too early to know who will rise and who will fall and for how long. One can imagine, however, that everywhere a settlement is agreed upon, the emerging ruler will have to explain where his legitimacy comes from. In Egypt and Tunisia, we saw a genuine effort to conduct a fair election campaign, to keep restraint, and to distance the military from the election process. These are signs of legitimization of government.

Conversely, in places where the struggle is continuing, there is no telling how it might be decided. But one thing is certain: the previous illegitimate rulers will not be back: there is necessity and urgency to replace them with others who can inspire legitimacy. But who are they? What do they stand for? Who can guarantee their behavior as long as the democratic game is not understood well enough to become an organic part of the local politics? And what is legitimacy after all? It can follow the Ferrero model of democracy, or the caliphate precedent as the fundamentalist would have it. Democracy has never been tried to its full in the Islamic world, and we are hardly watching its first steps and holding our collective breath for it to succeed. It is true that most current Spring movements in the Islamic world advocate slogans of democracy, but it is not clear at all whether any of them knows what they are talking about, for none of them had ever experienced Western-style democracy.

Democracy is not only elections, because, beyond a given method of electing leadership, it also means a state of mind that allows the media to act freely, respects the majority but protects the minority, does not pursue investigative journalists who publicize the corruption of the system, such as it is in the case of Pakistan and Turkey today, respects human rights, gives top adjudicating power to an independent judiciary, does not arbitrarily arrest its citizens, accusing them of plots against the government, refrains from incitement against its citizens and neighbors, advocates an open and liberal mode of government, and pursues a policy of good neighborliness with its neighbors. Where was there ever a paradise like this in the Islamic world? And where could such a regime materialize after so many years of oppression, corruption and travesty of justice? For a regime to be able to operate on such a standard, it has first to be legitimate. It is obvious that the

Spring broke out precisely in countries where the young people have had enough of tyrannical rule for decades, with no chance of change, for the rule of the fathers was to be taken up by their sons. In other words, the hopelessness of change was what pushed the young people to rebel. The demonstrators shouted: "Freedom! Democracy! Expel the Tyrant!" But we do not know what they meant, nor did they indicate what ought to be done to alter the situation. In most places we saw the same hypocrites and servile aides of the previous rulers, who had served them for years, suddenly turn over to the rebels. So people are suspicious and confused, not knowing whom to trust, convinced that whoever steals for you today will steal from you tomorrow.

At the height of the crisis, the only alternative to the crumbling rulers has seemed to be the Islamic state that the Muslim Brothers had consistently preached since their inception. They are on record as opposing democracy, for a human-made system cannot compete with divinely inspired Sharia. Thus, the latter, despite its problems and anachronism, still looks to the believers like the most trusted, known, and promising avenue. In other words, the caliphate was the only system that could lend legitimacy to the rulers, being based on Islamic tradition. For that reason, each time an existing system threatened to crumble, the caliphate alternative loomed in the horizon as the only acceptable alternative. But when we begin comparing it with democracy, we immediately realize that not only are they incompatible but they contradict each other in some very fundamental respects.

Some believe that fundamentalist movements that negate democracy would have stepped immediately into a Sharia caliphate-like state, as the Taliban did during their short stint in power (1996–2001) in Afghanistan. But the masses in the world of Islam have become so open to world media, to television, to the customs and standards of living in the West, to Internet and the social networks, and to the benefits of liberal democracy and human rights that they cannot be easily deprived from all that after decades of exposure. They are no longer prepared to accept oppression as a divine calamity; therefore the idea of a caliphate, which would be another kind of oppression from their point of view, would not be readily accepted without question.

Therefore, pragmatic Islamic movements, like those in Egypt and Tunisia, are compelled to pretend to behave democratically, to accustom the public to their style of rule before they begin imposing restrictions and gradually trapping the public into the incontrovertibility of Sharia law, which no individual in an Islamic society can resist without incurring the wrath of his environment. This method has already been dubbed: "One man, one vote, one time," meaning that following the one voluntary vote that has lent legitimacy to their rule, such fundamentalists would need no more legitimacy to rule, because they would be applying Sharia. For this reason, the early experiments we are witnessing in Egypt and Tunisia, as the test cases of the Islamic Spring, could be decisive for the fate of the entire Spring. For if these tests succeed in operating a modern and efficient Muslim society that enjoys freedom without the harassments that accompany puritanical Muslim societies, such as restrictions on women, public morals police, and fair elections in all levels of government, then the new, reformed style of the Muslim Brothers, which will be more moderate and sensitive than what they have been preaching for almost a century since their foundation, can perhaps produce a new, softer, feasible, and foundational Islam, a sort of revolutionary reform, instead of the restorative reform that they have advocated since their beginnings.

However, if the eternal values of Islam prevail with their conservative and fundamentalist leanings—as in the days of Ibn Taymiyyah in Egypt and Syria or the Wahhābis in Arabia, or the days of Banna and Qutb in Egypt again, and the clerics once again regard themselves as the watchdogs of the integrity of their faith in the face of Western cultural and civilizational onslaught—then major confrontations are to be expected between two styles of life, where not necessarily the stronger wins, but the one more doggedly committed to his version of Islam in the world, as has already been evident in many arenas of the Spring today. The days of the Islamic Spring have shown that even in Islamic societies that had taken large strides toward civil government, like Turkey and Tunisia, it was still possible to arrest the process with the help of the conservative and illiterate countryside, while the urban bourgeoisie watched with horror, helpless, as its great modernizing achievements rolled back toward their abrogation. What model of Islam these countries will choose when the dust settles, only time will tell.

The second issue the Islamic world will have to address in the post-Spring era is that of instability and weakness, especially of the failed states, as suggested by Yoel Guzansky and Benedetta Berti.[5] The authors claim that the uprisings across the Arab world that began in December 2010 were widely heralded as the catalyst for fundamental change in a region that desperately needed to be shaken. However, while the heterogeneous protest movements in the various Arab states were generally of one mind in demanding the end of authoritarian rule, in most cases they failed to produce a cohesive plan for the post-revolutionary transition. Apart from the partial exception of Tunisia (where the spark for the uprisings was first lit), the divisions within the protest movements, along with the absence of a functioning and developed civil society, have inhibited the process of political change. Further complicating efforts to establish a new political order has been the legitimacy deficit of existing political institutions and the resilience of networks of power and patronage.

As a result, the post-revolutionary period in countries where leaders have been toppled has been replete with challenges, including the exacerbation of preexisting divisions, rendering the creation of strong, functioning states extremely difficult. They claim that in general state weakness is not a new phenomenon in the Middle East and North Africa (MENA) region but has been significantly exacerbated during the last two years. State weakness can be measured by the degree of the regime's legitimacy, its capacity to deliver social and political goods, and its ability to guarantee a basic level of security. While states that fulfill these functions are considered strong and stable, a state that is utterly unable to meet any of these criteria is perceived as "failed."

They emphasize that pessimistic observers, including Henry Kissinger, have recently noted that lawlessness may come to dominate the Middle East. They point to Yemen, Libya, Iraq, and the Sinai Peninsula as examples of this "cascade of state failure." To be sure, this one-size-fits-all approach leaves much to be desired when referring to such a politically, economically, and culturally diverse region as the Middle East. Even so, there seems to be truth in the notion that the post-revolutionary stabilization period in most countries is witnessing the exacerbation of preexisting cleavages and weakening of central authority. Already prior to the Arab Spring events, the MENA region provided important examples for analyzing the problem of state weakness, with half of the twenty-two Arab League member states defined as weak states, varying between highly dysfunctional states like Yemen or Sudan and weak but far from collapsing countries like Lebanon. However, since the beginning of the Arab uprisings, there has been a general deterioration in the level of internal stability of MENA states.

For example, the new Libyan authorities have been confronting monumental difficulties in their effort to reassert control and accumulate sufficient legitimacy following their overthrow of the Qaddafi regime. The country is highly fragmented, with competing tribal loyalties having always taken precedence over a common national identity, and lacks strong, central political institutions. One of the toughest tasks the new government faces is how to assert authority over tribes, cities, and provinces, which are resisting attempts to bring about a measure of centralized control. This difficulty is related to the problem of establishing a monopoly on the use of force and dismantling existing armed groups. Their proliferation is especially a problem given that the Libyan security sector, already weak during the Qaddafi regime, has been in a nearly total state of disarray following Qaddafi's overthrow. Although security sector reforms are being implemented and a large-scale DDR (disarm, demobilize, reintegrate) program does exist, the establishment of a cohesive and well-functioning Libyan state seems to be a remote possibility for now.

Syria, of course, is currently the hottest of all Arab arenas. Even before the outbreak of the Syrian uprising in March 2011, Syria was listed as the forty-eighth most unstable state in the world by *Foreign Policy*'s index of Failed States. Now it ranks twenty-third. The initial clashes between the Syrian regime and the anti-Assad opposition forces have escalated exponentially in the past few months, leaving the country in a state of full civil war. The depth of the cleavage between the pro-regime forces and the opposition groups and the wounds that the ongoing war will leave on Syria's political and social fabric suggest that Syria's high degree of state weakness and instability will extend even to the post-conflict stage. Whoever will be left standing will face the daunting task of having to unite a deeply polarized country, rein in a vast number of active militias and armed groups, and rebuild social and political institutions. The case of Yemen, currently ranked as the eighth most unstable and weak state in the world, is even more extreme. The Yemeni authorities are trying to tackle simultaneously a violent uprising with sectarian connotations in the north, a separatist struggle in the south, and growing jihadist activities with global connections. This challenge is especially daunting as Yemen is also among the poorest and least developed states in region, with the central government lacking internal legitimacy or the capacity to deliver social and political goods. The ongoing turmoil in the region has accelerated existing trends that pose a number of important challenges to the human security of the region.

First, failing states represent a challenge to regional stability. This is especially the case because of the large involvement of external actors in the domestic affairs of weak and failing states. The weakness of the central government and the proliferation of groups competing with the state represent an excellent opportunity for external third parties seeking to expand their influence on the region. The Lebanese civil war between 1975 and 1990 serves as a reminder of the dangers of protagonists becoming surrogates for regional and international conflicts. Currently, both Iraq and Yemen are increasingly looking like potential arenas for similar struggles between the different regional and global powers invested in the region. Similarly, the conflict in Syria is becoming increasingly more regionalized.

Second, failing states are problematic from a human security and humanitarian perspective. Such states are often unable to provide security or basic social and political goods, contributing to precarious living conditions of the population. The recent example of famines in both Somalia and Yemen tragically highlight the human cost of prolonged internal instability and endemic state failure. Similarly, the ongoing war in Syria is resulting in a humanitarian crisis, with large numbers of both internally displaced persons within Syria and refugees seeking safety in neighboring states—Turkey, Jordan, Lebanon, and northern Iraq.

A third challenge stemming from failing states is terrorism. Failing states present international and regional terrorist organizations with a convenient base of operations and are more likely than other states to host such groups on their soil.

Fourth is the crime challenge. Similar to terrorist organizations, criminal organizations take advantage of governments' loose control in failing states to advance their interests.

A final security challenge is the increased threat of proliferation of nonconventional arms. As Syria implodes, the concern that Syria's chemical and biological weapons may not be secured or may be transferred by the regime to its Hezbollah ally has heightened.

The Islamic Spring has accelerated a preexisting trend within the MENA region, one characterized by state weakness and instability. This widespread weakness stems from a number of factors, including the unrepresentative and unpopular nature of the ruling political institutions, the lack of a cohesive citizenship discourse, the failure to provide social and political goods to all citizens, and the difficulties in preventing the proliferation of nonstate armed groups and alternative pockets of authority within the country's territory. Given the structural nature of the problems faced by MENA states, it is unlikely that the regime changes induced by the Arab uprisings will lead to a rapid improvement of the situation. As a result, at least in the short term, it is fair to expect continued instability and state weakness, with all that that implies for regional stability.

What's more, the longer and deeper the crisis, the greater the likelihood that other regional actors will become more involved by supporting one or another of the warring protagonists. This in turn will pose new challenges to regional peace and stability. Based on this analysis alone, the prospects for seeing the Spring as a positive watershed in the fortunes of these countries do not seem extremely bright. But perhaps some other additional elements will introduce some balancing points of variety, if not of optimism.

Few people realize how, in the long run, the current upheaval in the Muslim world will affect Israel in the most direct fashion. This is connected to the fact that Israel's 18 percent Muslim population (more than one million), which has seen both nationalism and Communism collapsing, has become so attached to the Muslim alternative that the Muslim Spring is its best occasion to see the wind blow in its sails and push it forward in unforeseeable directions. Already that undercurrent of Muslims in Israel has been on record as undermining state authority by acting in favor of Hamas, and their head, Sheikh Ra'id Salah, has been convicted for fund-raising for terrorist Islam. For example, in their fixation on the Judaization of Jerusalem, Salah and his movement has been inspiring Islamic causes of the Palestinians as echoed by Hamas. In one instance, pamphleteers wrote a 2006 piece in *Sawt al-Haq wa-l-Hurriya* (*Voice of Truth and Freedom*), the journal of the Islamic Movement centered in Umm al-Fahm in northern Israel and led by Ra'id Salah, where the "plan to Judaize Silwan" is discussed in great detail. The Islamic Movement, a local branch of the Muslim Brotherhood, brought to bear its standing in the forefront of organizing Israeli Arabs to identify themselves strictly as Palestinians, with Salah leading the campaign to "defend" Jerusalem from "destruction by Israel" and "liberate" it from Israeli "occupation," while the country in general, and Jerusalem in particular, had never known such an enormous development élan in all its history.[6]

Another unfounded claim of the Muslim movement against Israel, which is and will be further enhanced as the Muslim Spring unfolds, is the alleged Israeli plot to replace al-Aqsa Mosque with a third Jewish temple—despite the fact that the Israeli authorities have consistently restricted the movement of non-Muslims on the Temple Mount to the point where they have been accused of discrimination against Jews and Christians to favor Muslims. A pamphlet from the Islamic group

Jihad-Beit al-Makdas (the Jihad for Jerusalem) uses melodramatic language to further illustrate the evil intents of the Jews, accusing Zionists of attacking Jerusalem, Silwan—"the gateway to al-Aqsa Mosque"—and al-Aqsa Mosque itself, which is "the rock of grace of Jerusalem and the crown of the whole Islamic nation." The authors thank those "who protect al-Aqsa and its gates and the residents of the village of Silwan" and inform them that the way is clear "to the temple, from Silwan, the aristocratic, the symbol of steadfastness at the gates of al-Aqsa Mosque." The authors ask, "Would you like to be a guard [on watch] at the blessed al-Aqsa and nothing will pass by you?" and warn, "Do not let into your homes the flocks of the settlers." According to this line of thought, Silwan becomes the doorway through which the settlers are trying to Judaize Jerusalem and at the same time enter the Temple Mount in order to dismantle al-Aqsa and rebuild the temple. The steps that are being carried out, according to Islamic spokespersons, will lead to a third intifada.

As Shaul Bartal, a prominent researcher on Palestinian affairs, has often noted,[7] the Palestinian Arab assault on the Jewish connection to Jerusalem continues apace, aided and abetted not only by radical Muslims or angry Silwanites but by fellow travelers in the media and in academia, including Israeli Jews. Take for example the tours carried out by Emek Shaveh, an Israeli nonprofit organization, and Palestinian residents of Silwan, with a view to rebuffing the "political archaeology of the Jews" and to prove the area's "true" archaeological significance. Emek Shaveh's founder, Yonathan Mizrachi, who has voluntarily left his job at Israel's Antiquities Authority, spares no effort to downplay the Jewish biblical history of the area. As he put it: "After three hours on [an Israeli-organized] tour, you are convinced that you are at a totally Jewish site where evidence of Canaanite, Byzantine, and Muslim, and, of course, Palestinian [civilizations] are pushed aside. Jerusalem has 4,000 years of history. They only focus on the marvelous stories of King Solomon, David, and Hezekiyah, of which, by the way, they haven't found any archaeological evidence that ties them to the place."

Mizrachi's Website contains an essay of over 5,000 words—"Archaeology in Silwan"—which transforms archaeology into a handmaiden of social science pieties and criticizes even the use of the phrase City of David as "a manifestation of settler objectives." In doing so, he also manages to rewrite history, claiming falsely that "during the main periods of prosperity under the kingdom of Judah . . . the cultural identity of the town and its inhabitants was contested." Bartal concludes that "sadly, the battle over Silwan (and for that matter the wider Palestinian-Israeli conflict) is likely to continue as long as Palestinian Arabs and their brethren refuse to recognize that another people, the Jews, have a claim to the Land of Israel." Nothing has given more momentum to these anti-Israeli claims than the present Islamic Spring, hence the vitality for Israel's future or the turn it might take.

Sensing the fatefulness of that trend, even the non-Hamas Palestinian leaders who have negotiated and signed the Oslo Accords seized upon the nineteenth anniversary of that event (September 13, 2012), which coincided with the successes of the Islamic Spring in Tunisia, Egypt, and Libya, with more promise to come, to signal their desire to withdraw from the accords. For if they stand under the Spring to win it all, after the Jews are disinherited from the land, why should they hold on to their compromises?

They say that the accords, which were signed Sept 13, 1993, were meant to be an interim agreement leading to a final peace agreement and an independent Palestinian state within five years. Palestinian National Initiative leader Mustafa Barghouti said the accords turned out to be "a transition to nothing," and had been used as a cover by Israel "to consolidate a system of apartheid." "We as Palestinians need to liberate ourselves from the terrible conditions of the agreement," through popular resistance, national unity and boycott, divestment and sanctions, Barghouti told Ma'an News Agency. He charged that the Palestinian side has committed to the agreement while Israel selectively implemented the accords to its benefit, Barghouti said, adding that 19 years on the concept of the two-state solution was at risk due to Israeli settlement building. He just forgot to mention that Oslo was signed to commit all the Palestinians, while half the Palestinian people (the Hamas) has elected to reject it, and that the first clause of Oslo was the end to violence, while Israel has suffered more casualties from Palestinian terror after Oslo than before it.

Another Fatah leader, Mahmoud al-Aloul on the PA to abolish the Oslo Accords, as Israel had refused to commit to its obligations and instead continued land grabs and settlement expansion in the West Bank. He emphasized that negotiations toward a final peace agreement won't succeed because "Israel doesn't want peace", al-Aloul added. The Popular Front for the Liberation of Palestine also called on the PA to disengage from all agreements with Israel, and be free of political and economic restrictions imposed by the Oslo Accords. It also urged the

Ramallah government of the PA to end security coordination with Israel and implement national unity, the leftist faction said in a statement.

Palestinian negotiator, Saeb Arikat, noted "Israel's failure to abide by its signed commitments", in a statement marking the anniversary. "Most of the Israeli settlements and their associated infrastructure have been built during the past 19 years. The number of settlers has more than doubled during this time, while forced displacement, home demolitions, ID revocations and land confiscations continue to be a daily reality in Palestine." Arikat added: "The interim agreements were supposed to last for five years. But what we see two decades later is apartheid rather than freedom and independence." Arikat blamed the international community for failing to hold Israel accountable for its violations. "Our hope for peace and justice has been destroyed by Israeli bulldozers and a culture of racism and hatred espoused within Israeli society. This horrific reality has been facilitated by the immunity which Israel has been granted by the international community." He just forgot to mention, that the final results of negotiations cannot be pre-determined before negotiations started; that the West Bank is a disputed territory which only negotiations and compromise can settle; and that the Palestinians have signed Oslo II which divides the West Bank into three zones (A, B, C) between the parties until a new agreement supplants that arrangement. No new agreement is known to have emerged all those years.

Now, since the beginning of the upheaval in the West Bank in September, 2012, it is evident that the Islamic Spring (no longer a Palestinian Intifada) is unfolding within the walls, and that at some point not only the Palestinians will get rid of the present whimpy Abu Mazen and Fayyad, if they do not resign of their own volition, but Islam will come to sweep the scene and the Hamas renown will rocket skyhigh, with the support of the successful Muslim Brothers wherever they have already established themselves. The Oslo Accords have been the focus of demonstrations across the West Bank in September. Protesters angry at rising prices complained that the economic sections of the treaty have been implemented by Israel selectively and mostly to its benefit, a position shared by UN agencies and economists.

Israeli Arabs, led by Ra'id, will soon follow in open rebellion against Israel as part of the Islamic Spring, and their confrontation with Israel will become inevitable. Only following a bloodbath and total defeat would those manifestations of the Islamic Spring among the Palestinians be removed so they no longer pose a threat to the only country in the Middle East not directly participating in the Islamic Spring.

Notes

1. In the original: *mal nommer les choses c'est ajouter au malheur du monde.*
2. See, for example, R. Israeli, *Islamikaze: Manifestations of Islamic Martyrology,* Frank Cass, London, 2003, especially chap. 1, which samples the reactions in the Muslim world to the 9/11 horror.
3. For the significance of the term, see ibid.
4. During the Muslim Rebellion in Yunnan, China, in the nineteenth century, its leader, Du Wenxiu, assumed the title of *Qa'id Jami' al-Muslimin* (the Commander of all Muslims).
5. Moshe Dayan Center publishes *Tel Aviv Notes,* an analytical update on current affairs in the Middle East, on the tenth and twenty-sixth of every month, as well as the occasional special edition, *Instability and State Weakness*: http://www.dayan.tau.ac.il. "The 'Post-Revolutionary' Challenge in the Arab World," by Yoel Guzansky and Benedetta Berti.
6. See Raphael Israeli, "The Islamic Movement in Israel," *Jerusalem Letter,* Jerusalem Center for Public Affairs, Oct. 15, 1999; L. Barkan, "The Islamic Movement in Israel: Switching Focus from Jerusalem to the Palestinian Cause," Inquiry & Analysis Series, report no. 628, Middle East Media Research Institute, Washington DC, July 30, 2010.
7. Bartal is a lecturer on Palestinian affairs at Bar Ilan University and author of *The Fedayeen Emerge, The Palestine-Israel Conflict, 1949–1956* (Bloomington: Authorhouse, 2011).

6

The Islamic Axis of Change in the Midst of Conflict

One of the most remarkable manifestations of Islam on the international level as a result of the domestic upheaval it created after 1989 has been its new worldwide thrust of expansion, both demographically and culturally, as a way to strengthen its actual presence in the West, especially Europe, with a view of seeking dominance there. At stake has been the third Muslim invasion in Europe, which refers to the historical sequel whereby the first invasion into Europe was made by the Arabs in the seventh century from the south, when they launched the onslaught from Morocco on southern Europe until they were arrested by the Charles Martel victory in 732 near Poitiers, and the eight centuries of Muslim rule in Andalusia that ended with their final retreat from Grenada in 1492, under the relentless advance of the Spanish Reconquista.

But when they were removed from the Iberian Peninsula in the fifteenth century, they launched the second invasion by the Ottoman Muslims from the East, which led to the fall of Byzantine Constantinople in 1453 into their hands and went as far as the gates of Vienna before they were arrested and thwarted in 1683, ultimately leading to the breakup of the Ottoman Empire during World War I. The current third invasion is occurring through immigration and the demographic flooding of Europe and other Western countries,[1] together with a campaign of *da'wah* to propagate Islam, aided by a terrorist wave to intimidate the West.

International terrorism has not been limited to the confines of the Islamist struggle against the West in the international arena but has expanded into the domestic scene in Islamic countries where local Islamist oppositions aspire to seize power from current illegitimate rulers who are usually supported by the West. This is the genesis of the Bali, Casablanca, Istanbul, Sinai, Amman, Cairo, Riyadh, and Jeddah acts of terror that were primarily directed against visiting aliens after 9/11, in order to destroy the tourist source of income or the economic base of those hated regimes. More ominously, many a homegrown Islamist, who was allowed to sow lethal propaganda in Western democracies where he had initially sought asylum from oppression in his land of origin, has used his familiarity with his adoptive land to turn it into his object of terror. This is the background for the 9/11, Madrid (March 2004), and London (July 2005) horrors.

For too long the world had accepted the Palestinian hijackings of the 1970s and 1980s, which had inaugurated this era of international terrorism, as a "natural" calamity. Instead of fighting against them and uprooting them, Western governments and passengers accepted being stripped at airports and searched, having their otherwise sacrosanct privacy encroached upon and trampled in public, paying ever-increasing airfares in order to cover security costs, and repeating the mantra that a "solution to the Palestinian conflict will resolve the problem." The United States has reversed itself and resolved to fight only following the 9/11 attacks on its soil; Madrid has elected to yield to the terrorists' demands by ousting its prime minister, Aznar; and London changed the rules only after it was rocked by a series of attacks on its public transportation.

After the Van Gogh murder in the Netherlands in 2004 and then the anti-Denmark outburst of Muslim rage in the Cartoon Affair of early 2006, the public debate was turned on its head. Previously, far from recognizing that the fight against terrorism in Iraq, Afghanistan, and worldwide had been launched by the United States as a defensive measure after it was attacked on its home territory, US detractors in Europe and the Muslim world claimed that American offensive moves in those countries prompted terrorism, exactly as it was Israel's "injustices" toward the Palestinians that had triggered terrorism in the first place. Cause and effect were reversed. So instead of joining the United States in its universal struggle against terrorism and ridding themselves of a menace, they blamed the violence on American and Israeli policies, thus unwittingly becoming its unwilling accomplices and its unsuspecting next victims.

But the Cartoon Affair of early 2006 has dramatically demonstrated that the general Muslim wrath against the West and Israel had been convoluted for years due to the measures taken by Muslim governments who were afraid of American retribution. It is also likely that the wrath was restrained until Muslims were confident that their presence in the

West constituted a critical mass, for they became numerous enough to instill fear of potential civil disorder in the European governments. The fear from American retribution, which was brought to bear in Afghanistan and Iraq, may have been somewhat mitigated by the United States' proven constraint to absorb the atrocious behavior of Syria and Iran, like the havoc of the 1973 oil price rise in which it quadrupled. In that regard, one might say that the Arabs were constantly testing the limits of what the United States will tolerate, but they were also aware that the United States turned a blind eye to misdemeanors to secure uninterrupted oil supplies. Thus the United States (and other Western countries, for that matter) were seen to favor totalitarian rulers in the Middle East, fearful of the regimes that might replace them—the "devil they knew" approach. No American president wished to be responsible for creating another Iran, after the ignominious behavior of Carter vis-à-vis the shah in the 1970s.

The waves of recriminations of the Muslim world against the West and Israel have been expressed in the rise of Muslim parties in Turkey, Egypt, Jordan, and the Palestinian Authority; in the unbridled desire of the Iranians to go nuclear; and in the rhetoric of President Ahmadinejad against Western values and the Jews in general, to the point of denying the Shoah in blatant terms: all were indications of the spreading anti-Western antagonism in Islam. The zeal in the Islamic world was directed not only against Israel and the West but aimed primarily to sweep out of power their own Western-allied regimes, which were regarded as American stooges.

As the major Egyptian paper *al-Ahram* put it, "Religious identity has replaced nationalist ideology,"[2] and that applied not only in Muslim countries but also amid Muslim minorities throughout their diasporas. This meant that Muslim terrorism would continue to rise in both Europe and the Muslim world. One has to realize nevertheless the distortions of the basic tenets of Islam by both scholars and politicians, who wished to depict a more benign and less menacing picture of the Islamic rise than it is in fact. This was done through two distinctions that have become conventional wisdom among both critics and proponents of Islam. One is the artificial bifurcation between the so-called Islamists or radicals, who spoil the lot by their violent deeds and lend a bad reputation to the majority of their coreligionists by waging war against the West and Israel, and the majority itself, which is arguably peace-loving and shunning violence and has no quarrel with West. The other artificial, and equally spurious, distinction would have us believe that Judeophobia, which is an attenuated sort of anti-Semitism posing as anti-Zionist and anti-Israel, had nothing to do with anti-Semitism and that, while Islam as a whole carried no traces of anti-Semitism and claimed that its present anti-Jewish manifestations were no more than a much less lethal and vastly less threatening Judeophobia. It is clear that these "scientific" distinctions, though pursued by some scholars of reputation, have much more to do with political correctness with a degree of sheepish dhimmi-like submissiveness, for fear of being accused of racism, than with historical reality.

The fact is that throughout the Muslim world the legitimacy of Israel is challenged and the Holocaust is denied, as evidenced by the popularity there of such Holocaust deniers as Robert Faurisson, Roger Garaudy, or David Irving, by the prohibition of *Schindler's List* on their screens, and by the violent declarations of the Iranian leadership on both scores. This is a common denominator among most Muslims: nothing separates radicals and moderates there, exactly as anti-Jewish stereotypes, be they anti-Semitic or Judeophobic, are current among them all, with few exceptions. That is the reason why we find them contradicting themselves on the Shoah, denying it on the one hand and wishing Hitler had brought his anti-Jewish annihilation plan to completion on the other, and urging a "scholarly, free, and objective" research of the Holocaust in order to prove that it never was.

Similarly, the belief in and the spread of the *Protocols of the Elders of Zion,* the blood libel, the poisoning of wells by Jews, and conspiracy theories are recurring themes in Palestinian (not only Hamas) as well as mainstream Egyptian, Jordanian, Saudi, Pakistani, and others' writings, systems of beliefs, and propaganda. Genocidal threats against the Jews used to abound, not only in bin Laden's statements and in Ahmadinejad's delusions, but also in columns of Egyptian, Saudi, Palestinian, and other respectable, mainstream newspapers. Is this Judeophobia of the moderates or plain anti-Semitism of the Islamists? Words have a significance, and it is imperative to streamline our vocabulary; otherwise we are under the permanent threat of losing our ability to express what we mean or to comprehend what we are told.

Matters are further complicated and made less comprehensible to Western minds by the paranoia and conspiracy theories that are widespread in the Muslims world, among Islamists and others, whether modern and Western-educated or traditionalist and obscurantist. Those theories that are rampant even among Muslims living in the West insist that world leaders who support Israel are Jewish (like presidents Reagan and Bush), that the United Nations, of all places, is the mastermind of the Jews, who utilize it as a tool for their world dominion, and that the major violent acts that shook the world, such as the World Wars, world revolutions, and 9/11, are all the fruit of Jewish imagination and execution. Their minds are so permeated with these nonsensical theories that they become impervious to logical, rational debate that is open to argument, discussion, and conviction.

Therefore, the difficulty of dealing with Muslim minds consists not only in removing the mountains of pure delusion that choke and obstruct their free thinking, but also in persuading them that the very attempt to counter-argue those futilities is not necessarily part of the world conspiracy that is being woven against them. It is possible to explain their imaginary picture of the world through their need to project on their enemies the analytical shortcomings that bewitch them, but it is impossible to move them away from the illusory scenarios that they have constructed around themselves and then cling to with a tenacity that defies and contradicts Western standards of conduct. The result is that even when Muslims initiate and launch an act of violence, they accuse the West of what led to it as an act of aggression, of which they are the victims and which deserves their retaliation.

One has to consider not only the direct victims of terrorism, those who perished instantly, but also those left behind, either wounded or maimed or otherwise traumatized by the horror he or she experienced. There is no denying that the Muslims who shun violence and terror also suffer from the adverse effects that terrorism has on their reputation, on their collective consciousness, and on the circumspect conduct of their neighbors, colleagues, and passersby toward them when they are identified as Muslims. But their justified grievances have to be directed toward their fellow Muslims—terrorists who by their behavior have soiled the Muslim collective.

What of the individuals from the host-cultures of Europe, who see their hospitality to asylum-seekers rewarded with acts of terror? For example, the driver of the bus blown apart by one of the London bombs on July 7, 2005, spoke a year later about the devastating effects on his life and how he has been left permanently traumatized. George Psaradakis, fifty, bravely returned to work after the explosion, but he admitted that the events of a year earlier were always on his mind.

> The father-of-three recalled in graphic detail the shock of being in the driver's seat when "suicide bomber" Hasib Hussain, 18,

from Leeds, killed himself and 13 passengers in Tavistock Square. Mr Psaradakis believed it was a miracle he was still alive after surviving the carnage, but hoped his life would finally get back to some form of normality. "It has traumatized me so deeply—the events of a year ago are indelibly on my mind," he said during the longest interview he has given since the bombings. The Greek-born bus driver recalled how he moved to London in 1972 to stay with relatives after deciding to leave the rug trade where he had been employed most of his life. Remembering every detail of that fateful morning, he recalled being in a happy mood, partly because London had just won the race to stage the 2012 Olympics, and because he was due to have a long weekend break with his wife Andriani and children when his shift finished. He started work at 5.30am, completing two rounds before grabbing a cup of coffee and starting another journey on the number 30 bus from Marble Arch to Stratford. As he approached Baker Street he received a message from his central control that there was a problem on the underground and extra passengers would be using buses. "I remember thinking to myself that it was going to be a busy trip and I wanted to help the public as much as I could. There were only a few passengers on my bus, but as I approached Baker Street I could see hundreds of people waiting for buses."[3]

The driver went on with his chilling account: "I stopped and my bus quickly filled up, so I moved on toward Euston. I was driving very slowly because traffic was building up and the pavements were full of people. Pedestrians were in the road." Police had set up diversions around Euston because of the bombs which had exploded on the underground, forcing Mr Psaradakis to turn into Tavistock Square. "I thought something was wrong because I could sense it, but I did not know what had happened. I announced that it might be quicker to walk and a large number of passengers got off." Mr Psaradakis called to a traffic warden to ask the name of the road, and as he moved off the bomb exploded. "It was a bang. For a split second I thought I had hit something. It never crossed my mind that it was a bomb. Hundreds of things were going through my mind in slow motion. I saw debris flying around, the windscreen blew out, but absolutely nothing touched me" . . . "I felt dust in my hair. I was just stunned and puzzled. I thought, oh my God. I don't remember how I got out of my cab but I glanced to the back of the bus and I saw it was a bomb because of the devastation." Mr Psaradakis saw some horrific sights as passengers and bystanders lay on the road after being caught up in the blast, some obviously dead. "Another bomb exploded inside me—it was carnage, too gruesome to go into detail. It was death—I could feel it, I could smell it. Most of the people I saw were young, they had been so full of life. I felt devastated because they had been under my care. The fact that someone could jump on the bus and kill my passengers in such a cowardly way was devastating. I still have utter contempt for the people who carried out the bombings. It was

> barbaric and they achieved nothing but killing innocent people." Mr Psaradakis tried to help people who were lying injured in the road, but admitted he was in a state of panic. "I was shaking and crying—I was overwhelmed. Everyone treated each other like a sister or brother. A plain clothes policeman held me to stop me shaking. I learned later that he was injured. I saw him on a stretcher with an oxygen mask over his face. He looked at me and gave me a thumbs up sign." Mr Psaradakis phoned his wife and he said in a calm voice that many of his passengers had died. He paid tribute to the emergency services and other helpers who treated the survivors, adding that good had prevailed over the evil of the bombings. "It was human nature at its best. Everyone was caring for someone else." Mr Psaradakis was checked over at a hospital before going to his brother's house to be reunited with his family. George admitted the bombings had affected his entire family. He is moody, can no longer watch violent films or listen to loud music but has coped with being back at work, even when he drives on the same number 30 bus route. He has thought about finding a different job, but he loves driving buses in London and loves living in the capital in spite of the increased threat of terrorist attacks. Mr Psaradakis said his Christian faith had helped him cope with the past year and revealed that every Sunday he lights a candle in church for the victims. He feels sympathy for the parents of the bombers. "It must have been devastating for them." Like other people caught up in the bombings, George has still not received any compensation, but prefers to talk about the future. "I hope that after today the healing process will begin."[4]

All these facets of Muslim terrorism, which require not only an objective reporting for what they are but also an attempt to comprehend the mechanics, temptations, motivations, and aspirations evinced by the terrorists themselves. This information must then be supplemented by the role of the media in diffusing the data among the masses. The media create immediacy but also inaccuracy inasmuch as unchecked and unverified reports sometimes prove premature and have to be reversed or corrected. Very often a stand is taken by certain media toward acts of terror, either leaning toward understanding the terrorists or ruthlessly censuring them, often without preserving the equilibrium between report and commentary, fact and emotion, sympathy and criticism, manipulation and straightforward information, thereby supplying the terrorists with what Margaret Thatcher called the "oxygen of publicity." Ideological writing that relies on a political agenda to educate and influence readers instead of selflessly and honestly striving to inform them: this is the difference between good journalism and journalistic spins. Are the media actors in the scene or merely acting as mirrors (as the *Daily Mirror* suggests) of events? Consider the following excerpts from a lead article in a major British medium:

> Strangely, the story didn't appear on the BBC News website last night. But apparently the internet and digital TV have supplanted what is now called the "mainstream media" to the extent that BBC1 has lost a million viewers in the past year. Technology is responsible for a dual phenomenon. We are seeing a mass opening up as people are able to contribute directly to the reporting and discussion of news, whether through the internet or (as on July 7 last year) using camera- and video-phones. But we are also seeing a closing down. The proliferation of news outlets means we increasingly receive narrow-casting rather than broadcasting: news tailored not for everyone, but for us and people like us. These developments are entwined—we cannot have the one without the other. But they do make the idea of a monolithic state broadcaster seem sadly 20th century.[5]

People do not simply read, view, or listen to the media but respond to it, and their outrage must be heeded lest the medium lose its constituency. A case in point was the anniversary of the London bombings, when bereaved relatives and survivors reacted angrily after a video of one of the July 7 London bombers was broadcast on the eve of the first anniversary of the attacks. The statement of one the Islamikaze terrorists, Shehzad Tanweer from Leeds, was released and was obviously designed to cause "maximum hurt and distress" to the families of the victims, the way Hamas and Hezbollah terrorists in the Middle East delight in perturbing families of their victims and causing them pain and despair. Tanweer is seen in the video wearing a head scarf and jabbing his finger at the camera. "What you have witnessed now is only the beginning of a string of attacks that will continue and become stronger," he says.

The video, which also featured a statement from Ayman al-Zawahiri, al-Qaida's second-in-command, was broadcast by the Al Jazeera television station, which specializes in torturing families of victims, after being produced by sources associated with previous al-Qaida communications. Tanweer's statement was cut with footage of unidentified people experimenting with explosives and images of an unidentified man circling points on a map of London. It also showed armed terrorists. Scotland Yard said its anti-terrorist investigators would subject the video to the same scrutiny brought to bear on footage released in September 2005 by Mohammed Sidique Khan, Tanweer's fellow terrorist and the leader of the attackers.

Nader Mozakka, whose wife Behnaz died in the Tube attack near King's Cross, said the video and its timing were abhorrent. "It is like a smack in the face—the timing especially," he said. "They have released it at the time when a lot of survivors are going through hell." Jacqui Putnam, fifty-five, who was on the Tube at Edgware Road, said the video seemed designed to taint the first anniversary of the attacks. "Nothing is going to overshadow this anniversary," she said. "We are just going to mourn the dead and show they are not going to intimidate us. Whatever they think the reaction will be, it won't be. These people don't understand us, which is why they thought they could frighten people off the Underground." Like Khan, Tanweer used Islamic jihadi rhetoric on his video, knowing that it would be broadcast to make an impact of intimidation, threatening more attacks until troops leave Afghanistan and Iraq and British support for the United States and Israel stops.

Investigators have concluded that Khan's video was probably made when he and Tanweer were in Pakistan in late 2004 and in early 2005. Tanweer's recording is likely to have been made at the same time and by the same people. It has come as little surprise that Tanweer also made a video testament. Andy Hayman, the Metropolitan Police assistant commissioner, said: "We are aware of the tape and this will form part of our investigation. There can be no doubt that the release of the video at this time can only cause maximum hurt and distress to the families and friends of those who died on 7/7 and the hundreds who were injured." The fact that the video was released by those involved in, or close to, al-Qaida reinforces the suspicion that the London bombings were an al-Qaida-inspired episode. It is still unclear, however, what foreign direction, if any, the four bombers received. Investigators still believe the attackers were a self-contained unit who made their peroxide chemical bombs for around £8,000.[6]

When conscientious and knowledgeable journalists dare to confront, interesting reporting results, which sheds light on events and instructs the populace. BBC1's John Ware presented a *Panorama* program in which a healthy, no-frill confrontation with his Muslim panelists generated an immensely revealing trove of information and lessons that could be drawn from it.

> Panelist Iqbal Sacranie, secretary-general of the Muslim Council of Britain (MCB), said he did not believe in double standards, and if affiliates of the MCB, like *Markazi* Jamiat Ahle Hadith (the Central Association of the People of Hadith), want to say that the ways of Jews and Christians are "based on sick or deviant views," then, as

> far as he is concerned, it's merely part of the "diversity that exists in the community." Perhaps one should at least be thankful, according to a viewer, that he did not prefix *diversity* with that mindless adjective *rich*.
>
> This is the man who had been campaigning, with no little success, for the government to imprison people for seven years for inciting religious, that is Islamic, hatred. Yet at a time when Islamist fanatics were blowing up commuters, he was not bothered by his own members holding people of other faiths in moral contempt. This was the man who thought that death was "too easy" for Salman Rushdie. This was the man who still contended that the *Satanic Verses* should be banned. He thought that one ought to respect the freedom of expression but that one also expected freedom of expression to be exercised with responsibility (unless, it seemed, that freedom was exercised by one of the MCB's affiliates). This was the man who praised Hamas leader Sheikh Yassin, the architect of the suicide-bomb campaign in Israel, as a "renowned Islamic scholar." Another was Inayat Bunglawala, MCB media secretary, who only months before September 11, 2001, was a propagandist for Osama bin Laden.

Naturally, the MCB has accused the BBC of Islamophobia in screening John Ware's sharp and timely *Panorama* investigation into the ideology of so-called moderate community leaders. Said Andrew Anthony:

> The last time I checked my dictionary, "phobia" meant "fear" and it would seem entirely rational, if I were a Jew or a Christian, to fear anyone who called me sick or deviant. No doubt, by Sir Iqbal's reckoning, such logic is Islamophobic rather than, say, an example of the diversity that exists in the community. But then the MCB's standard response to any form of criticism is to shout "Islamophobia" at the top of its voice. It's to Ware's and the BBC's credit that they were not deterred by such shameless victim posturing. Sacranie has been at the forefront of many political campaigns of late and Ware gave him the kind of grilling that politicians routinely receive on Newsnight. He responded with all the incoherence and evasion of a man who has grown used to an easy ride from the media.
>
> One outraged "liberal" critic has since accused Ware of McCarthyism. However, there's a much better word to describe what Ware did in Panorama. It refers to the dogged process of finding out facts, scrutinising inconsistencies and asking difficult questions. It's called journalism.[7]

Europe, like the rest of the world, was stunned by the horrors of 9/11. Western delegations and leaders poured into Washington DC to present their condolences and sympathies to the United States. But as soon as the United States began to react to terrorism by fighting it actively, first in Afghanistan and then in Iraq, it found itself almost alone, but for the loyalty of Tony Blair and John Howard, who harnessed the resources of their countries (Britain and Australia) to that battle. Moreover, many Europeans elected their narrow and immediate national interests over the eradication of Saddam's regime, and, instead of instilling into their citizenry the need to stand up to new terrorist barbarians, they behaved like "soft" states that had lost the will to stand up for their values and future. It is worth recalling that the rich and powerful empires of Rome, Persia, Byzantium, and China, living in their self-contentment, had much to lose and were unwilling to fight anymore. These empires subsequently lost the battles to the Vandals, the Arabs, the Turks, and the Mongols (and then the Manchus), respectively, because the latter had nothing to lose and looked with contempt upon life, but coveted the wealth of their neighbors and concluded that it behooved them to inherit it: rather than abandon it in the hands of the declining empires, they attacked and destroyed.

People should learn, if not from others' experience, then at the very least from their own, from the antecedents that have tormented their own cultures when not heeded by their peers and cultural mates. Disturbing warning signs went unnoticed or denied in Western countries, then hit the peripheral areas of the Muslim world too. Canada and Australia, and to some extent the countries of Asia, fell into that syndrome of denial until they were shaken up and forced to listen, often at a price. At the core of Muslim presence in Europe are countries including Britain, France, and Germany, for example, which lacked law enforcement against terrorists, since they systematically preferred their human rights and apparent safety by appeasement over defensive measures to protect their citizens and way of life. Muslim immigrants, many of whom were accustomed to the often abusive law of their countries of origin, flooded by the millions to the heart of Europe; but even as clear threats of jihad were being heard in London and Paris, these threats were for the most part ignored by European governments.

The writing was on the wall, but British Home Secretary Jack Straw failed to read, see, and hear it. His liberal policy, for which he would repent after it was too late, was more convenient to dismiss than to heed the menace of terror. In so doing, he acted with irresponsibility, and that is the only measure to judge a government: not by its liberal intentions, good-hearted policies, or idealistic values, but by its failure to defend its citizens, by allowing terrorists to use Britain to wreak havoc on others, and by its myopic understanding of the situation that was due to its ideological blinders. It is a fact that too little and too late the same British government has had to reverse its policies and to seek even harsher measures than public opinion or the Parliament would allow, which is an indication of its inability to foresee what was coming and to prepare its citizenry before disaster struck.

The United States was no different, for in spite of the documentary evidence gathered on film by Steve Emerson in the early 1990s under the threatening title *Jihad in America,* the US approach to potential terrorists was very human and liberal: Muslim associations were allowed to collect money under the cover of "charitable" institutions, and even military training with live ammunition that Emerson documented in New Jersey, partly under the doctrinal supervision of the blind Sheikh Abdel-Rahman, a fugitive from Egyptian law. While this was not sufficient to awaken the FBI to its responsibilities of internal security, the first attempted sabotage of one of the Twin Towers in 1993 brought about the arrest of Sheikh Abdel-Rahman, who had masterminded it.

Both models of Western democracy, the United States and Britain, needed a traumatic jolt before they moved to act. In the United States, it would be the watershed event of 9/11; in London, the July 7, 2005 bombings. And in other countries: in Spain, the March 2004 Madrid train bombings; in France the violent riots of 2005; in the Netherlands, the van Gogh murder; and finally in Scandinavia, the Cartoon Affair. In all those instances, the jolt would be brutal, for it would totter the naiveté of the European populations, which had believed in peaceful coexistence with the Muslim immigrant populations and in the feasibility of their integration into European culture and society.

Take, for example, the case of Abu Hamza al-Masri, who took refuge in Britain in 1994. He never hid his destructive intentions or his subversive plans, but he was not heeded until he was convicted in early 2006 for the very same crimes that he had committed throughout the previous decade. That means that what had changed was not the man or his deeds but the permissive attitude of Jack Straw and his likes, which was reversed by the London terror of July 2005. It was, in effect, closing the doors of the barn after the horses had run away. Abu Hamza, of Egyptian origin, arrived in London and became the imam of the Finsbury Park Mosque. He headed the Ansar al-Sharia (Supporters of the Sharia), a movement that would have surely been outlawed in Cairo, wherein he propagated for the violent Algerian Armed Islamic Group (GIA). Both his native Egypt and Yemen demanded his extradition. He emerged from a background of moral corruption, something that is sure to have made him more radical than others.[8] He moved to Afghanistan with his family prior to the Taliban regime at a time when the Islamikaze[9] camps were disseminated in the various domains of the regional warlords.[10] He fought against the withdrawing Soviet forces and was severely injured by a landmine, which removed both his hands and destroyed one of his eyes.

In 1994, Abu Hamza, a civil engineer by training, found refuge in London at a time when the entire West was off its guard with respect to the international Islamic terrorist networks that were being erected in its midst. And there he founded his Ansar al-Sharia organization. Reminiscing on that period, he complained that while he had never lived off his hosts' money, those British "infidels" levied heavy taxes on him when he worked for them as an engineer, and that justified his latter attacks against the West which "had plundered the lands of Islam." He never explained why he chose to live in the land of his alleged "robbers," unless we take his words at face value: "I am a cripple and I use their country to spread good, to counter the British authorities who use it to spread corruption." In spite of his continuous complaints that he was persecuted by the authorities, his Muslim activities went unhindered, until he was briefly arrested in May 1999 and then released, and finally arrested again in May 2004, and indicted and convicted in 2005–06 in the aftermath of the London bombings.

On his Internet site he claimed that Yemen was the best launching pad after Afghanistan for the Islamic Revolution that was to spread worldwide.[11] And it was from Yemen that he directed his attention in 1998 after having left his London mosque to take care of his "Aden Abyan Muslim Army." He apparently masterminded an abortive attempt against the life of the Yemeni president and the kidnapping of foreign tourists. In a press conference that he conducted in London in January 2000, he called for the overthrow of the Yemeni regime and urged foreign visitors to leave Yemeni soil. And in a letter in the London-based Arabic daily *Al-Hayat,* he warned the ambassadors of Britain and the United States that they should leave Yemen, lest a painful strike against "the enemies of Islam" be carried out against them. He also attacked Arab monarchs and depicted the deceased King Hussein of Jordan as "roasting in Hell."[12]

Al-Masri has also shown aggressive concern for Muslim communities under pressure or threat. In 1999 he convened a conference on Chechen Muslims and incited his audience against a group of Russian reporters who were on hand to cover the debates. On the same occasion, he voiced support for the Chechen attacks in Moscow in the summer of that year.[13] All this took place under the open eyes of the British authorities, who saw not and cared not, foolishly believing that words did not hurt and that deeds would not follow incitement, contrary to all known precedents of hate literature, anti-Semitism, and terrorism, in which defining the enemy and dehumanizing him is a precursor to delegitimizing and ultimately to using violence against him.

Somehow, Jack Straw thought that Britain was immune to that law. Abu Hamza's choice of Yemen as the ideal place to launch the Muslim Revolution emanated from the fact that it was the only country in the Arabian Peninsula that had not yet "surrendered to the United Snakes [*sic*] of America," and he was certain that after the takeover of that country by the Islamists, other countries would fall through the domino effect. He denied in one of his interviews that he had called upon his followers to kill foreigners in Yemen, specifying that he meant infidels, unless they converted to Islam, paid the poll tax (*jizya*) that dhimmis (protected non-Muslims) were obliged to under the rules of the *dhimma,* or entered into a pact that guaranteed their safety in Sharia country. Otherwise, he asserted, "Their blood and wealth are not protected." He admitted that he had also operated from Algeria and Egypt, but because reform there was impossible from within due to the corrupt regimes in place, he came to the conclusion that only a Muslim invasion from the outside would trigger the Islamic Revolution and the warranted change. And that invasion he envisaged as stemming from Yemen and then fanning out worldwide.[14]

Abu Hamza's work consisted not only of promoting Muslim terrorism, recruiting volunteers, indoctrinating others, and collecting funds for Muslim organizations, but he also launched a campaign to recruit, convert, and train British Muslims, which he was sure British liberalism would digest and ignore. For that purpose he held "Islamic camps," usually in the grounds of his mosque, offering "military training for brothers, self-development skills, martial arts, map-reading etc," aimed at distracting the thirty young men in attendance from "television and the obscenity of Christmas." Incidentally, the Website that made the announcement was decorated with a picture of a hand grenade.[15] Some of those trainees found their way to Afghanistan and were killed there but did not come to the media attention until after the horrors of 9/11.[16]

During the Second Conference of the Islamic Movements held in London in February 1999, Abu Hamza told the gathering of five hundred Muslims of a plan to "blow up civil and military aircraft, so as to challenge western monopoly of the skies." He even gave details of "new flying mines connected to balloons, currently being experimented on in Afghanistan," and hinted that sometime in the future such an operation would be carried out in Britain or in the United States.[17] But Britain obviously thought that he was hallucinating and elected to look the other way. There are indications that he knew of the upcoming 9/11 plan, that he was involved in masterminding a scheme to kill President Bush during the G8 meeting in Genoa two days before the New York attack so that an America in disarray over the death of its president would be less able to respond to 9/11, and that he held a meeting in his mosque in London on June 29, 2001, in which the idea of attacks using aircraft was raised.[18]

The most relevant aspect of Abu Hamza from the Western point of view is his encouragement of violence, which he cultivated and elevated into an ideology in its own right. His advocated use of violence had a two-pronged purpose: to topple regimes in place in the Arab and Islamic worlds in order to replace them with Islamic governments and to boost the diffusion of Islam in the world. At a gathering in early 1999 commemorating the removal of the last Ottoman caliph by Kemal Ataturk, he openly urged Muslims to resort to the sword in order to achieve his blueprint for domestic and international upheaval. One of his supporters, Mohammed Yusuf, seconded his mentor's ideas by urging his followers not only to fight against the West in the Balkans and the Middle East, but also by establishing a "strong fifth column" within the Western world,[19] something that would have explained his own self-imposed "exile" in London and his cultivation of violent Islam there. But Jack Straw was still deep into his slumber; he neither heard nor saw.

In 2001 Abu Hamza became involved in a press debate geared to clear his name from the "abominable accusation" that he had relinquished the use of violence, something that would have been antithetical to the nature of his struggle. Indeed, according to the London-based *Al-Quds Al-Arabi,* Abu Hamza had been accused by another Egyptian fundamentalist ex-patriot who had also found refuge in London, Abdul Hakim Diab, of having dismissed a fatwa (religious verdict) by the Palestinian radical cleric Abu Qatada, who had decreed that Muslims should kill the wives and children of Egyptian police and army officers as part of the struggle against the Arab regimes.[20]

This accusation was too much of an affront for Abu Hamza. In his rebuttal in the same paper, he said that he did not recognize the term *violence* because it had become a weapon used by the world media to dub anyone who defends his faith and his honor in the face of the Arab regimes who rule through "legislative and oppressive measures." Therefore, the very term *violence* seemed deceptive in his eyes and incompatible with Islamic religious law and the struggle for the survival of Islam. He asserted that mujahideen have never recognized that term because it was used to sustain the monopoly of the ruling regime in the use of terrorism, and conversely to eliminate the religious precept of "doing good and avoiding evil." This was the clearest explanation yet of Muslim terrorism as an act of "good," and in consequence any attempt to fight it is inherently evil. This thinking also helps explain why, for the Muslim radicals, the Western definition of *terrorism* is unacceptable, inasmuch as it addresses itself to a means of combat or struggle (namely acting against innocent civilians to attain a political goal), instead of addressing the core issue of the struggle: that is Islamic "good" against Western or anti-Islamic "evil." It is instructive to heed Abu Hamza's own words:

> As a rule, Islam teaches that those holding opinions different from one's own should be treated gently and with flexibility, provided they are willing to listen and comply, and provided that one's tolerant efforts do not lead to a blurring of rights and borders . . . Treating gently anyone who blocks his ears and forces perversion, heresy, abomination and humiliation upon Muslims in their own countries by the use of force, is a kind of idiocy and loss of rights and of religious precepts . . . What can be said of Arab regimes who have enacted abominable laws and have given license to implement them, and use taxes to appoint military personnel to protect the abomination, instead of protecting Jerusalem and its people? . . . This is the mark of Cain, which is unprecedented in the history of Egypt.[21]

According to such analysis, Islam is thus tolerant only as long as the challenger to its rules ultimately accepts it and complies with it. For Islam alone can define right and wrong, holy and profane, acceptable and abominable, and anyone opposing it is no longer to be subject to the "gentle treatment and flexibility" suggested in al-Masri's definition of *tolerance.* Getting to the point of the use of violence that he had been "outrageously accused" of having abandoned, he stated:

> My position is as clear as the sun, praised be Allah, and it will not change . . . I do not recognize the term "violence" and will not agree to abandon *jihad* or to sign a truce with the regimes of the tyrants. As Allah said: "Fight them so there will be no internal strife (*fitna*)

> and so that their religion will be Allah's religion." The Muslim nation to which I belong cannot come to terms with anyone who does not have mercy on and respect for the people . . . Physical exile, far from my homeland, is much easier for me and for many like me than the exile of our souls, the slaughter of our faith and of our values, and the amputation of our tongues as the price for returning to our homeland.[22]

And finally, in defense of Islamic violence (jihad) against the West, he had this to say to the *Christian Science Monitor*:

> It was when the Americans took the knife out of the Russians [in Afghanistan] and stabbed us in our back . . . In the meantime they were bombing Iraq and occupying the Arabian Peninsula, and then with their witch-hunt against *mujahideen*, everything became clear: it was a full-scale war . . . The Americans wanted to fight the Russians with Muslim blood and they could justify that only by invoking the word *jihad.* Unfortunately for everyone, except Muslims, when the button of Jihad is pushed it does not come back that easily. It keeps going on and on until the Muslim Empire swallows every other existing Empire . . . I do not condone what happened [on September 11] nor do I condemn it. If somebody has done that just for mundane gain and political advancement, then obviously it is a cheap cause. But if it was done because people are desperate and their lives have been threatened, then it is a respectable cause . . . Then those people who carried out the attacks would be martyrs. Martyrdom is the highest form of Jihad, and if you do things for the cause of Allah, losing your life for it is the most sublime expression of faith. This is in the Qur'an. America thinks it comes first, but Muslims believe that Believers come first. When you damage a people and they have no home and no hope, and their babies and children are killed, then they retaliate. America took decisions to give arms to certain people and take arms away from others. What happened yesterday would be self-defense . . . I have sympathy for the victims, but also for Bin Laden who is the victim of an American witch-hunt, but who is unable to commit an act like this, though he probably has millions of sympathizers [who could have done it].[23]

Abu Hamza al-Masri was not the only writing on the wall that was ignored by the British authorities, who in their blindness elected to regard as mere rhetoric his ominous deeds that amounted to warnings of what was to come. Sheikh Omar al-Bakri, of Syrian origin, who also sought and obtained asylum in Britain, was no less dangerous and no less unclear in his designs. He too, in flight from the oppression in his own country, had to flee to the freedom of Europe in order to undermine it from within, without arousing the suspicions of the complacent West. He founded in London a local branch of the Palestinian-based Hizb ut-Tahrir (Liberation Party) and also Jama'at al-Muhajiroun (Association of Immigrants).[24] He has occasionally introduced himself to interlocutors as a spokesman for Osama bin Laden's International Islamic Front for Jihad against Jews and Crusaders, which is known to have raised funds for Hamas, Islamic Jihad, and Hezbollah and recruited volunteers for training in Islamikaze attacks. He left Syria for Beirut following the drowning in blood of the Muslim Brotherhood uprising in Hama in 1982. Then, under the name of Omar Fostock, he established his Muhajiroun group in Jeddah, Saudi Arabia, as a front for the Liberation Party, which spread thereafter to Europe, especially among the large concentrations of Muslims in Lille, France, and Hannover, Germany, with headquarters in Hamburg. In all, some forty-seven Muslim organizations in Western Europe come under the heading of the Liberation Party.[25] In 1985 he was evicted by the Saudis and landed in London, where he fell into disagreement with his fellow Islamic Party members, who wished to focus on the revival of the caliphate, while he meddled in all manner of Muslim organizations.

In 1996 Bakri applied for British citizenship after he had become a legal resident three years earlier. Since that time he has preached in London mosques and delivered fiery sermons to Muslim assemblies, the largest of which convened in Trafalgar Square and the Wembley Stadium. He founded the Khilafah (Caliphate) Publishing House and claimed service in the Sharia court of the United Kingdom. In an interview with the *Daily Mirror,* he admitted that he lived on a weekly state allowance of 300 pound sterling to provide for his family of eight, rationalizing that "Islam permits me to take the benefits the system offers. I am fully eligible. It is very difficult for me to find a job. Anyway, most of the leadership of the Islamic Movement [in Britain] is on state benefit."[26] But after seven radical terrorists, some of them Egyptians, were arrested in Britain in September 1998, Bakri began attacking his benefactors unabashedly, denouncing Great Britain as the "spearhead of blasphemy that seeks to overthrow the Muslims and the Islamic Caliphate." He explained that the arrested Egyptians were political refugees who were not involved in terrorist activities and that the Muslims in Great Britain "condemned the barbaric acts of the British government against innocent Muslims who . . . were lulled and betrayed into believing that they could seek sanctuary in Britain from their own corrupt regimes."[27]

This reversal of allegiance is what characterizes the behavior of Muslim terrorists who have sought refuge in the West that they detest and wish to undermine, while for the most part on the run from their home regimes that they tried unsuccessfully to topple. Since they are persuaded that they fight for the path of Allah, they certainly do not regard themselves as terrorists, and, when they are arrested for terrorist activities within their host countries that have generously, naively, and self-defeatingly given them shelter and provided for their needs, they accuse their benefactors of Islamophobia and condemn their "barbaric behavior." This mechanism of denial, which posits Western democracy as a milking cow that owes Muslim immigrants sustenance while they owe it nothing, allows them to deny the good and the protection they receive and to even mount subversive cells that are liable to act in the heart of their countries of refuge as of right and to cause havoc and terror upon the nations that took them in, in spite of their repeated commitment to refrain from political or subversive activity as a condition for being accorded the status of refugees.[28]

A political denial was adopted in the Western chanceries as well, under the belief that if they meant well for the Muslim refugees, they would encounter exemplary behavior on their part in return. Even the al-Qaida entrenchment in the United States and Europe and their illicit activities committed under various guises was not enough to stir suspicions and to instigate the slumbering Western governments to take measures of self-defense, until the Muslim radicals struck, first in the United States and then in Europe. The new Muslim terrorists put the blame on the West for rescuing them from their own corrupt regimes, and therefore the host countries that have tried to fight terrorism after realizing it too late are being accused of racism, an "anti-Islamic" drive, inhumanity, and the like. The democratic countries of shelter that have absorbed these streams of "refugees" who arrived uninvited, now become the "oppressors of the poor and peaceful Muslims," similar to the oppressive countries of Saudi Arabia, Egypt, and all the rest.[29]

The building tensions between Bakri and his peers on the one hand, and the British authorities on the other, did not begin with the 9/11 events or with the awakening of Europe to the danger of international terror that grew with its increasingly radicalized, foreign Muslim population. Already during the Gulf War of the early 1990s, the British MI5 had interrogated Bakri for his alleged call to assassinate British Prime Minister John Major. Indeed, Bakri was cited by the British press as declaring that Major was a "legitimate target. If one gets the opportunity to assassinate him . . . it is our Islamic duty and we will celebrate his death."[30] Bakri declared that he had been misquoted, specifying that Major would have been a legitimate target only if he "set foot in a Muslim country," and that applied to Tony Blair, his successor, as well. He confirmed that, in such a case, he would not condemn the killers.[31] The lenient British, instead of making it clear that they rejected the Muslim way of assassinating rivals as a legitimate comment on current politics, let things go and forgivingly dismissed that threat on their political system that they probably failed to recognize for the nth time. But similar Islamic patterns of behavior were not slow in coming to the surface and ultimately, but belatedly, convinced even the most diehard liberals to tighten the rules and supervision of those potentially subversive elements. Indeed, a spokesman for the Muhajiroun in England, Salim abd al-Rahman, also announced after 9/11 that Tony Blair had become a legitimate target for Muslims because of the British attacks on Afghanistan. In his words:

> Now that the Americans, the British and probably the French, have begun to bomb Muslims in Afghanistan, henceforth government buildings and military installations in Britain, even 10 Downing St, have become legitimate targets. If any Muslim wants to kill [the British Prime Minister] or get rid of him, I would not shed a tear for him. In the Islamic view, such a man would not be punished for his deeds but would be praised.[32]

In December 2000 Bakri went to Birmingham, under the open eye of British security, to preach his brand of Islamic radicalism. He was so sure of himself and of the numbing British indolence at the time that he gave an interview to the local newspaper and explained that he had come to Birmingham to recruit volunteers not only for his Muhajiroun group but also to fight for the Muslim cause in such foreign countries as Kashmir, Afghanistan, and Chechnya. He emphasized that in Britain there were only "physical training camps," but that volunteers were sent out from Britain for military training in South Africa, Nigeria, Afghanistan, Kashmir, and the United States.[33] This cleric, who depended on the generosity of the British government's welfare system, admitted in another interview that he was involved in financing the training of volunteers for his jihad network, who were dispatched to the United States, taking advantage of the fact that training with firearms and live ammunition was more readily available there than in Britain. The rationale was simple: "As they [the British] started to label us as terrorists when we went to Afghanistan, we now go on to the US." He gave details of that training: the use of firearms and explosives, surveillance, and other skills in order to join jihad fighting in countries such as Chechnya, Palestine, Kashmir, and South Lebanon. He emphasized that the choice of the battle arena depended on each individual fighter. He stressed that the US training camps were run by private firms in states like Michigan and Missouri, and Muslim recruits came from various countries but had European or American citizenship and therefore did not need visas. Recruits stayed for periods ranging from one week to three months.[34]

With a spirit of nonchalance that could certainly not be adopted in an Arab or Muslim setting and was borne out of the absolute certainty of the Muslims in the West that their Western nationality made them immune and gave them the right to subvert their countries of asylum, Bakri made explicit his military activities: "It is not illegal. We are not hiding anything. It should be looked at with an open mind. We are talking purely about helping people who would like to train. The skills they learn are part of the religious obligations every Muslim has. A Muslim must have military training at least once in his lifetime."[35]

But lest the reader should think that only military training was imperative for Muslims in their lands of dwelling and citizenship, a clarification follows: "In Muslim countries we can fulfill this obligation by joining the national armies. But some Muslims would not want to join British or American troops and would rather go to an independent training camp. Why call this terrorist training? All Americans can learn how to shoot so what happens when this American happens to be a Muslim? Unless, of course, you consider us second- or third class citizens."[36] The answer to those questions came fifteen months later, on September 11, 2001. In other press interviews Bakri admitted that the International Islamic Front Against Jews and Crusaders (IIF), created by bin Laden and with which he was himself connected, supported Hamas and Islamic Jihad in Palestine, who were the acknowledged masters of Islamikaze acts. The Front collected funds for them, recruited "militiamen," and took care of their propaganda needs in Europe. He related that in October 2000 alone, the month the Al-Aqsa Intifada was picking up steam against Israel, British "volunteers" were recruited and sent to Jordan, where they awaited "opportunities to infiltrate the West Bank" and join the Palestinian outburst of violence. He said that more recruits were sent to Lebanon, who joined training in Palestinian refugee camps with a view to opening up a new front with Israel in the southern part of the country, and confirmed that his group, the IIF, maintained connections with Hezbollah and other Islamic movements, such as Usbat al-Ansar (The Faction of Supporters [of Islam]) who are committed to fight for the "liberation of Jerusalem."[37] Bakri was also active on the Asian front. He claimed that it was he who recruited Muhammed Bilal to carry out the Islamikaze attack in Srinagar in Indian Kashmir in December 2000, in which a number of Indian soldiers were killed, that he also trained Bilal's brothers and cousins for similar operations, and that Bilal's parents were "proud of their son's sacrifice." According to Bakri, he also recruited six hundred British Muslims in universities and mosques to fight in Kashmir, and some media attributed to him the financing (again he who lives off British unemployment and social welfare benefits) of al-Madad (literally "assistance" or "supplies"), which, together with other groups, has recruited 2,000 other young men across Britain.[38]

Bakri's activities in Asia also encompassed the Malay Muslim rebel minority in southern Thailand, where reports surfaced of foreign supporters who "provided money and training to southern separatists" and of a training farm twenty kilometers from the Malay border linked with "the Middle East and with radical Muslims based in London," one of whose foreign supporters was Bakri.[39] He voiced his support of aircraft hijackings and in an interview gave his harrowing judgment on the worth of Muslim blood compared to that of others:

> The Islamic Movement has the right to sacrifice whomever it sees fit. The rule is that children, women and the weak should not be targeted, except in one situation: if it is difficult to win without sacrificing them. So, if hijackers find [Muslim] women, children and elderly people on the [hijacked] plane, they should set them free except if the goal of the hijackers is to free other women, children or elderly people held prisoners in other countries. In this case they can be kept because the blood of Muslims is equal, but they can sacrifice foreigners on the plane . . . If you study Sharia, you will know that. The ransom of a Muslim is 12,000 dirham while that of a *dhimmi* (Christian or Jew) is 4000 dirham.[40]

Bakri's renown as the "leader of the Islamic Movement" is widespread in the Islamic world.[41] Although he denied any organizational or hierarchical link to bin Laden, he has repeatedly declared that they were both committed to the same ideology, but he objected to defining bin Laden as a terrorist, explaining that "if one supports Muslims against the occupying forces in Somalia or Arabia I will never call him a terrorist. I will call him a freedom fighter. I will call him a hero."[42]

After the bombing of US embassies in Saudi Arabia and East Africa in 1998, Bakri insisted that even if it were proven that bin Laden was responsible, "Those still remained legitimate acts" because the US troops in the Gulf were there to fight against Muslims and Islam, and it was then the duty of every Muslim to fight them. He cited the US bombing of Sudan and Afghanistan, the war against Iraq, and the US "blind support" for Israel as "acts of war against Allah and his Prophet."[43] Following the US missile attack on Sudan and Afghanistan as a result of the 1998 destruction of the American embassies in Tanzania and Kenya, Bakri read a statement to the Italian press, allegedly coming directly from bin Laden:

> The war has begun. Our response to the barbaric bombardment against Muslims of Afghanistan and Sudan will be ruthless and violent . . . Our response could happen in any corner of the world. Retaliation for the US attacks will end only when the last American soldier has left Saudi Arabia and the Gulf, and when the embargo against Iraq is over . . . We will not accord a truce to America.[44]

In July 1999 Bakri published a letter to bin Laden on his Muhajiroun Website, calling upon him to act against the West. And though the letter was removed from the site following a US protest, it was read out in mosques in London, Bradford, Sheffield, and Leicester. Bakri warned in his letter that the Islamic movements had not used the "real weapon" yet, and addressed bin Laden thus:

> Oh Osama! . . . You and your brothers are now breathing new life and dignity into the body of the *umma* . . . Our main mission as Muslims is to carry the Islamic message to the entire world . . . We are an umma of Jihad, and beyond doubt we have been chosen by Allah to lead the whole world if we hold to His command . . . The opportunity is here and we must not miss it . . . Our Muslim brothers are firm in their Jihad so we must not lose time aimlessly and act now . . . Oh, Osama! Let us hear the good news from you and your brothers, for a new dawn is near at hand.[45]

Allegedly, that letter was heeded by bin Laden and answered in a circular read out in mosques in London and Pakistan. Another letter by bin Laden to Bakri was faxed in the summer of 1998 and later published in the *Los Angeles Times.* It allegedly contained the four specific objectives of jihad against the United States: "Bring down their airlines, prevent the safe passage of their ships, occupy their embassies and force the closure of their companies and banks."[46] Had the West heeded those threats and arrested those dangerous Muslim operatives, instead of sheltering them in its cities and letting them foment incitement and hatred in their midst, the events of 9/11 might never have taken place.

Journalists like Steve Emerson in the United States and a handful of academic writers who were warning during those years of the impending explosion of Muslim radical rage, were dismissed as alarmist, hysterical, racist, and Islamophobic. Even when, on occasion, a security apparatus in the West learned about the facts, it misinterpreted them and rejected them in disbelief, thus allowing one of the greatest strategic surprise attacks in modern times to come to pass, while the prosperous, complacent, hypocritical, shortsighted, and sycophant West, with the exception of the United States, looked on indolently and helplessly, although it had itself unwittingly bred the catastrophe by naively allowing in the Trojan horse, leaving itself open and vulnerable while hidden fighters surged forth and attacked.

Bakri, being at the time perhaps the most virulent and dangerous Western-based spokesman of the world war that radical Islam has declared against the West, made no effort to hide his program. Not only did he side openly with bin Laden and recruit and indoctrinate would-be Islamikaze in the heart of the West and in Islamic countries further afield, but he did not relent from his open campaign of hatred against Jews, and then the West in general, when the latter did not react decisively to this threat. He had posters that read "Kill the Jews!" plastered on walls around him, and to escape punishment he claimed that those were the words of the "Holy Scriptures," not his own.[47] He accused Jews of exploiting the Holocaust to achieve "hegemony over Muslims" and insisted that far worse war crimes had been perpetrated by others against Muslims in Chechnya, Kashmir, and Palestine than those Muslims were accused of in other parts of the globe.[48] He also said that he had no problem with Jewish communities as such, only against Israel, which was a "cancer in the heart of the Islamic world," and therefore it had to be "eradicated and removed." He told his demonstrating audiences in front of the Regent's Park Mosque, upon the outbreak of the Al-Aqsa Intifada, that "all Israeli targets are legitimate for you. All Israelis must be destroyed."[49] His campaign of incitement also included the playwright Terrence McNally for portraying Jesus Christ as a homosexual in his play *Corpus Christi*. Later, he suggested that all homosexuals ought to throw themselves down from Big Ben.[50]

The most relevant aspect of Bakri's teachings, however, as far as the use of violence is concerned, is his reliance on jihad. In a document entitled "Jihad" that he posted on the Muhajiroun Website, he offered a lengthy analysis of what he meant:

> Jihad, as a term, cannot be translated as "Holy War", nor can it be translated as "struggle" . . . At best, its legal meaning can be understood as "using military force where diplomacy fails, to remove the obstacles the Islamic state faces in carrying its ideology to mankind" . . . The aim of Jihad, unlike the Crusades, past and present, is not forcibly to convert to Islam the inhabitants of other lands. Rather, it is to provide them with the security that comes from the application of Islam, leaving them the choice or adopting Islam or keeping their own religions . . . History confirms that this is, and always has been, the role of Jihad, for it was in Muslim Spain that the Muslims, Christians and Jews could live peacefully under an Islamic authority . . . The difference between the use of force by the West and Islam is that the capitalist West uses violence covertly and overtly for the benefit of a few, such as corporations, while Islam uses force openly and justly to carry its mercy to others . . . Jihad is one of the Pillars of Islam after *tawhid* (the assertion of the unity of Allah) and *da'wa* (proselytizing).[51] In fact Jihad is *daw'a* by the Islamic state and its foreign policy.[52]

Unlike his fellow expatriate, Abu Hamza, who posited Yemen as the launching pad for the impending Islamic revolution, or al-Qaida leaders, who relied on the Taliban regime to kindle the world fire, Bakri thought it must all start in London, thus lending *ex post facto* rationale to his exile there. He aspired to establish a world Islamic caliphate, starting in the United Kingdom, as the first Islamic state in a new world order. Thus, he conveniently called British law and democracy that had allowed him to take up refuge there in the first place "phony rules," made up by the "monkeys in Parliament."[53] Indeed, he stated unequivocally to *Le Monde* his intention to "make the flag of Islam fly high at 10 Downing St and at the Elysee." In his view, "Islam is the supreme ideology facing an immoral West . . . and all contemporary leaders of the Islamic world, with no exception, are pawns of the West."[54] In interviews and public lectures, he made his doctrine clear and explicit:

> With thanks to Allah, we bring peace to all, and we help the world realize that Islam is the only way of life . . . Terrorism according to the West is defined as "the systematic use of violence to achieve political or religious goals" but *al-Muhajirun* define terrorism as "an attack without the divine right" . . . Clinton is a target of Jihad, and American forces are a target of Jihad wherever they are . . . The American people must reconsider their foreign policy, or their children will be sent back to them in coffins . . . Clinton is responsible and he will pay . . .

> The existence of Israel is a crime and must be removed . . . Our duty is to work to establish a Muslim state anywhere in the world, even in Britain . . . Life is protected under us. There will be no minorities or majorities as in America. Anti-Semitism in America is disgraceful. Synagogues and Churches will flourish in the Islamic Caliphate, as long as they yield to Islamic Law . . . We restored life for the Jews after the Crusades, and we plan to do so again . . . What President Clinton and Prime Minister Barak are doing [that is, negotiating peace] is putting themselves in the position of Allah, therefore they are now in a direct war with the people who believe in Allah . . .[55]

The horrors of 9/11 neither surprised Bakri, who had been consistently preaching for action of this sort, nor generated any remorse in him. Quite the contrary, he regarded them as "compensation for the atrocities the United States committed against Islam"[56] and warned that should the United States attack the Taliban in reprisal, the "verdict of Allah" would descend on American installations that would become legitimate targets. He exhorted all Muslims to unite in the fight, to sacrifice themselves and their wealth in order to get to paradise, and to "make clear the difference between Truth and falsehood, Belief and heresy, oppressors and oppressed, the Alliance of Satan and that of Allah."[57] After the US attack on Afghanistan began, Bakri issued a fatwa against Pakistani President Musharraf and other Muslim leaders who let their territories be used by the Americans against a fellow Muslim state. The verdict said:

> There is no doubt that America has attacked, and is still attacking, the Muslims in every place and is carrying out massacres against them . . . It is the obligation of all Muslims to be in a state or war against it. The minimal obligation is a total boycott, by means of annulling diplomatic relations . . . The only ones who claim that diplomatic relations are permitted are the clerics and the treacherous sultans, most of them are donkeys bearing books, and some behave like dogs. They have renounced the verses of Allah and have become like dogs that should be left to pant, as a place is already reserved for them, surely on the lowest level of the fires of hell . . . Those people are heretics (*murtaddun*), if they were Muslims at all in the first place. They are all involved in the war against Islam and Muslims, and therefore the sentence of *murtadd harbi* (a heretic who should be fought) applies to them.[58]

Viewed against this background of blatant intolerance and aggression, the soothing and sycophantic declarations made by the Prince of Wales vis-à-vis Islam not only sound hollow, naïve, and offensive to intelligence, but especially counterproductive, because when words of provocation and utter rejection are countered with acceptance, appeasement, and ignorance, they can only invite more friction, aggression, and conflict. Remember Munich 1938? In fact, sitting on a divan inside a Bedouin tent, the Prince of Wales called for greater respect between religions and gave warning that too much literal interpretation of religious tenets could lead to fundamentalist extremism, as if current interpretations of Islam were clear of extremism. How does he know and under whose authority did he speak? His plea for understanding and tolerance was familiar, an echo of his recent calls to senior Muslims in Egypt and Saudi Arabia, but set against the statements of intolerance from Muslim clerics and politicians in his own country and worldwide, it sounded absurdly naïve.

The tent from which he spoke was tucked among skyscrapers on a bombsite at the back of St. Ethelburga's, the oldest medieval church in London, which was destroyed in 1993 by the IRA Bishopsgate bomb and rebuilt as a center for reconciliation and peace. It must have been the only Arab tent pitched in London, not exactly an adequate site for tolerance in the heart of a Western city. Flanked by the bishop of London, the chief rabbi, and leaders of seven other world faiths, Prince Charles inaugurated the exotic new center for interfaith dialogue representing sacred geometric and astrological rather than religious symbols. It will be used by people of all religions for meditation, worship, storytelling, and discussion of religious conflicts, social issues, spiritual authority, women in faith, suffering, and other issues. This was Prince Charles's second visit to the center, which he opened officially in 2002. He also unveiled a plaque to the Reverend John Rodwell, the rector of St. Ethelburga's from 1843 to 1900 and an orientalist who published the first reliable translation of the Quran in English. While laudable as an idea, the whole ceremony did not address specifically the issue of Islamic militantism, it being known that none of the other faiths represented has ever used violence or threatened the public order in the United Kingdom. Indeed, no members of any faith other than Islam have killed, wounded, maimed, threatened violence, or promised the takeover of Britain, and also delivered on some of these promises.

Representatives in Britain of the Baha'is, Buddhists, Jains, Zoroastrians, Hindus, Sikhs, Muslims, and Jews recited prayers, read passages extolling tolerance, and ceremonially laid copies of their scriptures on a table at the center of the tent. President Clinton, Archbishop Desmond Tutu, the U2 singer Bono, and the president of the World Jewish

Congress sent messages saluting the center's use of religion to underpin dialogue and replace conflict with understanding. It only remained to clarify what Muslims meant by dialogue and tolerance. Richard Chartres, the bishop of London, who has been the driving force behind the rebuilding of St. Ethelburga's, noted that the three Abrahamic religions of Christianity, Judaism, and Islam began in desert tents. Sir Jonathan Sacks, the chief rabbi, spoke of the significance of the tabernacle—a form of tent—in the Old Testament. This tent, paid for by an anonymous benefactor and with windows inscribed with motifs and messages in Chinese, Sanskrit, Arabic, Japanese, Hebrew, English, and Inuit, is a far cry from the desert; however, it will be heated in winter, is able to withstand the London rain, and will be pitched permanently in one of the world's most densely populated cities.

Prince Charles told the faith leaders: "We are all trying to explain the nature of mystery and, in a sense, it is almost impossible to explain. If only we could understand each other's gropings, to comprehend the mystery, not try to overdo the way in which we decide that we know everything, we might, perhaps, reduce the level of conflict and violence and misunderstanding."[59] The problem is that dialogue has been treated in the West as if it were a real policy, whereas it is in fact a nonpolicy, designed only to fill an awkward vacuum and to make royal princes and legislators feel virtuous for doing something. But while Europeans have regularly entered a dialogue in good faith, fully intending to find common ground with their unruly Muslim interlocutors—for the Muslims, *dialogue* means something else entirely. For them, it signifies the submission of a lesser culture and religion to their own superior one. They hope to inspire in the Europeans a Damascene conversion to an Islamic view of the world.

Anything short of that is regarded by them as an abject failure of dialogue and a signal to resort to threats of violence or acts of terrorism. They are well practiced at both, while the Europeans have literally become pushovers at this stage in their history. They do not believe anything is worth fighting over, nor do they have a stomach for a fight of unlimited duration. They would rather capitulate than investigate the meaning of tolerance, understanding, dialogue, and peace to the Islamists. The problem today lies in the juxtaposition of a resurgent Islam on the one hand and a self-deprecating Europe on the other, unsure of itself, its values, or even what it stands for. Its people have made a virtue of instant self-gratification, and therefore they invest next to nothing in the future—hence they have stopped having children.

Their preferred way of life amounts to a "credit card culture." They want everything, and they want it instantly. Never mind that their governments no longer raise sufficient funds from taxation to cover exorbitant welfare entitlements or that a bleak financial future awaits tomorrow's pensioners. In short, Europe has become a disgrace to its own heritage, in sharp reversal of its fortunes when at the turn of the twentieth century the Muslim Ottoman Empire was considered the "sick man of Europe" and was therefore no match for a confident West. Defense Secretary Donald Rumsfeld was onto something apart from the obvious when he distinguished between old and new Europe—except that in their eagerness to grab some (necessarily short-term) economic benefits after emerging from Soviet control, the headlong rush of "new" Europe to join the European Union will inevitably contaminate them with the prevalent Western disease.

There is another drawback to this constant resort to dialogue. It lulls the Western populations into believing that their governments are doing something constructive to avert violence or threats of violence in the future. In reality, nothing could be further from the truth, for this nonpolicy simply serves to embolden and concomitantly empower those Muslims whom the government has chosen to act as intermediaries with the wider Muslim community. Invariably, the Western governments have chosen these Muslims largely because they are prominent activists (and often militants, or fundamentalists in another parlance), while the governments comfort themselves with the injudicious belief that these figures represent "moderate" Islam. However, these Muslims have been living in Europe long enough to have learned to tailor their vocabulary precisely according to whom they are facing across the table. They speak the language of peace, reconciliation, and goodwill to Westerners and reserve their true thoughts and beliefs for fellow Muslims. In other words, they have learned to work the system, and admirably so.

In effect, these "moderate" Muslim leaders are gradually extracting one concession after another from Western policy makers, rendering "dialogue" a one-way street. They enter each session with the full intention of testing the limits of the concessions they may extract, and it is a rare government minister who would risk disappointing them—or else the headlines in the papers the following day would be sure to inflame the Muslim community. Herein lies the value of the worldwide Muslim penchant for overreacting to every perceived slight, real or imagined, by demonstrating loudly and violently their "rage." Temperament comes into play here too, for unlike other peoples who experience anger or humiliation, Muslims are either unable or unwilling to contain those sentiments. One has only to recall the Arafat-orchestrated "Days of Rage" in the early days of the intifada against Israel (2000) to understand that, in sharp contrast to Westerners, Muslims make a fetish of celebrating their anger. Such an uncontrolled behavior is unthinkable in the West, not because of lack of provocation, particularly since 9/11. Funerals too are manipulated to vent wrath and fury, emotion, general mayhem, and impromptu rifle shooting. The total and shameless lack of dignity, even at what should be a somber occasion, is jarring to Western eyes. Bodies are held aloft and bounced along the route, in a manner that would be regarded as disrespectful to the deceased in other cultures. Bodies have been known to fall off the stretcher amid the melee, as was recorded for posterity in the case of Iran's Ayatollah Khomeini.

Iran's ambassador to Copenhagen, Ahmad Danialy, making his first public appearance in Denmark since being recalled by the Iranian foreign ministry in January 2006 following the Cartoon Affair, addressed a public gathering and noted that the crisis had "hurt the feelings of the Muslim world and caused a great deal of concern. Now after the lapse of this period of unpleasant and bitter experience, I am very pleased to witness a beautiful and jovial gathering of the erudite and learned here in Copenhagen . . . The conference is a step in the right direction for improving relations. The truth of the matter is that the world needs to direct new attention to one fundamental principle and that is: Respect for the sanctity of religions in all places and at all political, cultural and social levels."[60] And this when the ambassador was aware of how his president spoke about Jews and Israel and how his clerics deprecated Christianity and other faiths, and how the Iranian regime supported the burning down of Jewish synagogues in the West Bank and in European cities. But if the purpose of the conference was "to introduce the Prophet (the Muslim one, not all the rest) the proper way," then why should we expect any care or concern for any faith except the Islamic one? The conference in the United Arab Emirates, organized by the Tabah Foundation, brought sixty young people from Denmark and the Arab world together under the banner "The Search for Mutual Understanding," namely that the Danes should learn to respect Islam, never mind their own beliefs and culture. The delegates discussed a range of issues that the cartoon crisis revealed as sore points between religious Muslims and secular Western culture, such as freedom of expression and the role the media can play in hindering or facilitating global understanding. The four-day conference held in Abu Dhabi "exceeded the expectations of Jeppe Bruus Christensen," chairman of the Danish Youth Council, who naively and prematurely declared: "I don't think we should underestimate how important this is in the Arab world. It has gathered a great deal of attention."

What he did not realize was that his statements were interpreted throughout the Arab world as a desperate attempt by Denmark to apologize for its "horrible" deed, as a capitulation to Muslim demands. It did not earn Denmark any credit, but only scorn and contempt. Christensen felt that the two groups managed to "understand" each other and "accepted" mutual criticism, but he failed to comprehend that the Muslim goal was to assert its victory, not to compromise, because its system cannot recognize that it can be at fault, unlike other (lesser) faiths. Thus, his feeling that the whole exercise "had been very constructive and positive" and that "we have been able to agree upon common values, such as having the right to criticize each other" would have been in vain had he read the Arab reports of the conference. Other participants from Denmark and the Middle East were more realistic when they merely agreed that the conference "underscored the need for bridging the gaps that the conflict had revealed," and that "We have to accept that there are areas where we remain distant from each other." Moreover, to illustrate the depth of that gap, some Muslims continued to consider Denmark, one of the most open, tolerant, and hospitable countries of the world, to be "a racist and closed country."[61]

Much closer to the reality was the evaluation by some Danish participants who heard their country being deprecated albeit that it could be the model of tolerance for the entire Islamic world, when they said that "we have to acknowledge that that's the way it's going to be for some time." The conference also gave young Muslims the chance to meet their Danish counterparts and test the images presented by the media in their countries. "It's been very important for me to obtain the human aspect. To meet people and hear their opinion instead of seeing it in the media," said a nineteen-year-old Egyptian who admitted that preconceived notions, such as "the Danes hate us," were difficult to reject, but the conference's people-to-people approach helped.

Another Arab youth from Saudi Arabia, where Danish goods were initially boycotted, said that he was surprised in a positive way about the Danish young people, for "They were much more open and understanding about our culture than I had expected." But was he about theirs in the same way? He acknowledged that while dialogue and respect had been established at the conference, transferring the experience to his home country could prove difficult. He explained: "We'll be challenged when we come back to our countries, because some people have different attitudes. They use a different approach than dialogue, but we still need to work to spread the message that it is possible to live in this world together."[62] One wishes he were right.

The Danish queen, Margrethe, more reflective than the British Royal House, stated that Islam posed a challenge both globally and locally, and the challenge should be taken seriously. In her biography, based on interviews between the queen and the book's author, journalist Annelise Bistrup, the queen affirmed that "There is something impressive about people, whose existence is immersed in religion from dawn to dusk, from the cradle to the grave . . . but it is a challenge, which we need to take seriously. We have admittedly ignored it for too long. Because we are tolerant and a little lazy, I don't find it easy at all. Nor especially pleasant." Unlike other royals and politicians who make gratuitous declarations just to please their Muslim citizens or to placate their wrath, Queen Margrethe has studied Islam through her archaeological pursuits and says she does not feel entirely unprepared to enter the debate.

"There is something fascinating about people who go to such lengths to surrender themselves to a religion. But there is also something frightening about the all-encompassing side of Islam," she said, and then courageously added, "The challenge must be met, at the risk of getting some less flattering labels attached, for there are some things we should not meet with tolerance. When we are tolerant, we should be careful to note whether it stems from convenience or conviction." Queen Margrethe explained that we stand at a crossroads, and it needs to be recognized that crossroads often only reveal themselves once they have been crossed. She warned that "one doesn't always turn out to have taken the right road. But we have at least realized that we cannot let ourselves be shooed off by things that frighten us. We cannot compromise our notions of justice and legitimacy." Queen Margrethe said her interviews with her biographer brought up forgotten memories that could be worthwhile for others, especially young people, to hear.[63] She was certainly referring to the seeming nonchalance with which the young generation looked upon the multicultural societies that exacted an increasing price from present-day European societies.

This state of affairs allows British converts to Islam to take up the vocation of Abu Hamza and Bakri with the help of foreign financing, thus lending to Islamic radicalism the aura of a native religion, no longer introduced by foreigners into Britain, but followed by Britons and thus completely legitimate.

Indeed, a British Muslim convert has emerged as successor to Omar Bakri as the leader of a radical group that wants Britain ruled by Islamic law. *The Times* has obtained transcripts of Omar Brooks' utterances, now known as Abu Izzadeen, preaching holy war (Jihad) and discussing killing Tony Blair in a recent sermon in London. Abu Izzadeen had previously described the July 7 bombings as "completely praiseworthy" and organised demonstrations in support of the September 11 hijackers and killers. His organisation, the Saved Sect, of which he became head, was formed from the remnants of the disbanded extremist group al-Muhajirun, which the Government intended to proscribe. However, it is not on the Home Office's list of 40 banned terrorist organizsations, and an official spokeswoman refused to comment on whether it could be outlawed. The Crown Prosecution Service has not ruled out charges against Abu Izzadeen, which may include solicitation to murder and withholding information about acts of terrorism.

Abu Izzadeen, 31, was born into a Christian family of Jamaican origin, in Hackney, East London, and was known as Trevor to some acquaintances. He converted to Islam at the age of 17 and is believed to have become involved with Bakri at Finsbury Park mosque in the late 1990s. Before he was fully radicalised, Abu Izzadeen trained and worked as an electrician. He eventually chose a new name, which means "Might of the Faith" in Arabic, and immersed himself in his new religion. He married and now lives in Leyton, East London, with his wife and three young children. Vitriolic lectures for its website were recorded—until recently—by Bakri, who was sent in exile to Lebanon. But Abu Izzadeen has started preaching sermons and posting them on the website, suggesting that he has taken over as Emir of the Saved Sect. He is one of a generation of young British-born radical converts to step into the shoes of notorious clerics such as Bakri, Abu Qatada and Abu Hamza al-Masri. Abu Hamza is in jail and Abu Qatada is being held without charge under anti-terrorism laws. The Saved Sect, also known as the Saviour Sect, rejects democracy and wants Britain to adopt *Shari'a*, or Islamic law. It believes that it is the only group representing the true Islamic path, but has links with another al-Muhajirun successor, *al-Ghuraba'* (the Strangers), whose leader was arrested during extremist protests against the publication of cartoons depicting the Prophet Muhammad in early 2006.[64]

In lectures given at a London location, Abu Izzadeen said that a war was being fought to make Islamic law "completely dominant" in Britain, and that "all Jews and Christians are going to hell fire". He also praised Mullah Omar, the Taliban leader, saying: "This man is a winner." His lectures, entitled "The Christian Crusades"—parts 1 and 2, describe conflict in the Middle East and Britain as a present-day crusader. Abu Izzadeen said:

There is a war here [in Britain]. Maybe you don't have weapons, but there are arrests against the Muslim community, there is brutality by the police. It is a form of war against the Muslims here as well . . . If I said to you that we're going to conquer Rome, or if I said to you that we're going to kill George Bush and we're going to kill Tony Blair, you would say to me: 'Which come first brother?' . . . Muslims do not need to stand by the British flag . . . There is without doubt a war taking place between the Muslims and the non-Muslims . . . you must take part in the struggle . . . Tony Blair is a *taghoot* [believer of false religions]. The British forces in Iraq and Afghanistan, the police in the UK, they are all fighting for the sake of *taghoot*.[65]

When Mr Blair announced after the London bombings that he would ban "the successor organisation of al-Muhajirun," the group praised the September 11 terrorists, describing them as the "Magnificent 19". Legislation tightening the Terrorism Act came into force some months later, when it became illegal to glorify or incite terrorism. A Home Office spokeswoman said: "The list of proscribed organisations is kept under constant review. The Terrorism Act 2006 widens the criteria of proscription to include those groups which glorify terrorism. All possible candidates for proscription will be considered against these criteria." The Saved Sect website also carried a statement from Abu Musab al-Zarqawi, the commander of al-Qa'ida in Iraq. On the BBC programme Newsnight in 2005, Abu Izzadeen said that the July 7 bombings would make people "wake up and smell the coffee". He added that he would never denounce "suicide bombings", "even if my own family was to suffer, because we always stand with the Muslims regardless of the consequences", and he elaborated on his sect's program:

We can envisage that, if he were alive in the UK today, Jesus would undoubtedly have supported jihad in Afghanistan and Iraq, as opposed to the capitalist-driven US-led alliance . . . and would also have been no doubt interned under the Home Secretary Mr Clarke's new terrorism laws, thereby languishing in Belmarsh Prison . . . The call of moderate and apostate 'Muslims' [of the Muslim Council of Britain] upon the

Metropolitan Police to take action and arrest the 'extremists' behind the peaceful protests in central London (against the cartoons of Prophet Muhammad) was indeed a call for apostasy and betrayal. They have repeatedly called for the arrest and deportation of a vast number of Islamic activists, including scholars such as Sheikh Abu Hamza, Sheikh Faisal and Sheikh Abu Qatada—may Allah assist them and release them from captivity . . . Since the majority of Muslims living in the West are on the brink of committing apostasy (e.g., by voting for man-made laws and allying with the disbelievers), it is important for us to identify the ways in which they are leaving the fold of Islam and tackle these problems directly . . . If we look to the reality of the so-called mosques in Britain today, hardly any are built by Muslims . . . therefore, they cannot be considered to be mosques. These halls have become places of corruption, calling Muslims to vote, inviting *kuffar* (non-Muslim) MPs and prime ministers, as well as lying about Allah, His Messenger and the religion of Islam. It is even considered to be a form of heresy to call these places Houses of Allah . . . Sodomy, bestiality and incest are all crimes that are acceptable in un-Islamic societies. Recently the British government legalised homosexual marriages. It was not enough that they allowed homosexuals to practice their vile filth openly, but they felt the need to take a step further into the pits of humanity.[66]

All this causes much less outrage in Britain than if it occurred in Muslim lands, which execute their citizens for homosexuality and apostasy. A comparative story of two converts in Britain, who then became more fanatic than the most extremist Muslims, was reported by the *Times.*[67]

One of them, David Copeland, a Neo-Nazi whose ideas were said to be the inspiration for the man who let off a nail bomb in Central London in 1999, has converted to an extremist form of Islam. Another, David Myatt, a founder of the hardline British National Socialist Movement (NSM) who has been jailed for racist attacks, has changed his name to Abdul Aziz ibn Myatt. Copeland, who is serving six life sentences after three people died in his Soho bomb attacks, was a member of the NSM. Myatt is reportedly the author of a fascist terrorist handbook and a former leader of the violent far-right group Combat 18. But now he subscribes to radical Islamist views. In an internet essay entitled From Neo-Nazi to Muslim, Myatt asked:

How was it that I, a Westerner with a history of over 25 years of political involvement in extreme right-wing organisations, a former leader of the political wing of the neo-Nazi group Combat 18, came to be standing outside a mosque with a sincere desire to go inside and convert to Islam? These were the people who I had been fighting on the streets, I had sworn at and had used violence against—indeed, one of my terms of imprisonment was a result of me leading a gang of skinheads in a fight against 'Pakis'. [I support] the killing of any Muslim who breaks his oath of loyalty to Islam, and the setting up of a Muslim superstate. I had been staunchly opposed to non-white immigration into Britain and twice jailed for violence in pursuit of my political aims that I spent several decades of my life fighting for what I regarded as my people, my race and my nation, and endured two terms of imprisonment arising out of my political activities . . . But the pure authentic Islam of the revival, which recognises practical jihad (holy war) as a duty, is the only force that is capable of fighting and destroying the dishonour, the arrogance, the materialism of the West . . . For the West, nothing is sacred, except perhaps Zionists, Zionism, the hoax of the so-called Holocaust, and the idols which the West and its lackeys worship, or pretend to worship, such as democracy. They want, and demand, that we abandon the purity of authentic Islam and either bow down before them and their idols, or accept the tame, secularised, so-called Islam which they and their apostate lackeys have created. This may well be a long war, of decades or more—and we Muslims have to plan accordingly. We must affirm practical jihad—to take part in the fight to free our lands from the *kuffar* (Unbelievers). Jihad is our duty.[68]

Myatt, who briefly became a monk after his second spell in prison, said that he became a Muslim while working long hours alone on a farm. He grew up in Africa, moved to Britain in 1967 and spent time living in Worcestershire. In July 2000 *Searchlight*, the anti-fascist magazine, described him as "the most ideologically-driven Nazi in Britain, preaching race war and terrorism." He issued a statement in response to the Soho nail bombings saying: "Neither myself nor anyone else connected to the NSM can be held responsible for these bombs in any way. That responsibility lies with the person who constructed them, planted them and caused them to explode. Only that person, and God, know the motive behind the attacks." Myatt said that "all bombs are terrible and barbaric, whether detonated by lone bombers, Western governments in Iraq or Zionists in Palestine. The NSM considered the creation of a revolutionary situation in Britain as necessary since it wished to build an entirely new society, based upon personal honour, and believed this could only be done by destroying the dishonourable and corrupt society of the present. However, the NSM neither preached, nor sought to incite, what is called 'racial hatred'. Instead, it strove to propagate the warrior values of honour, loyalty and duty, and make the British people aware of, and come to value, their ancestral warrior culture and warrior heritage." Myatt also said that he had given up hope of a breakthrough by the far Right and believed that Muslims were the best hope for combating Zionism and the West. Echoing the current reality in Britain and elsewhere in Europe, where prisons have become fertile grounds for converts to Islam, Myatt appealed to other dysfunctional people like himself to rally to his new religion:

> There will not be an uprising, a revolution, in any Western nation, by nationalists, racial nationalists, or National Socialists—because these people lack the desire, the motivation, the ethos, to do this and because they do not have the support of even a large minority of their own folk . . . If these nationalists, or some of them, desire to aid us, to help us . . . they can do the right thing, the honourable thing, and convert, revert to Islam—accepting the superiority of Islam over and above each and every way of the West.[69]

Despite these voices that were widespread in Britain before July 7 struck, few were ready for the attacks; at the same time there was awareness in wide circles that it might happen. Take this account, for example, which makes the point that British authorities were slow to recognize the growing threat of terrorism by angry British Muslims before the deadly bombings in London of July 7, though there is no evidence that the attack could have been prevented, according to the report issued in May 2006.

"If more resources had been in place sooner, the chances of preventing the July attacks could have increased," stated the report by Parliament's Intelligence and Security Committee. Acknowledging that its determinations were reached "largely in hindsight," the committee also concluded that no matter how extensive the government's anti-terrorism efforts, "it seems highly unlikely that it will be possible to stop all attacks." The parliamentary report on the deadliest attack in Britain since World War II, and a separate report issued by the Home Office, concluded that two of the July 7 bombers probably had contact with al-Qa'ida during visits to Pakistan in 2003 and from late 2004 into early 2005. But they said there is no solid evidence to suggest that al-Qa'ida directly planned or directed the London attacks, in which 52 commuters were killed on three subway trains and a bus. The bombers, all young British Muslims who mixed chemicals for their crude bombs in a bathtub, were likely inspired by al-Qa'ida but acted on their own, motivated by "fierce antagonism to perceived injustices by the West against Muslims," the Home Office report stated. The long-awaited reports seemed unlikely to end speculation about the July 7 attack and a failed attack on July 21, in which five men are charged with getting onto London subways and a bus with bombs that failed to explode. Although British officials for years had warned of the likelihood of an attack by Islamic extremists, many Britons were shocked to learn that three of the four July 7 bombers were British-born.

Had the authorities and the public heeded the press reports and interviews by Masri and Abu Hamza, they would have certainly not been surprised.

> David Davis, the Shadow Home Secretary of the opposition Conservative Party, said the reports "raised more questions than answers" about what he called "a major failure of our intelligence services" to pick up earlier on the home-grown extremist threat. But he too was wrong, because the information was there, it was simply not taken seriously. He also questioned the reports' independence from Prime Minister Tony Blair's government and security services, which, despite being the focus of key aspects of the probes, provided much of the information used to compile the reports. "It is the government's view, not an independent view," Davis said in the House of Commons.[70]

Davis reiterated calls for a "fully resourced, independent inquiry" involving public hearings and witness testimony, similar to the 9/11 Commission that studied the Sept. 11, 2001 attacks in the United States. Families of some of the bombing victims have made similar demands, but Blair has said the incidents could be fully explored by the parliamentary committee investigation and the Home Office, which was in charge of domestic security. Home Secretary John Reid, also appearing in the House of Commons, said there was no need for a further inquiry into the bombings, although investigations by security services continued. The reports noted that some data were withheld because British law limits the release of information during criminal trials; five men faced attempted murder charges in the July 21 bombings, but the two reports found no connection between the July 7 and July 21 attacks. The parliamentary panel generally painted a picture of British security services as slow to recognize "the speed and scale" of the growing threat from home-grown radicals. Despite evidence that some British citizens might attempt "suicide" attacks—most notably the botched 2001 attempt to blow up an airliner by "shoe bomber"

Richard Reid—British security services predicted that such attacks would "not become the norm in Europe," the report said. "We are concerned that this judgment could have had an impact on the alertness of the authorities to the kind of threat they were facing and their ability to respond," the report added: "The chances of identifying attack planning and of preventing the 7 July attacks might have been greater had different investigative decisions been taken by the Security Service in 2003–2005." Perhaps the most intriguing sections of the two reports dealt with the July 7 bombers themselves, particularly Mohammed Sidique Khan, 30, the group's presumed ringleader, and Shehzad Tanweer, 22. The parliamentary report said Khan and Tanweer had been spotted as unidentified men "on the peripheries of other surveillance and investigative operations" in 2004. Security services did not investigate them further and focused instead on "higher investigative priorities," including attempts to disrupt "known plans to attack the UK," the report said. "In light of the other priority investigations being conducted and the limitations on Security Service resources, the decisions not to give greater investigative priority to these two individuals were understandable," the report said. The Home Office report said that Khan, Tanweer and bomber Hasib Hussain, 18, were all British-born children of Pakistani immigrants who lived middle-class lives in Beeston, on the outskirts of the English city of Leeds.[71]

Khan was a well-respected special-needs teacher and youth worker. Tanweer and Hussain were still living with their parents when they died; Tanweer played cricket and drove a red Mercedes given to him by his parents. While all were known for their strict religious observance and each was seen to become more religious in the months leading up to the attack, none was regarded by friends as a potential extremist, the report said. The fourth bomber, Jermaine Lindsay, 19, was born in Jamaica and moved to Britain with his mother in 1986. He converted to Islam in 2000 and took the name "Jamal." The report said Lindsay had handed out leaflets supporting al-Qaida and had been "strongly influenced" by Abdallah al-Faisal, an extremist preacher who was serving a prison sentence for incitement to murder and incitement to racial hatred. Khan visited Pakistan in 2003 and then spent time there with Tanweer between November 2004 and February 2005. The report said it is unclear who they met there, although it is "likely that they had some contact with al-Qa'ida figures." The report said that security officials believe both men underwent "some form of operational training" in terrorist activity during their time in Pakistan, or possibly over the border in Afghanistan. While planning for the July bombings seems to have started just after Khan and Tanweer returned to Britain, the Home Office report notes, "The extent to which the 7 July attacks were externally planned, directed or controlled by contacts in Pakistan or elsewhere remains unclear." The report states that the men had contact with someone in Pakistan before the attacks, but it does not elaborate. Further, the men likely had received some assistance in handling the chemicals they used to make their bombs. While the chemicals were cheap and readily available, they were volatile and required careful handling. The men's hair apparently lightened in color from handling the chemicals so closely, and the tops of plants just outside the bathroom died from exposure to fumes. The Home Office report concludes that "the best indications of the group's motivation" were contained in a video left by Khan that was aired on the Arabic television channel al-Jazeera on Sept. 1, which security agents believed he may have recorded during his trip to Pakistan. On the tape, Khan focused on "perceived injustices carried out by the West against Muslims" and justifying violence through his own interpretation of Islam. "We are at war and I am a soldier," Khan says on the video, speaking in a thick British accent. Shortly after the tape was aired, al-Qa'ida's number two official, Ayman Zawahiri, praised the bombers and implied that al-Qa'ida had been behind the attacks. The report said there was no evidence to support that claim, but emphasized that the July 7 bombing was "typical of al-Qa'ida and those inspired by its ideologies."[72]

As if all this incriminating evidence of the brewing Islamic subversion in Britain and elsewhere was not sufficient to stop terrorism before it erupted, it was accompanied by the distancing of Europe, except for Britain, from the furious American reprisals after 9/11, which indicated to the Islamists that they could pursue their anti-Western activities in the heart of the West almost undisturbed. For, while 9/11 traumatized the entire West, which began to awaken to the new dangers Islam posed to its security, the sense of urgency and immediacy of the issues was late in coming. Until 9/11, the Islamic world was considered friendly to the West, and the essentially Islamic struggles taking place in Bosnia, Kosovo, Palestine, Kashmir, or the Philippines were regarded as so remote, incomprehensible, and irrelevant to Western culture that few bothered to find those places in world atlases, let alone deepen their knowledge of them. But, as of 9/11, not only did these names begin to resound clearly in the minds of ordinary people in the West who had been unaware of them, but many rushed to read the Quran and works about Islam, or to visit Islamic centers in the West in a quest to comprehend what makes that faith tick, and it is believed that more than a few even asked to join the ranks of the believers. So, in a small measure, the "Islam Rush" was due not to an invading foreign Islam that one needed to understand, but to the shocking realization that the "enemy" emerged from within. After all, the nineteen Islamikaze who committed the Twin Towers horror were asylum seekers in the United States who were educated there or in Europe, had become acquainted with Western openness and democracy, and were expected to demonstrate loyalty to their countries of refuge. The fact that they did not and that their common denominator was their Islamic faith took the Americans, as well as the Europeans, by surprise, especially due to the Saudi and Egyptian identity of the perpetrators, and made them feel that a fifth column was growing in their midst, especially when it turned out that their operators, in this case al-Qaida, had organized, financed, indoctrinated, and dispatched them from the outside.

In Western Europe, Australia, and Canada—the main targets of legal and illegal immigration from Muslim countries—the first thoughts of putting strictures on those immigrants began to rise, as these countries realized that some Muslim immigrants did not move to Western democracies to improve their lot or to provide for their families who stayed behind, but that an entire scheme lay behind their move that would revolutionize the status of entire Muslim communities in the United States and Europe: from being asylum seekers, political refugees, and foreign workers to becoming a real social and security liability. For, while many of them were grateful for their new home and went about their business, the political and religious activists among them pressured the others to take a stand on current affairs of concern to all Muslims, encouraged them to demonstrate, even violently, against their new countries and in favor of their original ones, and strove to increase their numbers and make a dent on local demography and politics.

The difficulty of distinguishing the activists apart from the others made all of them suspicious in the eyes of the host countries, who, for the most part escaped the label of "racism" by not voicing in public their concerns of Islam, would venture to complain privately, as they began to feel like strangers in certain neighborhoods of their country, in which even police did not dare to enter and impose order and safety. Every wave of new immigrants, legal or illegal, was aided by the previous one, which under the humanitarian excuse of "family reunion" brought entire clans in their wake. If they had constituted negligible minorities, no one would have been overly concerned about their political or cultural impact on their host countries, but, as their great numbers alter the median age of the general population due to their high proportion of children, their demographic "threat" has become apparent in the long haul.

Had these minorities aspired to assimilate into their host societies and just become French, Swedes, or Spaniards, peacefully and individually following their cult of Islam as a personal endeavor, no one would have even noticed them. But as the Muslim communities grew larger, they also grew more vociferous and violent; they were no longer happy to be absorbed into their societies as individuals. Instead, they began to claim group rights and to justify their often violent behavior by their right to differ from the overwhelming majority. Many minorities had been absorbed by these countries over the centuries, especially the immigration-oriented among them, such as Canada, the United States, and Australia, but seldom has a minority clung to its original roots in an effort to force the host majority to yield to its will. For example, the Poles, Irish, Germans, Japanese, and Jews who flocked to the United States or Australia have willingly and wholeheartedly hoisted their new national colors, sung "America the Beautiful" or "God Save the Queen," and participated in the fighting forces of their adoptive countries in times or war. Now Arab youth in France (as in Israel), like other Muslims in other European countries, refuse to sing the anthems of their adoptive countries and demand that their ethnic and religious heritage be recognized in their school curricula, even if it contradicts the local national ethos, and think that they have the right to rip apart the national consensus and the basic values that hold the country together. Again, were it not for Muslim spokesmen who proclaim their blueprint for infiltrating Western societies to subvert them from within and take them over, one would have tended to believe that these manifestations of recalcitrance among Muslim youth in Europe were merely pangs of assimilation and demonstrations of passing displeasure with their lower living standard or with the prevailing discrimination against them.

Worst of all have been the violent methods that these groups have often been seen resorting to. In Western Europe, the native populations are terrified by the high rate of crime that is linked, according to statistics, with the immigrant Muslim population. There are recurrent, and increasingly public, complaints by Europeans in this regard, who no longer fear being branded racists if they share their thoughts with others, since the level of risk to their national identity has grown so perceptible and pressing.

Many of them are dismayed by the changing character of their cities and towns, where Muslim immigrants live, bring their religious rituals to the public square, and alter forever the cultural ambience that the local population had been accustomed to. Many Europeans now shun the use of public transportation in certain areas and at certain hours. Entire urban areas have brought the Muslim marketplace into Western cities, with the attending voices, sights, and smells, much to the disgust of many, though also to the delight of some, who would still laud cultural diversity if it were not for the accompanying atmosphere of violence and fear; the ugly sights of vandalism and littering in the heart of European cities previously famous for their neatness and public order; noises emanating from public squabbles or from shrieking muezzin calls for prayer from mosques in otherwise tranquil neighborhoods; the Muslims who squat for their Friday prayer in front of the most Italian or French Christian churches in the heart of Florence, Marseille, and other cities; security forces that dare not enter certain Muslim neighborhoods for fear of battling violent criminals and drug dealers; and, most importantly, the oppression that many feel from their inability to air their concerns in public for fear of being seen as bigots or politically incorrect.

Right-wing political parties in these countries have learned to tap these concerns and to strengthen themselves politically, because they dare to voice in public what liberals and left-wingers consider taboo. And so, paradoxically, the liberal and socialist parties, who are lenient toward immigration and have thus increased their constituencies when the newcomers were naturalized and began voting, now find themselves impoverished when their original European constituents turn their backs on them. This has happened in France, the Netherlands, Australia, and Italy, and is likely to spread into Germany and the United Kingdom if they do not tighten their restrictions on immigration into their respective territories. In the meantime, those who have immigrated—including Muslim radicals who admit in public their aspirations to subvert their benefactor states—have no qualms about milking the generous welfare systems that have absorbed them or of using taxpayers' money, which was earned by the hard work of the local populations, to cultivate a whole subculture of parasitic dependence on state allowances that builds up hatred against their naïve and well-meaning hosts. Thus, rapid breeding—in order for their community to grow demographically and to strengthen its electoral influence, so as to allow it to demand more funds and allocations—has become a way for these immigrants to exert political pressure and achieve political and economic goals. The children they have are taken care of by the welfare system of their host states, as are their housing, education, health-care, unemployment benefits, pensions, and minimum wages, which free them from work to sustain their unpublicized goals, including sabotage and terrorism, building up caches of weapons, increasing Muslim proselytization, and demonstrating, at times violently, for their fellow Arabs and Muslims around the world.

The most distressing aspects of these outbursts of violence have been that Western countries have been turned, by their Muslim communities, into violent arenas in which the Middle Eastern conflict has been exported and replayed. Not content with attacking American and Israeli symbols in most Western capitals and large cities, those hooligans who terrorize the downtown areas of their countries of residence turned to cruel and brutal onslaughts on the local Jewish communities in France, Britain, Germany, Belgium, and others, thus signaling to the world that Jews and Israel were to be equated and that anti-Semitism meant also anti-Zionism or pure and simple anti-Israeli outbursts. The worst hit were the Jewish communities of those countries, where hundreds of Jewish synagogues, cemeteries, schools, and other institutions were torched or otherwise desecrated; Jewish adults were attacked on their way to and from prayer and children on their way to and from school—all that under the eye of the local police, who did not dare to intervene forcefully for fear of the politically correct politicians on the eve of elections. One can only imagine what would have happened if a mosque or a church had been likewise burned, or non-Jewish worshippers or children attacked and harmed. Other places too have experienced the full extent of this pogrom, which in many Jewish circles was reminiscent of the infamous Kristallnacht of 1938. In most, though not all cases, these horrific anti-Semitic attacks were orchestrated by the Muslim communities of Europe, at times in conjunction with local inveterate anti-Semites.

The outcome of all this is that the Muslim communities in the Western democracies have shown that they can act in unison to undermine public order, to pose a real threat to national security, and to harm their fellow citizens, Jewish and otherwise. This means that they can organize and demonstrate in the same fashion in their host countries wherever they judge an issue important enough to them, or when the local authorities are too lenient or reluctant to confront them. Polls organized in the United States after 9/11 found that Americans overwhelmingly tied Islam and Muslims to those horrific events; 68 percent of them approved of randomly stopping people who might fit the profile of suspected terrorists; 83 percent of Americans favored stricter controls on Muslims entering the country; 58 percent wanted tighter controls on Muslims traveling on planes and trains; 35 percent of New Yorkers favored establishing internment camps for individuals who the authorities identified as sympathetic to terrorist causes; and 31 percent of all Americans favored detention camps for Arab Americans as a way of preventing terrorist attacks in the United States.[73]

This means that the threatened populations found themselves ahead of their authorities, which were more cautious in drastically limiting civil rights, and they were prepared to a great extent to replay the unfortunate experience of the internment of Japanese Americans in World War II. It was to be expected then that if and when more major acts of terror unfold in the West, the authorities would be compelled to curtail civil liberties and take radical measures against the Muslim minorities in their midst. Only in this light did the moderate measures taken by Israel against its demonstratively hostile Muslim minority, which had come under scathing criticism from the pre-9/11 world, look incredibly generous, perhaps even bordering at times on criminal neglect.

So after 9/11 we could observe two contradictory trends in the West: on the one hand Muslim minorities decried their "persecution and humiliation" for being lumped together with the terrorists of 9/11; but, on the other hand, Muslims who were stunned by the outcome of those events defied their countries of refuge, and some even began boasting of those feats and threatening a takeover of their host societies. The Arab French of North African origin, including the second and third generation of *beur*, as they call themselves, were either totally assimilated Frenchmen or whistled in contempt when they heard "La Marseillaise" sung or saw the French colors hoisted in international football matches. They began to congregate around Muslim fundamentalist leaders and to adhere to all sorts of shady Muslim organizations, some of which operated under the cover of "charitable" institutions, mostly financed by Saudi Arabia or by violent groups bent on underground activity to collect weapons and to train their fellow Muslims for acts of terrorism. The same trends were identifiable on the morning of 9/11 in the rest of Europe: England, France, Germany, Benelux, and the Balkans.[74]

It is significant that a columnist for the *Wall Street Journal* (European edition), Jonathan Stevenson, had to remind his readers after 9/11 that the subversive statements of Sheikh al-Bakri and his likes had gone unpunished in the United Kingdom (eleven out of the nineteen Islamikaze hijackers had stayed in Britain a few months prior to that day of horror), and emphasized that Abu Hamza, who acted from his Finsbury Park Mosque and was wanted in Yemen for terrorism, had called for jihad against Western infidels, but his call remained ignored by the authorities. Stevenson gave a detailed account of several of the hijackers, of their training and shelter in Britain, and, as British law did not permit their extradition, they were permitted to thrive instead of amending legislation to allow their preventive arrest and expulsion. They continued to raise funds, to purchase property, to publish their propaganda, and to escape scrutiny. He confirmed that since the 1970s Britain had concentrated on the terrorist threat of the IRA, thinking it could wean the Sinn Fein from terrorism by allowing them full expression of their agenda and believing it could carry this nonconfrontational policy over to al-Qaida and other Islamic groups who subscribe to its grand strategy. Stevenson concluded that since negotiable objectives did not fit that strategy and since bin Laden simply wanted to "debilitate the US and its allies through violence," those counterterrorism measures would not work. Only after 9/11 did London wake up and outlaw twenty-one terrorist front organizations—sixteen of them Islamic—but it still remained a staging and logistics center for al-Qaida. Over a hundred British Muslims had joined the Taliban in Afghanistan, and at least fifty-five British Muslims had received military training at terrorist bases in Afghanistan since 1996.[75]

The United States adopted stiff measures of screening its Muslim population or Muslim immigrants to the country and instilled other supervisory measures to curtail prospective terrorist activities. But the squeamish, hesitant, and disunited Europeans, in spite of their being, paradoxically, part of the European "Union," not only did not follow immediately in US footsteps but were quick to disparage American "hysteria" and castigate Washington for its "disproportionate" reactions. In their June 2002 conference in Spain, where they discussed clamping down on illegal Muslim immigration with a view to blocking entrance to fundamentalist elements, their disunity was rather disappointing. But it was also becoming clear that the emergency measures adopted by the United States, Britain, and Israel could not be sustained in the long run, not only because they were untenable in terms of civil liberties, but also because they demanded a long-term state of alert that would wear out innocent civilians who must pay the collective price for their leaders' incompetence, irresponsibility, and lack of foresight and courage in tackling a dangerous situation that had been in the making for years but which they chose not to confront. Hence the need to draw up a new policy, not a stop-gap, of reeducating the public; reorganizing state institutions to deal with the enemy from within, but without imposing new immigration limitations; surveillance of potentially subversive groups; repatriation to their countries of origin of inciters and promoters of violence; new legal systems to deal firmly and swiftly with subversive elements; testing of the allegiance of troublemakers to their host countries; and evincing resoluteness in battling the terrorists and their supporters in Western Europe. However, while President Bush had singled out the candidates for Western retaliation, including the countries of the "axis of Evil," Europe continued to avoid confrontation, hoping to continue to buy the goodwill of terrorist organizations by allowing them to operate on its soil.

These soft measures were bound to fail, however, because unlike the "carrot and stick" policy of the United States, which rewarded allies and came down harshly on terrorists and their supporters, European governments naively thought that not using the stick was the biggest carrot they could offer, not realizing that the terrified public in their countries had understood that the permissive policies of the past, which had allowed hundreds of thousands of potential terrorists to flock in unchecked, could no longer be pursued. The public began to clamor for security, that their cities be re-Westernized, and that the grounds lost to the hordes of terrorists by domestic oversight, blind "liberalism," or oblivious multiculturalism must be reclaimed. The public in Western Europe, Canada, and Australia has indeed rewarded its tougher politicians who have spoken out against unbridled immigration by electing right-wing parties and wiping out socialists, and this trend seems to have taken hold and forced some politicians to change course, while a rear-guard, including Cherie Blair and Jack Straw, was still expressing "compassion for the bombers" and "understanding" their "despair."[76] Should everyone who felt despair in this world be shown compassion for mass-murdering others, the world population would rapidly diminish. Bernard Lewis, the great luminary of Middle Eastern studies wrote back in the 1990s about the quandary of modern Islam, in which "traditional dignity and courtesy toward others turned into an explosive mixture of rage and hatred," impelling governments to "espouse kidnapping and assassination and try to find in the life of their Prophet, approval and indeed precedent for such an action."[77] Now, the most urgent question had become how to tame that rage, which prompted Muslim groups to blow up restaurants, buses, Buddha statues, and churches; to desecrate others' holy sites and call them names; to kidnap people and then chop off their heads live on video; and then to claim that they are the victims, not the perpetrators. This feeling was often reinforced by Western liberals, who instead of castigating terrorists, urged their compatriots to understand them, and, instead of helping to uproot them, elected to look at the "root causes" of terrorism, whatever they are, and to call upon their governments to alter their policies.

For their part, Muslims have quickly grasped that by wrapping themselves in the cloak of victimhood, they have achieved a license to kill and sow mayhem wherever they go, in the certainty that they will not be held accountable for their misdeeds. It is always the fault of others, or a result of the occupation, the aggression, the humiliation, the political degradation, the economic deprivation, the sanctions, the "fence of apartheid," ad nauseam, inflicted on "defenseless" Muslims by the United States, Israel, Britain, and Denmark. A visitor from another planet could be forgiven for thinking that Muslims have been passive actors throughout their 1,400-year history rather than occupiers, expansionists, founders of empires, eliminators of other nations and cultures, aggressors, and conquerors. Western liberals have not done the Muslims a favor by infantilizing them to such an extent. That the Muslims continue to live down to the low expectations of those who are volubly sympathetic to them has actually had the perverse effect of arresting their development. A cursory look at the UN Arab Human Development Report, for instance, will attest to a staggering level of backwardness for part of the Muslim world, which has benefited from enormous inflows of cash from oil sales over the past decades.

In Britain, immediately after 9/11, people were gripped by fear and began to prepare for the next terrorist attack, which many thought might be in London, as it indeed was on July 7, 2005. Shops began to sell gas masks and protective suits for biological, chemical, and even nuclear attacks. Iran's insistence on developing nuclear weapons and its possession of systems of delivery to the heart of Europe only make that fear more concrete. The authorities in London have updated the procedures for mass evacuation, at the same time that former Mayor Livingstone continued to embrace the top ideologue of the Islamikaze, Sheikh Yusuf al-Qaradawi. While those responsible for the underground system of

London prepared once again for it to fill the function of mass shelter as in World War II, July 7 has demonstrated that the subway tunnels are the least safe place for Londoners who remain complacent. While Tony Blair warned against "fanatics who are totally indifferent to the sanctity of life, and have few compunctions about how many people they kill,"[78] his determination turned into disarray when those feared terrorists hit on July 7, and he described them as criminals and voiced his astonishment that homegrown Britons should commit these horrors.

Criminals are people who break the law for their own gain, while the young Britons who committed the July 7 horrors did not seek gain. On the contrary, they were prepared to risk their lives for their ideas and beliefs (they were fanatics, as he had appropriately dubbed them before). The writing had been on the wall since 9/11, when John Stevens, the metropolitan police commissioner of London warned that his city was next in line.[79] On the face of it, bin Laden had attained his goal: to sow panic in the West and to force it not only to squander its resources and energies on defensive measures but also to be passive and wait for the next strike that the Islamikaze might deliver at any time and place of their choice. Truly, the London police have been on terrorist alert ever since, and many more have been patrolling the streets more than ever before in peace time. More security guards were posted in strategic areas, such as the stock exchange, telephone switchboards, water pumps, and electric power stations; passenger airplanes were prohibited from flying over the center of London; and regressive emergency legislation to compel everyone in Britain to carry an ID card was proposed. But all that was not sufficient, because terrorists look always for the soft spots in the defense system and hit wherever the alert leaves something to be desired. ID cards were proposed but not distributed to the population and entrances to subways, movie theaters, shopping malls, buses, and restaurants were left unguarded: it was there that the terrorists stuck on July 7.

It is certainly a heavy burden to do all that, but it is not impossible. It is too late to impose all those costly safeguards after the terrorists have succeeded. Now they will wait for the relaxation of these measures to hit again. What is more important is that security experts admitted that Britain had been a safe haven for terrorist networks for too many years due to its liberal immigration policies, the many breaches at border-crossing stations, the rigorous consideration shown for individual rights, the legislation that made extradition difficult, and the presence of a large Muslim population (well in excess of the stated two million, but no precise data are available). Those experts also realized that the link between Arab sheikhs and businessmen and the Home and Foreign Offices had for years allowed work permits to be liberally distributed, with the depleted police force rarely carrying out random checks of cars, trains, and other means of land transport.

London had also served as an international center of financial services, investment, and transactions for Muslim companies and organizations, which often use straw men to launder money in the service of terrorist groups. No wonder, then, that eleven of the nineteen terrorists who carried out the attacks on 9/11 had spent time in London before proceeding to their targets, and the fear is rife that more cells of bin Laden might still be operating clandestinely. The British distinguish between "mouths" and "brains" in these organizations: the former being extremist propaganda groups, such as the Muhajiroun already mentioned above, headed by al-Bakri, who was copiously cited above. These groups, though under surveillance, are active in recruiting believers and disseminating hate literature, especially against Jews and homosexuals, Israel and the United States. The "brains" are smaller, compartmentalized underground groups who keep a low profile.[80] Now the British might have to adjust their categorization and add a third group, that of active terrorists, especially after the July 7 terrorist attacks in London.

Much of what was depicted above regarding Britain would be recognizable, in terms of personalities, activities, ideologies, norms of behavior, and the denying attitudes of the public at large, to Western public opinions everywhere. Rosemary Righter was one of the few authors who criticized Europe for its lack of support for the American counterattack in Afghanistan after 9/11 and was full of praise for the US stand against terrorism on behalf of the entire West. She said that Saddam Hussein shared the goals of the fundamentalists in evicting the United States from the Middle East and that Europe should be made aware that some of the killers in New York had spent time in Britain, while others were plotting in Genoa, Hamburg, Milan, and Paris, because "this conspiracy found in European cities and suburbs a general welcome, space, privacy and financial support that is completely chilling." She castigated the US critics and triumphalists in Europe, whose view was shared by many Arabists there, who could not hide their pleasure at seeing "arrogant and bloody America finally getting it in the neck." She asked: "Would there have been as many armchair fatalists if Piccadilly Circus or Montmartre had been leveled on a crowded Saturday night?" and answered: "My necessary tentative answer is yes, quite probably, for one reason: Britain and France, Europe's only credible military powers, could not have taken the war to the enemy unless NATO declared the attack on American soil to be an assault on all." Only Tony Blair understood that, to her mind, and that was the reason he would not retreat from the position of unhesitant support for the United States and its policies against Iraq. For the US power, and especially its will to project it, has exposed not only Europe's vulnerability and the hollowness of the EU pretensions of military self-sufficiency but also how vital US power was for their security. She concluded that the rise in anti-Americanism in Europe and its corollary—anti-Israel prejudice—tended to distort the political prism through which Britain's national interest was seen and called upon the conservatives of the opposition in Britain to lend Bush their support.[81]

Even in the field of "regular" criminality, there was a great concern among some European populations of the sharp rise of crime in their communities due to Muslim immigrants who did not always show respect for the rule of law. Particularly alarming was a series of rapes of European women, which was claimed to be because they were not "properly veiled." *Front Page Magazine* brought to public attention a revealing debate between experts, headlined by an atrocious picture of a beaten and bleeding Swedish woman, who was said to be a "victim of Muslim gang rape." The participants, all specialists of various aspects of Islamic martyrdom, made some harrowing interpretations of the phenomenon.

Peter Raddatz, a German scholar of Islam, advanced the thesis that in Orthodox Islam there was a deep division between sexes, with Allah licensing men to be the masters of females, to go to them whenever they like, to enjoy them however they like, and to discipline them in case they developed their own ideas, like sexual self-determination. The woman was regarded as a "seed field" that under strict male surveillance entailed "Islamic correct" veiling for the continued survival and expansion of Islam.[82] Family honor, which is the province of men to protect, installs male control over women, which sometimes can end in brutal raping. Since the man is the pure element who supervises the impure women, sexuality becomes the double-edged way of both fertilizing and punishing. Therefore, just as Islamikaze bombings are a protest against the arrogance of the West, their perpetrators regarded rape as a jihad against women who, under Western influence, may drift out of male control. Raddatz cited as a corollary the sodomization of French officers by Algerian independence fighters as a way to achieve the enemy's degradation and lamented the Western mainstream propensity to accept these norms and to adjust to Muslim immigrant Sharia demands based on the growing Islamist influence in Europe.[83]

Another participant in that debate, journalist Gudrun Eussner from Berlin, thought that the attacks against European women by guest Muslims was related to the new definition of Western countries by fundamentalist Salafists, such as Tariq Ramadan of Geneva, who viewed them no longer as *Dar-al-Harb*, or the space of war, but rather as *Dar al-Da'wa,* the arena of the call, or mission on Islam's behalf, or *Dar-al-Shahada,* the space of "testimony," with its double meaning as "bearing witness that there is no God but Allah and Muhammad is his Messenger" and "to die as a *shahid* (martyr) in the path of Allah." This soft way of interpreting *Dar-al-Harb*, which otherwise obliges Muslims to fight until submission, calls upon the Muslims to wait and not challenge the enemy as long as they are not strong enough to defeat him, which is not to be understood as resignation from converting to Islam, but as what the French call *entrisme,* namely a patient and persistent long-term penetration that will gnaw at and exhaust the enemy from within.

Eussner cited the case of the inauguration of a mosque in Granada, Spain, in July 2003, in which a Turkish scholar who doubles up as a member of his parliament made the remark that Paris, Rome, and Madrid had become part of *Dar al-Islam* due to the erection of mosques there and the spread of the Word of Allah freely, under the protective wings of the liberties pursued by the unsuspecting and naïve Europeans. But when *Dar al-Da'wa* fails to produce compliance with the laws of Allah, then jihad is required to punish those who refuse to submit, among them those women who do not obey the laws of Islam by accepting male supremacy and remaining unveiled. Non-Muslim women, who by the definition of Danish Mufti Shahid Mehdi in 2004 "are asking for rape" by their public conduct, are then punishable by Muslim men who cannot accept their "obstruction" of the expansion of Muslim territory and morality. Eussner rejected Norwegian Professor Unni Wikan's dhimmi-like[84]contention that Norwegian women have to take their part of the blame for these rapes, because they are not dressing and behaving according to Muslim rules.

This very revealing debate, which from treating an issue of criminology grew to tackle very intriguing problems of religion, theology, mass psychology, and sociology, continued with Pierre Rehov, a French filmmaker who made Palestinian films on the intifada. He contends that in Muslim society there is a great temptation to rape as a result of female "provocation," the latter including anything from smiling and singing or being alone in a room with the rapist, to wearing inappropriate clothes, all these fashions of misconduct justifying revenge. In Muslim society, where any premarital or extramarital relationship is taboo, men are made in the image of God and women the closest thing to a devil to tempt them, thus playing the role of the carrier of the original sin. When a Muslim male rapes the improper woman, then, he is fighting the devil, and what happens is not the result of his own will, but against it, and because of that he is sure to get absolution for his deed. The tempted Muslim male must react, and since he is permanently frustrated by the limitations on sexual behavior, his reaction is violent and may end up in rape. Rehov cites the case of a district in southern France where 80 percent of the rapes were committed by Muslim men (a manifold higher proportion than their numbers in the population), and 30 percent of them involved gang rapes. The police often caught the rapists, who were young Muslims, and the parents not only backed their children but could not understand why their children were arrested in the first place. Those parents saw evil in the irresistible "temptation" that the non-Muslim victims posed to the rapists. They therefore viewed their children's behavior as a natural reaction to the unacceptable behavior of Western women.

Nancy Kobrin, an American psychoanalyst who has conducted years of fieldwork interviewing abused female Muslims in the United States, generally agrees with the above, but she adds that while female immigrant women in the United States would call the police when abused, then would turn around and defend the rapists as part of their mentality of identifying with the aggressors. Some of them justified wife-beating as educational, since they were probably brutalized as young girls and cannot find any reason to lift the blame for a rape from the unveiled Western woman. She says that every Muslim, male or female, she interviewed had witnessed their mother beaten and experienced brutality themselves. Therefore, rape becomes a learned behavior at home, implying male supremacy, the denigration of women, and the protection of the rapist in the family due to "family honor." There is nothing surprising, then, when those rapists move into European streets to commit their acts of violence. She also regards rape as an "additional weapon in the arsenal of Jihad" in *Dar-al-Shahada*.

She believes that Muslim rapists not only attack Western women but at the same time ambush the Western male. For example, when the Moroccan Mohammed Bouyeri killed Van Gogh, it was not only because, as claimed, of his movie *Submission*, in which he dubbed Muslims a "fifth column," but because he also accused them of being "goat f---ers," something that hurt the masculinity of Muslim men in more ways than one: a goat herder is the bottom of the social pile, the goat is slaughtered and eaten, children are often treated as if they were goats. She attacks the Western women in academe who have "sold out to political correctness" and go to extreme lengths to defend their male rapists. She thought that some of those feminists are terrified that if they took a hard look they might find themselves to be the next target of the rapists.

Further evidence was produced during the debate about Muslim women who, once in the West, feel free to open their hearts and report the abuses they have been subjected to since childhood with their parents and brothers, or in adulthood with their husbands, but public discussion of these issues has remained muted for the most part. Conversely, male Muslim immigrants into the West often hate their countries of refuge because they are not totally free to live in accordance to Sharia by dominating their women, with the latter often calling the police when they are abused. Due to their totalitarian heritage, they target the most vulnerable parts of society, who are the women.

It was feared that since government officials and media, many feminists, intellectuals, and political parties were submitting to Islamic laws and demands, the Islamization of Europe was already in the making. The handling of the cartoon crisis by the Danish authorities was seen as a sure sign of Europe pulling back and submitting to Muslim claims instead of fighting back, and the permissiveness toward things Islamic would certainly not put an end to the cases of rape, which are "understood," and sometimes even justified in both liberal and Muslim women's circles, who rush to the defense of their culture though they are its first victims. Some saw in the raping of European women by Muslim males a political act of racism, of conquest of the women of the oppressors as a way to punish them too. In addition, a society that creates equality between men and women is hated, because it challenges the male-dominated Muslim society and exposes its inadequacy to modern life, and at the same time incites Muslim women to emulate feminism by shaking off the burden of male domination. Therefore, raping a woman from another culture is a statement of contempt for, hatred to, and fear from that entire other culture.[85]

November 2001," he said, "and I could feel the brother next to me stare. After the prayers, the first thing out of his mouth was, 'How did you become a Muslim?' That was very strange to me. I didn't know how to answer him. I said, 'What do you mean, how did I become a Muslim?' And he said, 'How did you become a Muslim? You have to have a story of how you became a Muslim.' And I realized that he was right. There was a process I went through. Muslims know that it's not by chance that you come into this religion. I know that now too."[88]

This sort of state of mind has become so widespread in Europe that many articles began to appear either bemoaning the fate of sinking Europe or calling for its awakening. There is a view that maybe bin Laden did the European Muslims a disservice by precipitating his attack on the United States. Had he waited another ten years or so, they would have been far more firmly entrenched in the institutions and society of the various countries and may have also irreversibly infiltrated the security forces and apparatus, thus keeping the security services unaware for that much longer. Then they would have been in a much more advantageous position to strike.

But what happened happened, and public opinion in Europe woke up following 9/11 and began to wonder what was happening to their countries. A castigating article by George Weigel, which describes the caving in of Europe and its consequences, sums up the situation. He tells that at the height of the morning commute on March 11, 2004, when ten bombs exploded in and around four train stations in Madrid, almost 200 Spaniards were killed and some 2,000 wounded. Spain seemed to be standing firm against terror, with demonstrators around the country wielding signs denouncing the murderers and assassins. Yet things did not hold. Seventy-two hours after the bombs had strewn arms, legs, heads, and other body parts over three train stations and a marshaling yard, the Spanish government of Jose Maria Aznar, a staunch ally of the United States and Great Britain in Iraq, was soundly defeated in an election that the socialist opposition had long sought to turn into a referendum on Spain's role in the War on Terror. A fifty-four-page al-Qaida document, which came to light three months after the bombings, speculated that the Aznar government would be unable to "suffer more than two or three strikes before pulling out [of Iraq] under pressure from its own people." In the event, it was one strike and out—as it was for the Spanish troops in Iraq who were withdrawn shortly thereafter, just as the newly elected prime minister, Jose Luis Zapatero, had promised on the day after Spanish voters chose appeasement.

At first the Madrid bombings seemed to aggravate public opinion against a conservative government, and that led to the installation of a leftist prime minister, who then proceeded to do many of the things that aggressively secularizing governments in Spain have tried to do in the past. It turned out, however, that the events of the past two years in Spain were a microcosm of the two interrelated culture wars that beset Western Europe today. The first, Culture War A, is a war between the postmodern forces of moral relativism and the defenders of traditional moral conviction. The second, Culture War B, is the struggle to define the nature of civil society, the meaning of tolerance and pluralism, and the limits of multiculturalism in an aging Europe whose low fertility rates have opened the door to rapidly growing and assertive Muslim populations. The aggressors in Culture War A are radical secularists who aim to eliminate the vestiges of Europe's Judeo-Christian culture from a post-Christian European Union by demanding same-sex marriage in the name of equality, by restricting free speech in the name of civility, and by abrogating core aspects of religious freedom in the name of tolerance. The aggressors in Culture War B are radical and jihadist Muslims who detest the West, who are determined to impose Islamic taboos on Western societies by violent protest and other forms of coercion if necessary, and who see such operations as the first stage toward the Islamification of Europe—or, in the case of what they often refer to as Al Andalus, the restoration of the right order of things, temporarily reversed in 1492 by Ferdinand and Isabella when they completed the *reconquista* of Iberia and expelled the Muslims. The question Europe must face, seemingly reluctantly, is whether the aggressors in Culture War A have made it exceptionally difficult for the forces of true tolerance and authentic civil society to prevail in Culture War B.[89]

What is more, sixty years after the end of World War II, the European instinct for appeasement is alive and well. French public swimming pools have been segregated by sex because of Muslim protests. Piglet mugs have disappeared from certain British retailers after Muslim complaints that the A. A. Milne character was offensive to Islamic sensibilities. So have Burger King chocolate ice cream swirls, which reminded some Muslims of Arabic script from the Quran. Bawer reports that the British Red Cross banished Christmas trees and nativity scenes from its charity stores for fear of offending Muslims. For similar reasons, the Dutch police in the wake of the van Gogh murder destroyed a piece of Amsterdam street art that proclaimed, "Thou shalt not kill"; schoolchildren were forbidden to display Dutch flags on their backpacks because immigrants might think them provocative.

The European media frequently censor themselves in matters relating to domestic Islamic radicalism and crimes committed by Muslims, and, with rare exceptions, their coverage of the war against terrorism makes the American mainstream media look balanced. When domestic problems related to Muslim immigrants do come to light, the typical European reaction, according to Bawer, is usually one of self-critique. In Malmo, Sweden, the country's third-largest city, rapes, robberies, school burnings, honor killings, and anti-Semitic agitation got so out of hand that large numbers of native Swedes reportedly moved out; the government blamed Malmo's problems instead on Swedish racism and chastised those who had wrongly conceived of integration in "two hierarchically ordered categories, a 'we' who shall integrate and a 'they' who shall be integrated."

Belgium, for its part, has established a governmental Center for Equal Opportunities and Opposition to Racism (CEEOR) that recently sued a manufacturer of security garage gates whose Moroccan employees work only in the factory and are not sent out to install the gates in Belgian homes. By contrast, according to the Belgian journalist Paul Belien, whose online *Brussels Journal* (www.brusselsjournal.com) is an important source of information on Europe's culture wars, CEEOR declined to prosecute a Muslim who created an anti-Semitic cartoon series, on the grounds that doing so would "inflame the situation." Perhaps predictably, European Jews have frequently played the role of the canary in the mineshaft amid the trials of Islamic integration. In 2004, a Parisian disc jockey was brutally murdered, his assailant crying, "I have killed my Jew. I will go to heaven." That same night, another Muslim murdered a Jewish woman while her daughter watched, horrified. Yet at the time, as the columnist Mark Steyn has written, "No major French newspaper carried the story" of these homicides. In February 2006, the French media did report on the gruesome murder of a twenty-three-year-old Jewish man, Ilan Halimi, who had been tortured for three weeks by an Islamist gang; his screams under torture were heard by his family during phone calls demanding ransom while, Steyn reports, "The torturers read out verses from the Qur'an." He quoted one police detective shrugging off the jihadist dimension of the horror by saying that it was all rather simple: "Jews equal money."[90]

These patterns of sedition and appeasement finally came to global attention in early 2006 in the Danish cartoons jihad. The cartoons themselves, depicting Muhammad, caused little comment in Denmark or anywhere else when they were originally published months earlier in the Copenhagen daily *Jyllands-Posten.* But after Islamist Danish imams began agitating throughout the Middle East (aided by three additional and far more offensive cartoons of their own devising), an international furor erupted, with dozens of people killed by rioting Muslims in Europe, Africa, and Asia. As Henrik Bering put it in the *Weekly Standard,* "The Danes were suddenly the most hated people on earth, with their embassies under attack, their flag being burned, and their consciousness being raised by lectures on religious tolerance from Iran, Saudi Arabia, and other beacons of enlightenment." The response from Europe, in the main, was to intensify appeasement. Thus the Italian reforms minister, Roberto Calderoli, was forced to resign for having worn a T-shirt featuring one of the offending cartoons—a "thoughtless action" that, Prime Minister Silvio Berlusconi deduced, had caused a riot outside the Italian consulate in Benghazi in which eleven people were killed. Newspapers that ran the cartoons were put under intense political pressure; some journalists faced criminal charges; Websites were taken down. The pan-European Carrefour supermarket chain, bowing to Islamist demands for a boycott of Danish goods, placed signs in its stores in both Arabic and English expressing solidarity with the Islamic community and noting, inelegantly if revealingly, "Carrefour don't carry Danish products."

The Norwegian government forced the editor of a Christian publication to apologize publicly for printing the Danish cartoons; at his press conference, the hapless editor was surrounded by Norwegian cabinet ministers and imams. EU foreign minister Javier Solana groveled his way from one Arab nation to another, pleading that Europeans shared the anguish of Muslims offended by the Danish cartoons. Not to be outdone, the EU's justice minister, Franco Frattini, announced that the EU would establish a media code to encourage prudence—*prudence* being a synonym for *surrender,* regardless of one's view of the artistic merits of, or the cultural sensitivity displayed by, the world's most notorious cartoons. For all the blindness of the politicians who in the 1930s attempted to appease totalitarian aggression, they at least thought that they were thereby preserving their way of life. Bruce Bawer (following the researcher and author Bat Ye'or) suggested that twenty-first-century Europe's appeasement of Islamists amounts to a self-inflicted *dhimmitude*: in an attempt to slow the advance of a rising Islamic tide, many of Europe's national and transnational political leaders were surrendering core aspects of sovereignty and turning Europe's native populations into second- and third-class citizens in their own countries.[91] No one has nearly as brilliantly extracted from these sets of data the most exhaustive conclusions as George Weigel did. He wrote:

> Bawer blames Europe's appeasement mentality and its consequences on multiculturalist political correctness run amok, and there is surely something to that. For, in a nice piece of intellectual irony, European multiculturalism, based on postmodern theories of the alleged incoherence of knowledge (and thus the relativity of all truth claims), has itself become utterly incoherent, not to say self-contradictory. Take, for example, the case of Iqbal Sacranie, general secretary of the Muslim Council of Britain, whom Prime Minister Tony Blair appointed as one of his advisers on Muslim affairs and for whom Blair procured a knighthood. In a series of episodes that indeed seem like something from beyond Lewis Carroll's looking glass, Sir Iqbal soon went on the BBC to announce that homosexuality "damages the very foundation of society"; following the protests of a British gay lobby, he was investigated by the "community safety unit" of Scotland Yard, whose mandate includes "hate crimes and homophobia"; then, when a Muslim lobby demanded that Blair scrap the "Holocaust Memorial Day" he had created several years earlier, Sir Iqbal backed the demand, informing the *Daily Telegraph* that "Muslims feel hurt and excluded that their lives are not equally valuable to those lives lost in the Holocaust time." Yet to blame "multi-culti" p.c. for Europe's paralysis is to remain on the surface of things. Culture War A—the attempt to impose multiculturalism and "lifestyle" libertinism in Europe by limiting free speech, defining religious and moral conviction as bigotry, and using state power to enforce "inclusivity" and "sensitivity"—is a war over the very meaning of tolerance itself. What Bruce Bawer rightly deplores as out-of-control political correctness in Europe is rooted in a deeper malady: a rejection of the belief that human beings, however inadequately or incompletely, can grasp the truth of things—a belief that has, for almost two millennia, underwritten the European civilization that grew out of the interaction of Athens, Jerusalem, and Rome.
>
> Postmodern European high culture repudiates that belief. And because it can only conceive of "your truth" and "my truth" while determinedly rejecting any idea of "the truth," it can only conceive of tolerance as indifference to differences—an indifference to be enforced by coercive state power, if necessary . . . Those who would

defend the true tolerance of orderly public argument about contending truth claims (which include religious and moral convictions) risk being driven, and in many cases are driven, from the European public square by being branded as "bigots." But the problem goes deeper still. For one thing, however loudly European postmodernists may proclaim their devotion to the relativity of all truths, in practice this translates into something very different—namely, the deprecation of traditional Western truths, combined with a studied deference to non- or anti-Western ones. In the relativist mindset, it thus turns out, not all religious and moral conviction is bigotry that must be suppressed; only the Judeo-Christian variety is. In short, the moral relativism of Europe is often mere window-dressing, a mask for Western self-hatred. For another, related thing, Europe's soul-withering skepticism goes hand in hand with what Allan Bloom once styled "debonair nihilism"—a nihilism that, in its indifference to everything beyond the imperial self, has made its own contribution to the continent's unwillingness to create the future by creating successor generations. Bruce Bawer left America for Europe because of what he saw as the baleful influence of the religious Right on American politics, and because Europe was far more "open" than the United States to same-sex marriage. He cannot seem to grasp that what made Europe attractive to those like himself—its putative moral openness—is what has made it so vulnerable to radical Islam.

Bawer suggests that Europe can regain its nerve, and defend its free societies, by rejecting multicultural political correctness while retaining the political expression of skepticism and relativism: freedom concretized in law as radical personal autonomy. But it is radical personal autonomy that has helped lead Europe into steep demographic decline; it is radical personal autonomy that has brought Europe to denigrate its own civilizational achievements, seeing in its history only repression and intolerance; and it is radical personal autonomy that underwrites political correctness and its corrosive effects on Europe's capacity to defend itself against internal Islamist aggression . . . Do Europeans understand, that their very existence is at stake, their civilization has been targeted, their culture is under attack? Do they understand that what they are being called on to defend is their own identity? Through culture, education, diplomatic negotiations, political relations, economic exchange, dialogue, preaching, but also, if necessary, through force? . . . . Nihilism rooted in skepticism, issuing in the bad faith of moral relativism and Western self-loathing, comforting itself with a vacuous humanitarianism: not only is this not marvelous, it has contributed to killing Europe demographically, and to paralyzing Europe in the face of an aggressive ideology aimed at the eradication of Western humanism in the name of a lethally distorted understanding of God's will.[92]

Notes

1. For the cases of Canada and Australia, see R. Israeli, *Muslim Minorities in Modern States, the Challenge of Assimilation,* Transaction, 2009, chaps. 3 and 4.
2. *Al-Ahram Weekly,* "Beyond the Vacuum," April 13–16, 2006.
3. "Bus Driver Speaks of His Mental Torment," *Daily Telegraph*—July 7, 2006.
4. Ibid.
5. "News from Everywhere," *Daily Telegraph Leader,* July 8, 2006.
6. John Steele, "Suicide Bomber's Video Won't Frighten Us, Say July 7 Families," *Daily Telegraph*—July 7, 2006.
7. Andrew Anthony, "A Muslim at Bay: The Panorama Program on BBC1," *The Observer,* August 28, 20.
8. For Abu Hamza's background, see *al-Ayyam* (Yemen) August 8, 1999; the *Christian Science Monitor,* September 27, 2001. Both cited by MEMRI, No. 72, October 16, 2001.
9. For this term, the combination of Islam and Kamikaze, see R. Israeli, *Islamikaze: Manifestations of Islamic Martyrology,* Frank Cass, London, 2003.
10. For the description of those camps, see R. Israeli "Islamikaze and Their Significance," *Terrorism and Political Violence,* 9:3, 1997, pp. 96–121.
11. www.al-bab.com/yemen/hamza/hamza.htm.
12. Ibid.
13. *Online Journalism Review,* November 15, 1999.
14. *Al-Ayyam* (Yemen), August 11, 1999.
15. *Christian Science Monitor,* January 13, 1999.
16. *Daily Telegraph,* October 5, 2001.
17. *French News Agency (AFP),* February 28, 1999.
18. http://dsc.discovery.com/news/briefs/20010910/abroad.htlm.
19. *Middle East Times,* issue 13, 1999. MEMRI 72, October 16, 2001.
20. *Al Quds al-Arabi* (London), July 21, 2001.
21. Ibid.
22. Ibid.
23. Ibid and *The Radical,* September 13, 2001. Both in MEMRI 72, October 16, 2001.
24. Terminology is evasive and ambiguous for a reason. The original Muhajiroun are those who migrated with the Prophet Muhammad from Mecca to Medina in AD 622. In modern terms it has come to signify those Muslims who emigrate from what they term as "unbelieving societies," including their own Muslim countries that are ruled by tyrants who do not respect the Sharia laws. Exactly like the Prophet and his companions who had migrated from heretic Mecca to establish a society of believers in Medina, present-day Muhajiroun equate their act with his, which lends an aura of sanctity to their migration from an ostensibly Islamic land to the land of the unbelievers. In the London context, the move might signify that the Muslim immigrants are clustering there like the Prophet in Medina in order to build a base and use it to launch an attack on their home countries. The Muslims who left India upon its partition in 1947 to find refuge in the newly created Muslim country of Afghanistan were also dubbed Muhajiroun. This variety of possible interpretations lends multiple meanings to the term.

25. *The Observer,* August 13, 1995; and *Intelligence Newsletter,* no. 295, September 19, 1996. Both cited by MEMRI, October 24, 2001.
26. *Daily Mirror*, September 7, 1996.
27. *Al-Ahram Weekly,* October 1, 2001.
28. *Executive Intelligence Review,* September 4, 1998.
29. *Al-Ahram Weekly,* October 1, 2001.
30. *Mail on Sunday,* November 12, 1995.
31. http://artsweb.bham.ac.uk/bmms/sampleissue, January 2001, cited by MEMRI 73, October 24, 2001.
32. FP, cited by *Al-Hayat al-Jadida* (Palestinian Authority), October 10, 2001.
33. See website cited in MEMRI 73, October 24, 2001.
34. Ibid. Incidentally, the details remind one of the camps in Afghanistan described in R. Israeli, "Islamikaze and Their Significance," *Terrorism and Political Violence, 1997.*
35. Ibid.
36. CNNews.com, May 24, 2000.
37. *Middle East Intelligence Bulletin,* November 2000, citing Milan's *Il Giornale,* October 14, 2000.
38. Irfan Hussein, "The Battle for Hearts and Minds," *Dawn Weekly,* October 6, 2001.
39. *Periscope Daily Defense News Capsules,* September 4, 1996.
40. *Rose al-Yusuf* (Egypt), September 13, 1999.
41. *Al-Ahram Weekly,* November 19, 1999.
42. CNNews.com, May 24, 2000.
43. *Al-Ahram Weekly,* November 19, 1999.
44. *La Republica* (Italy) August 24, 1998.
45. www.terrorism.com/_trectforum5/000004b5.htm.
46. *C,* October 14, 2001.
47. http// artsweb.bham.ac.uk/bmms/sampleissuejanuary2001.asp.
48. Ibid.
49. BBC News, October 14, 2000.
50. For those fiery speeches and the reactions to them by unsuspecting Britons, see *The Times,* September 9, 1996, and *The Guardian* September 9, 1996.
51. Of course, the five pillars of Islam (*arkan*) are slightly different (statement of faith, prayer, fast, alms, and pilgrimage), but in the parlance of fundamentalist Muslims, *tawhis* and *da'wah* often take precedence.
52. www.almuhajiroun.com/islamictopics/islamicissues/jihad.htlm.
53. *The Mercury,* cited in http://artsweb.bham.ac.uk/bmms/sampleissuesJanuary 2002.asp.
54. *Le Monde,* September 9, 1998.
55. *The Jerusalem Post,* May 30, 2000.
56. AFP, September 14, 2001.
57. www.almuhajiroun.com/press_releases/index.html.
58. www.obm.clara/net/shariacourt/farwas/fa5.html.
59. Michael Binyon, "Prince Pitches for Religious Tolerance," *The Times,* May 5, 2006.
60. "The Clash of Civilisations Is Currently on Hold," *Copenhagen Post Online,* April 20, 2006, http://www.cphpost.dk/get/95174.html.

61. Ibid.
62. Ibid.
63. "In a New Biography, Denmark's Queen Margrethe II Says Should Be Challenged," *Copenhagen Post Online*, April 14, 2005, http://www.cphpost.dk/get/87253.html.
64. Nicola Woolcock and Sean O'Neill, "Once a Friendly Christian, He Now Backs the Bombers: Two Faces, Two Converts—Two Muslim Extremists in Britain," *The Times*, April 24, 2006.
65. Ibid.
66. Ibid.
67. Nicola Woolcock and Dominic Kennedy, "What the Neo-Nazi Fanatic Did Next: Switched to Islam, Two Faces, Two Converts—Two Muslim Extremists in Britain," *The Times*, April 24, 2006.
68. Ibid.
69. Nicola Woolcock and Sean O'Neill, "Two Faces, Two Converts—Two Muslim Extremists in Britain," *The Times*, April 24, 2006.
70. Kevin Sullivan, "British Slow to Recognize Threat of Terrorism: London Bombings Couldn't Have Been Prevented, Report Says," *Washington Post*, May 11, 2006.
71. Ibid.
72. Ibid.
73. See Daniel Pipes, "Fighting Militant Islam, Without Bias," *City Journal*, Autumn 2001. http://www.city-journal.org/htm/41/fightingmilitant.html.
74. For a basic survey of the Muslims in Europe, see the now outdated work of Gilles Keppel, *La Revanche de Dieu.*
75. Wall Street Journal, Europe, November 15, 2001. See also article by Jocelyne Cesari, in MSA News June 6, 2000, who drew a wide background of the situation of the Muslims in Western Europe.
76. *Associated Press*, cited by *Ha'aretz*, June 20, 2002.
77. Bernard Lewis, "The Roots of Muslim Rage," *Atlantic Monthly*, September 1990.
78. Sharon Sadeh, "The London Bridge Is Collapsing," *Haaretz*, September 30, 2015.
79. Ibid.
80. Ibid.
81. *The Spectator*, March 2002.
82. Incidentally, the Hamas Charter speaks in its Articles 17–18 about the role it assigned to Muslim women, consisting primarily of "manufacturing men" for the next generation of Jihad fighters. See "The Charter of Allah: The Platform of the Islamic Resistance Movement (Hamas)," in R. Israeli, *Fundamentalist Islam and Israel*, The University Press of America, 1993, *The Spectator*, March 2002.
83. Ibid.
84. For Dhimmi (the "protected people" under Islam, with their subservient legal, economic, political, and cultural status), and especially for the dhimmi state of mind, which obliges individuals and nations to submit to their persecutors, see Bat Ye'or's *The Dhimmi* and *Islam and Dhimmitude.*
85. Jamie Glazov, *FrontPage Magazine*, March 7, 2006.
86. Dr. Fatihi, *al-Ahram al-Arabi*, Cairo, October 20, 2001.

87. Brendan Bernhard, "White Muslim: How to Become a Muslim, from LA to New York, to . . . Jihad?" *LA Weekly*, December 2, 2004.
88. Brendan Bernhard, "White Muslim: How to Become a Muslim, from LA to New York, to . . . Jihad?" *LA Weekly*, December 2, 2004.
89. George Weigel, "Europe's Two Culture Wars," *Commentary*, May 2006.
90. Ibid.
91. Ibid.
92. Ibid.

7

The Islamic Watershed

Since the seventeenth century, when the Ottoman Empire attained the zenith of its power and was stopped at the gates of Vienna first (1683) and then resoundingly defeated by the Russians (1769), the Muslim world was sliding down toward its eclipse and turning from conqueror to conquered. By the end of WWI, the empire had lost the Middle East, as France and Britain carved up territories that became known as "mandates," with only Turkey and Iran remaining independent. Most painful for the Islamic world, however, was the establishment of the Jewish state of Israel in 1948. Humiliated and shaken to its foundations, the world of Islam sought solace, inter alia, in returning to the faith, as exemplified in the Islamic Conference convened in Cairo following the Muslim rout of 1967, in which thinker after thinker advocated the return to Islam as the panacea for all ills. Even before that, however, the Muslim Brothers had made their debut in Egypt, advocating Islamic piety and living according to Sharia law and using jihad as a tool of struggle against the West, with the added bonus of paradise if a believer falls in the course of jihad, so as to reassure young people that the loss of life in this world, when it is done in the path of Allah, will hold much more promise in the hereafter than does actual life at present.

Based on the Holy Word of Allah, which is not a mere recommendation but an imperative obligation, Muslims are commanded to exercise authority.[1] But, as Western authority continued to spread around the world, it was not practical for Muslims to shake it off. Therefore, a sense of gloom and despair spread among the countries of the *umma*[2] under colonial rule. The panacea was to revive Muslim society based on the values of the Quran, but this was easier said than done, because Muslims living under un-Islamic rule was not a situation readily envisaged by Muslim jurists. Moreover, the Islamic movements worldwide do not usually even recognize the legitimacy of their own domestic regimes, since they do not rule in the name of Islamic Sharia law and regard them as subservient to the decadent West. Therefore, some militant Islamic movements who seek to undermine their existing governments commit acts of sabotage, kill officials and foreign tourists, and terrorize people into submission. In countries like Syria, Libya, Yemen, and Iraq, where the devolution of power has been the main result of the Arab Spring, Islamic forces like al-Qaida, Jabhat al-Nusra, or the Islamic State of Iraq and Syria (ISIS) have been openly challenging the state authorities. In other words, the states have been falling apart, exposing the inability of those countries to govern themselves by a social contract that is acceptable to most of the population. Either an authoritarian ruler holds the country together by terror and force, or the country falls apart into its constituting components, an ideal situation for Islamic groups to enmesh themselves into the system and claim an alternative source of legitimacy of rule.

One of the earliest and most zealous attempts to revive Islam was that of Mohammed ibn Abd al-Wahhāb (1703–83), the founder of the Wahhābi Movement, which campaigned for puritan Islamic revivalism in the Ottoman Empire via a spiritual awakening in modern Arabia. Like other utopian revivalists, he thought to remove all modern accretions to Islam and to return it to its primitive origin where it was clear of saint worship and Sufi "idolatry," which had often pushed the believer to such a high degree of assimilation with Allah as to pretend to personify him. So zealous were his followers that they even destroyed the tomb of the Prophet in Medina, claiming that the cult of the shrine had replaced the worship of the defunct Messenger of Allah. Another wave of "reformists," or "modernists," followed, represented by al-Afghani (1839–97), Muhammed Abdu, the grand mufti of Egypt (1849–1905), and Rashid Rida (1865–1935), who all thought, each in his own way, to cleanse Islam from foreign influences with a view to creating a more perfect Islamic society. The greatest momentum to these trends was given when Hassan al-Banna (1906–49), a young and independent-minded imam from Ismailia, Egypt, inaugurated the Muslim Brotherhood in 1928, which within a few years grew from a handful of founders to a Middle East–wide and then to a worldwide movement of sweeping dimensions. After him, during the 1950s and 1960s until he was executed by Nasser in 1966, Sayyid Qutb (1906–66) inherited Banna's mantle. He radicalized the movement by rejecting lock, stock, and barrel the innovations of the West and felt he was in a position to judge Western values and dismiss them since he was himself partly educated in the United States.

Then came 1967, when the decisive rout suffered by the Arabs affected directly their return to Islam, as we have already discussed above, especially the Al-Aqsa Mosque in Jerusalem, considered the third holiest site of Islam, now fell under Jewish–Israeli jurisdiction and the Muslim world found itself impotent to salvage it from its new occupiers. Those days also saw the end of Nasser's pan-Arabism, nationalism, and glamour, and the return to the roots of Islam. But it was in 1979 that Iran proclaimed itself as the revolutionary Islamic Republic, overthrowing the pro-Western regime of the shah and installing Sharia as the law of the land. The great shift consisted in revolutionary Islam being the product of an Islamic state, not of an Islamic movement or party any longer; revolution had moved to become a state establishment and not an opposition to the state. Those years also saw the resurgence of Muslim Brothers in Jordan, Sudan, Afghanistan, Tunisia, Algeria, Egypt, and among the Palestinians. In sum, while many events were pivotal in the years leading to the 1989 axial year, the most important among them were the 1979 Iranian Revolution, the rise of the international manifestations of the Muslim Brotherhood, and the First Palestinian Intifada (1987–92). It would be worthwhile to dwell on each of these three components separately, beyond the general words said above.

1. The Iranian Revolution

The Iranian Islamic Revolution, declared in April 1979, was probably the most salient event in the history of modern Islamic radicalism. For, despite its being a particularly Shiite event, it proclaimed a new era in which revolution was embraced by a conservative Islamic country as the legitimate way to "progress." In a setting where the monarchies (including that of the shah) spelled out conservative Islam, while "revolutionary regimes" signified secularism (like Nasser's Egypt and Assad's Syria), the new compound of "Islamic revolution" was quite revolutionary indeed, especially as the Iranian Revolution declared itself fit for export, and it had an immediate impact on Islamic revival worldwide. So, though it would take another decade to get to the watershed year of 1989, the Iranian Revolution was clearly the trigger of the great changes to come. It was engineered by Ayatollah Khomeini, the spellbinding cleric and orator who had been gathering popularity since the 1940s, especially during his fifteen years in exile in Iraq (1963–1978), when his speeches and sermons were broadcast or recorded and then smuggled into Iran where they were avidly listened to.

When the shah initiated his peaceful and violence-less "White Revolution" in the 1960s, which consisted of wide-ranging reforms to be implemented piecemeal that aimed at modernity and secularism, Khomeini and other prominent clerics frowned upon them. The shah had them arrested in 1963, but, when riots culminated in eruptions of violence, he exiled Khomeini, who moved in 1965 to Najaf and worked there on his Islamic ideology and governance that was expressed in his *Islamic Governance* and then *Islamic Republic* books. The more the shah redoubled his efforts at modernization, the more Khomeini's scorn and backlash mounted. The latter, supported by 120,000 mullahs who preached from 80,000 mosques, saw his popularity swelling in absentia, his exile adding to his charisma and positing him as an independent force acting outside Iran against the shah instead of being given to his mercy inside the country.

Riots and demonstrations continued, both in the streets and on campuses, and the more they were quelled the more the cycle of violence escalated so as to turn into daily routine in the months leading up to the revolution, which being Islamic was nevertheless against symbols of conservatism, Western values and capitalism, like electronic stores and cinemas, and revolutionary ideas, which are usually anathema to conservatist Islam. As the demonstrations escalated, desertions from the shah's troops were stepped up in response to Khomeini's appeals from his exile in Paris, where he had moved from Najaf when he felt insecure after the Saddam–shah pact of 1978 for the partition of the Shatt al-Arab waterway. Demands began to be heard for the shah's resignation, which turned out to be the prelude of the Arab Spring of four decades later, in which the main demand of the populace to the tyrants in place was to "go away" (*Irhal!*) since they had become the symbols of oppression who should yield to popular will.

In December 1978 Iran witnessed the largest Ashura procession the country had ever seen. In the Shia, the day of Ashura commemorates the martyrdom of Hussein and his entourage by the envoys of Yazid ibn Muawiyah, who for the Shiites symbolizes the paradigm of tyrannical and oppressive rule. The commemoration of the massacres he had ordered against Hussein bin Ali and his entourage became analogous to the carnage ordered by the shah against the demonstrators in Iran. The only difference was that instead of the self-flagellation inflicted by the Ashura participants on their own bodies, in identification with the passion of Hussein, the demonstrators against the shah inflicted violence on the supporters of the shah to force him to abdicate. That was the transition from the passive and quietist Shiism of old to the active and violent Shiism that Khomeini advocated.

It took the shah a couple of weeks to abdicate in January 1979, with his administration collapsing and Khomeini's supporters taking over, a process that culminated on April 1, 1979, when the Islamic Revolution was proclaimed, based on Shiite Islamic ideology and Sharia of the Shiite brand. Two and a half months sufficed to draft the new constitution, once it was clear that the revolution would be based on Shiite Islamic ideology and the Sharia, as interpreted by the Shiites, and that Imami Shiism was the official state religion. In accordance with his principle of *wilayat al-faqih,* that is the right of the cleric to assume the ultimate rule, which Khomeini had always advocated, he set himself as the "supreme leader," distancing himself from the affinities of hierarchal and corroding power. He remained in his small Qum apartment, far from the luxury and corruption that had brought popular wrath upon the shah, and received his guests on a modest floor mat that spelled out simplicity, modesty, and a connection to the level of the people, which all added to his tremendous and mounting popularity and charisma. He appointed a Revolutionary Islamic Council as a temporary governing body, and Mehdi Bazargan, a veteran anti-establishment politician, as a prime minister, who enjoyed a vast acceptance among Iranians at large. But when radical students took over the American embassy in Tehran in November 1979, a saga that was to last more than a year, Bazargan tendered his resignation, thus leaving to Khomeini the exclusive monopoly of power and the satisfaction of savoring the greatest Shiite victory in modern times following almost thirteen centuries of downtrodden history.

The vigor of the Islamic Revolution was manifested not only in its domestic capacity to chart a new road by asserting the Sharia as a system capable of managing a large country with a thriving population, but also by its demonstrated ability to challenge the West in general, and the United States in particular, with impunity. It showed to the Islamic world, on the one hand, and to the West, on the other, that the new explosion of Islam had generated new unexplored and untapped energies that could induce the Muslims worldwide to manifest themselves with self-confidence while at the same time showing the world that Islam was not as hapless and helpless as it appeared to be. The idea was to encourage other Islamic countries to adopt without hesitation a system of Sharia law and to shed their inferiority complex vis-a-vis the West by challenging it as equals and demanding that they be respected as such. While the real watershed in Islam was to occur a decade later, there is no doubt that the Iranian Revolution, together with the other major developments in Islam (the surge of the Muslim Brothers and the Palestinian intifada) paved the way to it.

2. The Surge of the Muslim Brothers

Unlike the 1950s and the 1960s when the Muslim Brothers were repressed in Egypt, their birthplace, under the nationalistic and pan-Arab rule of Nasser, the 1970s and 1980s, namely on the eve of the axial year of 1989, there was a remarkable resurgence of the movement throughout the Islamic world. Though this revival was immanent in the Islamic environment, it was certainly fed by the tremendous worldwide impact of the Iranian Revolution and other subsequent developments. As we have already mentioned, the main ideological vigor of the Brothers had been set in motion by their founder, Hassan al-Banna, and then, after he was assassinated by the regime in 1948, by his fervent successor, Sayyid Qutb, who was in his turn sentenced to death by Nasser in 1966. The watershed occurred during the Six-Day War and its aftermath, as many Egyptians and other Muslims found solace in the faith following the devastating rout by Israel. That was the era when the Brothers, emerging from their underground status, surfaced in the open and established themselves, focusing on welfare and *da'wah* activities and distancing themselves from open opposition to the government by violent means. During Sadat's presidency in the 1970s, they gained legitimacy, for they were seen by the government as balancing leftists and Nasserite elements in Egyptian society. Indeed, compared to the more militant groups like Islamic Jihad and the Gama'at, which in the wake of the Iranian Revolution did not hesitate to launch jihad, to attack tourists, and to murder public figures, the Brothers seemed pragmatic and peaceful, engaged in charitable activities and respectful of public order.

Islamic Jihad assassinated Sadat in 1981, and his deputy Mubarak took over. He too sought accommodation with the Brothers while relentlessly combating the more militant groups. But he still banned the Brothers from joining the political arena by running for national elections as a political party, though he encouraged them to join other existing political formations and run with them. This stratagem brought them several seats in parliament at first, then when they ran in another coalition under the slogan of "Islam is the solution" in 1987, their group won thirty-six seats and became the main opposition to the government. Their excellent organizational prowess and expedient institutionalization of their ideas and activities were the infrastructure that allowed them to surge forcefully during the Arab Spring of 2011–13 and to take over the spontaneous demonstrations at Tahrir Square and turn them into an established revolution. That vigorous démarche was also to be the main tool that permitted them to take over the first elected post-Spring government in 2012, headed by President Mursi from their ranks, until they lost power by the counter-revolution initiated and led by General Sisi one year later.

The resurgence of the Muslim Brothers in Egypt was by no means limited to Egyptian territory and politics. The branches of the Brothers that were operating elsewhere, for instance, in Jordan and in the Palestinian territories, also showed signs of revival and unrest. Many of the leaders of the resurgence were refugees of the Brothers in Egypt, who had escaped Nasser's persecution and were welcomed by King Hussein as allies in resisting Communist, pan-Arab, and Nasserite onslaughts against his regime. In the 1970s and 1980s the Brothers in Jordan, following the Egyptian example, also established their welfare and da'wah activities in schools, clinics, trade unions, professional and student organizations, and mosques and Islamic centers—all organizations that did not seem threatening to the regime but at the same time enlarged the constituency of the Brothers and other Islamic organizations and built up a pool of goodwill toward them in view of the many social services that they were able to provide. So much so that in the wake of the Iranian Revolution, as the Islamic mood in the country continued to grow, a new Muslim radical group, Bayt al Muqaddas (the Holy House, Jerusalem), headed by Sheikh Tamimi, a deportee from the West Bank, was established. But the Brothers were still openly tolerated, like in Egypt, due to their seemingly pragmatic policies and peaceful ways. In fact, it was reported that they were allowed by the king to erect bases near the Syrian border in order to facilitate the training of their Syrian counterparts, who were persecuted by the Syrian regime,[3] after their predecessors had been brutally eliminated in Hama by Assad the father in 1982.

It was not until the mid-1980s, when the Brothers became increasingly radical due to aborted government economic reforms and blaring government corruption that they were harshly repressed by the authorities. In those years, the king sought closer relations with President Hafez al-Assad and was prepared in return to tighten control over the Brothers in Jordan. Many Brothers were then incarcerated and others put under surveillance. In 1988 another setback in the relations between Jordan and the Brothers set in as the king, frightened by the intifada that had broken out in the West Bank, announced the withdrawal of his claim to the Palestinian territory, in contradiction to the Brothers' stance, which viewed the unity of the two banks of the Jordan as essential. But in the meantime, the Brothers, who were the only political entity allowed to operate while all the parties were banned and the parliament suspended, had been so deeply and strongly established and institutionalized that they no longer needed the support of the regime to operate. Thus, when parliamentary activity was again allowed, they made stunning and unexpected gains in the elections of the axial year of 1989. The king had planned to make them play by his political rules, but they outsmarted him and came out on top, until he would be forced to devise other stratagems to cut down their power in the coming elections.

Thus, the rise of the Brothers in Egypt and Jordan, which also manifested itself during the Palestinian intifada, continued to expand into other parts of the Islamic world, notably the Sudan, which soon came under the tutelage of revolutionary Iran, in spite of its Sunnite brand of Islam, signifying that the cause of the Islamic Revolution proved stronger, as Tehran had hoped, than the theoretical bickerings that separated Shia from Sunna. The Brothers' branch in Sudan had been established in 1949 and joined by its eminent leader, Hassan al-Turabi, in 1951. The various Islamic trends that sprouted in those early days, voted in unity in 1954 to come under the umbrella of the Muslim Brotherhood while their opponents (for there can be no movement without its innate adversaries) rallied around a branch of the more radical Islamic Association. In 1956, Sudan became independent from the Anglo-Egyptian condominium that had ruled it since 1899, and in 1958 it ran its first parliamentary elections, with the unified Brothers remaining outside the circle of what they considered "corrupt politics." In 1964 al-Turabi emerged as the unchallenged leader of the Islamic Front, which professed a Sharia regime in the country, but in the 1965 elections his party did poorly and remained on the margins. In 1977, the dictator General Nimeiry proposed a government post to al-Turabi and banned alcohol and sanctioned the *zakat* (payment of alms, one of the five pillars of Islam) in an attempt to gain popularity for his government.

In 1977 the Brothers controlled most student unions, while al-Turabi was laboring to gain Islamic control of the state machinery, mainly by erecting his network in the military, which was viewed as the main avenue of power. In 1979, al-Turabi was appointed attorney general, which led him to assume the powerful function of Nimeiry's chief adviser on legal and foreign affairs due to his legal education in Europe and his vast knowledge of, and experience in, Western culture. His impact on government policies was manifested when the country adopted the "September Islamic Laws" as *hudud* (1983), which meant that criminal offences were punished according to the Quran (i.e., adulterers were stoned, thieves had their hands amputated, and apostasy was punishable by death). In addition, Nimeiry authorized the opening of a first Islamic bank, which prohibited interest. But by implementing these policies, which gained favor in northern Sudan, he provoked resentment among the southern Sudanese, who were Christian or animists and who erected their Sudan People's Liberation Army, which fought the north for decades from their capital in Juba and eventually brought about the creation of a separate South Sudan in the 2010s.

In 1984, relations went awry between Nimeiry and al-Turabi. The dictator reneged on his Sharia implementation and imprisoned al-Turabi, who was gaining popularity, but a year later the government was overthrown. The Brothers founded the National Islamic Front, a political party geared to run for the upcoming elections, which won 20 percent of the seats in the 1986 elections, while the secular Umma Party won double the votes and formed a government under Sadiq al-Mahdi, al-Turabi's brother-in-law with whom he was often at odds. But al-Turabi did not relent and constantly offered his Islamic alternative to the sitting government. The deadlock forced the two parties to coalesce in 1988, and al-Turabi was again the justice minister and the attorney general. The watershed year of 1989 saw the fall of the Mahdi government, which was replaced by a much more Islamic one in which al-Turabi called the shots, enabling Sudan to become the second Islamic Republic after Iran. No wonder then, that Iran hastened to sponsor its junior sister militarily and economically, thus contributing to the firming up of 1989 as an axial year and to the tremendous soaring of the Brothers worldwide, which would remain unmatched until the takeover of power by the Brothers in Egypt in 2012 under President Mursi. We have then seen the escalating power and reputation of the Muslim militants, represented by the Brothers, mainly in Egypt, Jordan, Sudan, and the Palestinian territories, all in the wake of the Iranian Revolution, reinforcing its credibility and inspiring hope in its future.

3. The Palestinian Uprising

Along with the Iranian Revolution and the emergence of militant and radical Islam as a crucial actor in the politics of Islamic lands, it is essential to cite the unrest in the Palestinian territories, otherwise known as the intifada, as a major contributing building block to the structure of 1989 as an axial year of modern Islam. Like its preceding factor—the rise of the Muslim Brotherhood (MB)—it was provoked by the Iranian Revolution, and it was in turn influenced by the prominence of the Brothers in domestic and international affairs, for the conditions for the intifada itself had been created by the Palestinian Islamic Jihad and then given impetus and maintained by Hamas, a declared wing of the MB. In short, the atmosphere of unrest and bitterness created by the combination of those elements and the daring to confront their adversaries in general, the West and Israel in particular, have shaped the fortunes of the intifada in all its stages of evolution and lent to the confrontation the sense that the downtrodden Palestinians had nothing to lose and that the Israelis had no choice but to quell the unrest or appease it in any way possible.

Following the takeover by Israel of the West Bank and the Gaza Strip, which had been until 1967 under the rule of Jordan and Egypt, respectively, about one third of the Palestinian people found themselves under what they considered as Israeli occupation. For about twenty years (1967–87), the economic interests of the Palestinians, who were mostly employed by Israel, kept them quiet. But the international rise of the PLO, under Yasser Arafat, and the Lebanese War of 1982, during which the PLO was compelled to leave its base there and exile itself to Tunisia, precipitated unrest in the Palestinian territories. The riots were instigated by exiled Arafat and his entourage, who could not wait to extricate themselves from their isolation in Tunisia, due to their inability to remain active on Israel's borders as they used to be in Jordan until Black September (1970), and since then until 1982 in Southern Lebanon. Though the Palestinian rebellion of December 1987 seemed to have broken out spontaneously as a result of a traffic accident in which there were Palestinian casualties, the PLO was quick to take it over and to make it its own. The unrest took the shape of stone throwing at Israeli troops by Palestinian children, strikes, roadblocks, and traffic disturbances due to the stone pelting of Israeli travelers. At first, the unrest was chaotic and sporadic, but, as it went on, local committees were created to organize and coordinate it and to extend economic and welfare assistance to the victims of the intifada. Ultimately, the Unified National Leadership of the intifada took over the burden of coordinating and issuing posters and announcements to keep their public informed. The Islamic groups, notably Hamas, played a key role in the recruitment, organization, guidance, and aid programs throughout the rebellion. Since the MB had been rooted in Palestine before 1948 and maintained its branches on both sides of the Jordan thereafter, it believed that it had the primary commitment to retrieve Palestine from the Israelis and to return it to *dar al-Islam.*

Though the Israeli takeover of the territories in 1967 had compelled the MB to alter its structure and modus operandi, for several years Israel had tolerated its activities, while the organization continued to refuse any suggestion that it join the armed struggle against Israel. But the new guard of the membership came up with a different strategy, claiming that it was essential to reconquer Palestine physically before it could be conquered spiritually, while the old leadership opted for the reverse process and contented itself with a quietist attitude of altering the spiritual makeup of the territories by *da'wah* and leaving the armed struggle for the second phase of recovery. The younger and impatient generation (passion is impatient) went its own way and established the Islamic Jihad faction, which, under the impact of the Iranian Revolution, advocated confrontation with Israel without delay. But in spite of some daring and successful engagements with Israel, the organization remained marginal, and so it stays to this day in the Gaza Strip, where it occasionally violates the cease-fire understandings between Israel and Hamas in order to keep up its armed struggle.

During the months that led up to the intifada in December 1987, Islamic Jihad (IJ) committed several acts of terror against Israel that were made possible by the foolish release by Israel of many IJ operatives in the 1985 deal of prisoner exchange with Jibril, of which they constituted an important part. As in other instances, released prisoners not only reverted to terrorism, but they became hardened by the jail experience and emerged from their incarceration more fanatic and more dedicated to their struggle.

After the intifada broke out, the Israel Defense Forces (IDF) severely retaliated against IJ members by deporting several of their leaders and having others killed in undercover operations abroad. In those days, Abu Jihad, Arafat's deputy in charge of the liaison with Islamic Jihad, was killed in Tunis by Israelis, thus contributing to a further weakening of the organization, which had unmistakably lent to the intifada its Islamic character and influenced the Brothers to adopt a more militant and activist stance against Israel during the unrest. Thus, Hamas was born, and the young generation of the leadership, which advocated confrontation and violence, took the lead of the movement, pushing the older, accommodating guard to the margin. Thenceforth, Hamas's impact on the intifada would be crucial, especially after it published its platform in early 1988, giving precedence to the retrieval of the entire land from Israel, due to its status as a holy waqf land, vowing never to compromise or negotiate with Israel, and threatening genocide against Jews in general unless they recognized and submitted to Islamic rule over the land. The newly inflamed intifada was further advanced and fueled when King Hussein announced in August 1988 that he was relinquishing his claim on the West Bank, wishing to keep the unrest from seeping into his kingdom on the East Bank.

Hamas's popularity continued to grow, both in the territories and abroad, to the point of appearing to take over the primacy from the PLO, demonstrating once again that in Arab politics the quietist and less militant voices always tended to align with the more extreme and less accommodating. Hamas's uncompromising platform and extremely negative stance toward any negotiation, let alone compromise with Israel, turned out to be more attractive and more credible to the rank-and-file Palestinians than the relatively moderate statements of the PLO, which was prepared to invoke SC Resolutions 181, 194, 242, and 331 and advocate negotiations with Israel. The harsh statements of Hamas leaders, like Ahmed Yassin, which spelled out sweat, blood, and tears were more readily accepted by the suffering population than the soothing promises of the PLO leaders, whose vision of peace began to be proclaimed. In fact, Arafat himself, seeing how the popularity of Hamas was growing at his expense, tried to adopt the same line of harsh statements when he declared that he was prepared to sacrifice a million Palestinians in order to liberate Jerusalem, hoping thereby to retrieve the zealous constituency that had abandoned him and joined Yassin. Moreover, Yassin's modest living and direct concern for his people, contrasted with Arafat's pompous ceremonials and his prosperous and detached confinement in his *mukataa,* surrounded by guards, helicopters, and luxury cars and maintained by a lavish budget; he could not have escaped the scrutiny of the miserable populace that accused him and his gang of corruption and gravitated toward Hamas.

All these major upheavals formed the infrastructure that led to 1989 as the axial year of modern Islam. But the major events that marked 1989 somehow converged on that year in a succession of extraordinary events that a stage director could not have planned better. Not all events necessarily had to do with Islam directly, such as the fall of Communism that year, which left a huge ideological vacuum that Islam immediately stepped in to fill. A dramatic example of that unfolded in Israel when, upon the collapse the Communist Party, which had been until then the main political party among the Arabs of Israel, a dramatic rise in radical Islam took its place and became the fastest growing political organization in the country. Directly connected to the rise of radical Islam, however, was the Rushdie fatwa of February 1989, issued by Khomeini himself, which was not only emitted as a matter of course, but also became an educational program to indoctrinate students and a worldwide summon of all Muslims to strive to eliminate that "apostate" who had dared to insult the Word of Allah by calling its holy phrases "Satanic verses."

After the 1979 revolution, Khomeini had censored the press and created an educational system that was more indoctrination than education. Nonetheless, no one imagined that his censorship would extend abroad with such a tenacity and obtuseness as to reveal in public his deep-rooted complex of inferiority in Islam, which necessitated recourse to violence and wrath every time some Muslim or non-Muslim seemed to deprecate Islam or its Prophet. Muslims seem to be so unsure of their convictions that they are not prepared to wage a war of ideas, and, like a disturbed child, they react with force every time their feelings are hurt or their truths challenged.

On February 14, 1989, when Khomeini learned of Salman Rushdie's book *Satanic Verses,* he immediately issued his fatwa of "death for blasphemy," as if the author were under his jurisdiction or as if any Muslims and all Muslims were by definition given to the supreme guide's judgment. It did not occur to him that any mufti in any country serves the cases brought before him within the confines of the territory under his jurisdiction. The guide issued a summons to "all Muslims" to execute the author rapidly and declared worthy of death also all the publishers who permitted the book to see the light of day in all tongues. The sanction being "less anyone dare to insult the Islamic sanctities," it was made clear that Islam was not open to argument, debate, disagreement, or dissention, that its sanctities were sacrosanct and that any violator deserved death, just as any thief was bound to have his limbs cut off and any adulterer had to submit to being stoned to death. These rules of conduct toward any contravener of the rules of Islam were not adopted ad hoc for this case only, but, in view of the outrage and number of casualties caused by the Cartoon Affair in 2006, it is evident that those violent Muslim reactions were the rule of thumb. The following day was declared a day of mourning in Iran, during which thousands of demonstrators poured into the streets, stoned the British embassy (Rushdie had British citizenship), and chanted repeatedly "Death to Britain!" much beyond the normal reaction for an "insult" in the civilized world.

The overreactions continued to spiral in Iran, as a $3 million bounty was put on Rushdie's head by the top clerics, Foreign Minister Velayati urged all countries to close down the British embassies and cultural centers, as if a country were obligated to pay for the noncriminal trespassing of its nationals, or as if "blaspheming" someone were deemed a criminal offence internationally and not only according to the primitive and inhuman laws of Iran. Both Pakistan and Iran banned Viking/Penguin Books, which published the book, while the main office of the publisher received a bomb threat. What was even more shameful was the capitulation of Western businessmen to the Iranian blackmail when on February 17, American booksellers B. Dalton, Waldenbooks, and Barnes and Noble decided not to stock Rushdie's book. For while they did so, they betrayed the author and the freedom of press and expression and evinced an open surrender to threats and pressures in their own country where they enjoy protection by law. Viking/Penguin soon closed its offices "in order to install a new security system." England stood firm when its House of Commons passed a motion condemning Khomeini for his incitement and verdict and passed another motion ensuring Rushdie's safety. Never was anyone so threatened by foreign powers requiring his country to wrap him within various layers of safety measures. All in vain, because in the end he had to move to the United States, followed by Ayaan Hirsi Ali, the renowned migrant from Somalia who ascended to membership of the Dutch parliament, but her life had become so impossible by the security arrangements that were imposed on her due to the threats she received for her free tongue concerning Islam that she too had to leave. Both cases were of avowed Muslims who had reneged on the practicalities of Islam and some of its customs in spite of remaining formally Muslims.

However, the affair kept snowballing, in spite of Rushdie's open apology for his "insensitivity," which was ignored by Khomeini, who repeated the same verdict. And an offense of this caliber was unforgettable and unforgivable in Khomeini's Islam. In 1989, just after the fatwa and before Khomeini died, he must have sensed that he was at the height of his authority and of the respect he inspired, and he could not soften at the end of his life on something that seemed absolutely essential for him to leave as part of his revolutionary heritage. No longer could the Islamic state overlook "blasphemy" and behave as if nothing had happened. It was absolutely imperative for Khomeini to heed the situation, to show that he cared, and to take all the steps he could toward the implementation of the fatwa, even if it proved vain. The proof is that decades after his death no one has dared yet to abrogate it, so great its impact and authority. On February 20, the International Rushdie Defense Committee was founded in London by writers, booksellers, journalists, and human rights activists who called the fatwa an "armed censorship." The next day, the EC withdrew its twelve heads of mission from Tehran. From then on, there was a marked increase in acts of violence and accusations on both sides.

On February 24, police killed twelve Muslims and fifty others were injured during a demonstration in Mumbai against Rushdie, and two day later, thousands demonstrated in New York and Paris against Rushdie, and Iran opted to sever all relations with Britain. But soon the Norwegian publisher of the book received death threats, a Pakistani guard was killed at the British Council Library in Karachi, and a protestor in Srinagar, India, was killed while others were injured. Bombs caused damage at a California bookstore, as well as to New York's *Riverdale Press* newspaper after it criticized the store for withdrawing the *Satanic Verses* from its shelves. The US Senate also unanimously adopted Resolution 72, condemning the threats against Rushdie and his publishers and stating its commitment to "protect the right of any person to write, publish, sell, buy and read books without fear of intimidation or violence." In March 1989, a large demonstration was held to protest the *Satanic Verses* in Bangladesh. More than a hundred Muslims were wounded as police fired on the mobs. Muslims and police also clashed in Kashmir, leaving one dead and eighty-four wounded. Other Muslim disturbances erupted worldwide, from Bonn to Bangkok and from Rotterdam to Sydney. On March 29, two Muslims from Belgium were gunned down after speaking out against the fatwa on television. Mere days after that, two London bookstores were firebombed for carrying copies of the *Satanic Verses.* On April 12 two Norwegian bookstores were set afire after releasing a translation of Rushdie's book. In Sydney, Australia, a bookstore was firebombed on May 21, and on the twenty-seventh a mammoth demonstration of 30,000 Muslims gathered in London's Hyde Park and clashed with various human rights groups.

The month after, Britain took the extreme measure of deporting three Iranians who engaged in "anti-Rushdie activities." When on August 3, a radical Muslim accidentally blew himself up in his London hotel room, the Iranian-backed Hezbollah [4] deemed him "the first martyr who died while preparing to attack the apostate, Salman Rushdie." Then a bomb exploded in a London department store, Muslims attacked four Penguin bookstores, and when several countries (Denmark, Finland, Portugal, Sweden, the Netherlands, and Spain) announced that they would allow the publishing of the *Verses*, demonstrations and protests continued unabated. This was to show that when one abandons his principles, he is not respected, but when one submits to other principles under threat, he is despised.

The alacrity with which the fatwa was encountered in the entire Islamic world and the shock it inflicted on the rest of the world could not help dividing it into the pro-fatwa Muslim world of darkness, which presumed to decide for its followers what to think and had no compunction about imposing its views on others, including non-Muslims, to think and behave according to Khomeini's strict standards; and the Western anti-fatwa world, which held free thinking and personal freedoms above all the rest and rejected any attempt to impose on it standards of thinking and conduct that are borrowed from the Muslim world. Thus, a wide and deep gap was created between the West and the world of Islam, especially frustrating for the West, which continued to see itself invaded by multitudes of Muslim immigrants who dictated their standards to their host countries: the numbers of demonstrations and burned bookstores by Muslim migrants in the West, as contrasted with the Islamic world, in which the occasional Western visitors do not dare to confront their hosts with Western ideas of tolerance, coexistence, and peace was striking.

The Rushdie fatwa focused the attention of the world in 1989, but that was not the only focus of interest of the Islamic world. Other developments occurred simultaneously and had a long-term impact on Muslim countries, among them the fundamentalist trends in North Africa and the rise of the Muslim Movement in Israel, which was quick to fill the yawning gap of the disintegrating Communist Party. Communism had been borrowed from the outside, and replacing it by a new ideologically oriented grouping could only be Islam, which leaned on internally inspired Islamic sources. One of the most dramatic examples of these developments happened on February 18, 1989, when Algeria declared the creation of the Islamic Salvation Front (FIS). The Algerian regime recognized the new grouping, thus lending to it encouragement and credibility after years of oppression. However, when the authorities rescinded that recognition, violence became inevitable, as the Muslim radicals grew to consider their acceptance as legitimate and its withdrawal as a vicious encroachment on their rights. Clashes emerged on campuses between leftists and Muslim radicals. In the early 1980s an Islamic unrest started in the countryside, which led to the arrest of many Muslim radical leaders. After the sudden fall of oil prices crippled the economy in 1986, riots swept the country in 1988 due to economic despair. Only when the riots subsided, did President Chadli Bendjedid promise reforms and a multi-party system. Within months, more than thirty parties formed, including the FIS. While the FIS was at first an outlet for the frustrated classes and a provider of social services, its popularity soon swelled the ranks and pushed the FLN, the ruling party, to withdraw its recognition of it, lest its membership outnumber its own. After 1989, the party turned violent and mounted a terrorist campaign against the FLN's repression.

In 1989 the Islamic Party also scored an impressive victory in the Tunisian elections. The regime, however, annulled the results, fearing the rise of an Islamic state, but the shock remained that a thoroughly Westernized and modern country like Tunisia should be so open to Islamizing. Tunisia had been a French protectorate since 1881, until its leader, Habib Bourguiba, launched a campaign from Cairo in 1943 to bring his country's plight to world attention. In March 1956 he achieved independence and returned home as a hero. A devout secularist, he made changes that reduced the role of Islam, turning the renowned Zitouna Mosque into a university, abolishing Sharia courts, confiscating waqf property by the state, banning polygamy, dismantling mosques, and discouraging women from wearing hijab.

But when he appeared on television in 1960 urging Tunisians to ignore the fast of Ramadan, claiming to wage jihad on poverty, an Islamic opposition rose that denounced him, sparking street fights in the city of Kairouan. As food shortages grew in 1960, Islam was seen as an alternative solution. And when pan-Arabism was discarded following the 1967 rout, Islam was again hailed as a viable alternative. Influenced by the Muslim Brothers of Egypt, the Muslim Movement of Tunisia soon produced cassettes, books, and two journals. They attacked government corruption and secularism. In the 1970s Rachid Ghannouchi rose to lead the movement. He was an adept of the Muslim Brothers and a specialist on al-Banna's ideas, as well as on the writings of Maududi and Qutb. He created the Quran Preservation Society and turned it into the center of his Islamic Movement.

The year of 1979 was pivotal for Tunisia in the sense that in the wake of food riots and the positive popular reaction to the Iranian Revolution in the Tunisian street, Bourguiba faced a general strike by the General Union of Tunisian Workers (UGTT). But when he called the military in to force the workers back to work, many were killed or wounded. When Ghannouchi expressed solidarity with the strikers, Bourguiba clamped down on the Quran Preservation Society, which brought the collision to a head. In 1980 the Jamaat al-Islamiyya (Muslim Association) was created as a political organization led by Ghannouchi and geared to address the social and economic problems of the country. A year later, Bourguiba called for the first multi-party elections in the country, in which the Islamic tendency took part, presenting Islam as a means to achieve social justice rather than advocating an Islamic state.

Nonetheless, Ghannouchi and other Muslim leaders were arrested, and Bourguiba "won" all 136 seats for parliament, permitting him to repress the Muslim opposition. The Muslim Tendency continued its *da'wah* activities nonetheless and continued to dominate the student unions in the country since 1980. In 1984 Ghannouchi and other incarcerated leaders were released from jail, but the ban over employing Muslim Tendency members was enforced, and women wearing the veil were barred from public places. Taxi drivers who were employed to distribute Muslim materials were seized and punished. The peak was reached in 1987 when Bourguiba arrested 3,000 members of the Islamic Tendency, including Ghannouchi, bringing to a head a major collision between the government and the Iran-influenced Muslim opposition.

In September 1987, twelve tourists were wounded in a bombing carried out by members of Islamic Jihad, following on the example of their Egyptian counterparts, who were active in terrorizing foreign tourists in Upper Egypt. Ghannouchi was again seized and sentenced to life due to his contact with Iran. In the midst of the riots that followed and in the wake of the bombing of four tourist hotels, General Ben Ali took over the rule and deposed old and senile Bourguiba. He released Ghannouchi, went on a hajj to Mecca, and ordered the observance of Ramadan, a festival that had been taken lightly by Bourguiba, which had caused much bitterness against him among the populace. However, the promises of democracy faded when the Islamic Party, under its new name, Al-Nahda (the Revival), was banned from participating in the April 1989 general elections. The Islamic candidates ran individually and captured some 15 percent of the vote, though it was estimated that their real strength amounted to double that number. But Ben

Ali abrogated those results and claimed that all seats were won by his Constitutional Democratic Party, and he himself was proclaimed to have been reelected to the presidency by 99 percent of the vote. He severed relations with Iran due to the financing, guidance, and advice she channeled to the Tunisian Islamic members. Again al-Nahda was suppressed as a step toward its elimination. So, unlike the hostile attitude of the regime to the Muslim Party, it is evident that under the direct impact of the Iranian Revolution, much influence had seeped from one end of the Islamic world to the other.

If in Algeria and Tunisia the challenge to the existing regimes could emanate from the questionable legitimacy of the rule, in Morocco, the more established and recognized legitimacy of the monarchy caused a delayed reaction to the Iranian Revolution in Rabat. It was not until two or three decades later that the Islamic Party there gained plurality in the elections and demanded a larger part of the rule at the expense of the king, who had placed himself at one apex of the triangle: Allah, the Fatherland, and the king, to make his legitimacy indestructible. The gains of the radical Muslims did not stop there; they spread all over the world arena: Sudan, Afghanistan, and even in the non-Islamic state of Israel.

Indeed, 1989 was the year when Sudan experienced two military upheavals. The first occurred when a military petition, signed by 150 officers, was presented to Prime Minister al-Mahdi, demanding several secular reforms and forcing the government to act contrary to the general trend of radicalizing Islam in North Africa. Al-Mahdi suspended Sharia law and ousted the Brothers from his government. But Hassan al-Turabi mounted a counter-coup, and in conjunction with General Omar al-Bashir, a long-standing member of the Muslim Brothers, formed a new regime in which radical Muslims held important positions in government, in universities, and in the security services. He reinstated the Sharia, strengthened relations with Iran, and became the only Sunni state that embraced absolute Islamic rule, until the Taliban in Kabul adopted that order in 1996. Al-Bashir's main concern was to protect his own rule; therefore he began to arrest anyone who seemed threatening, including his ally, al-Turabi.

Sudan's radical conduct was unmistakable; it began providing safe haven for other radical groups, including bin Laden, who was pushed out of his native Saudi Arabia due to his dealings with al-Qaida, which became anathema to his government; Sudan provided diplomatic passports to Islamic militants wanted by conservative Arab governments; and it accepted aid, in weapons and oil, from Libya and Iran, both supporters of militant Islam. Thus, 1989 also signaled the year when the United States desisted from its economic aid and military aid to Sudan. From the Iranian viewpoint, then, Sudan was a success story as long as their revolution was earmarked for exportation. For after that coup in Sudan, the latter began to export its brand of Islam to adjoining Islamic countries in Africa and the Middle East. A non-Islamic country that was swept by that trend was Israel, where in 1989 local electoral victories of militant Islamic groups gave them for the first time dominion over several local councils and drove the entire Islamic Movement into important political gains, which marked it as the fresh alternative to the now dismantled Communist Party.[5] In 1979, inspired by the Iranian Revolution, a group of Israeli Muslim radicals declared jihad against Israel and set out to establish a Muslim state in Palestine. They called themselves "The Family of Jihad," and under the leadership of Sheikh Darwish stockpiled weapons, burned Israeli fields, and even turned violent against other Muslims whom they viewed as remiss in their Islamic duties. But in 1981 all sixty members of the group were arrested and sentenced to jail, and they were not released before they pledged to abandon military action and subversive acts. In 1986 the group started the journal *al-Sirat (the Straight Path),* which spread the group's ideas. Following on the Egyptian Brothers' example, the group started to dispense welfare programs, which advanced their cause.

In February 1989, Israel's Islamic Movement experienced its first major victory through Israel's democratic system. The municipal elections signaled that the movement had evolved into a religio-political organization that sought power as a way to implement its program. The leaders who presented themselves for office ran under the slogans "Islam is the solution," "Islam is the truth," and "Islam is the alternative." Not coincidentally, the Jordanian Brothers had used the same slogans in 1979, as had the Egyptians in 1984. In the end, five Muslim radical mayors were elected, as well as forty-five councilmen in various locations. Umm al-Fahm, the largest town of the lot, elected Sheikh Mahajneh as its mayor, as well as eleven Muslim councilmen out of fifteen. In fact, the Muslim radicals of Umm al-Fahm took nearly 75 percent of the votes. In Rahat, a Bedouin town in southern Israel, Sheikh Jum'a al-Qassassi was elected mayor. In Kafr Qasim, seven Muslim radicals out of the eleven councilmen were elected, and thirty-one-year-old Sheikh Abdallah Sarsur was elected mayor. Islamic mayors were also elected in the towns of Jaljulya and Qalansawa, while Kafr Bara's mayor was elected to a second term. In Kafr Kanna, the radicals took six of the eighteen seats, but Kamal Khatib, the Islamic mayoral candidate, lost to the incumbent Communist. Had the community been purely Muslim, Khatib would have easily been swept into office by the overwhelming majority of the constituents.

Mahajneh, Sarsur, and Khatib became new leaders in the movement. Mahajneh and his followers rebuilt Umm al-Fahm with activities ranging from trash collection to fundraising. In 1988 he inspired fellow villagers when he made the hajj to Mecca. Sarsur, however, focused on new needs to try to isolate Israel's Muslims from their Jewish/Zionists compatriots, for he opposed Islamic involvement in the national elections to the Knesset, unlike the local elections in which he was engaged and chose instead to fill the leadership gap in Muslim towns in Israel. Khatib made his mark as he helped treat Kafr Kanna's drug addicts and created peace between warring clans. Following their victory in the elections, the newly elected leadership banded together with Darwish, their undisputed leader, to form the Committee of Arab Mayors and Heads of Local Councils, claiming to be the legitimate corporate leaders of the Arabs in Israel. In late 1989, Sarsur led a delegation to the United States to garner support from American Muslims. They met with dozens of organizations, lectured at universities, gave interviews to the media, and were even received by the US State Department. As the distribution of *al-Sirat* skyrocketed, it became a monthly and then a weekly publication, which in October 1989 was replaced by another weekly, *The Voice of Truth and Freedom,* which presented itself as the "Voice of the Islamic Movement in the Holy Land."

The year of 1989 also saw the erection of Islamic colleges in Israel. One of them was built in the town of Taibeh, to be followed by another at Umm al-Fahm, and a third at Baqa. Some of the infrastructure was made possible by Yusuf Islam, otherwise known as singer Cat Stevens, who donated $40,000 to the Islamic Movement at Umm al-Fahm. After the 1989 local elections, the Islamic Movement kept radicalizing as younger and more militant sheikhs began to upstage Sheikh Darwish, who was considered more conservative and pragmatic. This process climaxed in 1996, when the Islamic Movement splintered between the northern more radical and uncompromising branch, who refused to participate in national elections lest its candidates be compelled to swear allegiance to the state of Israel, versus the southern one, which was the continuation of the Darwish pragmatic current that ran for national elections together with other Arab factions. The northern stream became coterminous with Hamas, and in fact collaborated with it, collected funds for it, and joined hands with it on a platform that was overtly anti-Israel, which in the 2010s prompted the government to discuss a proposal to outlaw that branch of the movement altogether.

An extraordinary distribution of Islamic events also unfolded in various parts of the Islamic world in 1989, which lent prominence to that year as a climactic one. Most remarkable were the death of Khomeini, the transformation of Hamas, the end of the Soviet venture in Afghanistan, and the July bombings of Mecca. When the supreme guide died on June 3, 1989, his death signaled the end of an era in which he had "reversed the course of modernization and westernization in Iran, breathed a new life into Islamic movements throughout the world, and turned Islam into a new political and social force to be reckoned with."[6] He had also demonstrated to Third World countries and to superpowers that there were limits to superpowers' hegemony over mobilized masses. The victorious resistance of the Afghan mujahideen against superior Soviet forces, as well as the Palestinian intifada against Israel, were inspired by the supreme leader to an extent and enabled the struggling Muslims to conclude that once Muslim fighters had overwhelmed the Soviets, it was now their turn (and capacity) to rout the other superpower too, as they were to demonstrate later in Iraq and Afghanistan. Khomeini's death could not come at a less opportune time: He had just fired the heir apparent to the leadership of the revolution, Ayatollah Montazeri, and the Council for the Reappraisal of the Constitution was amid its revision of executive laws, so anarchy was feared. To maintain stability, the transitional government postponed the funeral arrangements for a few days, and, when they were announced, eight people lost their lives and hundreds were wounded in the frenzy to catch a last glimpse of the departed leader. Finally the body was taken by helicopter to the graveyard and put to rest. After the funeral, Ali Rafsanjani became the new president, and Ali Khamenei the new supreme guide, but Khomeini's spot remained vacant and his shoes were never filled by his pygmy successors.

Khomeini's legacy was strengthened by the will he left behind him. It outrageously assaulted the Saudi monarchy as traitors and the Americans as terrorists. He also denounced Iraq, Egypt, Jordan, and Morocco, concluding with "May the curse of Allah and his Angels be upon them all!" He left instructions on how to keep the revolution on course, which meant pursuing a terroristic policy that he sanctioned and was therefore sanctified by other clerics as the right one. In other words, Khomeini's death was a defining moment in the history of the Islamic movement as far as exporting the revolution was concerned. For that policy could be either pragmatic and adaptive to changing circumstances or radical, doctrinaire, and uncompromising at all costs. The radical path won out, since it was always possible to accuse the reformers and pragmatists of betraying Khomeini's legacy if anyone tried to stray from the road chartered by the great guide. After Khomeini's death, Rushdie's affair was pursued unabated and its furor did not recede, forcing Salman Rushdie, who could no longer entertain a reasonable life under the permanent threat of death in England, to migrate to the United States.

In May 1989 Hamas was forced to restructure as a result of overwhelming pressure by Israeli forces. At first it appeared that the loss of Hamas leadership as a result of target elimination by Israel would irretrievably weaken Hamas, but the remarkable fashion in which it rebounded and turned into an internationally recognized movement has become one of the Islamic feats of that apex year of 1989. Indeed, in that year, the first of the intifada, Hamas not only continued to lead it, but it also took credit for spreading Islam among the populace, to the point that it became evident that Hamas was not merely the agent of propagating Islam among the population, but that it took credit for advancing the radical brand of it. In the years 1986–89 the number of mosques in the Gaza Strip jumped from 150 to 200. February 1989 was also the month when during the municipal elections in Israel the radical Muslims scored major victories, which brought the writers of a Hamas leaflet in the West Bank to say: "What is happening today in this blessed land is but a new creation of the Islamic *Umma* and of the Muslim generation that carries the banner of Islam."[7] As its popularity continued to rise, Hamas pressured Palestinian women to dress modestly and attacked stores selling liquor. Some of its militant members clashed with leftists and wantonly killed those suspected of collaborating with Israel. It also became clear in the public arena that Hamas gained clout vis-à-vis the PLO, so much so that in the summer of 1989, while the intifada was raging, they challenged the United Leadership and refused to allow schools and universities to become staging grounds of civil disobedience and protest, preferring instead that studies continued as planned.

The year 1989 was also significant in that Hamas began to carry out acts of violence. February was the first time Hamas kidnapped Israeli soldiers, thus inaugurating what they called "the development of the movements' methods of resistance." In May, a Hamas operative stabbed to death an Israeli soldier, and in July another militant took control of a bus on the Tel-Aviv-Jerusalem highway and crashed it, killing sixteen people. Later that year, in October and November, Hamas operatives killed five Israeli soldiers. In retaliation, Israel made hundreds of arrests among Hamas members, including the spiritual head and the founder of the movement, Ahmed Yassin. As a result, the movement was forced to restructure its leadership so that the thinned-out ranks would not debilitate the vitality of the movement. For example, since the centralized stamina of the movement was neutralized by the arrest of central figures, each local cell was granted the power to manage its own affairs independently of the center. The crackdowns also forced the organization to move its headquarters to Springfield, Virginia, and to Amman, Jordan. September 1989 was the month when Israel declared Hamas an illegal organization after it had expressly rejected the pragmatic policies of the Egyptian Brotherhood. At the same time, Hamas gained international notoriety in 1989 through increased efforts to institutionalize the movement's presence in Arab and Palestinian communities in the United States and Europe. In November 1989, Hamas officially announced its alliance with Iran "in the war to liberate Palestine" and created ties with radical Muslims in Jordan, Egypt, Saudi Arabia, Sudan, Algeria, Tunisia, and other places.[8]

Maybe the most dramatic of Hamas's effects was the general strike it called for in Xmas 1989, which was obeyed despite the vigorous protests of Christian Palestinians. That showed that not only Muslims but also followers of other faiths obeyed the summons to strike. The power of Hamas and its support continued to grow after its restructuring and, together with the other contributing factors to the axial year, brought 1989 to its apex.

The next dramatic contributor was the Soviet debacle in Afghanistan that was announced on May 15. Moscow had been battling an ideological war there since Xmas 1979 similar to the United States in Vietnam a decade earlier, namely a desperate attempt to hold back its Islamic ideological rivals from gnawing at its Communist boundaries, which under the pressure of unsustainable losses necessitated a withdrawal. The breaking point was reached when the Afghani mujahideen, aided by the United States and Saudi Arabia, obtained shoulder-fired anti-aircraft missiles that erased the overwhelmingly superior Soviet might from the balance of power and decisively shifted the advantage to the Afghani side. For the mujahideen it meant that if Islam could sap the military might of a superpower, it was itself a superpower. That meant in the long run, as the Soviets were replaced by the Americans, that the other superpower would not be immune to a similar result, hence the self-confidence of the Taliban that the United States and NATO were bound to be defeated. That realization was one of the capital gains that made 1989 an axial year: a year after which the world was different from what it had been before it.

The staggering defeat of the Soviets in the Afghan War no doubt contributed to the eventual dismantling of the Soviet Union, an axial event in itself, but also constituted a decisive stage in the remolding of Afghani domestic politics from the previous ungovernability of the Afghan community, in which rival factions were at each other's throats. The Soviet defeat gave rise to the Taliban, who in one hugely popular sweep united the country and instituted a strong central power that enforced law and order and inspired an immensely authoritarian rule. True, when Afghan women were delivered from the strictures of that rule by the American incursion in Afghanistan in 2001, they emitted a sigh of relief, but seen in terms of the chaos and the civil war that had prevailed in the country previously, the Taliban regime was certainly an advance. And in any case, after thirteen years of American and NATO fighting, it seems, as of August 2014, that the Taliban continues to prevail, in defiance of the "democratic presidential rule" that the Americans helped institute. Another far-reaching result of the Soviet defeat was the emergence of Osama bin Laden as a local hero, who created a symbiotic relationship with the Taliban and survived as long as the Taliban regime did, after which he was chased by the Americans until they gunned him down in Abbottabad, Pakistan.

Notes

1. See Sura "the Creator," verse 38, which commands: "He has appointed you [Muslims] his vicegerents in the earth. And whoever believeth not, on him shall be his unbelief; and their unbelief shall only increase for the unbelievers of their own perdition." See Bernard Lewis, *Islam and the West,* Weidenfeld and Nicolson, London, 1963, p. 52.
2. Emanuel Sivan, *Radical Islam: Medieval Theology and Modern Politics,* New Haven, Yale University Press, 1985, p. 1.
3. Beverly Milton-Edwards, "A Temporary Alliance with the Crown: The Islamic Response in Jordan," in James Piscatori (ed.), *Islamic Fundamentalisms and the Gulf Crisis,* The American Academy of Arts and Sciences, Chicago, 1988, p. 90.
4. O'balance, Edgar, *Islamic Fundamentalist Connection, 1979–95, The Iranian Connection,* NYU Press, 1997, p. 11.

5. R. Israeli, *Muslim Fundamentalism in Israel,* Brassey's, London and Washington, 1993.
6. Farhang Jahanpour, "Iran after Khumeini," *Current Affairs Bulletin,* vol. 66, no. 9, February 1990, p. 20.
7. Ziad abu-Amr, *Islamic Fundamentalism in the West Bank and Gaza: Muslim Brotherhood and Islamic Jihad,* Indiana University Press, 1994, p. 59.
8. Abu Amr, op. cit, pp. 86–87.

Conclusion

Watershed toward Growth or Down to the Abyss?

Is an axial year by nature a positive or a negative one? Does a peak year connote a welcome development, or does it signal a tragic turn of events? It all depends on the eye of the beholder. When pondering the question of whether stability is good or bad, it all depends on the quality of the stability: if it is a stable government that is legitimate and enjoys a wide support of the people who chose it, then we say that it is desirable and responds to the needs of the people; but if it is dictatorial, has no legitimacy, and depends on the whims of a dictator, then we say that it is negative and that there should be no qualms about bringing it down. For example, the Soviet Bloc had provided stability for seventy years, but it was still viewed as an "empire of evil" and forced by Western competition to surrender to the capitalistic world. Conversely, the endemic instability of the political systems in such Western countries as Belgium and Italy, since they are manifestations of the erratic conduct of basically democratic and legitimacy-conscious peoples rather than of anti-democratic enforcement of illegitimate rule, they constitute a bearable evil that will always be preferable to authoritarian regime.

Though the list of events that made up the 1989 axial year was not exhaustive, even more important were the trends that began to crystallize and would characterize the decades that unfolded thereafter. For example, the emergence of the Army of Muhammad in Jordan in that year on the heels of the mujahideen victory in Afghanistan dramatically illustrated how Jordanian volunteers who had fought in Afghanistan since 1979 returned experienced and battle-hardened a decade later and created secret military cells that launched attacks against secularists and non-Islamic targets in the country. Other trends, like the Liberation Army and the Armed Vanguard of Islamic Youth, as well as the Jordanian Islamic Jihad, gained ground and followers and filled in for the Muslim Brothers, who had slipped into pragmatic policies and were practically removed from the top list of Muslim radicals. When the Brothers moved into the political scene, they became established and ran for elections, while fresh and enthusiastic new adepts of radicalism made their way into the vacant slot of radicalism. The general mood of zealous support for the radicals and the soaring recruitment to their ranks soon settled into molds of action and discourse that illuminated the way radicalism was going to chart:

a. Islamic radicalism was increasing in volume and intensity.
b. Even after Khomeini's death and the Mecca bombings, Iran remained the unquestioned champion, guide, hub, and focus of Islamic radicalism.
c. As a result of this atmosphere, Islamic radicalism grew in other places like Sudan, Tunisia, Algeria, Jordan, Israel, and among the Palestinians, tipping the balance in favor of Hamas over the PLO in the 2006 elections.
d. Violence has become the trademark of this radicalism, as exemplified by Hamas, al-Qaida, Lashkar-e-Taiba, Boko Haram, the Mali rebels, and the Somalian Al-Shabaab.
e. After the mujahideen victory in Afghanistan, the country not only took on a more Islamic course in the form of the Taliban regime, but the Afghani veterans of the war transferred their battle to European, Asian, African, and western and Middle Eastern countries; it was then that bin Laden inaugurated his universal terrorist network, which became a major tool in that struggle.
f. The end result has been that after the eclipse of the Soviet Union, radical Islam has taken its place as the next global threat.

Beyond these trends, which have been transforming the world of Islam and the world in general, one can examine in minute detail the effects of the watershed year and realize how and to what extent things have dramatically changed over the quarter century since. We shall provide illustrations of these transmutations in North Africa, Central Asia, the Middle East, and a medley of other Islamic lands, not to speak of the impact of these Islamic trends on non-Muslim countries, except Israel, despite its being part of the Middle Eastern setting.

Starting with North Africa, it was very paradoxical that while Islamic radicalism had seemed to take a step back after 1989, it came back in full force in the wake of the emergence of the Arab Spring on the eve of Xmas 2010, when a self-immolating Tunisian young man triggered that process. However, between 1990 and 1992, there had been mass arrests of Tunisian Islamic radicals under the ascent of the repressive regime of Ben Ali, who took over from Bourguiba. The radical party al-Nahda's operatives attacked the offices of the Constitutional Democratic Rally in 1991, and shortly thereafter the authorities quelled an Islamic radical plot to overthrow the government in place. Many Muslim radicals, including members of the military, were arrested after they were caught receiving arms training in Iran. Other Tunisians were accused of receiving Iranian military training in Sudan. Conversely, Rachid Ghannouchi, the head of al-Nahda, had been forced into exile since 1989.

In Algeria, by contrast, an explosion of Islamic activity unfolded right after 1989. The FIS rose in 1989, and it soon became a main channel for anti-regime frustration, providing at the same time much needed social services financed by Saudi Arabia and Iran. In the June 1990 elections, the FIS won control of 853 municipalities out of 1,541, which is the majority, and came to control thirty-two provinces out of forty-eight. The first round of the vote gave the FIS 49 percent of the popular vote, which translated into two thirds of the seats in parliament, which were won, inter alia, due to the aggressive intervention in the election campaign by the Iranian Revolutionary Guards. Thereupon, the FLN regime promptly cancelled the election results and arrested more than 2,500 FIS members, including its two leaders—Abbasi Madani and Ali Belhadj.

The accompanying background music was more disconcerting than the political repression itself, due to the traumatic fear in Western countries from Muslim radicals, which was more concerning than the lack of democracy. In fact, France squarely supported President Chadli Bendjedid in his repressive démarche and so did other European countries that were paralyzed by the Muslim threat and considered a Sharia state more dangerous than whatever similitude of democracy the FLN had evinced. Conversely, there was little international intervention or concern on behalf of the radicals who had won their vote democratically in an election initiated and run by the FLN regime. Even though many claimed, as in 2006 in Palestine, that the pro-FIS vote (like the pro-Hamas vote in 2006) was against corrupt government, not for an Islamic state, the FIS who were robbed from their power (unlike Hamas who took hold of it), erupted in an angry and brutal civil war that would rip the country apart and cost hundreds of thousands of lives in the coming decade.

When 1992 dawned, Algeria was deep into chaos. Bendjedid resigned and Boudiaf replaced him as president. A state of emergency was declared while the FIS embarked on a campaign of rampage that included burning schools, car bombings, outrageous killings, and wild hijackings, mostly carried out by the MIA (the Armed Islamic

Movement), all aiming at removing the FLN government in place and replacing it with an Islamic government. In response, the government deported some 5,000 people and arrested many others, including the underground Takfir wal-Hijra, those fanatics inspired by the mother organization in Egypt that treated their coreligionists as *kuffar* (heretics) and, like the precedent of the Prophet Muhammad who had migrated from the Mecca "heretic" environment to start a new life in Muslim Medina, they also proclaimed their ambition to migrate, at least spiritually, if not physically, from their heretical environment toward a Muslim one. To lend a legal legitimacy to the suppression of the FIS, the Algerian Supreme Court officially barred the FIS in April 1992 for entertaining a "political party with a religious platform," and their leaders were again arrested and incarcerated for inciting an armed rebellion. Three members of the local Hezbollah who were backed by Iran were simultaneously sentenced to death. Another radical group, the GIA (Armed Islamic Group), made up of veteran Afghanis, emerged in 1991 and attacked an army post in southern Algeria, killing three soldiers. They were intent on killing nonbelievers.

In June 1992, after the government cancelled the elections, a gunman assassinated Boudiaf. In August, a bomb exploded at the Algiers airport and killed ten and wounded many more, with the FIS claiming responsibility. Throughout that year, the GIA also engaged in many high-profile assassinations, including a former prime minister, with the violence imputed to Iranian and Sudanese instigation, in view of the many radicals who were being trained in Sudan since 1991. Algeria reacted by suspending its relations with both countries. In 1994, an Air Algerie flight to Spain was hijacked, and in that same year Muslim radicals killed seven Italian sailors docked near Algiers, and in mid-July the GIA abducted the ambassadors of Yemen and Oman in an attempt to secure the release of one of their leaders. In August, five Frenchmen were gunned down by the GIA at the French embassy, and in December the GIA again hijacked an Air France flight, demanding the release of two of their leaders and declaring their intention to blow up the plane over Paris.

At the outset of 1995, a car bomb exploded near the main police building in Algiers, killing forty-two people and injuring hundreds. It became abundantly clear that Muslim causes as expressed by Muslim radicals were unforgiving and uncompromising, justifying the most extremist means of violence and the most inhuman treatment of their fellow countrymen, let alone of foreigners, in order to achieve their ends. So much so that by the end of 1994 the death toll stood at 25,000 civilians, 7,000 terrorists, and 2,700 members of the security forces, namely more casualties than all the Israelis killed in all the wars combined since the creation of Israel and into the twenty-first century. There were times when 800 people were killed each week in Algeria: that is more than the Israeli toll of fatalities during the Six-Day War of 1967. The situation resembled more the civil war in Syria in the 2010s, in which the daily number of fatalities surpassed the hundreds.

In 1995 the FIS took part in a peace dialogue in Rome under the leadership of Ben Aicha and Madani, indicating the beginning of a process of moderation on its part. However, the more radical AIS (Islamic Salvation Army) and some dissidents from the GIA broke away from that group, and the violence continued in spite of the peace process. Another group emerged—the Islamic League for Call and Djihad (LIDD) in 1997 that was responsible for widespread terror in the late 1990s in Algeria. In 1998, another militant group—GSPC—was created. In 1999, after lengthy negotiations with newly elected President Bouteflika, a general amnesty was announced for Islamic militants, allowing close to 5,000 GIA operatives to surrender their weapons, while a similar number of diehards among the radical group were still holding out. In three months between January and March 2000, 600 civilians and Algerian soldiers were killed by GIA members. In sum, since the creation of FIS in 1989, Algeria has witnessed a tremendous increase in Islamic activity and violence. And when the government repressed the FIS, it triggered an eight-year civil war in which an estimated 150,000 fatalities have been accounted for. Paradoxically though, as the FIS grew more pragmatic and ready to negotiate and settle, it spawned more fanatic splinter groups, like the AIS and the GIA. Namely, since the peak year of 1989, the Algerian radical Islamic movement has continued to increase in leaps and bounds.

In the heart of the Middle East, the growth of Islamic radicalism was no less impressive. Obviously, the most remarkable gains by Muslim radicals have been registered by ISIS (the Islamic State of Iraq and Syria, also known as ISIL—the Islamic State of Iraq and the Levant), that amorphic entity that has taken control of northwest Iraq and northeast Syria since the 2010s and declared a caliphate in July 2014 in that unruly Sunni territory where war-torn Syria and Iraq have witnessed the eclipse of the central Arab state and the rise of radical Muslim groups that purport to take over governments through incredible violence and cruelty. While the Kurdish autonomy in northern Iraq and in northern

Syria and the Alawite regime in Damascus constitute obstacles to such a new polity, the amazing numbers of volunteer mujahideen flocking from all over the world to fight jihad there against the Assad regime demonstrate that the balance of power on the battleground is far from being decided. Especially worrisome is the mujahideen effort to lay their hands on the chemical, and maybe also biological, weapons that the Assad regime has pledged to eliminate from the Syrian arsenal. But before matters boiled down to a dramatic confrontation in ISIS-controlled territory, Muslim radicals had been making remarkable advances in Jordan among the Palestinian Hamas and in Israel Proper.

After the 1989 elections in Jordan, the power of the Brothers grew. In 1990 Brother Abd al-Latif Arabiyat became the speaker of parliament, and five of his fellow party members were included in the national unity government that King Hussein established to wade the crucial period of the Gulf War, in which he decided to throw in his lot with Saddam Hussein, even though officially he declared his neutrality in the war while the Brothers had decidedly taken a pro-Iraqi stance due to the desecration of the Muslim holy sites in Saudi Arabia by the massive presence of US troops. But when the king opted for participating in the Madrid peace conference after the war in October 1991, the Brothers declared a day of mourning. Another Muslim radical group, the Army of Muhammad, which had made its inception in 1989, also carried several attacks on non-Muslims in Jordan, notably in 1991 against Christians, liquor stores, and some officials. In 1992 some of its members were arrested and sentenced to life for plotting hostile operations against Western institutions in Amman. In 1993 they were accused of conspiring to murder the king.

The wavering king decided to legalize political parties in anticipation of the forthcoming elections in order to dilute the power of the Brothers, who had until then enjoyed the lone-party status, but the new elections law, which was often altered to fit changing interests and to encounter prospective dangers, also forbade the parties to accept foreign aid, aiming at the well-connected Brothers. But the latter were experienced enough to circumvent the new law by creating a new party—The Islamic Action Front (IAF), which was comprised almost exclusively of Brothers members. The new law, which was tailored to shrink the influence of the Brothers, also assured the one-man one-vote system to replace the bloc vote, which automatically reduced the number of IAF votes, and also banned public rallies and politically motivated mosque sermons to reduce the party's constituency.

Their aggressive election campaign did not yield them more than sixteen seats, about half of what they had secured previously, and another six seats went to Islamic independents. In protest for the setback they had suffered in parliament, the IAF walked out from parliament. When the peace treaty was signed between Jordan and Israel in 1994, the Brothers drew up a critique of the clauses of the treaty, claiming that it was disadvantageous for Jordan and that it did not consider itself bound by it. Their members boycotted the king's crown speech in parliament in October 1994 and also boycotted President Clinton's 1995 appearance in the Jordanian parliament. But that trend was not sufficient for the hawks among the radicals, who had resented the relative pragmatism of both the Brothers and their IAF substitutes, and drifted toward the Army of Muhammad and Islamic Jihad. Others, like the founders of the Dar al-Quran Bloc in parliament, drifted further apart and were arrested for possession of weapons and explosives.

In 1995 the Brothers came under fire from the regime due to their most natural rapprochement with Hamas, in view of the affiliation of both movements with the Egyptian Brothers and of both considering themselves branches of the mother organization. But the Brothers attacked the newly constituted Palestinian Authority (PA) for dealing with Israel and praised the terrorist attacks of Hamas on Israel. In 1996, bread riots unfolded in southern Jordan, and several Muslim Brothers were jailed for their involvement in them. As the 1997 elections neared, the IAF again threatened a boycott if the government did not yield to its demands that the one-man one-vote reform should be repealed, that media restrictions should be eased, that the parliament's authority should be enhanced, that the oppressive measures be ceased, that the economic policies be freed of Western influences, that civil liberties should be increased, and that relations with Israel be ended. The king expectedly rejected those demands, and the elections were boycotted. In 1998 reports surfaced that the Brothers had maintained links with terrorist groups in Pakistan, Iran, and Afghanistan, all hubs of radical Islamic militancy. In October 1998, after Israel and the Palestinian Authority signed the Wye Plantation Agreement, the Brothers organized rallies in opposition, and during the 1998 American Desert Fox Operation, the Brothers demonstrated in various parts of Jordan. In 1999–2000, Jordanian intelligence uncovered cells sponsored by bin Laden, as well as others by Hizb ut-Tahrir, Islamic Jihad, and other extremist groups.

In sum, radical Muslims have played a large part in Jordanian politics since 1989. Though, since King Abdallah was crowned in 1999, he has removed Hamas HQ from Amman and Jordan has increased its counter-terrorism activity, the radical Muslim movement has continued to grow, signaling the new contours of Jordanian politics since the new king took over. In the times of his father, the foundation of the regime had rested on the inalienable alliance between royalty and the Bedouins of Transjordan. But since then, Palestinian businessmen and politicians, who represent the majority of the population, have carved for themselves larger swaths of the political pie in the country, thereby shrinking the role of the old Bedouin nobility and expanding the role of the new Palestinian elites, including the Islamic one. Connected with this trend is the exponential growth of the role of Hamas in Palestine, which has not only challenged the prevalence of the PLO and the Palestinian Authority, but has also, via its direct link with the Jordanian Brothers, expanded the impact of radical Islamic tendencies on the circles of power in the kingdom.

Hamas, which had risen during the intifada, had seen the Palestinian uprising subside due to the eruption of the Gulf War in 1991, after which it established its "military wing"—the Izz ad-Din al-Qassam Brigades, named after a militant Muslim radical imam, who had led radical Muslims in Haifa and northern Palestine in the 1920s and 1930s until he was gunned down by the British Mandatory Power in 1935 near the village of Ya'bed in Samaria. Al-Qassam Brigades, who were meant to gain immunity from counter-attacks for the religious leadership of Hamas, under the false pretext that the imams did not engage in violence, brought Hamas much notoriety by the sheer atrocity and continuity of its acts of terror against Israelis. Those atrocities were harshly punished by targeted killings, deportation, and repression, but all the measures of restructuring adopted by Hamas permitted it to continue to operate and expand, much to the dissatisfaction of both Arafat, the head of the PLO, and the Israelis, against whom the crux of Hamas's wrath was directed. But while Arafat had evinced some readiness to participate in peace conferences with the Israelis, Hamas did everything in its power to block the peace efforts, and he was rewarded by the Iranians, who invited him to Tehran for a conference on the intifada. The new Israeli government headed by Rabin decided in December 1992 to deport to Lebanon the four hundred most radical Muslim leaders, most of whom were Hamas members. Hamas was quick, nonetheless, to refill the ranks with new cadres, and in 1992 announced its increased ties with the Iran-backed Hezbollah in Lebanon, which were ironically forged while Hamas deportees were exiled in Lebanon.

When Israel and the Palestinians agreed on the Oslo Declaration of Principles (DOP) in September 1993, Hamas continued to steadfastly oppose it and created the Democratic and Islamic National Front, which was dedicated to thwarting it. Indeed, Hamas restated its vow to carry out terrorist attacks against Israel as long as the PLO negotiated with it. At the same time, the four hundred Hamas leaders who were deported by Israel started to train under the auspices of Hezbollah, in addition to the thousands that Iran was training directly. In that year of 1993, Hamas launched its Islamikaze operations,[1] which were a new, shockingly violent tactic adopted from Shiite terrorists, so much so that Hamas was soon placed on the US State Department's list of terrorist organizations. A string of violent Islamikaze attacks continued into 1994 and 1995, and in 1994 the Palestinian Islamic Jihad also joined the anti-Israeli rampage, causing a mounting number of casualties. The Palestinians were not deterred by the negative effects of their acts, which were often followed by the closure of their territories to Israel for work or for trade activities. It was much more important to them to savor the suffering they inflicted upon Israel than to prevent the deterioration of their own situation. In other words, there was little Israel could do to cause deterrence to Hamas. If initially the common Palestinian anger was directed at Hamas, it ended up being vented at Israel, so much was Israel resented and Hamas supported by the Palestinian populace.

In 1996 the Palestinians held their first elections, which were boycotted by Hamas heads who were reluctant to lend legitimacy to the PA, which was itself the fruit of the Oslo Accords they boycotted. In January 1996, Israelis targeted and killed Yahya Ayyash, the engineer behind many Hamas attacks, which prompted a retaliation in both Tel-Aviv and Jerusalem, resulting in dozens of Israeli casualties. A pattern was set, since in Hamas and Arab thinking, only Hamas had the right to terrorize Israelis, and Israel must absorb its casualties and damage in silence; if it dared to retaliate, as it often did, then there would be a retaliation for the retaliation, an indefinitely prolonged cycle of tit-for-tat, in which Hamas must have the last word. That pattern was still alive in 2014, when Hamas launched rockets on Israel at a trickling pace, but only as long as there was no Israeli response; when Israel reacted, that was taken as an aggression and Hamas retaliated against it with hundreds of daily rockets and missiles for days on end. This was a repetition of the same pattern that had happened in spring and summer 1997 and in 1999. In September of that year, Hamas recruited Israeli Arabs to bomb two buses in Israel's north, and its activity did not wane despite the arrest and incarceration of many of its members by the PA.

In 1999, the HQ of Hamas, which had been located in Amman, was forced by newly crowned King Abdallah to leave town. In 2000, there was talk that Hamas would move from Islamikaze killings to hostage taking, with a view to securing the release of their members from Israeli jails. At the same time, members of Izz ad-Din al-Qassam continued to be trained in Sudan and Iran and often returned to the territories to mount terrorist operations. The organization expanded its recruiting and money-raising activities, especially in Kuwait, Saudi Arabia, and other Gulf states, as well as from Iran, and through American donors who were solicited by seemingly charitable organizations, who then deviated the money to terrorist uses. But since Hamas took over the rule of the Gaza Strip in 2007, the organization became the machinery of a state in the making, and through it shared its actual power in Gaza with the outer leadership of Hamas, which used to lodge in Damascus and now in Qatar. It is dedicated to jihad against Israel, both in an uncompromising propaganda of threats and promises of destruction and occasionally through a shower of missiles and rockets on Israel, which it hopes will remain unanswered by Israel. When Israel does respond, as on Xmas 1997, in November 2012, and in July 2014, a full-fledged conflict has erupted between Israel and Hamas, in which the latter suffers a great deal of casualties and damage.

Connected to Hamas and the Brothers in Jordan are also the Israeli Muslim radicals who take advantage of the liberties afforded by Israel to skate adroitly to the outer limits of law and occasionally to cross them and be pursued to justice by the legal authorities of the country. After the elections of 1989, in which the Islamic Movement gained a few mayorships in the country, the Arab villages experienced an explosion of Islamic identity as many men wore beards and women traditional Muslim garb, and schools segregated girls from boys. The movement made great strides in education, health care, media, and social services, affording many Islamic towns and villages the opportunity to segregate themselves from Israeli society, as if they had created a parallel local government. In 1990 the Islamic Film Festival took place in Tel Saba, the Bedouin town in the south, in a hostile environment. It featured a life-size model of the Ka'ba, the Muslim holy shrine of Mecca, and set pavilions glorifying the luminaries of Islamic radicalism, including al-Banna, Sayyid Qutb, al-Afghani, Abdu, and others. The Israeli members of the Islamic Movement joined with their counterparts on the West Bank and Gaza to sponsor the meals throughout the festival, thus joining together the Palestinian Muslim radicals on both sides of the international border between Israel and the PA.

In 1993, the movement expanded its hold in the country when the number of Islamic representatives in Israeli local government increased from fifty-one to fifty-nine and the number of communities in which the movement won representation rose from fourteen to sixteen, including six mayors and heads of councils, and Islamic activities increased in mixed cities such as Haifa, Jaffa, and Acre. However, as the movement grew and diversified, a split occurred between the pragmatic faction of Darwish and the more doctrinaire one of Mahajneh, based in Umm al-Fahm. The former was based in the Arab Triangle just east of Tel Aviv and comprised that area and the Bedouins of the Negev, while the latter comprised the Galilee in northern Israel. The one supported the Oslo process and negotiations between Israelis and Palestinians, while the latter, in line with their Hamas counterpart, negated any such contacts. The former coalesced with existing Arab parties in Israel to justify running with them in national elections, while Mahajneh and his ilk continued to boycott Knesset elections lest they would have to swear allegiance to the state of Israel when inaugurated. Thus, two different and separate branches of the Israeli Islamic Movement grew out of the same Islamic root planted by Darwish thirty years earlier. As a result, Darwish had to found his own journal, *al-Mithaq*, once he had to part with the movement's journal based in Umm al-Fahm. The more fiery and hyperactive Mahajneh also embraced projects that lent him visibility, like rehabilitating old and destroyed mosques and cemeteries, collecting funds internationally for his al-Aqsa foundation, and leading large-scale refurbishing works in the al-Aqsa Mosque in Jerusalem. Mahajneh also became the spokesman for the al-Aqsa foundation in Jerusalem, thus eliciting worldwide support throughout the Islamic world, especially Egypt and Turkey. As he progressed, his links with Hamas continued to strengthen.

In 1997, as a conflict developed between the Muslims, now the majority, and the Christians, who have become the minority in Nazareth, Muslim radicals in Israel were instrumental is exacerbating the moods. At that time, Muslim radicals in Nazareth, with a view of exhibiting the new demographics of the city, decided on the eve of Xmas 1997 to invade the plaza at the foot of the Basilica of Annunciation, the tallest and most sacred Christian site in town, and to erect there a tent mosque, pending the construction of a permanent structure that would dwarf the Basilica. The Christians were incensed and the Christian mayor of the city, outnumbered by the Muslim majority of his councilmen, was paralyzed, and the city operations came to a halt. This author was appointed by the Israeli government as a member of a Commission of Inquiry geared to sort the rift out and permit the smooth functioning of the city machinery. But the Muslims, incited by radical coreligionists across the country, refused any compromise or mediation, so it took the government two years of legal procedures to clear the plaza and return the situation to the status-quo. But many Christians sensed that they had become strangers in their own city and left. In 1998 Mahajneh's popularity was at its zenith, when he won his third term as mayor of Umm al-Fahm. In Nazareth too, ten out of the nineteen seats of the city council went to the Muslims. In international politics, Mahajneh and his faction rejected the Wye Plantation accords between Israelis and Palestinians, while his rival, Darwish, supported that framework for negotiations.

In Israel's national elections in 1999 the Islamic Movement was active and helped to shift the Bedouin vote toward its affiliated parties. Those years also saw an increase in violence by Muslim radicals against Israeli Jews, recruiting among their coreligionists to launch acts of terror in coordination with Hamas's cells in the West Bank. Mahajneh himself sat on the Board of Governors of Gaza University, an important stronghold of Hamas. His general conduct and his general abuse against the state of Israel and its institutions have created an atmosphere of permissiveness and lawlessness among his followers, assured as they were that their Islamic convictions immunized them from any prosecution. Since 1989 there has been a marked increase in the number of mosques and Islamic cultural centers in Israel and in their proliferation into every village, city, and neighborhood in the Arab environment, which are attended by young men wearing beards, the hallmark of the Muslim Brothers, and young new clerics disseminating Islamic teachings and manners among them. So much so, that with the outbreak of the Second Intifada in 2000, many young Muslims in many Israeli towns mimicked the uprising of the Palestinians by burning sites, waving Palestinian and Hezbollah flags, pelting rocks at Israeli police, blocking main roads, and shouting anti-Israeli slogans and abuses.

In 2014, Islamic anti-Israeli activities and demonstrations having come to their zenith and subversive acts by Mahajneh and his group having come to a saturation point, there was talk by the Israeli government of outlawing the Northern Islamic Branch, which in fact acts outside the state and incessantly undermines it. The significance may be grievous, because, compelled to act outside the law, the movement will go underground, and what is known today openly and officially might became a secretive and covert operation. Whether it is outlawed or not, the fact that the two branches function separately point to the fact that both are legal. But if one should be outlawed and the other remain legitimate, then the outer impression would be that there is only one Islamic Movement, while the illicit one would be ignored as nonexistent. What that would do to the expansion or the shrinkage of the radical element among the Muslims is still hard to envisage.

Other parts of the Middle East, too, like Iran and Sudan, have seen the reinforcement of Islamic radicalism after 1989. Iran continued, as it had vowed, to export revolution and terrorism, closely followed by its client and adept—Sudan, and often coordinating between them was the al-Qaida network that was set up and financed by Osama bin Laden. The connection between the rise of Islam in North Africa, the Levant, and Central Asia was also provided by bin Laden, the engine and the living link of fundamentalist Islam who operated from Afghanistan. The fall of the Soviet Union in 1990 led to the creation of the predominantly Muslim states of Uzbekistan, Tajikistan, Turkmenistan, Kazakhstan, Kyrgyzstan, and Azerbaijan, and all were inspired by the Taliban in Afghanistan and under the spell of bin Laden, who had himself taken shelter there.

After the departure of the Soviets in 1989, Afghanistan fell into chaos, the United States shut off its aid to the mujahideen, who now fought against each other for power while some joined jihad elsewhere: in Chechnya, Bosnia, Jordan, Algeria, Kashmir, and elsewhere.[2] Many of them, however, sought refuge in the madrasas of Pakistan, where their ideological training went in-depth, and they prepared themselves to become the Taliban of later years. In April 1992 the mujahideen leadership celebrated the Islamic State of Afghanistan, and in December an assembly of representatives elected Rabbani as president and Hekmatyar as prime minister, with the military leadership under Mas'ud. But the country remained divided into fiefs and Kabul into different parts that were ruled by the various factions. Tehran, for its part, supported the Shiite minority, hoping thereby to take control of the country. All in all, radical Muslims continued to flock to Afghanistan from all parts of the world, and the main bone of contention among them was between various militant factions, one more radical than the others. Thus, despite the infighting and the chaos it occasioned, militant

Islam continued to thrive in Afghanistan, and mujahideen from all over the world (Egypt, Yemen, Sudan, Jordan, the Philippines, Bangladesh, and some European countries) continued to flock to the training camps there, that were backed financially and spiritually by Saudi Arabia and Pakistan and by individual donors worldwide.

In 1994 these trends gave rise to the Taliban Movement in Kandahar under Mullah Omar, and in October he and fifty followers captured a mujahideen base in Speed Baldak and started to remove roadblocks and to thwart road robbers. Soon they took over the local rule of Kandahar, took over stockpiles of weapons, disarmed the population, and established law and order. At the same time, they imposed a strict practice of the Islamic Sharia, forbade women from working, banned music and games, and launched a campaign to conquer the rest of the country. By 1995 the Taliban had captured about half of Afghanistan, and their following was swelling. Then they captured Herat and enforced the strict Sharia *hudud* penalties, whereby thieves were punished with amputation of their limbs and adulterers were stoned. They also prohibited soccer, chess, flying kites, and television. The Sharia was enforced by the Department of Promotion of Good and the Fighting of Evil, in which breaking the fast of Ramadan could result in two months in prison. In September, the Taliban captured Jalalabad, and then Kabul, upon which they hunted down President Najibullah and executed him. Mullah Omar was now crowned as the commander of the faithful, like the caliphs of old, and gave shelter to bin Laden, who pursued his terrorism worldwide and was now wanted by the United States and other world factors. By 1997 the Taliban controlled 75 percent of Afghanistan, followed by most of the north in 1998, coming to control 90 percent by 1999, all the while continuing to produce three times more opium than the rest of the world combined.

The rule of militant Islam in Afghanistan, cruel and strict as it was, did establish some rule and order unknown there in the previous twenty-five years. It also seemed stable and durable until September 11, 2001, when bin Laden's operatives carried out the terrorist horror in New York and Washington, causing 3,000 deaths and provoking the massive retaliation of the United States by the end of that year, which brought an end to the Taliban regime but again threw the country into chaos. However, following fourteen years of US and NATO fighting, it seems that, upon the exit of foreign troops in 2015, the Taliban are poised to again contend for power against the regime that was installed by the Americans and is not certain to last. Whether the experience of participatory democracy will prevail over the strong and Islamic currents run by the Taliban is too early to guess, but judging from the performance of the Taliban thus far, even while foreign troops were at their zenith in the country, there seems to be an inexorable edging toward the native Islamic order of the Taliban rather than toward the Western-imposed democracy of the Americans.

In Iran after 1989, not only did the trend of exporting the revolution remain steady, but Iran's client, Sudan, became a main aid of Tehran in that mission, often with the collaboration of bin Laden. After the 1989 coup, human rights allegations surfaced against Sudan, as the regime continued to harass its Christian minority, to force its conversion, and to burn churches. These processes were relieved only since 2010, when Christian South Sudan achieved its independence, but since 2013 that independence has become questionable as local tribes have undertaken a civil war that is wrenching the new country apart. In 1990, radical Muslims trained in Sudan murdered the speaker of the Egyptian parliament and attempted to take the life of President Mubarak. After the Gulf War (1991), al-Turabi launched his Popular Arab and Islamic Congress, geared to revitalize Islam and respond to political and social challenges facing the Muslim world, but critics claimed that it was a front for an Islamic terrorist organization. In 1991 bin Laden had moved from his native Saudi Arabia, from which he had become disillusioned during the presence of American troops in the Gulf War, to Sudan, which had become an Islamic republic, headed by Omar al-Bashir, who installed the Sharia law there in 1991. He too, like Mullah Omar, forbade mixed dancing, announced that all female students and governmental workers were required to dress by Islamic standards, and installed *hudud* penalties.

Bin Laden set up a training camp in Soba, followed by others, which filled with mujahideen from all over the world. These bases trained their personnel in arms, explosives, communications, forgery, equipment, and other war requirements. He contributed from his own fortune to the infrastructure of Sudan, as well as funding international terrorism. In 1991, Iran's president visited Khartoum; he proclaimed Sudan's revolution as apt to promote the world Islamic Revolution and pledged aid to it in weapons and finances. In 1992 Sudan's New Army, the Popular Defense Forces, modeled after the Iranian Revolutionary Guards, was introduced to the public as holding the gun with one hand and the Quran in the other. More than ten camps had been built and run by the Iranians in Sudan, and they trained foreign Muslim militants for jihad, including African recruits from Kenya, Somalia, Tanzania, Chad, and Uganda. From 1993 the fruits of that effort were visible: Somalia was the first African nation affected by Sudan, as al-Turabi created there the Somali Islamic Party, an umbrella organization for the joint Iran–Sudan operations in Africa. In October 1993, US troops were ambushed by Somalis, and three American helicopters were brought down, eighteen American troops were killed, and seventy-eight wounded. That attack, which was mounted by bin Laden, Iran, and Sudan, had been preceded by the first attempt against the New York Trade Center in February 1993, whose mastermind, the blind Sheikh abd-al-Rahman, had spent several weeks in Sudan at the invitation of al-Turabi prior to his move to the United States. By the end of 1993, Sudan was on the list of state-sponsored terrorists.

Iran has also pursued its persecution of anyone connected with the Rushdie Affair. They attacked academics, translators, and publishers, and in 1991 a Japanese academic was killed and in 1993 a Turkish translator was almost killed in connection with the fatwa. Other knife attacks almost claimed the lives of Italian and Norwegian translators. But one must emphasize nonetheless that following the 1989 Mecca bombing, Iran's relations with Saudi Arabia have improved over the years, though underlying Saudi resentment persisted over Iran's continued effort to export revolution to the Horn of Africa, via its Hamas, Hezbollah, and Islamic Jihad agents. Sudan's reputation as a rogue regime invited more international resentment and pressure, however, in 1994, the case of the international terrorist Carlos the Jackal, who dwelt in Sudan, did bear fruit when Sudan yielded and extradited him to France. Sudan's endeavor to improve its image was undone when six of the twelve suspects who were accused of conspiring to blow up public buildings in New York were from the Sudan. In 1994 plots were also uncovered to murder US President Clinton in the Philippines and President Mubarak in Italy.

In 1994–95 Sudan convened with Iran on several occasions, in conjunction with other Muslim radicals from Jordan, Syria, Lebanon, the Palestinian territories, Yemen, Algeria, Tunisia, and Pakistan to discuss plots against Israel, Jordan, Saudi Arabia, and US interests. Bin Laden, by then a senior adviser to al-Turabi, participated in the terrorist conspiracies. In 1995, Iran, Sudan, and bin Laden again joined in a plot to assassinate President Mubarak and to bomb a Saudi military base in Riyadh that killed six, five of whom were Americans. Two days later, other radicals killed the Egyptian deputy chief of mission

(DCM) in Switzerland, and in November of that year Muslim terrorists detonated a bomb at the Egyptian embassy in Islamabad, Pakistan that killed nineteen and injured sixty. Those operations were the fruit of the Iran–Sudanese collaboration again Egypt and Saudi Arabia. In November 1995, another Iranian delegation visited Sudan to assess Khartoum's military needs, in the wake of which Iran supplied armored cars, heavy artillery, and radar equipment to its clients, followed by a bilateral agreement in May 1996 to broaden cooperation between them, something that caused the United States, inter alia, to remove its entire diplomatic staff from Sudan.

In 1996, the bombing of the Khobar Towers in Saudi Arabia, killing nineteen Americans and causing hundreds of injuries, shook the kingdom, the United States, and those concerned about world terrorism and about bin Laden's and Sudan's involvement in it. That same year, President Rafsanjani established the International Hezbollah Organization, which encompassed many terrorist organizations as well as bin Laden, with the latter being part of the trio responsible for operations. Rafsanjani also visited the six East African countries considered strategically important for the spread of Islam (South Africa, Zimbabwe, Sudan, Tanzania, Uganda, and Kenya) and allocated millions for intelligence gathering in those countries. In the meantime, bin Laden's active presence in Sudan sparked a conflict between it and Saudi Arabia, who demanded his deportation in return for a grant of free oil. In 1996 Sudan yielded and deported him, forcing him to move first to Bosnia and Albania and finally to Afghanistan in 1997, which offered him sanctuary in return for military and financial aid. He settled in Kandahar, where he maintained a close relationship with Mullah Omar. At the same time, Iran continued to hold annual jihad conferences in which terrorist groups coordinated their activities under the wings of Iran's political, military, and economic aid. Al-Turabi conducted parallel meetings in Sudan, in which operations were discussed against Israel, Egypt, and Saudi Arabia. One of the outcomes of those conferences was the aborted operation on the soccer world championship in 1998.

In 1998 bin Laden, with the financial and political support of Iran, created the World Islamic Front for Jihad against Jews and Crusaders, the precursor of al-Qaida, designated to "kill Americans and their allies, civil and military." In the same year, two bombs ripped through American embassies in Kenya and Tanzania, killing 300 people and injuring 5,000. The bombings were attributed to bin Laden and his Sudanese connection. The United States retaliated by destroying a chemical complex near Khartoum that belonged to bin Laden and also bombed a terrorist base in Afghanistan. Sudan and Iran continued their activity in East Africa, the Balkans, Kashmir, Chechnya, and as far away as the Philippines. After one decade of hyperintensive plots in Sudan, al-Turabi was removed from the helm by Omar al-Bashir in 1999, who also suspended the parliament and declared emergency. In 2000, bin Laden's operatives were caught in Canada trying to cross into the United States with car bombs, while others were seized trying to blow up sites in Amman and in Moscow. Bin Laden was at the peak of his power then, leading him to the Twin Towers horror in 2001, which pulled the United States into the fray and turned it into the major world factor fighting Muslim terrorism.

Although a long string of events has characterized that period since 1989, there has been no year similar to 1989 in the density of Islamic happenings. Nonetheless, one could point out major events like the fall of the Soviets, the victory of the Afghani mujahideen, the Islamic coup in Sudan, the death of Khomeini, and the Rushdie Affair as the main events in that year. The other occurrences, including the rise of Hamas and of the Israeli Muslims and the events in Algeria and Tunisia were all contributing factors, making 1989 an axial year, all driven by the triangular engines of Iran, Sudan, and bin Laden, and affecting the far reaches of the world, including Central and Southeast Asia, the Horn of Africa, Russia, and eventually the United States too. So much so that the fears and suspicions in international relations became focused on the Islamic threat, as it transpired with the American East African embassies, the Twin Towers and the Pentagon, the USS *Cole,* and the attacks against Americans in Somalia, which were all led by Iran and actively aided by Sudan and al-Qaida. Afghanistan, which joined the leaders during the decade of the Taliban, saw itself eclipsed since the United States and NATO have started to battle there in 2001. But, in view of the prospective debacle of the Western powers, one can assume that Afghanistan will rejoin those engines of Islamic terrorism as soon as the Americans leave.

Since the 2010s, new hubs of radical Islam have been emerging in other parts of the world, claiming their place in the international Islamic game. First of all, consider the Muslim radicals actually fighting in Syria, mainly Jabhat al-Nusra among them, who appear to attract to their ranks thousands of Muslim volunteers flocking there from all over the Islamic and the Western world to bring about the downfall of Assad and the capture of the government by radical Islam. Then there is ISIS, which purports to take over the rule from the Shiites in Iraq and proclaim in their stead a caliphate to govern both Iraq and Greater Syria. In these Arab states, in which the Arab Spring has shown that their governability is rapidly dwindling, it seems that only Islam of the radical, authoritarian, and anti-democratic brand can gain some legitimacy. In that regard, 1989 can be viewed as the true watershed in the fortunes of the Arab state and in the reemergence of Islam as the base of legitimacy of any new polity that might prevail in the future.

Notes

1. *Islamikaze* was coined by this author, as a combination of Islam and Kamikaze the Japanese self-immolating (not-suicidal) operatives of the Pacific War who were prepared to kill themselves in the process of hitting enemy ships. Phenomenologically, the Hamas operatives, who blew themselves up in the middle of Israeli civilians, came closest to the Kamikaze, hence the adaptation of the attribute of Islamikaze to them. See this author, *Islamikaze: Manifestations of Islamic Martyrology,* Frank Cass, London, 2003.
2. Rameen Moshref, "The Taliban," *The Afghanistan Forum,* Occasional Paper #35, May 1997, p. 1.

Bibliography

Documents

UN Watch Briefing, News and Analysis from UN Watch in Geneva, vol. 187, March 11, 2009.

The Holy Quran.

January 23, 1995, a leaflet was distributed in the Palestinian territories headed by a citation from the Repentance Sura in the Quran, which promises paradise to those who kill and are killed in the battles of Allah.

Qira'a fi Fiqh al-Shihada (Readings in Islamic Martyrology) was published in 1988 as a special addendum to *al-Islam wa Filastin* (Islam and Palestine) that appears in Nicosia, Cyprus, but has been the ideological supporter of the Islamikaze operations against Israel. See *Al-Islam wa-Filastin*, June 5, 1988, p. 9.

"Multan Conference, January 1972: The Birth of Nuclear Weapons Programme." *Pakistan Military Consortium* (Islamabad: Pakdef.info) 1 (1–2): 12–18. November 2006.

Newspapers, Broadcasts, and Magazines

The Afghanistan Forum
Africa of the Sub-Sahara
Al-Ahram Weekly
Al Alam al Arabi
Al-Ayyam (Yemen)
Al-Hayat al-Jadida
Al-Islam wa-Filast
Al Jazeerah
Al Quds al-Arabi (London)
Asian and African Studies
Asian Survey
Atlantic Monthly
BBC News
Christian Science Monitor
City Journal
CNN World News
Columbia Daily Tribune
Commentary
Copenhagen Post Online

Critique
Current Affairs Bulletin
Daily Mirror
Daily Telegraph
Dawn Weekly
Executive Intelligence Review
Fars News Agency
Foreign Affairs
Foreign Policy
French News Agency (AFP)
FrontPage Magazine
Il Giornale
Global Time
The Guardian
Haaretz
Intelligence Newsletter,
International Herald Tribune
International Journal
IRNA
Islamic Fundamentalism
Israel Defense
JAM News (Iran)
Jane's Intelligence Review
The Jerusalem Post
Jewish Political Studies Review
Jordan Times
Journal of Peace Research
Journal of Terrorism and Political Violence
Khaleej Times
La Republica
Los Angeles Times
LA Weekly
The Maghreb Review
Ma'ariv
Mail on Sunday
MEMRI
(The) Mercury
Middle East Insight
Middle East Journal
Middle East Quarterly
Middle East Review of International Affairs
Middle East Times
Midstream
(Le) Monde
(The) Muslim World
(The) News
(The) Observer

Online Journalism Review
Palestinian Authority (PA) Broadcasting
Periscope Daily Defense News Capsules
Policy Studies
Policywatch
(The) Radical
Rand Report
Risalat (Iran)
Rose al-Yusuf (Egypt)
(The) San Antonio Express News
(The) Scranton Times
(The) Seattle Times
(The) Spectator
Strategic Assessment
Sudan Tribune
Sunday Telegraph
Survey of Arab Affairs
Survival
Swiss Review of World Affairs
Terrorism and Political Violence
Third World Quarterly
The Times
Times of Israel
Times Online
Wall Street Journal
Washington Post
Weekly Standard
(The) Windsor Star
http://www.timesonline.co.uk/tol/news/worlf/asia/article6666787.ece
http://www.time.com/time/printout/0,8816,1912653,00.html
webaxy/sal/sal.pl?lang=he&ID=107345_memri&act=show&dbid=articles&dataid=3306
http://www.city-journal.org/htm/41/fightingmilitant.html

Books

Abu Amr, Ziad, *Islamic Fundamentalism in the West Bank and Gaza: Muslim Brotherhood and Islamic Jihad*, Indiana University Press, Indianapolis, 1994.

Alexander, Yonah, "Hamas," *Middle East Terrorism: Selected Group Profiles*, Washington DC, the Jewish Institute for National Security Affairs, 1994.

Alexander, Yonah, (ed.), *Middle East Terrorism: Current Threats and Future Prospects*, Aldershot, Hong Kong and Singapore, 1994, pp. 41–82.

Algar, Hamid, *Islam and Revolution*, UC Press, Berkeley, 1981, pp. 329–343.

Appleby, Scott, (ed.), *Spokesmen for the Despised*, The University of Chicago Press, 1997.

Arjomand, Said Amir, *The Turban for the Crown: The Islamic Revolution in Iran*, Oxford University Press, 1988.

Ayoub, Mahmoud, *Redemptive Suffering in Islam*, pp. 148–58.

Bar, Shmuel, *The Muslim Brotherhood in Jordan*, The Dayan Center, Tel Aviv University, 1998.
Bartal, Shaul, *The Fedayeen Emerge, The Palestine-Israel Conflict, 1949–1956*, Bloomington, Authorhouse, 2011.
Baranovitch, Nimrod, *China's New Voices*, UC Press, Berkeley, 2003, especially chapter 2, pp. 54 ff.
Bat Ye'or, *The Dhimmi*.
Bat Ye'or. *Islam and Dhimmitude*.
Bedford, Carmel, *Fiction, Fact, and the Fatwa: 2,000 Days of Censorship*, International Center against Censorship, August 1994.
Bhutto, Zulfiqar Ali, *The Myth of Independence*, Oxford University Press, 1969.
Bodansky, Yossef, *Bin Laden: The Man Who Declared War on America*, Prima Publishing, Rocklin, CA, 1999.
Borowiec, Andrew, *Modern Tunisia: A Democratic Apprenticeship*, Praeger, Westport, 1998.
Cohen, Amnon, *Political Parties in the West Bank*, Cornell University Press, 1982.
Cole, Juan and Nikki Keddie, (eds.), *Shiism and Social Protest*, Yale University Press, 1986.
Craig-Harris, Lillian, *China Considers the Middle East*, Tauris, London, 1993.
Ehteshami, Anoushiravan, *After Khumeini: The Iranian Second Republic*, Routledge, London, 1995.
El-Said, Sabah, *Between Pragmatism and Ideology: The Muslim Brothers in Jordan (1989–94)*, The Washington Institute Policy Papers, no. 39, 1995. Esposito, John, *The Islamic Threat: Myth or Reality*, Oxford University Press, 1992.
Friedman, Thomas, *From Beirut to Jerusalem*, Doubleday, NY, 1989.
Friedman, Thomas, *The Lexus and the Olive Tree*, Anchor Books, 2000.
Gerges, Fawaz, *America and Political Islam: Clash of Cultures or Clash of Interests?* Cambridge, 1999.
Gladney, Dru, *Ethnic Nationalism in the People's Republic*, Harvard, 1991.
Gul, Tursun, "Symbol of Uighur Defiance: I Just Want My Husband Back," http://www.timesonline.co.uk/tol/news/worlf/asia/article6666787.ece, July 8, 2009.
Hatina, Meir, *Palestinian Radicalism: The Islamic Jihad Movement* (Hebrew), Tel Aviv University, 1994, pp. 79–80.
Heikal, Mohamed, *The Return of the Ayatullah: The Iranian Revolution from Mossadeq to Khumeini*, Andre Deutch, London, 1981.
Israeli, Raphael, *Israel's New Strategic Dilemmas: Survival or Revival?* Strategic Books, Texas, 2012.
Israeli, Raphael, *The Spread of Islamikaze Terrorism in Europe*, Vallentine Mitchell, 2008.
Israeli, Raphael, *The Islamic Challenge in Europe*, Transaction, NJ, 2008.
Israeli, Raphael, *Islamikaze: Manifestations of Islamic Martyrology*, Frank Cass, London, 2003, chapter 1, pp. 11–32.
Israeli, Raphael, *Muslim Minorities in Modern States, The Challenge of Assimilation*, Transaction, 2009, chaps. 3 and 4.

Israeli, Raphael, *Fundamentalist Islam and Israel,* The University Press of America, 1993.

Israeli, Raphael, *Green Crescent over Nazareth: The Displacement of Christians by Muslims in the Holy Land,* Frank Cass, London, 2002.

Israeli, Raphael, *Muslim Fundamentalism in Israel,* Brassey's, London and Washington, 1993.

Keats, John, *Letters,* January 13, 1818.

Keppel, Gilles, *La Revanche de Dieu.*

Khomeini, Ayatollah, *The Islamic Republic.*

Kramer, Martin, (ed.), *Protest and Revolution in Shi'ite Islam* (Hebrew), Tel Aviv University.

Kramer, Martin, *Arab Awakening and Islamic Revival: The Politics of Ideas in the Middle East,* Transaction, NJ, 1996.

Kurtz, Anat and Nahman Tal, *Hamas: Radical Islam in a National Struggle,* Jaffe Center for Strategic Studies, no. 48, July 1997.

Lewis, Bernard, *Jews in Islam,* especially chapter 3. Princeton, 1984.

Lewis, Bernard, *The Middle East and the West,* Weidenfeld and Nicolson, London, 1963–64.

Lewis, Bernard, *Islam and the West,* Weidenfeld and Nicolson, London, 1993.

Maddy-Weitzman, Bruce and Ephraim Inbar, (eds.), *Religious Radicalism in the Greater Middle East,* Frank Cass, London 1997.

Marsden, Peter, *The Taliban: War, Religion and the New Order in Afghanistan,* Zed Books, London, 1998.

Menashri, David, *A Decade of War and Revolution,* Holmes and Meier, NY, 1990.

Mishal, Shaul and Avraham Sela, *The Palestinian Hamas: Vision, Violence and Coexistence,* Columbia University, 2000.

Mohaddesin, Muhammad, *Islamic Fundamentalism: The New Global Threat,* Seven Locks Press, Washington DC, 1993.

Moin, Baqer, *Khumeini: The Life of the Ayatullah,* Tauris, London, 1999.

Munson, Henry, *Islam and Revolution in the Middle East,* Yale University, 1888.

O'Balance, Edgar, *The Palestinian Intifada,* McMillan Press, UK, 1998.

O'Balance, Edgar, *Islamic Fundamentalist Terrorism, 1979–95, The Iranian Connection,* NYU Press, 1997.

Olesen, Asta, *Islam and Politics in Afghanistan,* Curzon Press, Surrey, 1995.

Piscatori, James, (ed.), *Islamic Fundamentalisms and the Gulf Crisis,* The American Academy of Arts and Sciences, Chicago, 1988.

Qutb, Sayyid, *Our War against the Jews.*

Robinson, Glenn, *Building a Palestinian State: The Incomplete Revolution,* Indianapolis, Indiana University Press, 1997.

Rubin, Michael and Daniel Benjamin, *The Taliban and Terrorism: Report from Afghanistan,* Special Policy Forum Report, the Washington Institute of Near East Studies, no. 450, April 2000.

Ruesh, Andreas, "Talibanistan-Afghanistan's Mysterious Government," *Swiss Review of World Affairs,* no. 5, May 1997, pp. 9–11.

Rushdie, Salman, *The Satanic Verses,* Viking, London, 1988.

Schiff, Zeev and Ehud Ya'ari, *Intifadah: The Palestinian Uprsing, Israel's Third Front,* Simon and Shuster, NY.

Sela, Avraham, (ed.), *Political Encyclopedia of the Middle East,* Jerusalem Publishing House, 1999.

Sidahmed, abd al Salam and Anoushiravan Ehteshami, (eds.), *Islamic Fundamentalism,* Westview Press, Boulder, CO, 1996.

Sivan, Emanuel, *Muslim Radicals* (in Hebrew), Am Oved, Tel Aviv, 1985, pp. 192–95.

Smith, Charles, *Palestine and the Arab-Israeli Conflict,* St. Charles Press, NY, 1992.

Taheri, Amir (a former pre-revolutionary editor of the daily *Kaihan), The Spirit of Allah* (in Hebrew translation), Am Oved, Tel Aviv, 1986, p. 148.

Tessler, Mark, *A History of the Israeli-Palestinian Conflict,* Indiana University Press, Indianapolis, 1994.

Tripp, Charles and Roger Owen, (eds.), *Egypt Under Mubarak,* Routledge, London, 1989.

Voll, John, (ed.), *Sudan: State and Society in Crisis,* The Middle East Institute, Bloomington, 1991.

Weissbrod, Amir, *Turabi: Spokesman of Radical Islam* (Hebrew), Dayan Center, Tel Aviv, 1999.

Yang, C. K., *Religion in Chinese Society,* UC Berkeley, 1967, chap. XII, pp. 294–340.

Ziad Abu Amr, *Islamic Fundamentalism in the West Bank and Gaza: Muslim Brotherhood and Islamic Jihad,* Indiana University Press, Indianapolis, 1994, p. 59.

Articles

Aly, Sbd al-Moneim Sais, and Wenner, Manfred, "Modern Islamic Reform Movements: The Muslim Brotherhood in Contemporary Egypt," *Middle East Journal,* vol. 36, no. 3, Summer 1982, pp. 336–61.

Amidror, Maj. Gen. (res.) Yaacov, a former National Security Adviser for PM Netanyahu. Amidror joined the Begin-Sadat Center for Strategic Studies this month as the Anne and Greg Rosshandler Senior Fellow. His thoughts were uttered at his inaugural talk at the BESA Center on March 2, 2014.

Amir, Menashe, "Iran," in Sela, Avraham, (ed.), *Political Encyclopedia of the Middle East,* Jerusalem Publishing House, 1999.

Anderson, Betty, "The Status of Democracy on Jordan," *Critique,* Spring.

Anthony, Andrew, "A Muslim at Bay: The *Panorama* program on BBC1," *The Observer,* August 28, 20.

Babar, Farhatullah, "Bhutto's Footprints on Nuclear Pakistan," *The News,* (Islamabad), April 4, 2006.

Barghouti, Iyad, "Islamic Movements in Historical Palestine," in abd al Salam Sidahmed and Anoushiravan Ehteshami, (eds.), *Islamic Fundamentalism,* Westview Press, Boulder, CO, 1996, pp. 163–64.

Barkan, L. "The Islamic Movement in Israel: Switching Focus from Jerusalem to the Palestinian Cause," *Inquiry & Analysis Series,* report no. 628, Middle East Media Research Institute, Washington DC, July 30, 2010.

Bechor, Guy, *Haaretz,* December 6, 1995, p. b2.

Binyon, Michael, "Prince Pitches for Religious Tolerance," *The Times*, May 5, 2006.
Branch, John, *The San Antonio Express News*, February 10, 2006.
Brendan, Bernhard, "White Muslim: How to Become a Muslim, From LA to New York, to . . . Jihad?" *LA Weekly*, December 2, 2004.
Brumberg, Daniel, "Khumeini's Legacy: Islamic Rule and Islamic Social Justice," Scott Appleby, (ed.), *Spokesmen for the Despised*, The University of Chicago Press, 1997.
"Bus Driver Speaks of His Mental Torment," *Daily Telegraph*, July 7, 2006.
Cesari, Jocelyne, in MSA News, June 6, 2000.
Cole, John, *The Scranton Times*, February 8, 2006.
Collard, Tim, *Daily Telegraph*, July 29, 2009.
Cottam, Richard, "The Iranian Revolution," in Juan Cole and Nikki Keddie, (eds.), *Shiism and Social Protest*, Yale University Press, 1986.
Cullen, Kevin, "Salman Rushdie's Latest Moves Stirs Chorus of Howls," *International Herald Tribune*, September 29, 2000.
Darkow, John, *The Columbia Daily Tribune*, February 9, 2006.
Devericks, Eric, *The Seattle Times*, February 10, 2006.
Dunn, Michael Collins, "Usama Bin Laden: The Nature of the Challenge," *Middle East Policy*, vol. 6, no. 2, October 1998, pp. 23–28.
Ebeid, Mona Makram, "The Role of the Official Opposition," in Charles Tripp and Roger Owen, (eds.), *Egypt Under Mubarak*, Routledge, London, 1989.
Eimer, David, "China Admits That Police Shot Dead 12 Uighurs During the Recent Riots in Urumqi," *Sunday Telegraph*, July 19, 2009.
Elst, Koenraad, "The Rushdie Rules," *Middle East Quarterly*, vol. 5, no. 2, June 1998, pp. 31–42.
Enjung Cha, Ariana, "China Unrest Tied to Labor Program: Uighur Sent to Work in Other Regions," *Washington Post*, July 15, 2009.
Faksh, Mahmud, "The Prospects of Islamic Fundamentalism in the Post Gulf War Period," *International Journal*, vol. 49, no. 2, 1994, pp. 183–218.
Fatihi, Dr., in *Al-Alam al-Arabi*, Cairo, October 20, 2001.
Fluehr-Lobban, Carolyn, "Islamization in Sudan: A Critical Assessment," in John Voll, (ed.), *Sudan: State and Society in Crisis*, The Middle East Institute, Bloomington, 1991.
Foster, David, *Daily Telegraph*, July 7, 2007.
Foster, Peter in Urumqi and Malcolm Moore in Shanghai, "China Arrests 1,400 in Aftermath of Xinjiang Riots: Chinese Police Have Arrested 1,134 Suspects after the Worst Ethnic Violence in Decades Left 156 Dead in the Far Western Province of Xinjiang," *The Daily Telegraph*, July 7, 2009.
Freij, Hanna and Leonard Robinson, "Liberalization, Islamists and the Stability of the Arab State: Jordan as a Case Study," *The Muslim World*, vol. 86, no. 1, January 1996, pp. 1–32.
Ganor, Boaz, "Hamas—The Islamic Resistance Movement in the Territories," *Survey of Arab Affairs*, Feb 2, 1992, pp. 1–7.
Glazov, Jamie, *FrontPage Magazine*, March 7, 2006.
Graston, Mike, *The Windsor Star*, February 10, 2006.

Harel, Amos, "Local Ben Laden Group Planned Suicide Bombings," *Haaretz*, August 22, 2000.

Harpviken, Kristian Berg, "Transcending Traditionalism: The Emergence of non-State Military Formations in Afghanistan," *Journal of Peace Research*, vol. 34, no. 3, 1997, pp. 271–87.

Harris, Paul, "Algeria Faces the Challenges of Peace," *Jane's Intelligence Review*, vol. 12, no. 3, March 2000, pp. 47–49.

Hauslohner, Abigail, "Uighurs: Middle East Ignores China's Oppressed Muslims," *Time*, July 16, 2009.

Hoffman, Bruce, "Recent Trends and Future Prospects of Iranian Sponsored International Terrorism," *Rand Report*, in Yonah Alexander, (ed.), *Middle East Terrorism: Current Threats and Future Prospects*, Aldershot, Hong Kong, and Singapore, 1994, pp. 41–82.

Honig, Sarah, *The Jerusalem Post*, November 11, 2010.

Horovitz, David, *Times of Israel*, July 9, 2012.

Howard, Roger, "Ben Laden Expected to Retaliate for US Missile Attacks Sooner Rather than Later," *Jane's Intelligence Review*, vol. 10, no. 6, June 1999, p. 6.

Howard, Roger, "Entertaining Osama: Testing the Limits of Taliban Hospitality," *Jane's Intelligence Review*, vol. 10, no. 11, November 1998, pp. 14–16.

Hussein, Irfan, "The Battle for Hearts and Minds," *Dawn Weekly*, October 6, 2001.

Ibrahim, Saad Eddin, "Egypt's Islamic Activism in the 1980s," *Third World Quarterly*, vol. 10, no. 2, April 1988, pp. 632–57.

Israeli, Raphael, "The Islamic Movement in Israel," *Jerusalem Letter*, Jerusalem Center for Public Affairs, Oct. 15, 1999.

Israeli, Raphael, "Islamikaze and Their Significance," *Terrorism and Political Violence*, 9:3, 1997, pp. 96–121.

Israeli, Raphael, "Islamic Fundamentalism in the Public Square," *Jewish Political Studies Review*, vol. 11, no. 3–4, Fall 1999, pp. 141–62.

Israeli, Raphael, "Muslim Fundamentalists as Social Revolutionaries," *Journal of Terrorism and Political Violence*, 6:4, 1994, pp. 462–65.

Israeli, Raphael, "The New Wave of Islam," *International Journal*, Summer 1979, pp. 369–90.

Israeli, Raphael, "The Charter of Allah: The Platform of the Islamic Resistance Movement (Hamas)," in R. Israeli, *Fundamentalist Islam and Israel*, The University Press of America, 1993.

Jahanpour, Farhang, "Iran after Khumeini," *Current Affairs Bulletin*, vol. 66, no. 9, February 1990, p. 20.

Janabi, Ahmed, "Xinjiang Unrest 'Not Ethnic,'" *Al-Jazeera*, July 26, 2009.

"Jihad and Terrorism Threat Monitor," MEMRI, July 17, 2009, Special dispatch 2450.

Karmon, Ely, "Hamas' Terrorism Strategy: Operational Limitations and Political Restraints," *Middle East Review of International Affairs*, vol. 4, no. 1, March 4, 2000.

Keddie, Nikki, "The Islamic Movement in Tunisia," *The Maghreb Review*, vol. 11, no. 1, 1986, pp. 26–39.

Khamenei, in a public speech, February 20, 2006.

Kuntzel, Mathias, "The Iranian Holy War," an address at Columbia University on March 6, 2008, under the auspices of Scholars for Peace in the Middle East.

Lesch, Ann Moselely, "Sudan's Foreign Policy: In Search of Arms, Aid and Allies," in John Voll, (ed.), *Sudan: State and Society in Crisis*, Bloomington, 1991.

Lewis, Bernard, "The Roots of Muslim Rage," *Atlantic Monthly*, September 1990.

Macartney, Jane, "Rabiya Kadeer Accused of Being behind Uighur Violence in East Turkestan," *The Times*, July 7, 2009.

Macartney, Jane, "Han Chinese as the Main Victims as Urumqi Riots Death Toll Rises," *Times Online*, July 11, 2007.

Maddy-Weitzman, Bruce, "The Islamist Challenge in North Africa," in Maddy-Weitzman, Bruce and Ephraim Inbar, (eds.), *Religious Radicalism in the Greater Middle East*, Frank Cass, London, 1997.

Magnus, Ralph, "Afghanistan in 1996: Year of the Taliban," *Asian Survey*, vol. 38, no. 2, February 1997, pp. 111–17.

Makovsky, Michael and Blaise Misztal, *Wall Street Journal*, July 8, 2012.

Meyr, Eitan, "Israel, Hamas May Clash over Kidnapping," *Jane Intelligence Review*, vol. 12, no. 2, February 2000, pp. 28–30.

Miller, Judith, "Global Islamic Awakening or Sudanese Nightmare? The Curious Case of Hassan Turabi," in Scott Appleby, (ed.), *Spokesmen for the Despised; Fundamentalist Leaders of the Middle East*, Chicago, 1997.

Milton-Edwards, Beverly, "A Temporary Alliance with the Crown: The Islamic Response in Jordan," in James Piscatri, (ed.), *Islamic Fundamentalisms and the Gulf Crisis*, The American Academy of Arts and Sciences, Chicago, 1988, p. 90.

Milton-Edwards, Beverly, "Climate of Change in Jordan's Islamist Movement," in *Islamic Fundamentalism*, Westview Press, Boulder, 1996.

Mo, Lingjiao, "Turkey, Another Axis of Evil?" *Global Times*, July 10, 2009.

Pelin, Turgut, "Turkey No Longer a Safe Haven for Chinese Uighurs," July 27, 2009, http://www.time.com/time/printout/0,8816,1912653,00.html (Istanbul).

Moore, Malcolm, *Daily Telegraph*, July 14, 2009. See also Jane Macartney, *Online*, July 14, 2009.

Moshref, Rameen, "The Taliban," *The Afghanistan Forum*, Occasional Paper #35, May 1997, p. 1.

Mozaffari, Mehdi, "Islamism in Algeria and Iran," in Sidahmed and Ehteshami, (eds.), *Islamic Fundamentalism*, Westview Press, NY, 1996, pp. 229–47.

Nader, George, "Interview with President Ali Akbar Hashemi Rafsanjani," *Middle East Insight*, vol. 11, no. 5, 1995.

Naim, Moises, "Mute Muslims: Why Doesn't the Islamic World Speak about the Uighurs?" *Foreign Policy*, July 13, 2009.

"News from Everywhere," *Daily Telegraph Leader*, July 8, 2006.

Ofcansky, Thomas, "Sudan, Recent History," *Africa of the Sub-Sahara, 2000*, Europa Publications, London, 1999.

"On the Trail of the Black Market Bombs," *BBC News*, February 12, 2004.
Oster, Shai and Gordon Fairclough, *Wall Street Journal*, July 7, 2009.
Parry, Richard Lloyd, "Exiled Uighur Leader Rebiya Kadeer in a Hurry to Bring Freedom to Her People," *The Times*, July 30, 2009.
Paz, Reuven, "Hamas' Lessons from Lebanon," *Policywatch*, The Washington Institute of Near East Policy, no. 262, May 25, 2000.
Pinto, Maria de Ceu, "Some Concerns Regarding Islamist and Middle Eastern Terrorism," *Terrorism and Political Violence*, vol. 11, no. 3, Fall 1999, pp. 72–96.
Pipes, Daniel, "Fighting Militant Islam, Without Bias," *City Journal*, Autumn 2001. http://www.city-journal.org/htm/41/fightingmilitant.html.
Ramati, Yohanan, "Islamic Fundamentalism Gaining," *Midstream*, vol. 39, no. 2, March 1993, pp. 2–3.
Rashid, Ahmed, "The Taliban: Exporting Extremism," *Foreign Affairs*, vol. 78, no. 6, December 1999, pp. 22–35.
Rekhes, Elie, "Resurgent Islam in Israel," *Asian and African Studies*, vol. 27, no. 2, 1993, pp. 189–206.
Restall, Hugo, "The Urumqi Effect," *Wall Street Journal*, July 10, 2009.
Ronen, Yehudit, "The Struggle for Power within Sudan's Top Leadership," *Policywatch*, December 1999.
Ross, Terrill, "The Empire Strikes Back," *Weekly Standard*, July 27, 2009.
Sadeh, Sharon, "The London Bridge Is Collapsing," *Haaretz*, September 30, 2009.
Schemm, Paul, "Algeria's Return to Its Past: Can the FIS Break the Vicious Circle of History?" *Middle East Insight*, vol. 11, no. 2, 1995, pp. 36–39.
Schenker, David, "The State Department's 1999 Terrorism Report: Issues to Watch," *Policywatch*, The Washington Institute for Near East Policy, no. 457, April 26, 2000.
Shadid, Mohammed, "The Muslim Brotherhood Movement in the West Bank and Gaza," *Third World Quarterly*, vol. 10, no. 2, April 1988, pp. 658–82.
Shahin, Emad Eldin, "Tunisia's Renaissance Party: The Rise and Repression of an Islamic Movement," *Middle East Insight*, vol. 11, no. 2. 1995, pp. 29–35.
Shichor, Y., "Ethno-diplomacy: The Uyghur Hitch in Sino-Turkish Relations," in *Policy Studies* 53, East-West Center, 2009, pp. 1–53.
Sidahmed, Abdel Salam, "Sudan: Ideology and Pragmatism," in Sidahmed and Others, (eds.), *Islamic Fundamentalism*, Westview Press, Boulder, 1996.
Smyth, Frank, "Culture Clash: Bin Laden, Khartoum and the War against the West," *Jane's Intelligence Review*, vol. 10, no. 10, 1998, pp. 22–25.
Steele, John, "Suicide Bomber's Video Won't Frighten Us, Say July 7 Families," *Daily Telegraph*, July 7, 2006.
Sullivan, Kevin, "British Slow to Recognize Threat of Terrorism: London Bombings Couldn't Have Been Prevented, Report Says," *Washington Post*, May 11, 2006.
Sultan, Wafa, "Interview with *AL Jazeera*." February 2006. See MEMRI, Special Dispatch Series 1107, March 7, 2006.
Szpiro, George, "Israeli Arabs Turn to Islam," *Swiss Review of World Affairs*, vol. 39, no. 3, June 1989, pp. 29–30.
Tal, Lawrence, "Dealing with Radical Islam: The Case of Jordan," *Survival*, vol. 31, no. 3, 1995, pp. 139–55.

Tal, Nahman, "The Islamic Movement in Israel," *Strategic Assessment*, vol. 2, no. 4, February 2000, pp. 10–15.

"The Clash of Civilisations Is Currently on Hold," *Copenhagen Post Online*, April 20, 2006.

"Uprising in Urumqi," *Wall Street Journal*, July 8, 2009.

Weigel, George, "Europe's Two Culture Wars," *Commentary*, May 2006.

Woolcock, Nicola and Sean O'Neill, "Once a Friendly Christian, He Now Backs the Bombers: Two Faces, Two Converts, Two Muslim Extremists in Britain," *The Times*, April 24, 2006.

Zigron, and A. Savion, "The Jewish Image in the Eyes of the Iranian Regime: Theological Roots," http://www.Memri.org.il/cgi-webaxy/sal/sal.pl?lang=he&ID=107345_memri&act=show&dbid=articles&dataid=3306.

Index